W9-AVR-837

The Two Mr. Gladstones

The Two Mr. Gladstones

A Study in Psychology and History

Travis L. Crosby

Yale University Press   New Haven and London

Designed by Sonia L. Scanlon
Set in Caslon type by Rainsford Type, Danbury, Connecticut
Printed in the United States of America by Edwards Brothers, Inc.,
Ann Arbor, Michigan

Library of Congress Cataloging-in-Publication Data
Crosby, Travis L., 1936–
      The two Mr. Gladstones : a study in psychology and history /
Travis L. Crosby.
          p.   cm.
      Includes bibliographical references and index.
      ISBN 0-300-06827-1 (hc : alk. paper)
      1. Gladstone, W. E. (William Ewart), 1809–1898—Psychology.
2. Great Britain—Politics and government—1837–1901.   3. Prime
ministers—Great Britain—Psychology.   4. Political psychology.
I. Title.
DA563.4.C76   1997
941.081'092—dc20   96-26547
[B]   CIP

A catalogue record for this book is available
from the British Library.
The paper in this book meets the guidelines for permanence
and durability of the Committee on Production Guidelines for
Book Longevity of the Council on Library Resources.

10 9 8 7 6 5 4 3 2 1

Figures 1, 3, 6, 7, 9, 10, 13, 14, 15, and 17 courtesy Flintshire Record Office.
Figure 2 courtesy Liverpool Libraries and Information Service.

To Matthew and Timothy,
Daniel and Ian,
and Susan,
in gratitude for helping to create
a tolerant environment
for a preoccupied author.

Contents

Acknowledgments

In a work of this complexity—which stretches widely over two distinct fields of inquiry, psychology and history—I have incurred an unusual number of intellectual and personal debts. To all those who have given generously of their time, I am profoundly grateful. In gathering information—the initial stage of this project—I am especially grateful to the Reverend Dr. Peter J. Jagger, Warden and Chief Librarian of St. Deiniol's Library, Hawarden, Wales; to A. Geoffrey Veysey, County Archivist, and to Christopher Williams, then Assistant Archivist, of the Flintshire Record Office at Hawarden. For many months in Welsh winters and summers, they were unfailingly welcoming and helpful in providing access to the Gladstone family papers. In the later stages of the manuscript preparation, Paul F. Mason, Archivist of the Flintshire Record Office, provided invaluable services. Sir William Gladstone was more than cooperative; he showed a fellow historian's interest in my work. Thanks to him for permission to use and to quote from his ancestor's correspondence. The Manuscript Division of the British Library, London, always with efficiency and good cheer fully facilitated my numerous requests for Gladstone's political papers. College and university libraries, both in the United Kingdom and the United States, provided crucial assistance in secondary materials; these include the libraries of the University of London, Northwestern University Library, University of Massachusetts (Amherst) Library, and the libraries of Amherst, Smith, and Wheaton Colleges.

Numerous colleagues have given encouragement, and some have taken on the daunting task of reading the manuscript. I particularly wish to thank Abigail Stewart of the University of Michigan and Gerald Zuriff of Wheaton College for their thoughtful comments on the psychological side of things. Peter Marsh of Syracuse University generously gave the manuscript a careful reading and made numerous useful suggestions, as did A. Geoffrey Veysey and Christopher Williams. Conversations with Colin Matthew and Richard Shannon clarified for me their larger perspective on Gladstone. T. W. Heyck of Northwestern University and Emmet Larkin at the University of Chicago read parts of the manuscript and shared their special knowledge of Britain and Ireland in the nineteenth century. Exchanges with scholars from different perspectives are always useful and can even be exhilarating, as was true at the Gladstone Seminar held at Christ Church, Oxford, in the summer of 1991. I wish to thank the sponsors of the conference for their invitation to participate.

Valuable time for research and writing was provided by a summer grant from the National Endowment for the Humanities, by a grant from the American Philosophical Society, and by the Carter-Wallace History Faculty Fund at Wheaton College. Wheaton also granted two sabbatical leaves and a leave of absence for extended work on this project. I wish to thank the Provost of Wheaton College, Hannah Goldberg, for her lively interest and support in this work. Nancy Shepardson and the secretarial staff at Wheaton were heroic, especially in the high summer days of 1995, in undertaking the bibliographical and copying tasks associated with the completion of the manuscript. Kathy Ebert-Zawasky of the Academic Computing Center at Wheaton was crucial to the solution of computer mysteries known only to the initiated. Many thanks to Elaine Dezenski (Wheaton '92) for checking citations from the *Gladstone Diaries*. I am also grateful for those students who enrolled over the years in my psychohistory seminar at Wheaton for providing a forum for thinking out loud about some of the problems of explaining the past in psychological terms. Their enthusiasm and industry gave me more encouragement than they knew.

To Jenya Weinreb, my manuscript editor at Yale University Press, who became my colleague in an extended telephonic writing seminar, my gratitude and thanks. And finally, my heartfelt thanks to Gladys Topkis, Senior Editor at Yale University Press, who has been steadfast and persevering in helping to bring about a new view of Gladstone.

The Two Mr. Gladstones

1

The Two Mr. Gladstones

More than any other historical figure in modern British history, William Gladstone has been prey to myth and mystery. In his own time, the great Liberal statesman was most often seen, especially in the last decades of his long life, as a titan—a moral colossus striding across the political stage. Newspapers and popular periodicals filled their pages with reports of his public utterances and his parliamentary exploits. His speeches were read not merely for their political content; they were viewed as oracular. Gladstone was—according to the well-known English journalist W. T. Stead—a "kind of secular pope."[1] Trainloads of sightseers made their way to Hawarden, Gladstone's estate in north Wales, to catch a glimpse of the great man. A special treat was to see him at work chopping down the majestic trees that grew in abundance on his land. His favorite exercise became symbolic of his ability to hack and hew his way through the knottiest of problems. Slivers of fallen Hawarden oaks were sold as souvenirs to the most enthusiastic among the crowds of admirers. By the end of his life, Gladstone had become the center of a cult that extended far beyond his political reputation. All the world, wrote Albert H. Broadwell in the *Strand Magazine*, admired him "as a man, as a great English statesman, as a kind husband and loving father."[2]

Contemporary biographies were equally laudatory of Gladstone's life and work. Justin McCarthy's first sentence sets the tone for the biography to follow: Gladstone was, he wrote, the "greatest English statesman" during Queen Victoria's reign. Herbert Paul believed him to be incapable of making an uncharitable judgment. G. W. E. Russell thought that Gladstone's "love of power" had nothing to do with the "vulgar eagerness for place and pay and social standing which governs the lesser luminaries of the political heaven" but could be attributed to "his deliberate theory of the public good." John Morley's admirable *Life of William Ewart Gladstone* is also filled with adulatory comments. "He was not only a political force," Morley wrote of Gladstone, "but a moral force" as well. Most later biographers have followed this complimentary line. Sir Philip Magnus reaffirmed Gladstone's stature as a "moral giant" in an author's note to the ninth printing of his popular biography. J. L. Hammond and M. R. D. Foot contrast the liberalism of Gladstone's moral order to Bismarck's espousal of "perpetual struggle . . . and perpetual fear." Even the more detached E. J. Feuchtwanger saw Gladstone as a man who could "move mountains."[3]

But recent biographies have begun to portray a different Gladstone. The first volume of Richard Shannon's life of Gladstone, based substantially on the *Gladstone Diaries,* offers an interpretation distinctly at odds with those of Morley, Magnus, and others. Not denying Gladstone's substantial achievements, Shannon also speaks of Gladstone's "anxieties," moods of "near despair," "emotional distemper," "repressed aggression," and "pent-up aggressive energy."[4] Colin Matthew, editor of the *Diaries,* also finds evidence in Gladstone of "despair," "high nervous excitement," "private torments," "underlying restlessness," and "guilt." He was a man, as Matthew notes, "prone to tension," who during the 1840s and 1850s had evidently suffered a "severe psychological crisis."[5]

This side of Gladstone, the tense and moody part of him, if unnoticed by his earlier biographers, was not surprising to his contemporaries. The jarring impression he made at social events and political meetings and, most remarkably, his angry outbursts in the House of Commons were matters of frequent comment. The journalist Henry Lucy, who spent his career observing the House of Commons, once described Gladstone during a parliamentary debate as "fuming and fretting in a white heat of passion, . . . throwing oil on the flames by interjecting remarks, or making undignified gestures."[6] He would leap up from his seat "with catapultic celerity" to answer an opponent, his face "darkened into a scowl of passionate anger."[7] Even in apparent repose, Gladstone hummed with a kind of restrained violence. Lucy once followed him through the hours of a particularly important parliamentary sitting toward the end of his second administration, taking notes of his "manifold gyrations." Entering the House, Gladstone strode to the front bench, sat down quickly, and abruptly took up the Orders of the day. Turning "with a sudden bound of his whole body," he began a conversation with a colleague, his face "working with excitement." At the same time, he beat the open palm of his left hand with his right "as if he were literally pulverising an adversary." His conversation finished, he flung himself back into his seat for a moment. Then, as swiftly as before, he turned to another colleague, thrust his hand into his breast pocket "as if he had suddenly become conscious of a live coal secreted there," pulled out a folded letter, opened it with a "violent flick of extended forefingers," and began to discourse upon it to his neighboring listener.

Gladstone's excitable nature was made much of by erstwhile friends and political enemies. The earl of Selborne, Lord Chancellor in two of Gladstone's administrations before breaking with him over the Irish question, characterized Gladstone as a man with "something volcanic in the underground currents of his mind."[8] Lord Stanley went further. He harbored suspicions about Gladstone's sanity, as he filled his diary with observations of Gladstone's "peculiar vehemence," "excessive irritability," and loss of temper.[9] Tories generally thought Gladstone quite unlike other politicians: his apparent lack of control, they believed, lay behind his fervent and too frequent espousal of political causes.[10] They even claimed that his "impetuosity" could doom legislation that he himself had supported, as happened when the Liberal franchise reform plan failed in 1866.[11]

That most acute of Victorian observers, Walter Bagehot, summed up best the general reservations about Gladstone's behavior. "Mr. Gladstone," he wrote in 1860, "is a problem: . . . we are all of us in doubt about him." Gladstone's talents were obvious: his industry, his seriousness of purpose, his mastery of detail, his oratorical skill. Perhaps these would raise him to the pinnacle of success. But he was also "impressible, impetuous, and unfixed." And he had a "vehement temperament." Would he in later life be found in isolated opposition, uttering "unintelligible discourses," pouring forth "during many hopeless years a bitter, a splendid, and a vituperative eloquence?"[12] Only time would tell.

Bagehot need not have worried. In December 1868, Gladstone formed the first of his four ministries. One of the most significant reforming governments of the century, it disestablished the Church of Ireland, legislated an Irish land bill, passed a comprehensive education bill, and enacted the secret ballot. His later administrations, if with less success and with fewer constructive monuments to the future, struggled actively with the important issues of the time: the movement for Irish independence, global imperialism, and further extensions of the right to vote. In all his governments Gladstone played a central legislative role, and in all of them he added to his reputation as a master of governmental finance. Yet these achievements were not without controversy. On such substantial issues as franchise reform, free trade, and Home Rule for Ireland, he changed his original views. These shifts of opinion, sometimes precipitately announced, alarmed even his political allies.

Gladstone's leaps ahead—into the dark, his opponents would say—reinforced the notion that he could be irresponsibly impulsive.

Gladstone's reversals were striking enough to suggest to some observers a divided soul. An anonymous article written early during his first administration noted that any character study of Gladstone was a "social puzzle, an ethical problem," because there was no man "against whom greater contradictions and inconsistencies are alleged." So profound were these divisions that he appeared to have a "dual character."[13] Toward the end of Gladstone's life, John Robertson voiced a similar theme: "It is this perceived combination, as it were, of rectitude and crookedness in Mr. Gladstone's mental processes, the consistence in him of admitted moral elevation with a curious moral versatility, which looks like levity of principle and conviction—it is this that makes his character such a theme of dispute. If we can explain that duality, we shall understand and explain Mr. Gladstone."[14]

Gladstone's duality was seen variously. An old Whig once remarked after one of Gladstone's budget speeches, "Ah, Oxford on the surface, but Liverpool below." As Bagehot explained this cryptic remark, beneath Gladstone's scholastic polish lay the industry and robustness of the Lancashire merchant.[15] A twentieth-century biography expanded this theme: although the Liverpudlian Gladstone was dominant in his ambition and shrewdness in politics or business, occasionally the Oxford Gladstone would burst through with its searchings of conscience and quixotic political or moral campaigns.[16] Or, as another of Gladstone's contemporaries put it, Gladstone was a highlander in the custody of a lowlander: the highlander might brood and dream, but the lowlander was a man of calculation and practicality.[17] Gladstone's duality of disposition was recognized in his own family. His wife, Catherine, once remarked to John Morley that a key to understanding her husband was to remember that he had two sides: "one impetuous, impatient, irrestrainable, the other all self-control, able to dismiss all but the great central aim, able to put aside what is weakening or disturbing."[18]

The theme of duality in Gladstone's private and public life is a primary focus of this book. My first object is to see Gladstone as his contemporaries saw him and to penetrate the mysteries of his personality insofar as they affected his life and work. There is little doubt that in his own time, Gladstone's behavior, both public and private, was a matter of wide speculation. His fits of temper and aggressive verbal attacks were well known.

Yet Gladstone also manifested discipline of an unusual order. Many events in his life—coming to terms with the death of his baby daughter, coping with the loss of office, preparing his famous budgets, negotiating the terms of Irish legislation—demonstrated a high degree of self-control. It would seem that Gladstone, fearing a loss of control and knowing its potential for harm in his political life, sought to gain a strict mastery over the circumstances in his life.

These characteristics suggest an aspect of Gladstone's life that has hitherto been unexamined by any previous biographer. We know Gladstone as moralist, as politician, and as public spokesman; we do not know him psychologically. To understand Gladstone's behavior in psychological terms is, however, a daunting task. The application of psychological principles and concepts to historical studies has been plagued with theoretical inadequacies and simplistic explanations.[19] A misuse of Freudian and neo-Freudian theory and its attendant therapeutic paradigm has presented particular problems. The subtle complexities of human behavior have been denied by an emphasis on pathological portrayals and the diagnostic labeling of historical actors. It is not surprising that joint efforts in psychology and history have fallen into disrepute.

My second major objective, therefore, is to suggest a psychological approach to the past that is less reductionistic and more genuinely attuned to historical studies than has heretofore been the case. The approach that follows is based on a loosely knit group of ideas known as stress and coping theory. These will be supplemented by life-course and life-cycle theories, the psychology of control, and cognitive dissonance theories.

Simply put, stress and coping theory postulates that external "stressors" impinging on individuals call forth a set of cognitive responses. A stressor may be any tension-filled or discordant event, including work-related problems, marital difficulties, or misunderstandings with friends. Stressors engender within individuals varying degrees of psychological stress, which may be defined as a perception of impending harm.[20] To mediate stress, individuals engage in a two-stage process. First is cognitive appraisal, by which an individual reflects on the nature of the stress. Second is coping, a process by which individuals manage the perceived stress and thereby restore a sense of coherence and balance to their lives. Coping styles vary, depending on family background, religious beliefs, social skills, and differing stressful circumstances. Coping may be a relatively benign mechanism such as humor, crying, boasting, talking randomly at length, or withdrawal. Coping mechanisms may also be straightforwardly negative, aggressive, angry, and generally antisocial.[21]

Coping is not always successful: individuals may misidentify the source of stress or misconstrue the circumstances in which they find themselves. Thus, coping mechanisms may sometimes appear to be inappropriate or even pathological. If a politician were to pursue a continuous strategy of withdrawal in public life in order to avoid perceived threats, he or she would surely offend political allies and seriously damage career prospects. In contrast, a brief withdrawal might provide a temporary haven for a troubled politician. A short-term political loss might be acceptable to secure long-term psychological gains. Thus, successful stress management can occasionally appear to be dysfunctional. This was most certainly true of Gladstone. He commonly followed a strategy of withdrawal. Diplomatic illnesses, avoidance of cabinet meetings, threats of resignation, and flights from England were as characteristic of his behavior as his mastery of parliamentary practices, his rousing speeches in the countryside, or his assiduously prepared budgets.

Gladstone sometimes employed an entirely different strategy, however: he engaged in attacks on his political opponents. Indeed, Gladstone's vehemence and anger were commonly noticed by his contemporaries. But it is important to identify the kind of anger that characterized Gladstone's outbursts. As traditionally defined, anger is usually thought to be caused by frustration, that is, by a cancellation of something planned or an interruption of an activity already under way. Psychoanalytic theory sees anger as a subset of aggression. As a natural expression of human beings, anger must be periodically released to prevent it from causing debilitating illness. It is thus usually seen as a negative emotion.

From the point of view of social constructivism, however, anger (as a socially constituted emotion) may in some cases have beneficial effects.[22] That is not to say that all anger is socially useful: some anger can lead to physical aggression and violence. But within an accepted context, anger can be an appropriate instrumental device for securing certain psychological ends. So defined, anger is not atavistic, part of some biological residue of a far-distant ancestral past. Rather, it is an emotional response that is drawn on, and reflective of, cognitive behavior. Anger is thus "chosen." It is a way of fighting back, of repelling the invasion of destructive stress. Angry people often consider themselves morally justified in being angry: they may choose anger as a reproach for a perceived misdeed. Anger can also be an attribution of blame. A politician may use anger as a strategy to unnerve and intimidate opponents or to unmask suspected opposition policies or threats to legislative programs.[23]

For Gladstone, anger was probably used on occasion to intimidate but more frequently to fend off threatening events or behaviors. Anger also fueled his passionate advocacy for various political and social causes. As Morley noted of Gladstone, "In native capacity for righteous Anger he abounded."[24] Anger can thus be viewed, in Gladstone's case, as a reasonably effective way of managing the various stresses of political life, especially within the House of Commons. His angry outbursts were, therefore, not a sign of insanity, as his severest critics might claim.

With its emphasis on coping, or fighting back, stress and coping theory lends a more optimistic, less pathological cast to the inevitable psychological struggles of life. The most effective stress managers are those who have developed what Antonovsky has called a sense of coherence—the notion that things will generally work out well.[25] Gladstone, despite moments of pessimism and occasional depression, had a sustaining belief in religion and morality that provided for him a sense of coherence important to his psychological well-being. Gladstone also likely had a complementary sense of self-efficacy; that is, he believed in his own capacity to master events, a construct similar to what another psychologist has called hardiness.[26] Hardy persons are not only confident that they can influence the circumstances of their lives, but they also have a deep commitment to a system of beliefs that tends to minimize perceived threats radiating from stressful events. Indeed, the belief in a just world substantiates the notion that good things happen to those who do good. If one plans carefully, strategizes effectively, and behaves "mindfully," then psychological and perhaps even material rewards are sure to follow.[27]

Hardy people are thus "healthier" than those who feel powerless in the face of external forces. They tend to be cognitively flexible and to meet change with a sense of exhilaration. They have developed a capacity to see life circumstances as connected, not disjointed. They construct linear, progressive narratives of their lives to impart a sense of direction and movement; such narratives reinforce their sense of coherence. These narratives also engage others. There is a reciprocity in relationships, an ability to incorporate family, friends, and colleagues easily into the texture of one's life. Such a life not only "unfolds" but also "opens out."[28] Such characteristics are crucial to the successful politician. How Gladstone acquired them is undoubtedly related to his early experiences within his family of origin, during his schooling, and at university.

It will be readily noted from this discussion that stress and coping theories are more modest than psychoanalytically based models in their claims of explaining past lives. Stress and coping theories, for example, pay relatively little attention to childhood experiences and their putative effects on adult behaviors. These theories thus have an advantage over Freudian models with their attempts to draw consequences for adults from inadequate toilet training, bungled breast feeding, or foreshortened oedipal development. Stress and coping theories have other advantages, too. By emphasizing the positive adaptive qualities of individuals, they decrease the emphasis on pathology, also characteristic of Freudian approaches. And by allowing for cognitive appraisals, they reduce the reliance on unconscious motivations. Stress and coping theories, while more limited in their application, are also far less speculative than psychoanalytic approaches.

If Freudian models of past behavior have erred in overemphasizing the formative effects of childhood experiences on adult behavior, it is nevertheless true that a careful appeal to psychological modeling can be useful in gathering together the disparate threads of Gladstone's early life. In recent years, plausible alternative models to psychoanalytic theories have begun to make their appearance in biographical studies. A promising example is Elisabeth Griffith's use of social learning theory in suggesting ways of explaining early influences on Elizabeth Cady Stanton, the nineteenth-century American suffragist and reformer. Griffith bases her model on the work of Albert Bandura, who postulates that individuals, even as young children, learn appropriate behavior by observation and reward. Approval for an act or word reinforces that act or word; disapproval discourages such behavior. As one masters a difficulty or copes with stress, patterns of behavior are strengthened. Thus one learns. Most important, Bandura emphasizes that learning is cognitive and lifelong. Individuals "code and store" information, and they thoughtfully mediate the meaning of external stimuli, rather than respond automatically. In Stanton's case, she patterned her own behavior on the lives of others. In time, these adopted behaviors were successfully internalized to become her own.[29]

As one moves through the life cycle, behavioral changes are possible. Indeed, life-course and life-cycle theorists argue that individuals undergo distinct changes related to chronological stages. Erik Erikson's famous eight-stage epigenetic chart demonstrates how individuals may evolve into succeeding stages of life, each stage eliciting discrete needs and prescribing certain roles. Other theorists have devised variants on this theme. Dan Levinson has portrayed a dialectical process in male development, and George Vaillant has analyzed the effectiveness of ego defense mechanisms in achieving maturity over time.[30] Although these studies are grounded in the psychoanalytic tradition, they nevertheless demonstrate the new thinking in ego psychology that emphasizes adult development.

If, then, we join the programmatic schema of life-cycle studies to the stress and coping model, we ought to be able to predict stages in past lives when stress was most likely to occur. A Victorian politician such as Gladstone might have expected a parliamentary seat, or a high office, or a cabinet post at a certain time in his life. When these expectations were not met, frustration and curtailed ambition could have been a powerful stressor. As we know from his famous diary, Gladstone was almost obsessively determined to make the best use of his time. He was extremely conscious of the fleeting moments of the day as they impinged on his work. Every task he undertook, he performed intensely. Each minute for Gladstone, a contemporary wrote, "had its employment, each book (of the many he read in the day) its appointed hour, each paper, letter, and document its proper place."[31] It is not too much to suggest that Gladstone was a Victorian workaholic.

Gladstone was, however, relatively free from role stress—a dominant form of tension among members of late twentieth-century middle- and upper-class families, who often face conflict between work and family life.[32] Gladstone expected—and received—his due as the head of a large, deferential Victorian family. Gladstone's wife and children, pressed into service as readers, secretaries, or social assistants, were knit together into a strong familial support system to facilitate his work and leisure.

Gladstone, therefore, manifests certain consistent personality traits and behaviors that are characteristic of his private self; these same characteristics are also important to his public policy. Such a flexible paradigm as stress and coping theory should make it possible to draw a connection between the private Gladstone and the public Gladstone—that is, between the two Mr. Gladstones. Only in this way can the apparent inconsistencies in his life and work be explained.

In attempting to construct a psychological portrait of Gladstone and to determine its relation to public policy, a student of Gladstone's life is fortunate in the diversity and depth of the relevant historical evidence. The most important source is the diary that Gladstone kept virtually every day of his adult life.[33] Much of the diary is simply a catalogue in telegrammatic style of daily events. We know where he was, what he did, the books he read, to whom he wrote for nearly three-quarters of a century. But there is much else. We also know the track of his daily thoughts and the private image he had of himself and of others. We can follow Gladstone in his most ebullient mood and in the depths of his most morbid introspection. Later volumes of the diary also contain letters between Gladstone and a wide variety of correspondents—an invaluable addition to the record of his life.

The details of the diary reveal Gladstone as less assured than we would expect from a statesman and politician of his stature. He often seemed tentative about the meaning of his life. He worried about the loss of time spent on unworthy or frivolous activities. Some of this worry is undoubtedly due to the dour Evangelical habit of religious introspection: an emphasis on his sin and depravity appears in the first volume of the diary and continues well into adulthood and old age. Apart from anguish and doubt at the state of his own salvation, he also wrote of his deeply felt "oppression" when rejected for a second time by a prospective bride, of his impatience when serving as amanuensis to his ailing and demanding father, of his annoyance and then anger at the religious apostasy of his sister Helen. He reflected on the nature of pain and whether it can be enjoyed. He noted with sadness the loss of his closest friends. He wrote year-end summations of his life, sometimes in elegiac mood, sometimes in hopeful anticipation of what was yet to come. These summations became formulaic in time, but in his earlier years they were clear expressions of strong emotional tides.

Though frequent, his diary entries are tantalizingly brief. This is particularly problematic when analyzing Gladstone's affective life. Thus, for example, the significance of his episodes with London prostitutes remains obscure. Nevertheless, the diary is informative. It becomes a record for an outpouring of guilt, self-justification, and mordant self-pity. To purge the guilt, he sometimes scourged himself with a whip when he returned from the most tempting of his late-night vigils. His intimate association with women outside his married life was not a thing of the moment or a youthful sowing of wild oats: in his sixtieth year, Gladstone corresponded secretly with a former courtesan turned religious revivalist.

In a psychological sense, the diary not only presents Gladstone's ruminations on the state of his own emotions; it may also be argued that the very act of keeping such a diary was in a rough way an act of coping. By sorting out and setting down his daily activities, Gladstone could impose order on the events that crowded in on him during his impossibly busy life. A man who so highly valued his time would equally value a strict accounting of it. Such a system would help promote a sense of coherence not only for each day that passed but for the day to follow. The diary taken as a whole is a monument to his determination to control the events of his life.

To say that Gladstone confided in his diary and revealed surprising emotional diversity may not seem unusual when we remember that other Victorian diarists have also done as much. The rollicking Walter of *My Secret Life* is rich in sexual fantasy and illusion. Arthur Munby's diary is even more revealing of obsessional behavior; not far behind is Munby's servant, partner in fetishism, and eventual wife, Hannah Culwick. Equally intriguing is the diary of the American Mabel Loomis Todd, whose carefully chronicled sexual proclivities (and those of her husband) were hidden from the prying eyes of a quiet Massachusetts town.[34] All these diaries are affective journals; that is, they speak of emotions. What sets Gladstone apart from these and other diarists is his identity. What Gladstone said or did, even as a private individual, had influence. When Gladstone wrestled with himself in the pages of his diary, grappling with the nature of sin and temptation or with desire and duty, the outcome could not help but be more important for the world than for almost any other diarist we may encounter in his era.

A second important source for the details of Gladstone's life is the extensive collection of family correspondence housed at St. Deniol's Library, Hawarden, and viewed at the Flintshire Record Office nearby. Most helpful to the research for this book was the correspondence between Gladstone and his wife, extending over many decades, and the letters between Gladstone and his sons and daughters. Correspondence also exists between Gladstone and members of his family of origin, including his father, his brothers, his sister Helen, and others of his extended family. This correspondence is crucial for interpreting the Gladstone family context. Less important for exploring the psychological side of Gladstone but still important for understanding his role in the formation of public policy and his day-to-day administration, is the enormous collection (750 volumes) of political correspondence at the British Library.[35]

Without his diary and personal papers, a psychological portrait of Gladstone would be impossible. Yet some caution is in order. To rely exclusively on the diary for its affective content is to take Gladstone at his word. Corroborative evidence is essential. Luckily, Gladstone was often a topic of absorbing interest among his contemporaries. References to him emerge frequently in letters, political memoirs, country house gossip, and newspapers. Friends and enemies alike were exasperated, mystified, or merely puzzled by his behavior and political decisions. Their comments are happily accessible in the published secondary works of the nineteenth century, especially in the multivolume biographies so characteristic of that era. Hundreds of relevant works were written by people within Gladstone's extensive circle: cabinet colleagues, junior ministers, journalists and other political observers, and nonpolitical members of political families.

The extensive evidence on Gladstone, when viewed in psychological terms, leads inescapably to the conclusion that he was a man of great volatility and passion. Equally important is that his active and stressful life forced him to develop a sophisticated range of responses to stress. His interest in rescue work, his enthusiastic collecting of fine porcelain, the happy hours spent in arranging an extensive collection of books, his habit of tree felling at Hawarden all suggest diverse means of coping, of relieving stress in some fashion. Within his political life, his habit of threatened and real resignations from office likely were also coping devices, as was his occasional withdrawal from the parliamentary battles. His rich emotional life ranged from introspective fears on existential matters to guilt and remorse for dabbling in the most forbidden of Victorian pleasures. He was a man of great cognitive complexity. We can no longer believe, as Morley did, that "nobody had fewer secrets, nobody ever lived and wrought in fuller sunlight."[36]

2

Willingly to School

William Gladstone's early life was not an unusual one for a child in his circumstances. His family was wealthy, although only a generation removed from humbler origins. His paternal grand-father, Thomas, was a Scots corn dealer. Of Thomas' sixteen children, John, the eldest, proved the most commercially adept. From an early age, John was active in his father's business. After learning the trade, John traveled south to try his luck, like many energetic and ambitious Scotsmen before him. Settling in Liverpool, John Gladstone soon became a partner in a firm of corn merchants. When the partnership ended after fourteen years, he established his own business.

A man of obvious intelligence, immense drive, and calculating shrewdness, John Gladstone prospered during a time of commercial uncertainty. Using both the American and French Revolutions to his advantage, he traveled widely in North America, the Baltic, and elsewhere, anticipating shortages and making purchases for the market at home. The transatlantic grain trade became the staple of his initial fortune, which he parlayed into a greater one by lucrative investments and capital diversification. His interests included property, shipping, and West Indian sugar, cotton, and slavery—the latter a Liverpool specialty because of that port's long association with the slave trade. His net worth increased from approximately sixteen thousand pounds in 1795 to more than five hundred thousand pounds in 1828. He purchased several fine houses: residences in Edinburgh and Liverpool; Seaforth House in the Liverpool suburbs; and in 1829 the estate of Fasque, in Kincardineshire on the east coast of Scotland. His career and remarkable accumulation of assets represent one of the most notable of the entrepreneurial success stories characteristic of Britain's emerging commercial and industrial power.

Although he was ceaselessly active in making money, John Gladstone's energy found other outlets as well. Most important was his growing political ambition. As a leading Liverpool merchant, it was natural for him to cap his rise to economic prominence with a comparable political achievement. In those unreformed days, corrupt boroughs offered unique opportunities. From 1818 to 1827, he sat for a variety of seats. His ultimate goal, to become the member of Parliament for Liverpool, was never realized, although he became an election agent for the moderate Tory George Canning, M.P. for Liverpool, who served briefly as prime minister in 1827. John Gladstone's support for the Tories was ultimately rewarded when Sir Robert Peel granted him a baronetcy in 1846, a distinction held to the present day by the Gladstone family.

John was married twice, first in 1792 to Jane Hall, daughter of a Liverpool merchant. She died childless six years later. In 1800, John Gladstone married Anne Robertson, who came from a genteel landed family of Highland descent. Anne was a study in contrast to her husband. Where he was bluff, domineering, and quarrelsome, she was shy and retiring, and often ill. She bore John six children; William was the fifth, born in 1809 at the Rodney Street house in Liverpool.

Although it is impossible to be certain about the influence of parents on children, more than adequate evidence suggests a correspondence between some traits and ideas in William's parents and some in his own adulthood. Perhaps the most significant example is William's religious development. The Gladstones were members of the established Church of England. But it was not the languid state religion of the eighteenth century that the Gladstones practiced. Though Anglican, they were part of the more dogmatic, more Calvinistically inclined wing of the church known as Evangelicals—a form of Anglicanism that emphasized a consciousness of ever-present sin. Through frequent church attendance, daily prayer, and family Bible reading, Evangelicals hoped to avoid the most tempting snares of a wicked world. Yet with a sure understanding of human depravity, they knew that failure was inevitable. Thus it fell to each Evangelical to be personally responsible for his or her state of sin: continuous self-scrutiny and a strict accountability were necessary to guard against Satanic wiles. A careful life, organized around godly principles, gave hope of—if not a blameless life on earth—salvation in another life.

Such a method of strict introspection was not only at the service of discovering and expunging sin in individual lives; it was also designed to find the working of God's will in the events of everyday life. Happier times were a manifestation of divine mercy. When things went wrong, it was an example of the wrath of God or, at best, of a time of testing and strengthening for the benefit of the life of the spirit. Evangelicalism was the religion of Job. Accordingly, in the frequent illness of Anne Gladstone a strong Evangelical message could be found. To bear physical burdens, to submit to the will of God, and to be tested for one's faith could even be signs of God's favor. From her sickbed, Anne Gladstone spoke often to her children of the cleansing blood of the Savior and the crown of glory for his redeemed.[1]

If William learned at his mother's knee the lessons of duty and obligation within the religious framework, these lessons were confirmed by the precepts of his father, who also had an Evangelical lineage. John Gladstone's father, Thomas, had been an austere Evangelical, who read his gathered family a chapter from the Bible each night. Thomas, a dogmatic moralist, condemned the theater, novel reading, and other "vain appetites." Such a view of life effectively insulated the Gladstones from the critical and literary movements associated with the Enlightenment thinkers of the eighteenth century. The astringent notions of David Hume, a fellow Scotsman, would have been especially distasteful to these practitioners of earnest religion. Because Evangelicalism was strongly didactic and proselytizing, it had a powerful effect in socializing family members. Not surprisingly, then, John Gladstone followed his father's belief—although generally he was far less ascetic in his practice. John enjoyed playing cards, especially whist; took a glass of wine now and then; and encouraged the musical talents of his children. Sketching, novel reading, and poetry were accepted part-time activities in William's childhood. In some ways, however, John was a far more dynamic Evangelical than his father. As a successful merchant, he was able put into practice the precepts of Evangelicalism. Dissatisfied by the routine Anglican services in Liverpool churches, John Gladstone built two churches and placed his own preachers in the pulpit. Each of the new churches had an affiliated school: at St. Andrew's Episcopal Church the children of the deserving poor were to be educated, and St. Thomas' was for the sons of gentlemen. By these acts, John Gladstone was recognized as the founder of Evangelicalism in Liverpool. Other charitable interests drew John's financial support, including the Society for Bettering the Condition of the Poor in Liverpool, and the Female School of Industry, probably formed to give poor women options other than joining the growing ranks of urban prostitutes.

Not only the propagation of religious belief and philanthropic obligation was served by John Gladstone's churches and schools. They also were a source of profit, bringing him a return of £750 annually from pew rentals and sales of burial plots. In fact, his religious life often complemented his commercial instincts. His fellow worshipers benefited from his entrepreneurial gifts: St.

Andrew's Church was one of the first Liverpool churches to be illuminated by gas. John took care to encourage in his children this potent combination of Evangelical moral rigor and commercial acumen. He also inculcated in them the importance of striving, the wise use of time and money, and the benefits of secular ambition. To dislike waste and to spend wisely every minute nicely complemented the Evangelical creed. In teaching his children to record money earned and spent, for example, John Gladstone extended the idea of spiritual accountability to more mundane matters. To lead a life for Jesus Christ did not preclude success in secular concerns.

Deep within the Evangelical view of life, however, was a hidden sin—the sin of pride. Linked uneasily to the overpowering sense of sin was a belief that once a person had received salvation as a gift of God, that salvation was personally known to the sinner. They knew that their Redeemer lived, and that knowledge gave to Evangelicals a certain confidence in their life's work. To participate in the struggles of devotion and self-betterment enjoined by the Evangelical creed might even indicate that God himself had designated certain sinners for special missions in the world.[2] Thus the paradox of the firm Evangelical believer: a keen sense of personal unworthiness joined to a highly developed self-righteousness. This was a characteristic often seen as arrogance in William's later life.

Equally important as a part of the affective inheritance of Evangelicalism was its unintentional inculcation of anger and hostility.[3] Evangelical parents, who were ever watchful for the manifestations of sin, who taught their children to doubt their own self-worth, and who, at their most extreme, sought to break the spirit of potential young rebels against the will of God, exerted an immense pressure to conform. Parental authority, thus designed to subjugate the natural growth of autonomy, emphasized the virtues of control and discipline—control over one's sinful nature, and discipline over one's actions in the sinful secular world. Parental authority of this kind, continuously exerted upon offspring even as adults, could feed a pooled reservoir of rage. But because that rage could not be directed against their parents, children vented their aggression against others who in some way symbolized parental authority and who were more appropriate targets. Seen in this light, Gladstone's heritage of anger, originating within his family, appears significant in familiarizing him with that emotion. Thus, as an adult, he might well "choose" such a familiar emotion as a device for coping with stress.[4]

It is not difficult to imagine how John Gladstone would have provided a model for the use of anger as a method of control. John never avoided confrontation—indeed, he seemed to seek it out—with either business associates or family members. To go against his wishes in business was especially risky. He rarely acted in concert with his various partners unless his was the final word. He once broke up a partnership with one of his brothers simply because the latter had attempted to mediate in a quarrel between John and a third party. Six of John's other brothers were ultimately brought into his Liverpool business in positions of dependence.[5] He was a man of strict routine and order, never leaving his desk for the day until it had been cleared. As in business, in family matters too he sought an established dominance. Both his wives were invalids, as though in illness they could escape from John Gladstone's driving personality. Escape was less easy for his children, as he managed their lives into adulthood. Even in his charities, he played a supervisory role, acting alone and controlling their funding and direction.

By observation and emulation, young William learned from his parents. He could not help but assimilate the precepts of the Evangelical-commercial creed, most likely the most formative influence on him. Long after he had surrendered the substance of the Evangelical faith, he retained its tortuous introspective demands. He also learned other lessons from his father's business practices: the rewards of assiduous labor, the efficacy of controlling the circumstances of one's life, perhaps even the usefulness of well-directed anger. Issues of anger, control, and authority remained problematic for William though much of his life.

This characteristic should not suggest that William had an unhappy childhood. In fact, he held a favored position as a younger child in the family. His place in the birth order guaranteed some distance from the parental expectations traditionally bestowed on elder sons: his brothers buffered him from the excessive demands of an overpowering father.[6] In addition, as the child of aging parents—John was forty-five at William's birth, and approaching sixty when he was in early adolescence—William occupied a position in the family more analogous to that of a grandson than a son. This may have meant that he was singularly adept at earning his parents' praises, thus reinforcing the natural propensity to model himself upon their expectations. William was also fortunate in that he found a rare comradeship with his older sister, Anne, who matched his unusual combination of intelligence and piety. In Anne, William found a confidant from whom he could seek advice and support within the family. In this sense, Gladstone may be said to have manifested early signs of developing a strategy of withdrawal for coping with unpleasantness.

William's early schooling did not take him far from home. He was put into St. Thomas' School at Seaforth, as were all his brothers, cousins, and other relations. Supervised by John Gladstone, the school and its master followed Evangelical principles. In effect, the school was simply an extension of the Gladstone family circle. Eventually, this rigorous domestic socialization had to end. John Gladstone, well aware of his own lack of cultural polish, entertained wider ambitions for his sons. Only Eton and Oxford would serve: they would provide his sons with the advantages he had lacked at their age. William's oldest brother, Tom, was the first to leave for Eton, in 1817. Eton proved a shock to Tom, as it had for generations of schoolboys. Perhaps it was worse for shy boys like Tom, whose only education had been in the sheltered school founded by his father. Eton was a Spartan world of freezing dormitories and poor food, rigid behavioral codes and obligatory rituals, humiliating submissions to senior boys, and a frightful social conformity. Infractions of house rules drew a severe caning by the master; more serious offenses could mean expulsion from the school. There was no religious comfort at Eton. Officially practicing a starched Anglicanism, it was effectively in a state of paganism. Lonely and isolated, Tom lacked the academic abilities that would provide a focus for his energies. In his first year, he fell into a bout of delinquency that nearly brought about his expulsion. Tom's time at Eton never eased, and he rose no higher than the fifth form. But he was able to perform a valuable service for William, who entered Eton in 1821, at the age of eleven.

As William's fagmaster, Tom smoothed the way for his younger brother. In the long run, however, William's success at Eton had more to do with his own intelligence and capacity for adaptation. He quickly learned the conditions for survival, avoiding difficulties that could bring him before the authorities: he was flogged only once in his six years at Eton. Bright and industrious, he took up the classical curriculum with enthusiasm. Modern languages—especially French—also attracted his interest. He was equally assiduous in his own reading: British history, literature, and political and philosophical topics were staples. Daily Bible reading on his own fleshed out his religious obligations, supplemented by rigorous study of the sermons of well-known divines. William was not a dreary swot, however. He was elected to the elite Eton Society, made captain of the fifth form, and promoted to the sixth form the year before he left Eton. He made many friends, some of whom he kept for a lifetime. He found time for long walks, sculling on the river, and extensive debates in the Eton Society—particularly valuable training for a political career.

William's success not only marked his ability to meet Eton's scholastic and social expectations; he had also obviously mastered the more subtle requirements Eton imposed on its students. Like other public schools of its day, Eton expected those who matriculated to become leaders and members of an established elite. This was largely assured by the prominent background of most of the boys. Eton merely provided the opportunity for these scions of great families to rub shoulders. In addition, the very structure of the school socialized its pupils to have certain expectations. Its hierarchical system, a microcosm of the British ruling class, was based on privilege.[7] To master the intricacies of this complex organization—which boys were expected to learn on their own—was a significant training for later careers. Where possible, Eton provided opportunities for boys to cultivate outside contacts while they remained in school. The Eton Society, for example, allowed former pupils to remain members; in William's day, the society included eight members of Parliament.

Socialization for later life was at least partly a conscious policy of public school education. Less obvious was the psychological effect this schooling may have had on some pupils. William's wholehearted acceptance of the Etonian world, its mode, and its values suggests that he was drawn to the system of rewards and punishments at Eton. Excelling at studies and feeling the consequent sense of achievement, receiving admiration from one's fellows especially in games, being selected as head boy, and winning the honor of election to the most prestigious societies were significant recognitions for those who worked hard. All in all, it was a perfect conditioning environment. If William accepted the rewards, he also seems to have accepted the system of punishments. This is not to say that he was masochistic. For him, rather, the system, by guaranteeing an accepted behavior, preserved order. Already disposed to expect a sense of order and coherence from his family and religious background, William took naturally to the Etonian system. He left Eton with regret, remembering it fondly to the end of his days.

As at Eton, so at Oxford William enjoyed success. He entered in 1828, after some delay because of crowding in the Oxford colleges. His father had chosen Christ Church, then the dominant college at Oxford and the one most determined to prepare a governing elite.[8] The ruling political creed at Christ Church was a solidly grounded toryism based on the maintenance of church and Crown. But it was also a nonideological toryism, pledged to a practical approach to the problems of governing. Thus reform was acceptable if measured and guided from above; a kind of administrative reform was the preferred method of change. Sir Robert Peel, one of the illustrious alumni of the college—who later became William's political mentor—was representative of this moderate brand of toryism.

Christ Church was also an intellectual center of the highest quality; a man could, therefore, either undertake the scholarly life or become involved in essentially political activities. William, then as later, chose both. His days were usually spent in reading the classics, theology, and some mathematics. His extracurricular activities included the university debating society (later the Oxford Union), of which he became president in 1830. He also founded a short-lived essay club, known by his own initials: the WEG. For recreation and health, he became a champion walker. His diary contains almost routine accounts of walks of eight miles, or fifteen, or, in one case, twenty-two miles. As at Eton, he made many good friends, with whom he delighted in conversing on a wide range of topics.

If William had a reputation at Oxford as an intellectual, he was also considered a young man of religious and censorious attitudes, who saw the hand of God actively at work in the university. Cautionary tales on the wages of sin in letters home, however, must have warmed his parents' hearts. In early 1831, he wrote his father about a "most awful death" of a young noble-man at Christ Church who "passed from perfect health into eternity on Wednesday night about twelve o'clock in *one or two minutes*. This alone were enough to render the event awful: What will you say when you learn . . . that he was called to meet God from the very midst of intoxication and profane-ness!" What would be the lesson of this "appalling event"? William wondered. He could hope only that God in his mercy might "touch some thoughtless and reckless heart."[9]

The most dramatic moment of his time at Oxford came in the spring of 1831 during the national debate on the great reform bill. Political temperatures had risen around the country with the dissolution of Parliament over the House of Lords' rejection of the bill. John Gladstone testified in a letter to his son that "the Reform fever seems to be an epidemic everywhere." That was not to his liking. "I expect, now, that this Democracy have felt their weight in the State." He predicted that a reformed Parliament would repeal the Corn Laws, alter the tithe system, abolish the plurality of church livings, "and God only knows what, for the principle will be a leveling one in the hands of a power that will neither submit to be controuled or restrained."[10]

Taking the lead from his father, William plunged into the thick of the ensuing election campaign as an antireformer. Perhaps to his surprise, Wil-liam discovered that he was passionate about the conservative cause. During the exciting days of May 1831, he joined in election processions, shouted himself hoarse, and experienced some minor assaults from the opposing fac-tion. As he reported to his father, there had been clashes "more or less every night with the mob. . . . I got pelted, though very slightly." He added, with some pride, that he had earned the reputation "of being a noisy character in these disturbances."[11] It was all very exhilarating. The climax for William came during a three-day debate in the Oxford Union on the reform bill. His forty-five-minute speech against reform electrified the union, a foretoken of his great oratorical career to come. The substance of his remarks was to refine further the question before the union: that the reformist Whig ministers were incompetent to carry on the government. William sharpened the attack by declaring that the reform bill threatened to change the structure of the British government and would ultimately break up the whole frame of society.[12]

In the months that followed, he continued his active support for the Tories. He collected signatures for a petition against the second reform bill, introduced in Parliament in June 1831. He went to London to hear the famous five nights' debate in the House of Lords in October 1831. To keep his phil-osophical grounding in conservatism up to the mark (if this were needed), he read Edmund Burke. Political excitement did not deter William from his academic goals, however. He spent the autumn of 1831 preparing for the oral and written examinations for the final honors schools. Here we find the first documented example of his quite remarkable capacity for concentrated work.

In spite of the distractions of the reform agitation, William averaged ten to twelve hours a day of study. His efforts were well rewarded. The capstone of his Oxford career was a Double First in Litterae Humaniores and in Mathematics and Physics—a testament to both his intelligence and his industry.

Upon graduation, William was widely recognized as one of the most promising young men of his Oxford generation. The question now before him was, for what vocation did his successes best prepare him? Early on in his university career, he leaned strongly toward the church. In a long letter to his father in August 1830, he declared his belief "that the work of spreading religion has a claim infinitely transcending all others in dignity, in solemnity, and in usefulness."[13] His mind constantly reverted, as he wrote to his father, "to the sad and solemn conviction that a fearfully great portion of the world" was "dying in sin": "day after day" his fellow creatures were "sinking into death." John Gladstone's reply suggests surprise and some disappointment.[14] For his youngest son, John had greater ambitions than could be met by priestly devotions in some obscure parish. "Let nothing be done rashly," he advised. Once his studies were completed, William could then decide. This temperate and shrewd advice bore fruit.

A second letter in early 1832 from William to his father contained a different message.[15] No longer did William see his duty in the "clerical profession." His attitude had clearly been changed by the events of the reform bill. He had become politicized by the attendant dangers of a wider franchise. The reform bill could lead, he believed, "to the destruction of the Church Establishment, to the overthrow of our own kingly government in this country . . . ; to the degradation of its National Character and through the depredation of the British Nation, to wide and irreversible ruin throughout the world." William feared for the future of traditional society—"of parent and child: of landlord and tenant: of master and servant." These ranks of society "extending from the highest person . . . to the lowest, and involving authority on one side, and a subordination and obedience on the other, have . . . formed a pervading bond of union, under whose constraint . . . the lower classes of different communities have been retained for the most part content in their station and have acquiesced in a life of labour." But now there was emerging a different philosophy—"a kind of calculation of interests, which is from its very nature necessarily shortsighted." It was "gradually and silently taking the place of those feelings of obedience and attachment under whose influence men had hitherto been content to act." This subversion of the "ancient principles of political union" seemed especially dangerous because it did not substitute anything better; it merely freed human beings to follow their own "ungoverned and uninstructed self will."

This strongly felt conservative manifesto justified William's change of heart from a contemplative religious life to political activism. Only by becoming a "public man" could he enlist himself in the struggle for sound principles of government. But he was unsure how best to bring about his chosen career. He had no immediate prospects at the end of his final term at Oxford. In February 1832, therefore, he set off on a six-month grand tour of Europe, a traditional valedictory to formal education among the aristocracy and the upper classes. William took his travels seriously, and his diary indicates an introspective mood. As he toured the great cities of Catholic Italy and France, he felt drawn to their beauty and tradition enshrined in the cathedrals. St. Peter's in Rome seems in particular to have made a deep impression on him. The glorious panoply of the Easter benediction was to William not only beautiful; it also struck him as a powerful reminder of a time when religion was at the heart of human experience. Yet he was also repelled by what he considered the overly sacerdotal quality of Roman Catholic services—much as Martin Luther had been repelled on his trip to Rome in 1512. Like Luther, William saw pomp and pride and ceremony frequently taking the place of genuine religious faith, especially when the services were so often performed in an offhanded manner. William's religious paradox was to remain a lifelong characteristic—an attraction toward the worldly beauty and order of the Roman Church combined with a distrust of what he considered the corrupting tendency of papal authority.

While abroad, William kept himself informed of the progress in Britain of the reform bill; in Venice he learned of its final passage through the House of Lords. Shortly afterward, he received word from an Oxford friend, Lord Lincoln, that Lincoln's father, the duke of Newcastle, was prepared to use his considerable influence to secure William a parliamentary seat in the forthcoming general election. Lincoln, who had been present as a union member during William's celebrated Oxford speech, had informed his father of his friend's accomplishments in general, and of his conservative views in particular. Newcastle, a curmudgeonly and possibly unbalanced ultra-Tory, was eager to stem the reformist tide and was willing to take a chance on the untried and presumably compliant young man.[16] William, who could not but be flattered by this sign of favor from one of Britain's premier families, set off at once for home. By August, he had drawn up his election address. In September, he was on the ground at Newark in Nottinghamshire, campaigning vigorously as he had done at Oxford the previous year—this time for his own parliamentary seat. By December 1832, he was elected member for Newark. William was just short of his twenty-third birthday.

John Gladstone was understandably pleased at his son's successes at school, university, and politics. William had met every challenge without faltering, vindicating his father's ambition for him. When William moved to London to take up his seat in the House of Commons, his father transferred to his account ten thousand pounds of Gladstone and Company stock. He continued to be generous throughout his life to his youngest, most promising son. William's gratitude toward his father was evident during his early years in Parliament. He kept his father fully informed in dozens of detailed letters, filled with parliamentary gossip and observations about the political scene.[17] In some ways, Parliament was for William an extension of the learning atmosphere of home and school. Writing many years later in an autobiographical note, William observed that his first years in the Commons reminded him of his school days: the bashfulness and timidity he felt toward the august position of the Speaker seemed not unlike his feelings in the presence of his Eton schoolmaster.[18]

As a young M.P. and the son of an affluent and ambitious father, Gladstone lived in London a life of leisured privilege when not attending to his parliamentary duties. He quickly moved into comfortable lodgings at the Albany, near Piccadilly (the lease was purchased by his father), and engaged a valet soon after. He entered Lincoln's Inn, taking occasional dinners there for several years before giving up his intention of being called to the bar.[19] He joined the Oxford and Cambridge Club and was elected to the Carlton Club, the Tory analogue to the Reform Club. He dined out frequently with acquaintances, family, and old Eton and Oxford friends. He took up singing and German lessons and maintained the course of wide reading that he had already developed. He walked a good deal, attended Sunday services, and kept regular habits—when his parliamentary duties did not intrude.

Parliament, of course, captured his main interest. He spent his first two years in unremitting opposition as one of a small number of conservatives who attempted to resist the Whig reformers. Reform of the franchise in 1832, factory reform in 1833, the Poor Law Amendment Act of 1834, municipal reform in 1835, the establishment of the Ecclesiastical Commission in 1836— all challenged William's closely held conservative views. The record of political and social reform in the 1830s made the decade uncongenial to a man of William's turn of mind. His voting record was marked by what he would call principle—that is, an almost unvarying defense of things as they were. He voted against the admission of Jews and dissenters to Parliament, against Corn Law revision, against the abolition of military and naval sinecures, against the publication of the division lists in the House of Commons, against the ballot, and against shorter Parliaments.

Within this reformist Parliament, William nevertheless found a recognizable voice. He emerged as one of the steadfast defenders of West Indian plantation owners, in deference to his father's economic interests. During the 1820s, John Gladstone's stake in the West Indies had increased substantially. Some sixty percent of his entire fortune—nearly three hundred thousand pounds—was invested in the Demerara sugar plantations by 1830. The larger his plantations, the more slaves he owned. Eventually, well over a thousand slaves lived and worked on Gladstone's plantations. On 3 June 1833, William gave his maiden speech in the House of Commons in defense of the West Indian planters against Whig proposals for the abolition of slavery. William's speech showed a mind divided. It was difficult to defend the West Indian interest without defending the institution of slavery itself; that far William could not go because it ran counter to the Evangelical abolitionist creed. But he could defend slavery as a form of property for which adequate compensation must be granted when slavery ended. His speech was well received, if the substance of it was not universally praised.

Although he had shown to advantage his mastery of detail and his fluency, this was his last speech of any consequence for several sessions. Indeed, he made less than a dozen speeches in his first two years—a matter of some discouragement to William himself. But he made his way forward by other means. He was scrupulous in attending the House of Commons; when once he missed a division of the Commons while dining out, he felt "excessively disgusted" and vowed it would not happen again.[20] He was faithful, too, in his other duties: receiving petitions to Parliament, reading papers relevant to the West Indian question, and attending innumerable meetings concerning the West Indies. William's intelligence and attention to parliamentary duties did not go unnoticed. As the months passed, his potential was recognized by the leader of the Conservative minority, Sir Robert Peel. When the reformist Whig ministry was dismissed and the Conservatives formed a minority government in November 1834, Peel made him a Junior Lord of the Treasury. Within two months, he rose to be an undersecretary of War and Colonies. Because Lord Aberdeen, who was secretary of state for War and Colonies, sat in the House of Lords, William was effectively responsible for that department in the House of Commons. It was a remarkable recognition for so inexperienced an M.P.

As a junior minister, William was particularly impressed by Peel's qualities as a political leader. Peel struck him as both pious and manly. Peel's conduct in the Commons was "masterly." When the Conservative government weakened in the spring of 1835, William harshly condemned the Whig opposition's tactics against Peel: "They have pressed, worried, and persecuted their noble antagonist as vermin tease creatures of a higher order than themselves." He closely observed his leader during a privileged visit to Peel's estate, Drayton Manor, in Staffordshire. Peel's reputation of coldness, William wrote to his father, was unmerited. Indeed, the reverse was true, although Peel's "shyness and thoughtfulness" could produce the impression of coldness.[21] William's association with Peel had clearly turned him into a disciple.

William's first term of office was brief: the Whigs were in again by April 1835. William used his unexpected time in opposition wisely. He began a course of reading that was in effect (as Colin Matthew notes) a second education. Much of his reading was theoretical in nature, designed to puzzle out the great issues of the age in which he lived. Most particularly, he concentrated on the place of ethics and morality in the state. Prompted by the legislative achievements of the reforming Whig government, he hoped to place his parliamentary experiences within the framework of his emerging conservative doctrine. His conservatism came to him naturally, from his family background and from his privileged position in society. He also seems to have had what may be called a conservative temperament. Although his experience of life was limited, he was convinced that society needed to be ordered, disciplined, and hierarchical to a degree. Society had to remain stable: rapid change could be unpredictably threatening. Samuel Coleridge and Burke were his modern authorities, Aristotle the ancient. Given these beliefs, it was not surprising that William justified his adherence to the Conservatives, a party held together, he believed, by a principle of obedience.[22]

It is not impossible to imagine, too, that William was drawn to conservatism because of another, equally significant reason: he feared chaos and disorder. It was a distinctively personal matter. His vehement antireformism was not merely the sign of an enthusiastic conservative partisan. Order and tradition represented safety, control, and the maintenance of a personal coherence. Schooled by his father in the virtues of an orderly life, William had learned his lessons well. Reform could not only cast off the traditional moorings of society but could also cut him loose from his own psychological groundings, rooted as they were in Evangelical teaching and parental influence.

The behavioral manifestations of William's need for order and control in politics first began to appear during the decade of the 1830s. That the young parliamentarian was tightly controlled—even rigid—in his relations with his colleagues can be illustrated by two suggestive episodes. The first was a deteriorating relationship with his constituency agents in Newark, which came to the surface in the summer of 1834 and apparently continued for some months. In August, William wrote in his diary that E. S. Godfrey, chairman of his election committee in Newark (and brother to the mayor of Newark), was "at the centre of offence" in some unnamed point of disagreement: "I am really and sorely tried in this matter," Gladstone noted.[23] Godfrey, for his part, charged that William was "too precise . . . too *particular* & too *close*" in his instructions to the committee, especially on the matter of election expenses. The disagreement arose over the electoral practice of treating: William believed firmly that unlimited meat and drink should not be provided to voters out of the election funds he supplied. He disliked both the bribery and the drunkenness that treating encouraged and had been at odds with the committee over this issue during the general election of 1832.[24] Clearly, Godfrey believed that treating won elections. Discourse between William and Godfrey worsened to the point that the duke of Newcastle was forced to mediate—an unusual position for the duke and a testament to the seriousness of the affair. Newcastle recommended that William confide more often in his election committee and give them a greater latitude and discretion.

Otherwise, Newcastle feared, the committee would continue to "draw conclusions . . . unfavourable to you."[25]

In another incident a few months later, William again showed an unmistakable propensity to control tightly the circumstances of his political life. During his short term of office in Peel's ministry, he took direct issue with his cabinet superior, Lord Aberdeen, the secretary for War and Colonies. In early March 1835, William held two "ominous" conversations with him when he learned that Aberdeen was considering a scheme of state-aided education to the West Indian former slaves once emancipation had been granted.[26] Indeed, Aberdeen was required to do so by a parliamentary resolution pledging assistance "on liberal and comprehensive principles." The plan would make no religious distinction among those benefited. Methodists, Baptists, and Roman Catholics, as well as Anglicans, would be eligible. To William, such a scheme would set a dangerous precedent. If the government—which financially sustained the official state religion, the Church of England—were to support from public funds other religious sects among the West Indians, then the Roman Catholics in Ireland "may at once call, upon the maxims of equal justice, for a participation in the Revenues in the Church [of England]." This, to William, was unacceptable: "Honour and religion [would] unite in imperatively enjoining me to decline participation in giving effect to that arrangement."[27] In short, he would resign.[28] He gave no hint here of compromise, or a willingness to consider differing points of view. It was as though William were determined either to force Aberdeen to his opinion or, if he was unsuccessful, to withdraw. The ministry was turned out before the matter came to a head.

Overall, William managed the circumstances of his political life during the 1830s with reasonable success. In his personal life, however, there were decided failures. An important priority for him in the late 1830s was to find a wife, not only because he desired companionship but also because he could not imagine sexual contact outside the bounds of matrimony. He had already experienced sufficient guilt with masturbatory practices; whoring (as he would call it) would be worse still. He set about his task with the intensity that he had given to the antireform movement. His first candidate was the beautiful Caroline Farquhar, an Eton friend's sister, whom he had met in 1835. The active phase of the courtship was in the summer and autumn of that year. Not much is known about the events, but William was obviously smitten. In July 1835, he spent a fair amount of time at the Farquhar house at Roehampton (near Dorking) and at their London town house in King Street, St. James. By August, he worked himself toward a decision. A diary entry for 22 August recorded, "Much rumination at home in evg. wrote a paper on my position: and driven to prayer."[29] The paper to which he refers set out not only his hopes for marriage but—what was essential to William—the justification of his choice of a life's partner in religious terms.[30] Although he had seen Miss Farquhar but little, he had been assured by others "of her incorruptible religious and social character, which has passed unharmed through the furnace of London amusement." William was convinced that at the root of her soul lay the "love of God and of his will and word: that she is growing therefore into his image, an heir of God and a coheir with Christ." Consulting with his friend W. K. Hamilton, William wrote to Sir Thomas Farquhar, asking for his daughter's hand in marriage. "I hope earnestly & believe that the hand of God points the way," he wrote in his diary.[31]

While awaiting the answer, William continued to place himself in Caroline's company by visiting the Farquhar family, following these visits by furtive confidences (in Italian) to his diary. In early September, he received from Lady Farquhar a letter "which puts an end to it all."[32] He immediately set out by ship for the Gladstone home at Fasque in Scotland. During the following months, William's hopes were occasionally raised when he received communications from the Farquhars, indicating that they were sorry things had gone awry. William mistook their politeness for a rekindled interest in the match. The Farquhars were then forced to disentangle themselves once again from William's persistent suit. Intensive discussions between William and Walter Farquhar, Caroline's brother, began in February 1836. His diary charts the progress of what William hoped were renewed negotiations. At first the news was bad. "Now it is finished—it is extinct," he wrote in Italian.[33] Yet within the next four days, five meetings took place between William and Walter, for there seems to have been an "unexpected change."[34] In a letter to his father on 18 February, William absolved the Farquhars from any responsibility "for the extremely embarrassed position which matters have assumed." "I am rather the party responsible," he wrote. "They do not shut the door upon me, and have made no retraction whatever of the proffered intercourse."[35] But on 24 February, he noted, "It is wholly concluded" (in Greek). And on 29 February: "Final conv. with W. R. F." But on 5 March: "Saw WRF: pressed my point." The entry of 9 March brought the last word: "Saw W. R. F.—finalmente." The final blow, however, did not come until August, when he received word that Caroline had married. In exemplary Evangelical fashion, William sought a lesson: "I see distinct reasons for glorifying God: I therefore hope that even the pain will in his good time turn to good." This theme he pursued in an additional diary entry (this time in French): "Henceforward I pray to God that he may begin by deflecting my mind from this aspect, making me rather feel that he has taken this cherished hope from me for my own good, because of my sins and of his love. So may sorrow for these sins stifle regret for need and loss."[36]

During these months of failed courtship, William suffered another loss. His mother died at Fasque in September 1835. His response is rather surprising: he seems scarcely to have noticed. Apart from a few clinical descriptions about his mother's failing medical condition, the event is barely recorded in the diary, even though he was at her side at the moment of death. "We gathered finally in the evening to see her die," was his inscription on the evening of 22 September. William himself seems to have realized that his feelings for his mother were unnaturally cool. A few days after her funeral, he wrote, almost in a justification: "Illness removed her from our eyes. . . . The flight of the spirit was less felt because it came at the close of long and intense expectation."[37] But perhaps the truth is that, after all, he was bound to her by bonds of duty, not bonds of love. His father had clearly played the greater role in his life, and his mother was by contrast a pale shadow.

Still, it is likely that the loss of his mother had some impact on his life. Perhaps her death, as well as the loss of an intended bride, explains his relative inactivity during the parliamentary session of 1836: he made but two interventions, neither of much moment. Indeed, Shannon credits William's "extraordinary feebleness" during the session to his "emotional distemper" brought on by his failure with Caroline Farquhar.[38] Certainly his failed courtship seems to have made him touchy on the subject of marriage. When his brother Tom became engaged in the summer of 1835 to the daughter of a member of the Norfolk gentry, William seemed to object. He objected more strongly to his brother Robertson's engagement to a Unitarian in November 1835.[39] William protested on ostensibly religious grounds. Only in the doctrine of redemption, he believed, did Christianity have any adequate foundation, that is, in the "*purchase* of our souls by Jesus Christ, and the power of His Spirit to cure the radical *disease* of our wills and hearts."[40] Because Unitarians did not hold with this doctrine, such a marriage could be no true union of souls. "Either this is not marriage—or that is not belief."[41] Robertson quite rightly believed that William should have kept his reservations to himself. John Gladstone insisted that William attend the wedding, whatever he may have felt. This he did, but with less than good grace. "Would to God that I had been able to lift up my hands to bless them, and to pray for them with an affectionate heart," he wrote in his diary, "but my [blessing], such as it was, at least got out of my mouth."[42]

His brothers' successes no doubt rankled, especially so when William's second venture into proposed matrimony also failed. In the autumn of 1837, he was attracted to Lady Frances Douglas, daughter of the earl of Morton. During the first week in November, he visited Dalmahoy, the Morton mansion west of Edinburgh. The impression William made was unfortunate. Doubtless shaken by the memory of his initial failure at marriage, he seems to have translated his nervousness into a kind of excitable intrusion on Lady Frances, interrupting her painting with learned discourses on Italian culture and insisting that she display her musical talents. Not only was his precipitant earnestness off-putting to Lady Frances, but the Mortons may have felt the match would have been a misalliance as well. Within a week of his departure from Dalmahoy, William received through an intermediary a "crushing" discouragement from the Mortons.[43] Lady Frances eventually married the heir of Earl Fitzwilliam.

Disheartened, William was determined to withdraw completely from the country of his humiliations: he asked his father for permission to visit the Gladstone plantations in the West Indies. But his father refused. In the weeks that followed, William recorded in his diary moods of discouragement and even despair. Not long after his rejection in November, he noted, "A day of oppression and pain."[44] As the months dragged on, he felt continuing sadness. After a successful speech of some length in the Commons in March 1838, he was congratulated on all sides, but he could not savor his triumph: "Isolated from love," he wrote, "and my greedy heart unappeased by a thousand consolations, I am half insensible even in the moment of delight to such pleasures as this kind of occasion affords."[45] His mood had not eased during the spring and summer. In May he mentioned the "daily sadness that is upon me in the midst of this painted life of inward trouble."[46] In June his despair deepened momentarily when he attended a funeral. The cemetery, he thought, was "beautiful and soothing." The scene prompted thoughts of suicide: "I am tempted to desire to follow, I ought to be happy here, . . . yet I live almost perpetually restless and depressed."[47]

It could be argued that these sentiments were self-indulgent posturings, a legacy of Evangelical morbidity. But in fact, his feelings were symptomatic of a world gone wrong. The early promise of success that he had once enjoyed was unfulfilled. By late 1838, his political party had been nearly four years out of office. His own chances for political advancement had been struck down. The prospects for marriage and a family were dimmer than ever. The death of his personal and political prospects drove him into a depressive mood. Yet in the midst of these gloomy events, William records in his diary the emergence of a strategy that was to stand him in good stead for much of his life. "Active duty brings peace," he wrote, and "what I have then to pray for is to be kept always at it."[48] In activity he found solace. He had already begun a work of importance that increasingly filled his days and, in so doing, gave him a measure of hope and a restored sense of coherence to his life.

William had decided to refine his ideas on conservative philosophy in 1835. In the spring of 1837, he intensified his efforts, concentrating for illustrative purposes on the state and the church. There seems little doubt that the spur to completing the task was his growing loneliness and sense of inadequacy in his personal life.[49] The fruit of his labors was a puzzling, subtly argued, and controversial work. In *The State in Its Relations with the Church,* published in 1838, he asserted that the Anglican Church was the conscience of the British state and, as such, was justified in its favored position within the state. The national religion, he maintained, was the true religion—at least for Britain—and it must be upheld. This was equally the case for the Church of Ireland: the task of the Anglican Church in that island must be to win the Irish from their unfortunate preference for a corrupt form of religion. To this end, the penal laws ought to be invigorated in the service of converting the Irish. Clearly, not only the Irish but also Jews and dissenters could be ridden hard on the points of his argument.[50]

Given William's premises, the book was the logical outcome of a logical mind. But it was a harsh book and placed him in ecclesiastical matters—as he well understood—firmly in the camp of the ultraconservatives. Thus T. B. Macaulay's famous review of the book in which he called William the "rising hope of those stern and unbending Tories" was not far off the mark. Although *State and Church* was well received in certain quarters, it was an unfortunate episode for his career, at least in the short term.[51] As William moved toward uncompromising positions, the leader of the Conservative Party had simultaneously moved toward a more moderate brand of conservatism. Sir Robert Peel understood that the reformism of the 1830s called for accommodation and a willingness to adapt to the times. Since the publication of his widely disseminated "Tamworth Manifesto" in 1834, Peel had worked gradually within his party to adjust to change. The appearance of William's book could not but be an embarrassment to Peel. The dogmatic and speculative nature of *State and Church* went against the growing practicality of Peel's ideas. It was said that after a perusal of the book, Peel threw it to the floor, exclaiming, "That young man will ruin his fine political career if he persists in writing trash like this."[52]

State and Church can be explained in purely intellectual or religious terms. William was pushed in part by the uncongenial reformist temper of the times to take such an extreme stand. But a hidden motive for writing the book was to become passionately involved with his work in order to avoid (in William's words) oppression and pain. The religious nature of the subject matter must have given William, psychologically speaking, an even greater satisfaction and sense of coping with the stresses of his life. If writing *State and Church* was politically unwise, it may have been psychologically beneficial.

As he was completing *State and Church,* William put into play an additional strategy to ease the strains of his life. He withdrew from the scenes of his humiliation. We have already encountered his proposal—refused by his father—to leave England in 1837 after the failure of his second courtship. A year later, he was more successful. In August 1838, with the drafts of *State and Church* in hand, William left for a recuperative European tour. By withdrawing from the venue of personal defeats and political uncertainty, he could hope to regain at a distance the sense of coherence and stability he had momentarily lost.

The tour had the desired effect: William always enjoyed foreign travel. While in Italy, he met by prearrangement the Glynnes, a Flintshire family. Sir Stephen Glynne, Glynne's mother, his brother, and his two sisters, Catherine and Mary, made William welcome. Sir Stephen was a conservative

Whig M.P. for his county, distantly related to Pitt the younger. He was also an antiquarian whose special interest lay in the old churches of Great Britain.[53] He proved to be a charming host to his younger parliamentary colleague as their paths crossed and recrossed on the Continent. William was soon taken with Catherine Glynne, the older sister. After a whirlwind courtship, he proposed to Catherine in January 1839 in what must be one of the most incomprehensible love letters ever penned.[54] No one could be easily won by this approach, and Catherine was wary. He left Europe without an affirmative answer. His diary records his despair in February: "Here again—yes, even a third time—it would appear that in incorrigible stupidity, I have been precipitate."[55] But characteristically he persisted. After nearly six months of wooing, William at last had the answer he sought. Withdrawal from the arena of his earlier defeats had brought unexpected rewards.

3

The Need for Control

The myths that surrounded Gladstone as a man and a statesman
extended to his marriage with Catherine Glynne. Contemporary
comment particularly praised Gladstone and his wife for their
complementary natures: William was the oak and Catherine the
ivy; the orderly mind of William was offset by the charming carelessness of Catherine; he was the public man, she the domestic
woman. On Catherine's double wedding day (her younger sister,
Mary, wed George Lyttelton) William's groomsman Francis
Hastings Doyle composed a poem outlining Catherine's duties.
Among the stanzas are these:

> High hopes are thine, oh! eldest flower,
> Great duties to be greatly done;
> To soothe, in many a toil-worn hour,
> The noble heart which thou hast won.

> He presses on through calm and storm
> Unshaken, let what will betide;
> Thou hast an office to perform,
> To be his answering spirit-bride.

> Be thou a balmy breeze to him,
> A fountain singing at his side;

A star, whose light is never dim,
A pillar, to uphold and guide.[1]

Thus enjoined, Catherine fully expected to become an "answering spirit-bride" to William and a "fountain singing at his side." Catherine was expected to live for her husband and her children, and especially to make sacrifices for the sake of William's well-being and political career. How well she fulfilled these expectations in the eyes of contemporaries may be illustrated by Edwin Pratt's biography of Catherine, published in the year of William's death. According to Pratt, Catherine "merged her existence in that of her husband, watching over him with the most devoted solicitude, anticipating his every wish, sustaining him in his arduous duties, fortifying him for his great political conflicts, and, what was all-important for a man of his temperament, guarding him against all possible risk." She made sure nothing marred the "perfect peace of his home life." William's health and happiness were to her a "sacred trust." In this way, Catherine contributed substantially to William's "prolonged efficiency in the public service." Catherine was, above all, his "inseparable companion, shrinking from no fatigue, provided she could be of service to him."[2]

Her life, thus described, was lived wholly within the Victorian notion of the women's sphere. As W. T. Stead put it, had William been married to a cleverer woman, she probably would have been less helpful to him: an "overpowering individuality" of her own would have interfered with the smooth operation of William's career. "As iron sharpeneth iron, so a man sharpeneth the countenance of his friend; but Mr. Gladstone was not particularly in need of being sharpened; he was in need of being rested. Therefore Mrs. Gladstone was not so much another sword-blade clashing with his," Stead wrote in an unintentional double entendre, "as [she was] the scabbard of his blade." Because Catherine lacked the intellect of her husband, she never aspired to be more than a sympathetic listener to him. As a "capital house-mother, faithful and attentive," and an "admirable nurse, who studied her husband as a doctor studies his patient," she provided for all his physical wants. Catherine "recognized her limitations and never attempted to interfere with matters beyond her capacity."[3] To contemporary observers, they were the perfect match. "There have never been any serious differences of thought or feeling between Mr. and Mrs. Gladstone," we are assured.[4]

How true was this picture of the Gladstones? Did perfect union and harmony exist between husband and wife throughout their days? Or was their relationship representative of the strains of a typical Victorian family, where subordinate women and dominant men played unequal and sometimes unhappy roles? To ask this question is to answer it. As their letters reveal, there were indeed times of happiness and companionship.[5] William was often an attentive husband: he frequently wrote Catherine when apart from her. If not overtly affectionate, he was obviously concerned with her health and welfare. But he was also in the early years of their marriage a preoccupied and ambitious young man who disliked any interruption in his public life. On her part, if Catherine was never less than dutiful, she also disliked the enforced separations from her husband, and she could be sharp in reminding him of his responsibility to their growing family.

In the early years of their marriage, the Gladstones lived in London at 13 Carlton House Terrace, almost adjacent to Whitehall, a short distance from the Houses of Parliament and Westminster Bridge to the south. Thus their residence was convenient both to the center of Gladstone's work and to the surrounding houses of London society. They remained there, or next door at 11 Carlton House Terrace, or at John Gladstone's house nearby at 6 Carlton Gardens, during much of their life in the capital city. Wherever they were, the Gladstone household was managed with rigor. A strict adherence to house rules was expected. These included attendance at church by all servants at least once a day, although it was hoped "that as many as can arrange it will go twice." Daily prayers at home were held, supplemented by Sunday sermons given by Gladstone. Meals were strictly prescribed. Meals downstairs included breakfasts at half past eight, dinner at one o'clock, tea at five, and supper at nine. For breakfasts, tea and sugar were served with bread and butter. Meat was allowed only at dinner and supper, as was beer. Merchants' accounts were strictly regulated, and bills were "*to be laid weekly on Mr Wm Gladstone's table.*" Furthermore, an account would be kept "of all things broken: with the names of those by whom they were broken."[6] Rules of this sort were doubtless common enough, although one may hazard a guess that many house rules were less punctilious than the Gladstones'.

At times Catherine Gladstone was no more than an infrequent guest in her husband's rule-ridden house. Within a few months of their wedding, William began the pattern of separation from his young wife that was a major cause of stress in their early years. He was often in London for parliamentary sessions or cabinet meetings while she remained at Hawarden, her brother's Welsh estate, where the couple had decided to live when not in London. Conferences with political allies at various country houses also kept William away from home. Frequent election campaigns put him on the road. Yet his political agenda, as full as it was, formed only a part of his busy life. Literary men and religious leaders were high on William's social list. Business affairs were often pressing. His aging father was sometimes a heavy responsibility: he occasionally spent several weeks each year at Fasque, the Gladstone family home in Scotland. Extensive reading, pamphlet writing, his Homeric studies, china and picture collecting, his rescue work, and an enormous correspondence were all activities that William performed without Catherine. In order to complete his work, he fell into the habit of reading at mealtimes, and he kept something in his pocket to peruse during such intervals of enforced leisure as the time spent waiting for trains. He was also said to have "five minute books" placed in every room of his house, which he would pick up in stray moments.[7]

This is not to say that William avoided Catherine. Nor was he necessarily much different from other Victorian politicians of the time. Still, it is easy to sympathize with Catherine. Especially hard to bear were William's excuses for remaining in London when he had no obvious official duties. William explained that as a rising man in Parliament, he often found it necessary to be on call. His desire for high office could be harmed by an untimely absence from the political center of things. As he explained it to Catherine in early 1840, "You will be disappointed by my not coming down today: but I well know from experience that there is . . . no dependence whatever to be placed upon any desire or prospect of escape, unless one is determined to go at all hazards and to have one's duties, as they call it in Lancashire, in the lurch."[8] Two days later, William apologized again for staying "until the fag end of the session," but these delays were, he feared, a "practical exemplification of the difficulty of reconciling domestic & political engagements."[9]

William's letters to Catherine sometimes struck a tone that seems to modern eyes thoroughly paternal. When Catherine wanted a pianoforte so that she could occupy herself during his absences, he urged hiring rather than buying. "You remember how it was with the last one," he reminded her. But even should she hire one, William cautioned her that "until the next session of Parliament is over *I* must not dream of having any thing to do with your performances."[10] Child-rearing advice he passed on frequently in absentia. After Catherine's return to Hawarden from Rhyl, where she had gone bathing in the summer of 1841, William wrote that her account of their firstborn, William Henry, was "most acceptable." But he was soon cautioning her to deal firmly with an outburst of temper from the young Willy: "*Now* I am *convinced* is the time to subdue that foe."[11] William also made it clear that it was Catherine's duty to maintain domestic order during his hours at home. Catherine reassured him on that point. "I quite understand all you say respecting yr self and the necessity of quiet at home: it will ever be my endeavour to promote it as much as can be for you." She sympathized, she wrote, with the "necessity of repose after the mental work you go through."[12]

Nevertheless, Catherine resented the demands and restrictions imposed on her. William, on his part, was increasingly exasperated by his wife's requests for his company. Prior to his departure for Newcastle during the election campaign of 1841, they had a conversation about the issue. Afterward, Catherine wrote William a characteristically apologetic and submissive letter: "I thought over & over again your words & I feel I was *very weak* to give way as I did. . . . You make great allowances for me far greater than I deserve." She concluded her poignant letter thus: "I will try to be stronger minded but when you are away it seems as if a part of me was wanting."[13]

Catherine's strategies in dealing with her position were limited. Although she was a well-educated woman by the standards of her day, she had no special training or skills. Like many upper-class women of the time, she was responsible for organizing an extensive household and for serving as an ornament to her family and husband, but she had little opportunity for self-fulfillment. Her husband had his vocation; she had none. Yet she was a woman of great energy and persuasive power. Her bottled frustrations flowed from her inability to express those talents. Her initial option was to play the subordinate wife, as society dictated. The tenor of a note she wrote in 1840 reveals her strategy: "So my precious thing does not arrive till tomorrow. I *will* be patient but somehow I feel a blank! It is childish perhaps to be disappointed when I have everything, but it is right you should see what a weak thing you have got." This coy, worshipful, grateful, and submissive attitude was typical, as was her farewell, "your old wifey."[14]

William's public preoccupations and his domestic demands may have contributed to a lingering malaise that Catherine felt throughout much of 1841. Motherhood (their oldest son was born in June 1840) and another pregnancy wore her down physically. In December 1841 she consulted a doctor. Perhaps on his advice, she decided to spend more time at her sister Mary's house at Hagley in Worcestershire. William approved of this, hoping it would alleviate her condition. "I am anxious that you should not suffer loneliness because of my absorption," he wrote, "but absorbed I must be."[15] Thus began for Catherine the support of and growing intimacy with her sister Mary, the mainstay of her young married life.

Catherine, in managing her separations from William, also began to spend time at Brighton, where she particularly enjoyed sea bathing. Mary would often join her there. Because Brighton was closer to London than the comparable beach at Rhyl, Catherine hoped to lure William more frequently to her, at least for day trips by train. In urging him to Brighton in the spring of 1842, she wrote: "I have set my heart upon this. . . . I think you will try to do this for poor Wifie just now especially. Oh, how I dislike separations! A man's vast occupation I suppose naturally prevents the gt. void we [women] feel."[16] William, however, was in the midst of tariff legislation for the Peel ministry: "The pressure is now such that it is hard either to snatch a moment, or to keep a tolerably clear head for what one has to do—we also keep very late hours at the House of Commons."[17] Within a fortnight William was more sharply critical: "I have great misgivings about going down on Saturday," he wrote, "and I do not really think you quite comprehend the speciality of the present time. A person, who professes to have more to do than he can actually get through, & who in consequence is obliged to refuse seeing many who have a claim to be seen, ought not to be found cutting off beginnings and endings of days."[18] But Catherine was insistent. The next day, she replied at length, playing on William's sympathy. "I have just read yr. letter & shall not be telling truth if I concealed disappointment that I could not help feeling when I read of your *mis-givings* about coming here: . . . it would be such a sad disappointment to me that you should not see Willy for another week & he has been talking so much of you—poor darling with his poor pale cheeks for this cold has pulled him down in looks after having been so ruddy." William need only come a short time. "If I thought that by yr. coming here on Saturday evening till Monday morning you will not [be] acting consistently in consideration of the immense quantity [you] have to do—I should not press it but I do believe I comprehend the speciality of the present time & that it is not for want of being aware of it that I am brought to the conclusion that you might come here." He would lose "little if any time." In any case, he would not come to waste his time or to amuse himself but to "look after your little boy, & bring home poor wifie whom you have not seen for all but 3 weeks."[19] Her pleas had some effect: within a few days, Catherine and the infant Willy were in London, where they remained for the remainder of the spring and into the summer. For Catherine these months in London were no doubt what she had hoped: walks and drives in the park, prayers at home, chapel going, and visits to friends provided opportunities for the young couple to be together.

After the birth of their second child, Agnes, in October 1842, Catherine was freed for a time from the most confining of her domestic duties. She hoped to be with William during part of the parliamentary session of 1843, leaving the children at Hawarden. But he discouraged her. His days were "crammed from one end to the other," he wrote. "I am afraid this is the reason, and not self mastery and a sense of duty, why I am *hard* about absence. If you had been here I should scarcely have had five minutes to speak to you since I came here!"[20] Later in the session, William was once again exasperated: "At present I can give myself fully to business, without restraint or distraction of mind which of course I cannot do when you are sitting twelve or thirteen hours in loneliness at home."[21] Two days later, William thought of another reason why Catherine should remain at Hawarden. The children, he wrote, could become ill during her absence, and this would be an extra burden on her, forcing her to return from London to nurse them.[22]

Catherine occasionally protested William's absences strongly, but these were invariably brief episodes; she relented almost immediately. During a ministerial crisis in late 1845, for example, William was brought into the cabinet with the likelihood of missing holidays at Hawarden. "You will come home for *Christmas day* even should you have to return," she wrote rather sternly. "We must not be apart then if possible." A softer tone followed. "But I need not urge this. You will feel a desire to be with poor old wifie & your children upon that day of days."[23] A note to William on Christmas Eve further revealed her compliance to his wishes: "Oh I will not say how delightful it would be if you can get away! but if you cannot I shall be perfectly satisfied that it is *best* as it is."[24] This seems to have moved him. By taking the mail train at night, William arrived at Hawarden at seven o'clock on Christmas morning. After sleeping a few hours, he attended late morning Holy Communion, then dinner and tea, followed by a walk with Catherine "& a little time for the children." This "was not a tranquil" holiday, however: it was too "forced."[25]

The Gladstones' separations have been explained in various ways. Joyce Marlow maintains that the initiative came from Catherine because of her sense of independence, her preference for the countryside, and the domestic needs of her growing family.[26] This was clearly not the case. Georgina Battiscombe, in contrast, recognizes Catherine's reluctance to be apart from William, but she defends his decision to place duty above family obligations. Battiscombe seems to suggest that Catherine ought to have been satisfied with her role as marriage partner, even if she was kept at a distance: "Marriage . . . can of itself become a woman's life-work."[27] To Catherine Gladstone, however, her marriage must have seemed increasingly one of convenience.

William's excuses to Catherine for his absences were entirely justified in his eyes by the demands of his public and political life—demands that increased in the early 1840s. His hopes for a return to office, held in abeyance since 1835, quickened in 1840 as the fortunes of the Whig government faded. The Whigs had lost the reform impetus of their earlier days and—as is true of every ministry—had also alienated various sections of the electorate. By 1841 their days were numbered: on 7 June of that year, they lost a no-confidence motion by a single vote. In the ensuing general election, the Conservatives gained a notable victory, winning 124 of the 144 county seats. The agricultural community, made up of farmers and landlords, had thrown its support in overwhelming numbers to the Conservatives. They also won nearly half the borough seats.

As Peel assembled his cabinet and made junior ministerial appointments, it was clear that the cabinet would be dominated by Peel himself, staunchly aided by his home secretary, Sir James Graham. Others in the cabinet included the duke of Wellington, Lord Stanley, Henry Goulburn, and such lesser lights as the agricultural protectionist, the duke of Buckingham. This cabinet was to prove greater than the sum of its parts: in its own way, it was one of the most important reforming ministries of the age, perhaps on a par with its Whig predecessors a decade earlier. It provided a model for conservative reform self-consciously followed by Gladstone during his own later ministries. It was also a ministry pledged to uphold social order, an aim as dear to the heart of Peel as to that of Gladstone.[28] Gladstone, entertaining hopes of high office, aspired to an Irish post with cabinet rank. But Peel realized that placing his ambitious young colleague in Ireland after his outbursts in *State and Church* would be unwise. Instead, he was given the vice-presidency of the Board of Trade and mastership of the Mint, which was less prestigious than an Irish position but which give him a chance to prove his mettle. He accepted only reluctantly.

Gladstone's record at the Board of Trade was, from the first, a noteworthy success. He met the challenge at the board in the same methodical and assiduous way that he tackled his studies at Oxford. In his first two years, he mastered the intricacies of customs duties, commercial treaties, and especially the politically sensitive topic of corn importation. He soon developed the habit of working all day—fourteen hours was not uncommon. As it happened, he was strategically placed: one of the important programs of the Peel ministry was tariff reform, which fell within the purview of the Board of Trade.

When Gladstone came to the board, he was a protectionist, believing that domestic producers—in both manufacturing and agricultural sectors—ought to receive preference over foreign imports. He had inherited this view from his father. The right-wing members of the Conservative Party, especially the agricultural interest, were also firm supporters of the Corn Laws and favored protection. Rural protectionists were especially vociferous in their belief that cheap foreign grain, imported in quantity since 1815, had driven down the prices of domestic produce.[29] Should foreign grain continue to flow into Britain, prices would likely tumble further. Conservative landlords and farmers believed they had a pledge from Peel to raise (or at least maintain) farm prices by exclusionary tariffs.

Unknown to his agricultural supporters, however, Peel was moving toward a relaxation of protection. The prime minister was less concerned about maintaining profits on the land than he was in maintaining social stability in the newly industrializing urban centers of Britain. Recurring cycles of unemployment among factory workers had already led to dangerous riots and incidents of unrest. Peel was convinced that tariff restrictions on raw materials must be reduced; otherwise, manufacturing would continue to be impaired and more jobs would be lost. Once a reduced tariff structure as it related to manufacturing was in place, it was sure to set a precedent for excluding corn and other grains from similar tariffs. Peel also doubted the capacity of British agriculture to feed a growing domestic population single-handedly. Cheap agricultural imports must make up the difference. Lost revenue from reduced tariffs could be offset, Peel believed, by a moderate income tax.

Such a policy, however, posed serious political risks. If the agricultural interests were to unite under the banner of protection, the ministry itself could be endangered. But Peel was encouraged by the support of his cabinet, and perhaps encouraged especially by support from an unexpected source: his new vice-president of the Board of Trade. As Gladstone familiarized himself with the effects of protection, he had gradually altered his views. He disliked the clumsy administrative tangle that the Corn Laws required. A simplified system of free trade would make more orderly and efficient the entire process of trade for the country, including trade in corn.

Peel and Gladstone acted as a team during the later part of the parliamentary session of 1842. Throughout the ensuing debates, Gladstone performed invaluable service by expounding to the House of Commons the intricacies of the tariff law and explaining precisely how Britain would gain by their revision. During the session, Gladstone spoke 129 times.[30] Although support from their agricultural friends wavered, the government successfully reduced the tariff on imported corn and on 750 other dutiable articles. Through his hard work on the campaign for tariff reform, Gladstone had regained the trust of his chief, which he had momentarily lost on the publication of *State and Church*.[31]

Gladstone's capacity for detailed administrative work at the Board of Trade, the development of his skill as an eloquent debater in the House of Commons, and his role as voice for the Peel government demonstrated a powerful combination of talents. "Zeal and toil and knowledge, working with an inborn faculty of powerful expression," was Morley's concise evaluation.[32] Gladstone continued to please Peel, especially in fending off the radical free traders in Parliament who wanted to carry forward the logic of the 1842 tariff revision.

Complementary to Gladstone's work in Parliament was the first of many of his public writings on government policy. In *The Foreign and Colonial Quarterly Review*, Gladstone launched an attack on protectionism, arguing that the "trade of foreign countries is essential to England" just as the "trade of England is essential to foreign countries." The high place that England held among the commercial nations of the world, he asserted, had been assigned to her "in the order of providence": thus, England had nothing to fear from a free exchange of goods with the nations of the world.[33] In May 1843, Gladstone had his reward: he was promoted to the presidency of the Board of Trade, which carried him into the cabinet.

Gladstone continued his work during the next two years of what might be called Peelite reform—sound administrative procedures designed to facilitate government efficiency and the maintenance of order in society. In July 1844, for example, Gladstone brought forward a measure to regulate joint stock companies by creating a Registrar for Companies that dispensed official information about the companies. The legislation also provided tighter regulatory procedures to protect the public from unscrupulous company directors. In the same year, Gladstone's Railway Act brought the burgeoning and largely uncontrolled system of railways under the general scheme for regulating joint stock companies. The most famous provision of the Railway Act established the so-called parliamentary trains: railway companies were required to run at least one train daily at a minimum fare per mile, thus providing a cheap and regular service for the poorer sections of the population.

Yet Gladstone occasionally wandered off his apparent path of success. Perhaps these deviations were lapses in judgment or signs of unfamiliarity with parliamentary procedure. But viewed in the longer term, the following three incidents were part of a pattern suggesting that Gladstone continued to manifest some unease relating to matters of control and authority. The first occurred in early 1842 when the ministry began its policy discussions on a proposed new Corn Law. The general aim was to reduce agricultural tariffs. But tariff revision had to strike a delicate balance between cheap and abundant food for consumers, and the legitimate interests of farmers and landlords as producers. Peel believed that the balance could best be achieved by using the sliding scale (in effect since 1828), which varied inversely with the price of corn in the domestic market. That is, as the price of grain fell in Britain, tariffs would be incrementally imposed to keep foreign grain from flooding the market and lowering prices still further; this benefited the farmer. In a rising domestic grain market, however, consumers could benefit as tariffs were relaxed, allowing the importation of some foreign grain.

The existing Corn Law imposed a duty of twenty shillings and eight pence per quarter when the price of domestic wheat reached the pivot point of sixty-six shillings per quarter. As the domestic price of wheat rose, the duty declined in graduated stages. When the domestic price reached seventy-three shillings, only a nominal duty of one shilling remained. Conversely, as the domestic price of wheat fell below sixty-six shillings, the duty was increased. The law also provided for other types of grain (barley, oats, and so on) in the same manner, each with a specified pivot point. Peel initially proposed lowering both the pivot point—from sixty-six shillings to sixty-two shillings—and reducing the tariff from twenty shillings and eight pence to ten shillings. Peel won the cabinet over to his point of view, with one important exception. Gladstone opposed Peel's proposal, not on protectionist grounds but because he thought Peel did not go far enough in removing tariffs in favor of the consumer: he preferred sixty shillings as the pivot point and six shillings as the proposed tariff. Thus Gladstone, mastering these confusing and complicated statistics, had accepted the logic of freer trade: the existing Corn Law, he concluded, was "very stringent and severe."[34] He was determined to force his conclusions upon the cabinet.

Gladstone records in his diary several conferences with cabinet colleagues and with Peel alone in January and February 1842. The climax occurred on 5 February in a meeting at Peel's London house. Peel was clearly unsympathetic to Gladstone's position. "I fear Peel was much annoyed & displeased," Gladstone wrote in his diary, "for he would not give me a word of help or of favourable supposition as to my own motives and belief." After a lengthy discussion, Gladstone offered to resign his office. Peel was "thunderstruck" at this news from his junior minister, even hinting that his resignation could endanger the government itself. The whole conversation, as Gladstone noted, "had a chilling effect on my feeble mind." He returned home "sick at heart" and told everything to his wife.[35] Years afterward, Gladstone still remembered the event well, admitting that he acted "like a schoolboy."[36] The following day, Gladstone wrote a thorough apology to Peel and pledged his loyal support to the government, thereafter arguing effectively in the House for the Peel program.[37]

A second incident, not unlike the first, occurred the following year in connection with Peel's offer of the cabinet to Gladstone. The promotion was well deserved and had been eagerly anticipated, yet it was met with some reservation on Gladstone's part. He seemed to set conditions for the appointment. He told Peel that it was his "duty" to examine his mind for possible exceptions to any policy, which might embarrass the government. Gladstone's implicit suggestion—that if the government did not sanction his views, he could not join it—must have been trying to Peel; nevertheless, he responded with good grace to his young colleague. No cabinet could expect unanimity, he assured Gladstone, citing several examples of individual cabinet members who held different opinions on important issues. But Gladstone persisted, raising several issues one by one, so that Peel had to comment on each. Gladstone was satisfied on all but the last—a proposed merger of two dioceses in north Wales, St. Asaph and Bangor. He wanted them preserved as they were, arguing that the merger would be an intrusion by the state into the affairs of the Church of England. Because Hawarden lay within St. Asaph, Gladstone was doubtless especially sensitive to its fate. In any case, Peel, whose patience was probably at last exhausted, indicated that Gladstone's reservations on the merger were serious. Following a lengthy discussion on the bishoprics, Gladstone asked for forty-eight hours to think the matter over—"whether to enter the Cabinet, or to retire altogether."[38] After consulting with friends, he accepted. On that Monday, 15 May 1843, he attended his first cabinet meeting.

Within several months, however, a train of events began that led Gladstone once again to talk of resignation. In this, his third threat of resignation during the Peel ministry, he acted in a sensational and puzzling manner. The origins of Gladstone's actions lay in the government's decision, after months of repressive actions in Ireland, to initiate a conciliatory policy toward Daniel O'Connell's movement for the repeal of the Anglo-Irish Union. Peel believed that a series of moderate concessions could dampen the enthusiasm for repeal. Cabinet discussion developed along several lines: reforming the Irish franchise; opening more positions of public responsibility to Irish Catholics; encouraging the solvency of Catholic institutions, such as the privately endowed Catholic chapels and benefices; and improving both secular and clerical educational facilities. Peel believed that the key to conciliation lay with the Irish clergy, many of whom supported repeal. He therefore proposed a permanent government subsidy for the Royal College of St. Patrick at Maynooth in

County Kildare. Maynooth was the national seminary for Catholic priests, but it had long been underfunded and neglected by successive British ministries. Its educational buildings were dilapidated, salaries were poor, and living conditions were below standard. Peel did not propose a new endowment; annual subsidies had been granted to Maynooth since its establishment in 1795. But by making the endowment permanent and simultaneously increasing it threefold, Peel hoped to encourage a friendlier Catholic hierarchy. He also proposed increasing the salaries of the principals and professors at the seminary, and doubling the scholarships for the seminary students. A special grant for new buildings rounded out the program. The Maynooth proposal was very much in the spirit of Peelite reform—change for the purpose of preservation.[39]

As the cabinet discussed Maynooth, however, divisions of opinion emerged: both Goulburn and Graham had reservations. But Gladstone carried his opposition much further. Should the British state, sworn to uphold the Church of England, perpetuate a hostile religion by supporting its educational mission? Gladstone's answer in *State and Church* had been no. His pledge to the public as outlined in his book remained firm. He could not, he told his colleagues, go against those principles. In a private interview with Peel on 2 March 1844, he carried his argument further. Underscoring his reluctance to vote for a plan of Roman Catholic education in Ireland, he intimated resignation if the plan went forward. Peel was unmoved and told Gladstone that no one would remember his former pledges. To another cabinet meeting that same day, Gladstone reiterated the likelihood of his resignation, but he also declared that it would be based on the grounds of *former* pledges and that he reserved the right of a "free and unfettered judgement" on the final proposal. That is, he hinted that he would support Maynooth as a private member of Parliament—something he could not do as a member of the cabinet.[40]

As a result of Gladstone's objections, the cabinet decided to postpone action. In the weeks and months that followed, Gladstone wrestled with the issues of Maynooth. In a conversation with Peel in July, for example, he seemed to be backpedaling: he suggested that there might be a way of "disposing myself in such manner so as not to go out [of office] upon that question."[41] Clearly he was angling for a face-saving device. A few days later, he indicated to Peel what it might be. He suggested that he be sent as a plenipotentiary to the Papal See in lieu of his presidency of the Board of Trade. From there, Gladstone presumably thought he could win an audience with the pope and work more effectively for a conciliatory Ireland. For a man of his talents to step down from the cabinet to assume an inconsequential post of this sort was not only an astonishing abrogation of responsibility but was personally damaging as well.[42] This proposal was, of course, similar to his decision to withdraw from England in the late 1830s. Peel deflected the issue by simply ignoring it.

Gladstone still had hopes as late as the autumn cabinet meetings of 1844 that Peel might compromise. But the prime minister remained silent. Anguished letters to his wife revealed Gladstone's mood of despair. "I have had a long battle with Peel on the matters of my office," he wrote in November. "You will see that whatever turns up, I am sure to be in the wrong."[43] In early January 1845, Peel informed the cabinet that a Maynooth bill was in preparation and would be presented early in the forthcoming parliamentary session, most certainly within a few weeks. On 28 January, Gladstone recorded his "official catastrophe": on that day, Peel informed him that his cabinet position had been offered to another party member.[44] Two days later, the news was leaked to the *Times*.

On 4 February, Gladstone explained his resignation from the cabinet in a short speech to an eager House of Commons. The government's bill for Maynooth, he maintained, was "at variance" with the system that he believed best for relations between a "Christian state and the Christian Religion," a system that he had written about in detail "in a published treatise." In passing, he denied that he favored legislation that discriminated against Roman Catholicism; indeed, he favored a religious pluralism.[45] His performance shed no light on the reasons for his resignation. Few had read his *State and Church*, and fewer still understood it. Some members of Parliament thought that Gladstone had resigned for no discernible reason at all or, at best, that the reason was slight. One observer said that the event reminded him of the story of a man who jumped off a train going forty miles an hour merely to retrieve his hat.[46] Most members of the largely uncomprehending House, however, gathered that he had resigned on a matter of principle, which appeared to be based on opposition to the Roman Catholic religion. This made Gladstone briefly a hero of the anti-Catholic right in the Conservative Party. He even received an invitation from Sir Robert Inglis—one of the firmest advocates for the established religion and a right-wing Conservative—to lead the fight against Maynooth.

During the debates that followed in the House of Commons on the Maynooth bill, Gladstone did not speak often, preferring to remain, as he put it, an "anxious listener."[47] But when he did speak, it was once again to astonish the House. He announced on 11 April that, after all, he planned to vote for the Maynooth proposal: he was now prepared to give a "deliberate and even an anxious support" to it. The ministry had not changed the bill; Gladstone, it seemed, had changed his mind. As he explained it, the old principle of exclusive state support for the national religion of England was no longer possible to hold: it had been repeatedly whittled away by acts of the state itself. Therefore, "viewing the practice of the State in Ireland as it is, and as it is likely to remain, I find it has cut away from under me any ground of religion upon which a stand might have been made." This Burkean argument he followed with another: that the Commons should decide what action to take based on what they consider to be just and right "with an equitable and comprehensive regard to the actual circumstances of the period and of the country."[48]

Whatever face he attempted to put on it, Gladstone's decision was by and large unfathomable to his colleagues. Colin Matthew's comment that his reversal was "perplexing and casuistic" as well as "idiosyncratic and perverse" does not seem too strongly phrased.[49] How, indeed, can one explain Gladstone's actions? Are they an example of mere fickleness? Or poor judgment? Were they a matter of tension between the man of theory and the man of government?[50] There may be something to this. Certainly Gladstone manifested a struggle of some sort: a dance of such tentativeness suggests at least a divided mind. He appeared to be both presumptuous and self-defeating. In arguing from a presumed right against a perceived wrong, he denied himself something he very much wanted: the retention of high office.

One may argue, however, that Gladstone's tug of war between his religious belief and his political common sense simply created such stress that he employed a coping mechanism that manifested both withdrawal (resigning office or departing for Rome) and engagement (supporting the bill). Both strategies had advantages. Withdrawal can reduce stress by serving as a delaying tactic: the time thus gained can be used to rethink a position or to mobilize resources for an alternative solution. Gladstone's resignation from the ministry may have relieved stress in precisely this way. Yet Gladstone was also politically ambitious. He must have realized—no less than his contemporaries—that questionable resignations could jeopardize his reputation as a loyal party member. Hence his engagement during the April debates, and hence his declaration of support for the bill. Complicating these strategic maneuvers was the psychologically enigmatic role of Peel. Admired, respected, perhaps even feared as a figure of authority, Peel was central to Gladstone's dilemma. In a sense, Gladstone's resignations were rebellions against the authority of Peel—rebellions that he could never entertain against the authority of his own father, who was strikingly similar to Peel.

The Maynooth episode is additionally significant for what it reveals about the underlying religious tremors of the age as they affected Gladstone. The Anglican Church, strongly challenged by the increasingly Erastian policies of the Whig governments of the 1830s, had responded by becoming introspective of its origins and its role in the wider world. The Oxford Movement, led by a group of Oxford divines who expounded their beliefs in a series of *Tracts for the Times,* sought to demonstrate the apostolic integrity of the Church of England and its independence from both Roman Catholicism and Erastian thinking. These Tractarians—as they also came to be known—were traditionally oriented because their task was historically grounded: they tended to be high church with an emphasis on ceremony and orderliness. They disliked the chaotic nature of Protestant sectarianism. To them, Protestantism lacked the beauty, order, holiness, authority, and dogma of an ancient system of beliefs; they preferred what they called an "ordered sanctity." Some of the most stellar religious intellects of the time were drawn into the Tractarian orbit. Among them were John Henry Newman, E. B. Pusey, John Keble, Henry Manning, and the Wilberforce brothers, Samuel and Henry.[51]

Gladstone was strongly influenced by the theoretical bent and the intellectual quality of the Tractarians.[52] Although his Evangelical habits of Bible study, private prayers, household sermons, and philanthropic activities remained with him throughout his life, by the mid-1830s he had moved away from some of the most noticeable Evangelical precepts.[53] He was increasingly attracted to practices more common among Anglo-Catholics, such as regular Eucharistic communion, a joy in clerical architecture, and an appreciation of the mystery and beauty of ancient rites of worship.[54]

Gladstone had developed this shift in religious beliefs and practices during his years at Oxford. Through an intensive program of systematic reading, he had come to question some of his earlier theological notions. For many Evangelicals, a conversion experience and the Calvinist doctrine of predestination were essential tests of salvation. But Gladstone doubted that he had ever been "converted." Nor could he accept the idea that the omnipotence of a good and just God would ever be used to redeem only a selected few, as predestination assumed. Once he had moved away from conversion and predestination, Gladstone found it easier to reverse a third previously held Evangelical prescript, the denial of baptismal regeneration. Evangelicals believed that the act of baptism was merely symbolic of conversion. Gladstone gradually came to believe that baptism was far more important in the life of a Christian, that it was indeed a sacramental act. Accepting baptismal regeneration not only strengthened his disavowal of predestination but also meant logically that God could convey grace through all the sacraments.

Gladstone emerged from his religious introspection believing that God was not a determinist, and that God provided numerous opportunities for sinners to exercise their faith within a sacramental framework. Salvation by faith under this doctrine allowed greater play on the part of the sinner. Erring humans could, to some extent at least, make decisions and engage in daily actions and behavior that might directly affect the condition of their immortal souls. In other words, Gladstone, on entering young adulthood, had remade his personal theology to conform to his own tendency for controlling and managing his life's circumstances. By living a holy life, by upholding the rigorous precepts of a Christian in the secular world, and by actively disseminating religious truths, Gladstone could hope to ensure the salvation that he so desperately desired. In religion, as in politics and in his personal relations, Gladstone manifested his need for command.

Religion was for Gladstone an important instrument of stress reduction. The church, in its institutional form, provided opportunities for Gladstone (as for so many others) to engage in formal dialogues with like-minded participants. Collective participation in ritual events encourages a commonly accepted belief system that enhances self-esteem and self-efficacy; thus, strong religious beliefs deepen a sense of meaning and coherence in individual lives. Religious groups also maintain informal social networks that support their members during times of adversity and doubt. For all these reasons, religion was significant to Gladstone throughout his life.[55]

As Gladstone wound his way toward his personal religious via media, he faced many temptations. Perhaps the most threatening was the lure of Rome. That ordered and traditional religion drew him from across the centuries. Unlike many of his Tractarian friends who joined the Roman Catholic Church, however, he resisted. Why he halted halfway on the road to Rome is an important question. It has been suggested that Gladstone, imbued with the nature of sin and depravity (as attested by his own self-disparagement in the his diary), was so convinced of the fallibility of humankind that he could never accept any human pretension to supreme religious or moral authority. He could, therefore, never accept the kind of authority claimed by the pope. Ultimately, he believed that every Christian must be individually responsible for making the choice and exerting the will to strive for righteous behavior.[56] A plausible alternative reason could also have barred Gladstone's full acceptance of Catholicism. To him, Roman Catholicism was a hegemonic religion: surrendering to papal authority would mean some loss of control in an important part of his life. To be relatively autonomous in his religion, as in his personal and private lives, was psychologically necessary to Gladstone. This interpretation helps to explain the curious paradox of his simultaneous attraction toward and repulsion from Roman Catholicism.

Although Gladstone was never anti-Catholic, some part of him reacted strongly to Anglicans who became converts to the Roman Catholic Church. He felt a surge of fear and distrust of apostasy. Even members of his own family were not immune to his censure. No example is more apt than the conversion of his younger sister, Helen, to Catholicism in 1842. Their relationship, it must be said, had never been smooth. Gladstone had always taken a strong hand in Helen's rearing. Not long after the death of their elder sister, Anne, William and Helen made a covenant to be candid about one another's faults with a view to improvement. William made use of the covenant with a vengeance. In one heavily officious letter, written while he was still at Oxford, he carefully categorized his remarks by topic: Helen's dress, her use of time, and her management of money. Gladstone believed that Helen was a "good deal beyond" those of her age in her manner of dress. She had, in Gladstone's eyes, "ideas of propriety" that were "a little overstrained" in fashion. "Be a Christian and a lady," he admonished. On the topic of money, he was briefer: "Save all you can." Her besetting sin, however, was her use of time. Although "far from accusing" her of idleness, Gladstone urged her to determine specific goals in life and then to pursue them: "*Aim at the moon*," he suggested. Above all, he wrote, "may you carry through all your dealings with all men the blessed principle of submission, and resignation of your own desires, & unqualified disregard of your own convenience, when these may come into collision with duty."[57] This was unwelcome advice for a high-spirited young woman who had few opportunities for her own fulfillment. It is not surprising that in her reply, she admitted that she did not at first take her brother's advice kindly: "When I first read it, my natural pride and self love were awakened fully." But she submitted dutifully, even abjectly, in the conclusion of her letter.[58]

The crucial event that divided brother and sister, however, was Helen's conversion to Catholicism.[59] Gladstone's letters to Helen thereafter take on a harsher tone; they are unkind and defensive. When he first learned of her attendance at Catholic services in 1841, Gladstone warned her of the "sin of schism." The "Romish worship" was "replete with peril of idolatry." "If their worship be lawful, the Church of England is an accursed thing."[60] Once her conversion became public the following year, Gladstone was more severe. He attacked her character. He charged her with lack of discipline, humility, and patience in her religious quest. "Have you yet to learn, that it is along the path of obedience and docility, of self-denial and self subjugation, that God leads His children into truth?" Gladstone appeared to be enraged by Helen's demonstration of independence in her decision to become Catholic. Her conversion, Gladstone wrote, merely proved that she was living a "life of utter self deception. Not in religion alone—but in all bodily, in all mental habits—in all personal and in all social relations."[61] Believing Helen to be a malign influence on the family, Gladstone urged his father to expel her from the household. Helen's promise not to proselytize among the children and servants would not be upheld, Gladstone wrote, because it would "be liable to be cancelled at the will of any priest to whom she might refer & over whom you could have no possible control."[62] The old man refused, condemning his son's uncharitable attitude. Gladstone defended his own behavior as someone who "would drag a woman by the hair, to save her from drowning."[63]

In a long interview with Helen in June 1842, Gladstone raised additional questions about the origins of her new religion. He seemed intent on absolving himself from any blame. Had he influenced her in any way? She admitted to reading parts of *State and Church* when it came out—"rather an extraordinary catechism," she thought. She recalled having gone often to church with him in London. "Perhaps six or eight times," corrected Gladstone. Helen was shrewd as to her brother's motives. His comments respecting her, she said, could be "construed into an anxiety" to save his "worldly position."[64] Indeed, he feared that he had been damaged in some significant way by Helen's conversion. A month after his interview with her, he wrote his father that several weekly newspapers had recently carried the "record of our shame. Helen is described as my sister in two [of them] . . . and in one of them as your daughter."[65]

Gladstone never forgave Helen. Time and again in later correspondence, he referred in hostile terms to her apostasy. In a letter written on Helen's birthday in 1847—ostensibly to wish her well—he could not refrain from touching on the topic. "The change which took place in 1842," he wrote, was "not an isolated calamity: it was one in a series: it added to the mass of evil, and it shut up the avenues of influence." And now, "what a spectacle of ruin" she was! Gladstone justified these harsh words on Helen's birthday thus: "To aim at anything, which presents the slightest hope of rescuing you from your profound, subtle & hitherto impenetrable delusions, is the office of love & duty."[66] Even in the last years of her life, Gladstone could not pardon her smallest misdeeds. In a brutal letter he wrote in 1878, he refused her parcel of gifts to the family because she had neglected to repay a loan of twenty pounds and had failed to send a promised contribution for the Belgian relief fund. As Matthew has observed, Gladstone acted as though his sister were still in the nursery.[67] The cycle of rebellion and recrimination ended only with Helen's death in 1880.

The effect of apostasy on Gladstone can be further illustrated by the conversion to Rome of his close friends James Hope and Henry Manning. Hope was an acquaintance of Gladstone's from their undergraduate days at Christ Church. In 1836, the two young Oxonians became fast friends. Their closest bond was their interest in the church. Hope had at one time, like Gladstone, thought of taking orders; instead, he became a barrister but remained active in the Church of England as a lay apostolate. During his crucial shift in religious beliefs in the 1830s, Gladstone frequently sought out Hope's opinion. Indeed, Hope may have been the most influential person in moving Gladstone along the path of Anglo-Catholicism.[68] They were inseparable intellectually as their friendship deepened into the 1840s. They confided in one another their hopes not only for religious renovation but for the shape of politics as well. When Peel offered Gladstone the cabinet post in 1843, it was Hope (along with Manning) to whom he turned for consultation. As Gladstone wrestled with the intricacies of tariff reform and the gradual dawning in his mind of the need for free trade in corn, it was from Hope that he sought advice.

Gradually and at first imperceptibly, however, Hope slipped from his Anglican moorings. As the Oxford Movement claimed its converts, Hope was drawn to them. In a long and impassioned letter in the spring of 1845, Gladstone pleaded with Hope to remember his obligations both to the Church of England and to his friends. Years ago, Gladstone wrote, "I began to form not only high but definite anticipations of the services which you would render to the Church in the deep and searching processes through which she has had and yet has to pass." He reminded Hope of the solemn oath he made in 1840 to advance the welfare of the church: "You placed no limit upon the extent of such cooperation." To that promise, Gladstone had assigned a "value scarcely to be described"; in fact, on that promise he had based all his "views of the future course of public affairs in their bearing upon religion." Should he ever be in a position to do good for the church, he would look to Hope for aid, under the promise Hope had given. Should Hope ever withdraw, it would increase Gladstone's "sense of desolation which as matters now stand often approaches to being intolerable."[69] The tone of his letter, allowing for the status of its recipient, is not so distant from the tone that Gladstone had adopted toward his sister. It includes elements of emotional blackmail, suggested betrayal, and implied blame. As in the case of Helen, Hope's increasing attraction toward Roman Catholicism struck Gladstone deeply and personally.

A remarkably similar story concerns Henry Manning, who eventually rose high in the Catholic Church to become cardinal-archbishop of Westminster. Manning, like both Gladstone and Hope, was at Oxford, and he had moved from an Evangelical bent toward a high church position. President of the Oxford Union and a Balliol man, Manning demonstrated a power of intellect and habit of work that matched Gladstone's own. Manning differed from both Hope and Gladstone, however, in that he took clerical orders in the Church of England early on, in 1832. After serving as rector of a small Sussex parish, he became archdeacon of Chichester in 1840. As with Hope, Gladstone found in Manning a constant fount of inspiration and unrestrained intellectual camaraderie. Gladstone relied on Manning perhaps more than on Hope as an informed source into the religious controversies of that era. Manning served as an intermediary between Gladstone and Newman during Newman's long and tortuous route to Catholicism, as Gladstone tried to stay Newman's decision. When it became clear that Manning was tempted to embrace Roman Catholicism, Gladstone used subtle pressures to bind him closer to the Church of England. He suggested, for example, that Manning should take the lead in striking a blow for Anglicanism by refuting Newman's ideas.[70]

The climax of Gladstone's struggle for his friends came in the spring of 1851. By then, they were on the point of "going over." On 6 March, Gladstone argued for two hours with Hope. A few weeks later, Gladstone reported he had been smitten "to the ground" with Manning's news that he was "now on the *brink:* and Hope too." On 6 April came the news that Gladstone feared: "A day of pain! Manning and Hope!" He no doubt felt the loss for the church of his two friends, but the greater loss was to himself. "They were my two props. Their going may be to me a sign that my work is going with them."[71] In a letter to another friend, he wrote: "Nothing like it can ever happen to me again. Arrived now at middle life, I never *can* form I suppose with any other two men the habits of communication, counsel, and dependence, in which I have now for from fifteen to eighteen years lived with them both."[72] Within forty-eight hours of the news of their apostasy, Gladstone struck Hope from his will as his executor, and he refused to see or write to Manning for a decade. Thus did Gladstone withdraw completely from his two closest friends.

Their apostasy was an intolerable threat to Gladstone's perception of himself as the upholder of religious constancy, and a reminder to himself of his own perilous religious journey. That men of such sanctity and intelligence as Hope and Manning questioned (at least implicitly) his religion raised disturbing questions for Gladstone, although he denied that doubts were sown. The Church of England represented order, an ethical system, and a certain and regulated set of rules for behavior. It was important for a man of Gladstone's character to rely on a bulwark outside himself in times of weakness or travail. For Gladstone, religion was the ultimate source of his belief in an orderly system in the midst of a disordered world. A threat or shift in his religious beliefs was a threat to his psychological well-being and to his coherent view of life. Not merely an abstract belief was threatened by the apostasy of friends or family: apostasy struck directly at his belief in himself. On the eve of his friends' conversion, he confessed that such "terrible blows not only overset & oppress but I fear also demoralise me." Their conversion caused the "loss of all resolution to carry forward the little self-discipline I ever had." Months later the feeling of desolation had not abated. He wrote in his diary in Italian (as he often did for the most sensitive passages): "These two terrible years have really displaced and uprooted my heart from the Anglican Church, seen as a personal and *living* Church in the *body* of its Priests and members; and at the same time the two friends whom I might call the only supports for my intellect have been wrenched away from me, leaving me lacerated, and I may say barely conscious morally."[73]

4

"In Respect of Things of a Certain Kind"

The loss of friends and their perceived betrayal of religious principles were a severe shock to Gladstone, contributing to his sense of spiritual malaise during the late 1840s and early 1850s. No less jarring were the painful illness and death of his young daughter in 1850; the accidental death of his political mentor, Sir Robert Peel, in that same year; and the death of his father a year later. He was additionally beset by more mundane affairs, such as the collapse of a substantial investment, which brought about severe financial embarrassment, if not ruin. Perhaps the most disturbing development was his descent into the seamier side of a Victorian underworld. Gladstone's obsession with London prostitutes, threatening not only his sense of self-worth but his political career as well, was both a release from the personal and financial stresses that hounded him and an additional stress in itself. How he struggled against these sexual temptations, and the guilt that followed, is a remarkable story of his capacity to adapt within the limits of his religious beliefs and practice.

Religious apostasy and consorting with prostitutes were at first less worrisome to Gladstone than family finances. Problems had begun through no fault of his. He was dependent for virtually all his wealth on his father's generosity. Over the years, he had received a considerable amount of capital stock and a share in a large trust fund, supplemented by occasional gifts of cash. In addition, he received at his marriage several thousand pounds from Catherine's marriage portion. By 1846, Gladstone estimated his annual income at nearly seven thousand pounds and his expenditure at about four thousand pounds, a testament to his prudent management. Potentially the most lucrative source of revenue for Gladstone was Oak Farm, a coal and ironstone works in Staffordshire owned by Sir Stephen Glynne, the squire of Hawarden and Catherine's brother. Gladstone, who had been presented with Oak Farm shares as a supplementary part of the marriage settlement, had a direct interest in its profitability. Unfortunately, Sir Stephen was not a wise money manager and had not lived within his means since he attained his majority. Nor was Sir Stephen a sound judge of character: he allowed James Boydell, his agent at Oak Farm, a free hand. Throughout the early 1840s, Boydell wildly extended the works, building furnaces and rolling mills, and sinking new mine shafts.

In 1847, the Oak Farm enterprise failed entirely when a national speculative boom collapsed. Gladstone's personal loss was considerable—more than £12,000. But more important was the danger to the Hawarden estate, which had been heavily mortgaged to pay for the Oak Farm operation. Sir Stephen faced bankruptcy and the consequent dissolution of Hawarden. Selling Hawarden would have been the easiest option, but Gladstone—though not its owner—considered it his home. In the years that followed, difficult financial decisions were made to pay off the Oak Farm debts. Land had to be sold, which eventually brought in some £200,000. Gladstone himself purchased land for £72,330, thus directly linking himself to the salvation of Hawarden. His financial involvement caused him to take part in the day-to-day management of the estate. In effect, he assumed the responsibilities of ownership for Hawarden, displacing his brother-in-law. Sir Stephen was given an annual income of only seven hundred pounds. Hawarden Castle for a time was boarded up, the park was let, and the herd of deer sold. Ultimately most of Gladstone's personal fortune was pledged to making Hawarden solvent.[1]

At times, energies given to Oak Farm affected Gladstone's parliamentary duties. On a single day, 21 February 1848, he wrote six letters concerning Oak Farm, two of them to J. W. Freshfield, a solicitor to the Bank of England.[2] Later that afternoon, he went to the City to see Freshfield personally. Although he squeezed in a few hours of attendance at the House of Commons in the early evening, he was unable to examine revenue papers relating to the debate on estimates because, as he phrased it, he was "too much distracted by the O. F. matters & correspondence to make progress. They make it quite impossible for me to discharge my duties properly in Parliament."[3] He penned almost identical words to his father two days later: "The state of politics is very interesting . . . but my mind is too much absorbed by the constant correspondence & interviews connected with the Oak Farm business to allow me to do any justice to my public duties."4 By spring, there was no change. "I do not think I have strength of mind," William wrote again to his father, "to go on for a series of years with my public duties on the one hand & with those which the crash of the Oak Farm & the complicated state of Stephen's affairs have brought upon me on the other."5 Between 1847 and 1852, as he once confessed, he "was scarcely a member of Parliament" because his "time & mind" was principally occupied "in bearing the sole responsibility & chief labour of this complicated business."6

Gladstone was obviously under severe financial and legal pressure during these years. Additional strains were placed on him by his father.7 Visits to his father's home at Fasque were often filled with petty domestic squabbles involving servants or relatives, punctuated by the old man's need for attention. While at Fasque in early April 1847, for example, Gladstone witnessed his father at lunch one day railing about domestic disorder to such an extent that his aunt had to lead the servants from the room. His father also "launched out about the Corn Law, full of the most extravagant & exaggerated apprehensions." To Catherine, he confided, "Though I thought I was coming to a quiet place, it has proved far otherwise."8 His father's increasing deafness made it difficult to meet his desire for extended conversations. During that spring visit, he once talked with his father for six continuous hours, and they had lengthy conversations on succeeding days. All the while, Gladstone was suffering from a heavy cold, sore throat, and deep cough.9

Particularly upsetting were his father's political criticisms. The elder Gladstone especially attacked his son's advocacy of free trade. He also abused Sir Robert Peel, the former prime minister. William was thus often forced to defend his own actions. In early 1847, when temporarily without a parliamentary seat, he wrote to his father that it was a "great relief to my feelings to be out of a position in which I must necessarily say & do what would be opposed to your views of the public interest."10 He then hinted that—should his father desire it—he would refuse to stand again for Parliament. This implied threat of resignation from an active political life did not stem the flow of criticism, however. Not long after William's election to Parliament from Oxford University in late 1847, father and son engaged in a public altercation on the merits of the Navigation Acts. William believed that abolition of the acts was a natural conclusion to the free trade legislation of recent years, and he spoke to this effect in Parliament. But the acts were especially dear to John Gladstone's heart because of their protective advantage in his own commercial days as a corn merchant. He sent a letter to a local newspaper, the *Montrose Standard,* taking issue with his son's opinion. Their quarrel lasted for some months. Gladstone reacted in a familiar manner: he fully justified his actions and then hinted again at resignation. The only way he could "avoid both the evils of acting against your view and against my own conviction," he wrote to his father, "was by retiring from parliament."[11] This threat apparently concluded the argument.

In spite of these disagreements, William faithfully honored his filial duties by visiting with his aging father. He was at Fasque during much of the autumn and early winter of 1849–50. He reported to Catherine in September that his father was often "excitable about mere trifles" and that there was "certainly a *great* decay of mental power since you saw him . . . it is now *all but* a case of second childhood."[12] The state of his father's condition had not altered several months later: "Generally he is very like a spent cannonball," although he still "hits a very hard knock to those who come across him."[13] In the summer and autumn of 1851, William was again in attendance. Sir John's irascibility was largely unabated: he spent his time making codicils to his will, complaining about the state of affairs, and being read to.

In the last weeks of his father's life, William was with him, noting in great clinical detail the final physical and mental deterioration.[14] The dying man frequently suffered from profuse vomiting and was often exhausted. He could keep down only chicken tea, a little brandy, and "once a piece of pear, with great relish." The doctors prescribed pills, injections, mustard plasters, and blisters. The patient's mind began to wander. Prayers were increased to twice daily, and William began sleeping in his father's room. As close family members were summoned, William pressed upon his father the Holy Sacrament. On 6 December 1851, the intervals of Sir John's breath began to shorten, his pulse weakened, and he grew cold. "There was no rapid decline: all was by steps till the very last—an effort at breathing, weaker than a dying infant might have made, air entering the mouth but not reaching the lungs: not a sound of pain. About an hour before there was the very faintest rattle, but it soon subsided. And so he died, upon the morning of the Lord's rest."[15]

These solemn details of his father's death William concluded with a brief description of the funeral. The order of the service did not please him; he compared it unfavorably to the service for his dead daughter scarcely a year past. Before his father was laid at his mother's side in the family vault, William remembered that he had kissed his father's cheek and forehead just before and just after his death: "the only kisses I can remember." William and his family remained a few weeks longer at Fasque, now his brother's house by inheritance. The day after Christmas, as he noted in his diary, "we bid our final adieu to Fasque as a home: the thought of it must for me ever be full of moving recollections."[16]

The death of his father was a climax to the personal and family anxieties that affected Gladstone at the beginning of the 1850s. It was also a time when he was increasingly at loose ends in his political life. Not only had he been without cabinet office since 1845, but he was also a member of a divided opposition party with no obvious prospects. The Whig government was once again in power. For any ambitious politician, this lack of prospects would have been a serious blow; for Gladstone, who had high expectations of his role in the world at large and who had already tasted the delights of cabinet office at an unusually early age, it was especially frustrating.

Gladstone, responding to these stresses in his private and public life, turned in confusion to an unusual form of coping. It was so strikingly aberrant that even modern scholars have refused to grapple fully with its meaning. In the late 1840s he began a series of systematic rescue missions among what were termed fallen women. Given Gladstone's professed public standards of morality and well-developed sense of scruple, which had brought him to the point of resigning from office, it would be easy enough to damn him for hypocrisy. Indeed, in his own day, there were many—especially among his political opponents—who condemned him, drawing the obvious conclusions from his well-known nocturnal rambles in London streets. His apologists have fallen back on his moral reputation to explain his high-minded rescue work. Basset believed in the "fearless rectitude and purity of Gladstone's motives." Magnus wrote that his "radiant integrity" upheld the "purity of his motives" in his relations with London prostitutes. Beales, more recently, thought Gladstone's charity showed his "real innocence."[17]

The truth about Gladstone and his interest in prostitutes falls somewhere between these divergent views. There is no doubt that he was genuinely taken up with prostitution as a legitimate charity. Fallen women had become a topic of public debate, and prostitutes were legitimate objects of philanthropic interest. Gladstone helped to found several homes of refuge for prostitutes, and his personal quest was a testament to his active commitment to this particular charity—a commitment no doubt based on his enduring Evangelical heritage. But the publication of the *Diaries* has made incontestable his private longing for prostitutes or, more accurately, for specific prostitutes. Gladstone was drawn imperceptibly from an initially genuine charitable impulse into a behavior that represented for him a kind of escape from the stresses and disappointments of his political and social life.[18] These episodes, however, became in themselves additional stressors, especially in their impact on the religious view that he had of himself as a sinner who must resist temptation. Increasingly, his encounters with certain prostitutes called into question—at least in his own mind—his sincerity as a Christian believer. This dark underside of his life was a potentially dangerous fragmentation of Gladstone's coherent view of his world.

Gladstone's early encounters with prostitutes were initially accidental and surely unremarkable. Only a few days after he had gone up to Oxford in 1828, he recorded in his diary that he "met a woman & had a long conversation with her." The following evening he "met the poor creature again, who is determined to go home"—presumably after his encouragement to do so.[19] The following year he had a similar encounter with two prostitutes, "both really, I believe, in great distress."[20] He made only two other brief references to prostitutes in Oxford.[21] Chance encounters with prostitutes in early nineteenth-century Oxford would not have been surprising. Like many cities, Oxford had drawn from its rural surroundings young women who sought work, perhaps as domestic servants; later, many of them took to the streets. One estimate puts the number of prostitutes in Oxford during Gladstone's undergraduate years at between three and five hundred in a city of approximately fifteen hundred students and twenty-five thousand inhabitants. Prostitution was the town's second leading offense—the first being pubs' staying illegally open after hours.[22] Gladstone's initial tone of disinterested philanthropy also characterized his first encounters with prostitutes in London once he had moved there to undertake his parliamentary duties. Accosted in a London park in 1837 by two women, Gladstone merely reported of them that "both ... had taken to their miserable calling from losing their livelihood by the death of their husbands."[23]

Gladstone's first sustained rescue case was Rebecca Ayscough, whom he first saw on the streets in October 1842. He visited her a few days later in jail. Her name does not appear in the diary again for another two years, when Gladstone saw her several times in late 1844. His last mention of her was in March 1845, when he noted despairingly that she had recently relapsed into her old habits after brief employment as a servant of Manning's.[24] About the time that Ayscough faded from Gladstone's view, he became a member of a secret lay Tractarian brotherhood. Known as the Engagement, the organization required regular acts of charity.[25] Its rules further bound its members to intense self-examination in pursuit of their common activities. This was a congenial arrangement for someone of an Evangelical temperament like Gladstone. As he explained its purpose to his wife, the Engagement would provide for him a discipline. "My conscience is weak and wants aid," he wrote.[26]

Perhaps Gladstone had already felt the temptation to be with fallen women for purposes other than rescue work, and it may have been this that prompted his decision to join the Engagement in early 1845 as a way of seeking an external discipline to strengthen his weakening resolve: thus the oblique reference in the letter to his wife. In any case, his diary records that in the summer of 1845 he met the prostitute E. Reynolds five times within a six-week span. It is quite possible that his experience with Reynolds was the first rescue case in which he felt other than a philanthropic interest. This would not be surprising, given the stress of the Maynooth debate during the previous year and his own resignation from the cabinet. In addition, relations with his sister Helen had worsened. In October 1845, Gladstone followed Helen to Baden, Germany, in a fruitless effort to rescue her from Roman Catholicism and from her growing addiction to laudanum. While there, he drew up the first of several remarkable documents of self-appraisal of the temptations that had begun to assail him.

He described these Baden Rules as a "sketch on my chief besetting sin": they were designed to recognize the conditions in which temptations might arise and to propose remedies. These conditions and remedies he organized under four categories. The first was "Channels" by which temptations might arise, such as thought, conversation, seeing, or touch. The second, "Incentives," outlined the circumstances of his own condition that would predispose him to be tempted, such as idleness, exhaustion, absence from usual places, interruption of usual habits, or curiosity of knowledge. Under this last circumstance, he included knowledge "in respect of things of a certain kind." Written in Greek in the diary, this phrase refers to an Aristotelian logical term but here obviously has a specific reference to the temptations that prompted the Baden Rules in the first place, that is, sexual temptations. The third category, "Chief Actual Dangers," identified specific conditions to which he was immediately vulnerable. These included impulses of thought, or seeing in form, movement, or language "things of a certain kind." His final category, "Remedies," set out the ways he might overcome these temptations. These included prayer, focusing on the presence of the crucified Lord, immediate pain, abstinence, examination, and a specific injunction not to look at certain books in bookshops, or into particular printshop windows.[27]

Gladstone was clearly performing a thorough and well-organized process of self-examination in trying to understand the stresses (or, in his words, temptations) that had come upon him. Even more important, he undertook to work out a series of remedies or coping devices, varied in their nature and application, that would relieve the stresses. It may be that Gladstone, far from home in Germany and under the immediate impact of distressing scenes of his sister's drug addiction, had turned suddenly to the sexual temptations of a foreign city. But the likelihood is that for some time he had been acutely aware of temptation. His caution to himself not to look at certain books or into the windows of printshops demonstrates that before 1845 he had already been attracted to erotic literature and pictures, as well as to the seductive forbidden fruit of certain prostitutes. To twentieth-century readers, Gladstone's determination to deny himself even a curious glance at mildly pornographic material may seem overwrought. But, from his point of view, succumbing to a trickle of temptation could lead to the floodgates of hell.

After the episodes with Ayscough and Reynolds in 1845, Gladstone seems to have had reasonable success in refraining both from seeing prostitutes and from reading racy literature. Perhaps the self-imposed restraints of the Baden Rules, complemented by the fellowship of the Engagement, stiffened his resolve. The next rescue case does not appear in the diary until 23 July 1848. Sins of reading appear only once more in 1845, once in 1846, and three times in 1847. His reading Petronius on 15 January 1847, with the ostensible aim of consulting it for his studies in Homer and Hesiod, drew from Gladstone a fairly long and agonized reproach. It was, he noted, a violation of the rules he had made for himself at Baden eighteen months before. In spite of this self-criticism, he calculatedly set out to find and read blatantly erotic writings during the spring of the following year. In a single week in May 1848, he read a four-volume set of the collected works of eleventh- and fifteenth-century French *fabliaux*. These verse fables, often explicitly bawdy, were considered pornographic by the Victorians. Gladstone confided to his diary (in Italian) his thoughts about his behavior: "I drank the poison, sinfully, . . . I have stained my memory and my soul—which may it please God to cleanse for me, as I have need. . . . I have found beastliness under the most innocent headings; I should have sheered off at the first hints of evil. . . . I read sinfully, although with disgust, under the pretext of hunting solely for what was innocent; but—criminal that I am—with a prurient curiosity against all the rules of pious prudence." Thus he concluded remorsefully, having finished the volumes.[28] Altogether, he recorded ten days in 1848 when he read for pornographic reasons.

It seems clear that Gladstone consciously sought a forbidden distraction as a release from increased stressors, as he himself admitted in an important piece of self-analysis in the summer of 1848. "It has been a year of over-pressure upon me, . . . I have been sore, feeble, and worried: I have lost courage to look my daily duties in the face: the disposition to turn my back on them lurks within me: and this . . . predisposes me to that vague habit of mind which seeks relief in some kind of counter-excitement."[29]

This "counter-excitement" created a second, deeper level of tension—a guilt at succumbing to thoughts of impurity, his "principal besetting sin."[30] How did Gladstone deal with this second level of tension? Here he fell back upon his Evangelical habits of thought. A sinful creature could be absolved, or have at least the hope of absolution, by recognizing his sin and asking God's forgiveness. His diary conveys the notion of his sinfulness and even has an abject tone. Gladstone, however, was ultimately a religious optimist: he believed that he would be forgiven if he was repentant enough. His diary thus became in part a record of repentance for his sins. As he looked back on the troubled year of 1848, he expressed this paradoxical point of view. His besetting sin—impurity or lust—had been much in evidence; his discipline had been weakened and his power of resisting sin endangered. But God continued to grant blessings, "leaving therefore the door of hope open."[31] The moral was clear. A sinful nature could be subdued by a penitent heart: forgiveness would follow. To this venerable Christian creed, Gladstone added his mite. He would do his part in restoring discipline and control.

Within weeks of writing the preceding diary entry, Gladstone began an experiment in control that remained with him for the next ten years. On 13 January 1849 he scourged himself with a small whip—pain being one of the options listed in the Baden Rules. His use of the whip he justified in his diary: "Having been much tempted during the week I made a slight application in new form of the principle of discipline: with a good effect at the time." It is not entirely clear why he chose that particular device to allay temptation. Matthew argues convincingly that it probably was suggested to him within a Tractarian context; Newman used a scourge, and Pusey apparently intended to do so. This technique may also have been used by other members of the Engagement.[32]

Gladstone used the whip eight times in 1849; in April alone there were five incidents. This high number suggests that the new physical deterrent was not working well. He reappraised the method, concluding that he had relied too much on the strength of the whip.[33] He needed to employ more fully the Baden Rules. In the face of temptation, for example, he ought to have broken contact "upon first presumptions of contamination or excitement from without." By contact he presumably meant any sexual excitement, whether by word or picture or sight of women. Gladstone was not yet apprehensive of physical contact with women: the danger lay rather with "adultery in the heart." His right-minded attempts to regulate the "sin of impurity" were thus far only moderately successful. Neither scourging nor the Baden Rules nor the Engagement had given permanent help. Even his marriage was not proof against temptation. "An ideal above the ordinary married state is commonly before me & ever returns upon me: while the very perils from which it commonly delivers still beset me as snares and pitfalls among which I walk."

Gladstone was somewhat puzzled by his lustful nature. But he was determined to grapple with the pain and shame that it engendered. It is within the context of Gladstone's struggle for a means for control that an unusual incident in the summer of 1849 may be explained. For several years the marriage of his close friend Lord Lincoln had been failing.[34] Lady Lincoln had reacted to her unhappiness by engaging in a series of infidelities and becoming increasingly dependent on laudanum. In August 1848, she left her family for Germany. Over the next several months, she traveled by leisurely stages to Italy with her reputed lover, Lord Walpole. Lincoln, already despondent over an estrangement with his father, the duke of Newcastle, turned to his friends, among them the Peels and the Gladstones, for advice. A plan, or "Mission," as Gladstone put it, soon evolved. The idea was either to confirm the rumors about Lady Lincoln and thus lay the groundwork for divorce proceedings, or to induce her to return to her family. Lincoln, whose character resembled Gladstone's in many ways, recommended either Manning or Gladstone for the job. Gladstone wrote Manning, indicating his willingness to go; indeed, he seemed eager to take up the task.[35]

Gladstone, in crossing the Channel on 13 July 1849 and journeying thence to Paris and Marseilles, then by boat to Genoa and on to Rome and Naples, traveled three thousand miles in twenty-seven days in a futile quest for Lady Lincoln. It was an unusual trip for someone like him to take; his father apparently thought it unseemly and was strongly opposed. Gladstone's reasons were probably various. Perhaps he took the trip merely in response to Lincoln's evident need. Perhaps he fancied himself as a latter-day knight-errant.[36] Or the adventure may have appealed to his growing urge to rescue unfortunate women: it would not have been difficult for him to see the attractive Lady Lincoln in the same desirable but damnable aura of the tempting prostitutes. Gladstone had been charmed by her over the years. When they were first introduced in 1833, he was struck by her manner and beauty. Four years later, he was no less fascinated. While visiting the Lincolns at Clumber, the estate of the Newcastles in Nottinghamshire, he wrote sympathetically, "Lady Lincoln has much of her usual buoyancy: but suffers much I believe—bravely & in secret."[37] The lure of travel, finally, could have been a reason for his mission. Travel was always for Gladstone a refreshing break. He clearly enjoyed the trip. He commented on the beautiful scenery south of Lyon, the architecture of the cathedral at Genoa, and various churches throughout France and Italy. He purchased Roman bronzes and casks of wine and had them sent home. His adventure may have been undertaken as much for himself as it was for Lincoln.

Although he never caught a glance of the fleeing Lady Lincoln, Gladstone had ascertained that she was pregnant. The next year, the charge of adultery was proven against her in both the Ecclesiastical Court and the House of Lords with Gladstone offering evidence. The marriage was officially dissolved in August 1850. Lady Lincoln, deserted by Lord Walpole after the birth of their son, married her Belgian courier in 1860. She returned to England sometime in the 1880s, living in a lodging house in Keymer, Sussex, until her death in 1889. Gladstone had already drawn the appropriate moral long before the final act of the scandal: "Oh that poor miserable Lady L.—once the dream of dreams, the image that to my young eye combined everything that earth could offer of beauty and of joy. What is she now!"[38]

Whatever relief the Lincoln mission may have brought to Gladstone was temporary. Beginning in the summer of 1850, his tension heightened markedly as he embarked on a substantial number of rescue cases. The pattern of his encounters was also altering. Although he continued to see some prostitutes at random by placing himself in well-known haunts, he increasingly sought out specific individuals to whom he had become attracted. From the diaries it is clear that the nature of his contacts with certain prostitutes had become almost obsessional.

The immediate stimulus to reinvigorated encounters with prostitutes was likely the death of his four-year-old daughter, Jessy, who died of cerebral meningitis in London on 9 April 1850. In the days before her death, the diary entries convey the emotional burden of the Gladstones as they attended the sick child. Gladstone noted her progressive loss of appetite, her fever, and her increasing pain. On 2 April, he entered into his diary that "dear little Jessy" had spent the night "tossing, moaning, & screaming, chiefly in C.s arms, the rest in mine."[39] In the last moments, both parents could only watch as Jessy endured successive convulsions. The final death agony was a prolonged spasm of half an hour. Gladstone met Jessy's death in a characteristic way: he immediately plunged into strenuous activity. He wrote letters, arranged for the funeral and burial at Fasque, and began a brief recollection of Jessy's life.[40] He alone took Jessy in her coffin on the journey north from Euston Square, traveling all night with her body in a railway carriage with blinds drawn. It was an exercise in control. But several less controlled, more private, violent bouts of grief caused some to fear for his life.[41] Added to this private anguish were the continuing worrisome news about Hope's and Manning's wavering allegiances to the Church of England and his own unresolved financial troubles. This was, as he wrote many years later, a "terrible time" in his life.[42]

In reaction to these trying events, Gladstone again fell into "counter-excitement." He broke his rules nine times in June alone. Twice that month he used the whip. In July, Gladstone met with prostitutes on seven occasions. On 23 July, he first noted in his diary his meeting with Emma Clifton, a prostitute who became the center of his attention during the next several months. He sought her out time after time, not always successfully. On the evening of 1 August, for example, he went to her lodgings twice without luck. The third try late that night found her at home. He spent his time (as he tells it) trying to persuade her and her child to enter the rescue house at Clewer. After only two and a half hours of sleep, he caught the train the next morning to Birmingham. He went thence to the Lytteltons at Hagley and thereafter to Hawarden. Two weeks later, Gladstone received word that Clifton had not entered Clewer. After consulting with Catherine, he thought it his "duty to go to town."[43] Upon his arrival, he set out to find Clifton, but without success. The remainder of August and September, he was at Hawarden and Fasque. Returning to London in early October for a few days, he immediately sought out Clifton. "Could I do otherwise in common humanity?" he queried himself.[44] On three separate days he looked for her without luck.

Suddenly, Gladstone seems to have reached a decision to turn abruptly away from his life in London. He left in mid-October for an extended journey to the Continent. The stresses of his life and his increasing need for repose likely enough prompted the trip, although it was ostensibly undertaken for the health of his daughter Mary, who had been suffering from a severe case of inflamed eyes.[45] Also traveling with him were Mary's older sister Agnes, his wife Catherine, and two servants, Edward and Emily. The Gladstones crossed the Channel to Boulogne on 18 October and then went by train to Paris. Thereafter, they pursued a strenuous round of sight-seeing. They visited Notre Dame, the Louvre, and Versailles—where they lost themselves "amidst the bewilderments of that wonderful palace."[46] Soon they steamed southward by rail, this time for Nevers, where they detrained at dusk and boarded a coach for Moulins, which they reached near midnight on 25 October. Following roughly the line of the Loire, they reached Roanne, where they remained for two days. Now bearing southeast, they headed for Lyons on the twenty-eighth, then Chambéry, and on the twenty-ninth they crossed the Sardinian border. France was left behind. Within the week, and by slow stages, they made their way to Genoa. On 7 November, they boarded a ship bound for their ultimate destination, the sunnier climate of Naples. There they remained until winter had passed.

However eagerly the trip began as a means of withdrawal from the pressures mounting at home, it soon forced upon Gladstone an outward expression of his own internal turmoil. Even in the earliest stages of the journey, Gladstone seemed peevish and out of sorts.[47] He was continually embroiled in one argument or another, caught up in the inevitable complications, misunderstandings, and shortchanging that can mar a tourist's holiday. He was "much incensed" at the "impudence" of the captain of their ship on the Channel crossing for hugging and kissing Agnes. Their baggage arrived in Boulogne "sadly rummaged." Dinner at the Victoria Hotel in Paris was "interminable," and the largely English clientele was "not of a high order of travellers." He had trouble with his passport. Things were often too expensive. French coaches were "sluggish heavy & extortionate." He had a row with a French postillion who tried to overcharge by twelve sous. Delays of horses occurred at staging points along the way. Turin was filled with "noxious smells."[48]

Gladstone was still simmering when he reached Naples. He felt unnecessarily caught up in making living arrangements, "the consequence of not feeling able to *trust* people freely." Once installed in an apartment, Gladstone had a contretemps with the porter about deliveries of milk and butter. After attending a local theater, he traduced not only the production of a "loathsome Comedy" but also the audience for putting up with it for so long. He left midway through the performance. The moral he drew was that the "Italian taste and character where they degenerate at all have a very gross and materialistic tone." Gradually, however, his tone became less splenetic as he settled into a routine. Sight-seeing, visiting, and churchgoing were favorite pastimes. He also began the translation of L. C. Farini's three-volume work on the early nineteenth-century Roman state: he later published it in four volumes as *The Roman State from 1815 to 1850*.

An unexpected event, however, changed the tenor of his holiday. It began at a tea party at Lady Leven's. There he met Giacomo Lacaita, legal adviser to the British embassy. Lacaita had recently been released from prison, where he and 150 others had been sent for advocating moderate political reforms. Lacaita's firsthand account of the practices of the archaic and dictatorial Neapolitan government electrified Gladstone. Soon he was visiting prisoners of the government, interviewing inmates, and taking extensive notes to substantiate Lacaita's information. Most appalling to Gladstone was the condition of the political prisoners, many of whom were respectable middle-class citizens like Lacaita. In the midst of his investigations, Gladstone received word that his father was in deteriorating health. He departed for England on 18 February 1851, leaving behind his family, as his wife was too ill to travel owing to a miscarriage suffered ten days earlier. The others were to follow him within a month.

Shortly after his arrival in England, Gladstone showed that he had not forgotten conditions in Naples. He published two blistering condemnations of the Neapolitan monarchy in the form of long letters addressed to his friend and Peelite colleague Lord Aberdeen. His judgment was harsh. The government of Naples, he wrote, was an "outrage upon religion, upon civilisation, upon humanity, and upon decency."[49] Neapolitan authorities, although empowered to uphold the law, were in continual, systematic, and deliberate violation of it. They were "in bitter and cruel, as well as utterly illegal, hostility to whatever in the nation really lives and moves, and forms the main-spring of practical progress and improvement." Violating every moral law through the machinery of fear and vengeance, the government employed a "savage and cowardly" system of torture to gain its own ends; it perverted its own judicial system to destroy the lives of those citizens who were among the "most virtuous, upright, intelligent, distinguished, and refined of the whole community." The police spied on and dogged the people, paid domiciliary visits (often at night), ransacked houses, and imprisoned men "by the score, by the hundred, by the thousand, without any warrant whatever." Those arrested, often for fabricated crimes, were placed in prisons known for their "filth and horror," where one found "scenes fitter for hell than earth." Lest some think him exaggerated, Gladstone made it clear that this was not so: "I here speak of what I know to have happened, and have imagined or heightened *nothing*." In summary, the Neapolitan government was a perversion of all that governments should be. "Law, instead of being respected, is odious. Force, and not affection, is the foundation of Government. There is no association, but a violent antagonism, between the idea of freedom and that of order."

Gladstone's indictment was certainly not unmerited, but the attack was excitable, ferocious, and, in Aberdeen's opinion, rash, impulsive, and probably unhelpful to the cause Gladstone espoused. As Aberdeen explained it, Gladstone had come to him before publication, imploring his help. Perhaps Aberdeen could exert some influence in the diplomatic community? Aberdeen agreed, provided that Gladstone remained silent. Aberdeen further asked for a letter describing the conditions as Gladstone found them in Naples; he would then forward the letter to responsible officials. Aberdeen feared that Gladstone's exposure "might injure the cause of Monarchical government throughout Europe." But Gladstone, impatient with diplomatic niceties, could not remain silent.[50]

However distasteful to Aberdeen, the *Letters to the Earl of Aberdeen* had an undoubted public impact. For the first time Gladstone was revealed as a passionate advocate of popular rights. Hitherto his writings and public pronouncements had been reserved, almost stately, as he wrote and spoke to the political and religious elite. His remote conservative political ideology seemed to place him above the hurly-burly of ordinary political strife. But his *Letters* were almost demagogic. Indeed, for a conservative spokesman, he sounded suspiciously liberal. It goes too far to suggest that with the *Letters* Gladstone simply thrust his private doubts and frustrations onto the public stage, but there is some truth to this. It was his moral certainty—or, rather, the anger that lay behind it—that gave strength to his argument. It was as though Gladstone saw in a flash that his passionate engagement in righting an obvious wrong would bring certainty to his own life.[51]

The tone of his letters was somewhat misleading, however. Gladstone did not intend his pamphlets to sound the trumpet for a broadly based liberal nationalist movement in Italy. His own personal predilection complemented his political beliefs on this issue: he placed more emphasis on order, stability, and tradition than on any abstract principle of national freedom. He preferred good government to the doctrine of self-determination. The solution to governmental corruption everywhere—as in the specific instance of Naples—was sensible reform, led by such moderate men as Count Cavour rather than such revolutionaries as Giuseppe Mazzini or Giuseppe Garibaldi. His aim was not to topple the Neapolitan monarchy and establish a revolutionary republic but to push the existing authorities toward a program of moderate reform. Otherwise, the tyrannical Neapolitan monarchy could cut its own throat through its repressive measures, raising up a host of radical enemies.[52]

Gladstone's foray into political pamphleteering did not distract him from his rescue work. Within forty-eight hours of his return from Naples, he was busy among London's prostitutes.[53] Again and again, Gladstone was drawn almost involuntarily to the seductions of his secret life during the spring and summer of 1851. In June, he entered into his most intensely personal relationship with a prostitute up to that time. During the next twelve months, he not only visited her frequently, but he also wrote to her. Sometimes, he hurried away from official duties or cut them short so that he could be with her. He spent hours in her rooms; sometimes they had tea. Once he invited her to meet his wife.

From the first, Gladstone declared himself "much interested" in Elizabeth Collins. Not the least reason for his interest was her beauty; "lovely beyond measure" was his description of her (to his diary in Italian).[54] The first weeks of his acquaintance with Collins were probably the most emotionally charged in the history of Gladstone's rescue work. For a month beginning in late June

1851, Gladstone saw her twelve times, almost every other day. She was obviously much on his mind. The events of 4 July are not untypical: he wrote her a note in the morning, went to the House that afternoon to speak against the Ecclesiastical Titles Bill, then left immediately to find Collins, who was not in. Three weeks later a similar sequence of events occurred. Gladstone, dining in the evening at the Clarendon Hotel to meet the American ambassador and Lord Palmerston, was the first to leave. He met Collins and spent two "strange, questionable" hours with her.[55] On this occasion, he flogged himself when he returned home to Carlton Gardens. This was the third time in ten days that he had used the lash after visits with Collins. The first occurred on 13 July. After dining with friends in Berkeley Square, he had gone to Collins' place to drop off a note. She was in, and he spent two hours with her—"a strange and humbling scene"—before returning to scourge himself. Two days later, again after dining out with a friend, he "fell in with" Collins and experienced "another mixed scene somewhat like that of 48 hours before," including another use of the lash. Gladstone thus extended the use of flagellation: he scourged himself not only after reading pornography but after visiting Collins as well.

His pattern of frequent visits to prostitutes continued during the remainder of that year and into the early months of 1852. From January to July 1852, he met with various prostitutes fifty times, an average of twice weekly for six months. The nature of the encounters changed somewhat, however. Collins was no longer the only object of Gladstone's attention. In April 1852, a prostitute named E. Scott caught his eye: she appears more often for a time in the diary than any other name. In addition to the frequently mentioned Watson, Lightfoot, and Collins, new names appear: A. Loader, E. Lee, and "Horton & Malins." It is likely, as before, that some of these prostitutes were genuine objects of charity. On 22 June, Gladstone discussed with E. Reynolds the possibility of another line of work: he recommended drawing—as unlikely as it may seem—and gave her one pound toward artists' materials. A week later, he took two pounds to Watson along with a copy of an uplifting work, "Jer. Taylors Holy Living." On 4 November 1852, he "saw a most beautiful unnamed girl of 18." He accompanied her home, where they "lingered over a talk." (This, too, was written in Italian in the diary.) But above all, his attraction to Collins persisted. As he himself once described his feelings late one night after tea with her, "I am surely self-bewildered." A few months later, he again was with Collins in the evening after a busy day: "Remained some time mainly I hope to muse but ever with shame." The next week he gave her a copy of Uncle Tom's Cabin. In November he again had tea with her late at night—by now this was a ritual—and returned home to cleanse his conscience with a flogging.[56]

The apparent freedom that Gladstone had in his nocturnal adventures is striking. How was he able to get away with it? No doubt his behavior would be quickly exposed by twentieth-century investigative reporting, but in his own time, Gladstone could always claim that he was engaged in legitimate charity. In addition, he could operate under the cloak of his religious reputation and his authority as a member of Parliament. When once threatened with blackmail in May 1853 by someone who had followed him on his nightly rounds, Gladstone simply marched the man to the police station and pressed charges. When the story reached the newspapers, editors protected him.[57]

Gladstone's late-night visits would certainly have been a matter of concern to his own family had they been aware of them. But the Gladstones were often separated. While William was in London, Catherine and the children were either at Hawarden, at her sister's home in Hagley, or vacationing at Brighton or traveling elsewhere. In addition, Catherine was pregnant nine times in fourteen years (some of these pregnancies ended in miscarriages). It was a Victorian convention to abstain from sexual relations during most of pregnancy, nursing, and menstruation. During these periods—and during Catherine's absences—Gladstone's rescue work flourished.[58]

The intensity of his rescue work and especially his relationship with Collins tapered off for a time in the mid-1850s. This likely was attributable to increased official work: in February 1853, he became chancellor of the Exchequer in the Aberdeen Coalition, the highest political office he had held to that time. This is not to say that he ceased his rescue work. Indeed, his diaries show fifty-six encounters in 1853 and sixty-four in 1854. In this period he was more prone than in the past to give money to those whom he met on the street—a pound here, five or ten shillings there. Some of these are new names: Williams, Harford, Robinson, Bishop, Whitnall, Edwards, Osborne, Griffin, Car, Bywater, Berkeley, Blanchard, Harrington, Dumin. Some familiar names, such as Loader and Lightfoot, reappear. But these entries are little more than perfunctory. No longer does Gladstone seem tormented over his behavior. There remains only occasionally a wistful remark about Collins, whom he continued to see irregularly. In January 1854, for example, he reported that she "goes on well" and that her case was thus "a source of real though I must add ill-deserved satisfaction."[59] Not for another five years, during a time of revived stressful events, did Gladstone find himself once again powerfully drawn to a woman of the streets.

Gladstone's dalliance with London prostitutes during the stressful years of the late 1840s and early 1850s has been set within a context of stress and coping theory. Gladstone, drawn to prostitutes at first through a legitimate channel of philanthropic concern, in time found some prostitutes attractive objects of desire. One question yet remains. How was it that he was able to cross the immense class and cultural divisions between his own upper-class background and those of London prostitutes? How could Gladstone, a man of prudish notions and a puritanical cast of mind, find it within himself even to speak to such women? There are several possible answers. Bernard C.

Meyer argues that erotic attraction for forbidden women may be the only way that some men can obtain sexual gratification. Wives, whom men love but cannot desire, remain pure; prostitutes, whom they cannot love, are darkly desired. This divergence in an erotic life is a consequence of repressed libidinal impulses toward the mother. In an attempt to remove the angelic mother from notions of sexuality, some men can relate only to a professional sensualism found in prostitution. By being the antithesis of the mother image, women of the streets make sex seem distant from any unconscious incestuous urges. Yet all women are mother surrogates: within the whore lies the mother. Thus there exists the impulse for rescue—to retrieve the mother within the prostitute. Meyer concludes that Gladstone's saintly mother drummed into her son ideas of womanly purity that tainted his relations with women for the remainder of his life in just the way that Freud hypothesized.[60] Thus was Gladstone driven to seek a form of sexual relief on the streets.

This psychoanalytic dichotomy between angel and whore has become a standard explanation in analyzing Victorian sexuality. Eric Trudgill, for example, has described an interdependence between what he calls the "angel woman and the outcast." He follows essentially the same argument outlined by Meyers: love for a wife chosen on the model of a mother and sister diminished erotic feelings, which could be released only by contact with a less exalted sexual object.[61] Peter Gay, although he does not take up the issue of Gladstone's night walking, suggests the powerful influence of his mother, which created within him a "punitive evangelical superego."[62]

The difficulty of discussing sexual mores in terms of the Freudian paradigm is that such an approach is often ahistorical. Freudian constructs too readily ignore empirical evidence. By assuming the primacy of what Gay has called the "propulsive power of erotic and aggressive urges,"[63] historians may distort the context of social life. Thus viewed, sexual habits remain constant, fixed over time, and cannot be altered. This represents what Jeffrey Weeks has called an essentialist view of sex; that is, a view that sees sex always as an overpowering, instinctual force that shapes not only personal but social life as well—no matter what the culture, no matter when the time.[64]

In short, a psychoanalytical perspective may raise questions about the past behavior of historical actors, but it lacks plausibility: it cannot easily answer the questions it raises. It remains grounded in abstraction and theory. To answer the riddle of Gladstone's attraction to forbidden lower-class women, the characteristics of the Victorian class system must be taken into account.[65] Broadly speaking, in nineteenth-century Britain a burgeoning commercial and industrial middle class was thrusting its way forward. The Gladstones were representative of this newly affluent middle class: they were thoroughly and consciously bourgeois. Yet within that family and virtually every other middle-class family were representatives of a much larger and less respectable class, that is, servants. In close proximity to family members, servants were simultaneously removed from the family circle, separated by the invisible barrier of class. This was true not only in the family but in the workplace, on the streets, and in the clubs as well. Many domestic servants were women; indeed, the numbers of women "in service" were growing throughout the nineteenth century. Middle-class children had frequent contact with female servants in the early years of their lives, whether as nannies, cooks, or scullery maids. Doubtless, a rough familiarity grew up between the children and household servants, although the class barrier was always in place.

Although life in service was a usual route from rural poverty to a more affluent and exciting life in town, it was a hard life. Long hours, low pay, and constant rituals of submission to their social superiors drove servants to hope for something better. But they were ill prepared for an advance in the urban job market. Many female servants, who were usually young, without formal education, and only roughly skilled, fell into prostitution as one of the few opportunities for independent work. It was a more attractive option than long hours of servile factory labor.[66] Young Gladstone no doubt had frequent contacts with servants: his mother, often ill, could not have managed the children on her own. In any case, his first encounter with working-class women likely enough was with servants. When Gladstone began his rescue work among prostitutes, he may have found it easy to initiate conversations with them. Speaking in his pedantic way to women of a lower station on the street was not unlike speaking to servants at his own house or his father's. (Prostitutes, too, were not shy. They were professionally inclined to interest and comfort gentlemen; they often would take the initiative.)

Equally suggestive of Gladstone's sense of ease in perambulating the city streets of nighttime London is Judith Walkowitz's recent gender map of urban Victorian centers.[67] She notes that women (or, more accurately, respectable women) were expected to remain within the narrow spheres of home and hearth. The dark and labyrinthine metropolis was potentially dangerous to women. Men, in contrast, could enter self-confidently the public spaces of cities. With a kind of masculine swagger, men took possession of cities, even at night. Because prostitutes were virtually the only women out late, they were a natural object of curiosity.

As a middle-class Victorian male, then, Gladstone was probably not untypical in his choice of charity. Nor was he unusual in selecting the urban landscape as an object of investigation, as Walkowitz points out.[68] And because his haunts were those of the select West End prostitutes who catered to the wealthy, the likelihood is that Gladstone found a high proportion of women among his rescue cases who were more privileged than the "proletariat of prostitution" that Walkowitz has identified. Elizabeth Collins was likely one of these. Gladstone may have been drawn to prostitutes like Collins, in short, because they were attractive and interesting. He may also have found their style of life intriguing. They represented a type of woman that he rarely met in his more conventional parliamentary and social circles. As a man of wealth and position, Gladstone may well have believed that he could control any outcome of such encounters, but the relief from stress that rescue cases had promised had dangerous side effects.

5

"The Stained Course of My Life"

The Oak Farm disaster, apostasy and death among friends and family, and the tension caused by a lack of control in his rescue work combined to make Gladstone a victim of what psychologists might term multiple concurrent stress.[1] Historians, too, have observed the "chronic anxieties" in the texture of his life that gave rise to an "underlying restlessness." Gladstone's "wayward and bewildering" behavior during the "untidy years" of his middle life have also drawn attention.[2] His contemporaries were puzzled by his actions. Few seemed to understand Gladstone and his intentions; some were suspicious of them. Yet he remained full of potential. Brilliant episodes reminded politicians and the public alike of those talents that could make him a prime minister. But the way remained difficult, in part because of self-inflicted wounds. A more detailed examination of Gladstone's political fortunes in the late 1840s and 1850s will make this clear.

The most salient fact for Gladstone's political ambitions in these decades was the dim prospect of high office after the fall of Sir Robert Peel's Conservative government in 1846. Although his free trade policy was widely supported in the country, Peel had alienated large numbers of the Conservative party faithful, especially farmers and landowners who made up the agricultural interest. Conservatives were bitterly divided after 1846 between a protectionist majority and a smaller Peelite minority, whose free trade members included Gladstone. Because his patron at Newark, the duke of Newcastle, was a rabid protectionist, Gladstone was forced to resign his seat. He was out of Parliament for some months until the general election of 1847, when he was elected for Oxford University.

During his several years of parliamentary opposition to the Whig-Liberal majority, Gladstone repeatedly sought a political vehicle for his ambitions. He had three options: to rejoin the protectionist Conservatives, to remain with the Peelite free trade Conservatives, or to break completely with conservatism and become a Whig-Liberal. None of these was immediately attractive. The protectionists would never offer a congenial home as long as Gladstone was a free trader. Yet to remain a Peelite became increasingly difficult as their numbers and influence were steadily reduced by death, electoral defeat, or defection. With the Whig-Liberal party, Gladstone felt out of step: he did not favor their erratic bouts of reformist energy and was not at ease with their leadership.

By the early 1850s, Gladstone was increasingly restless and dissatisfied; of all the Peelites, he was the most eager in seeking some kind of political accommodation.[3] Particularly alarming to Peelite (and Gladstonian) ambition was the growing strength of Benjamin Disraeli, an opportunistic but singularly able politician who had adopted the protectionist mantle in order to insinuate himself into the Conservative leadership. The longer the Peelites held aloof from the main body of Conservatives, the stronger was Disraeli's grip on the party. Disraeli's emerging political authority gave an added urgency to Gladstone's determination to seek a party that could fulfill his personal and political needs.

An opportunity for Gladstone's return to office came at last in 1852. In February of that year, the weakened Whig ministry of Lord John Russell fell and was replaced by Lord Derby (Lord Stanley, Peel's former colonial minister, had succeeded his father to the earldom in 1851). For the first time in nearly six years a Conservative ministry held office. The new ministry, however, was neither experienced nor distinguished. Should the ministry fail on the grounds of an unsuccessful protectionist platform, the long-standing hopes of the Peelites might be realized. Out of the ashes of a discredited protectionist Conservative party could rise a free trade conservatism. Throughout February and March 1852, Gladstone was intensely active in corresponding, arranging meetings, and soliciting opinions among leading Peelites about the most appropriate tactical response to the Derby government.[4]

In making his rounds, Gladstone discovered distinct variations of opinion. Sir James Graham, for example, leaned increasingly toward the Liberals, but Lord Hardinge—a former cabinet minister under Peel—had already accepted office under Derby. Newcastle (Gladstone's old friend Lord Lincoln had succeeded to the dukedom on the death of his father in January 1851) hoped for an independent third party, while the earl of Aberdeen wanted the Peelites to act independently until the question of protectionism had been settled. Gladstone himself favored Aberdeen's position, with a more pronounced tilt toward the Conservatives. Gladstone well understood that this Peelite disunity threatened his own political prospects. He was determined to rein in any errant Peelites. When Sir James Graham's flirtation with the Liberals turned serious, for example, and he accepted a Liberal platform as a parliamentary candidate at the forthcoming general election, Gladstone was appalled.[5] He called a meeting of Peelite leaders in an attempt to read Graham out of the Peelite connection. Gladstone also wrote a letter to Graham declaring that so long as Graham held his present views, Gladstone could no longer associate politically with him. Not surprisingly, a coolness grew between the former political allies. Graham's actions had the faint glimmerings of a kind of secular apostasy.

Gladstone's dislike of Graham's Liberal inclination left little doubt of his Conservative preference. During the brief life of the Derby ministry, he supported its measures for the most part and was sympathetic with Derby's antidemocratic and nonreformist notions. Graham believed that Gladstone was mainly eager to carry a free trade amendment against the Derby government not to bring down the government but to remove the main barrier between him and the Conservatives. Additionally, Gladstone had numerous friendly interchanges with Derby but none, significantly enough, with Disraeli. Indeed, Gladstone's antipathy to Disraeli—fueled in part by political rivalry—was developing into a personal animosity. To Gladstone, Disraeli was an unsavory, exotic, alien, loose charmer of men and women. Disraeli's early reputation as a philanderer, his political adventurism, and his moral cynicism were anathema to Gladstone. That Disraeli, an "impure" character, should block his way to political advancement was doubly distasteful.[6]

Gladstone's frustration and anger at Disraeli reached a climax during a dramatic parliamentary confrontation in late 1852. On 3 December, Disraeli presented his first full budget as chancellor of the Exchequer. Disraeli's budget brought praise from farmers for its reductions of malt and hop duties, but the middle class were confused by his tax reductions on earned incomes, which were offset by an increase on the house tax. Parliamentary critics were numerous, but the most unsparing critic of all was Gladstone.[7] Even allowing for the normal party rhetoric, Gladstone was harsh and unforgiving. The substance of letters to his wife in early December showed Gladstone in an angry mood. Reduction of the malt tax he believed was "essentially bad." Differentiating between earned and unearned income in one of the tax schedules was "flagrantly vicious." He thought Disraeli's speeches "full of trumpery," "disgusting and repulsive," and containing "fundamental faults of principle." The budget was the "least conservative" he had "ever known." He professed himself to be especially angry at Disraeli's carelessness and neglect of detail.[8] On 16 December—the final night of the budget debate—Gladstone showed his distaste for Disraeli in a most unusual way. Shortly after ten that evening, Disraeli rose to conclude the debate: he finished at one o'clock in the morning to the cheers of his supporters. Custom dictated that a vote should follow immediately after the concluding speech by the leader of the House. But this was prevented by Gladstone, who sprang up from his seat unannounced and launched an attack on the budget. He was met by what Victorian stenographers called "loud cries," "interruptions," and "confusion."[9] The protectionist ranks were outraged at this breach of parliamentary propriety. He was eventually allowed to continue, however, because his speech broke no formal rules of the House.

In an echo of his letters to his wife, Gladstone took Disraeli to task for devising a budget filled with structural flaws and characterized by a "hopeless obscurity." He declared that Disraeli was a "mere panderer to public opinion." Because the budget lacked a surplus from which one could draw in times of emergencies, it was also reckless, overthrowing "all those rules of prudence heretofore deemed necessary" in conducting the financial affairs of the country. "I vote against the Budget of the Chancellor of the Exchequer," he thundered, "not only because I disapprove upon general grounds of the principles of that Budget, but emphatically and peculiarly because . . . it is my firm conviction that the Budget is . . . the most subversive in its tendencies and ultimate effects which I have ever known submitted to this House."

Some historians believe that Gladstone's speech sealed the fate of the Derby ministry, which fell within days. But for the purposes of this argument, his criticisms of the substantive part of the budget are less important than the tone and manner of his proceeding, and what they may have revealed about his feelings toward Disraeli. Before and during the budgetary debates, Gladstone had worked himself into an unusual frenzy. The strain began to tell: he complained of neuralgia pains in his face, and of a "feeling in my teeth (as if some of them were half out)."[10] The parliamentary atmosphere became increasingly contentious; this, too, no doubt affected Gladstone when he rose to speak on the final night. His appearance was remarkable. His features, according to one parliamentary observer, "were livid and distorted with passion, his voice shook, and those who watched him feared an outbreak incompatible with parliamentary rules."[11] Gladstone's version confirms the tension he felt: "I have never gone through so exciting a passage of parliamentary life," he confided to his wife.[12] The evening following his concluding speech he could sleep only two hours. As he explained it, "My nervous system was too powerfully acted upon by the scene of last night."[13]

How can we explain Gladstone's behavior? He was not notably nervous in his public speeches. He was not new to parliamentary debate. His oratorical talents were widely acknowledged. Nor was he an inexperienced politician. Yet the prospect of confronting Disraeli directly on the floor of the House of Commons seems to have created within him exceptional tensions. Part of this can be explained by the fact that the budget debates of 1852 represented the Peelites' best opportunity since 1846 of exorcising from the Conservative Party the demon of protectionism. It was also an opportunity for bringing down its adventurist leader, Disraeli.

Disraeli not only represented a hindrance to Gladstone's ambition for high office but had become somehow a symbol for the ills that had so severely beset Gladstone in recent years. High office was for Gladstone neither an end in itself nor merely a sign of success in politics: it also had psychological utility. Quite simply, Disraeli barred Gladstone's return to a sense of coherence in his life, to order, and to stability. We can only guess why Disraeli should have assumed this role for Gladstone. No doubt Disraeli's apparent success within the Conservative Party was galling to Gladstone, especially so because Disraeli had achieved it at the expense of Peel and of Gladstone himself. Equally displeasing may have been Disraeli's ascension to chancellor of the Exchequer before Gladstone had a turn at that important office. It seems, too, that Disraeli's personal reputation played a role. In any case, Gladstone never abandoned his repugnance of Disraeli. Even at the end of his life, he could not recall Disraeli without a "strong sentiment of revulsion," a sentiment "quite distinct from that of dislike."[14]

Gladstone's response to the threat of Disraeli did occur within an appropriate parliamentary context. Debates, rude queries, interruptions, and heckling in Parliament between members of opposite parties are the stuff of political life. Such circumstances encouraged confrontation. Gladstone would unlikely have vented his anger against family, servants, friends, or rescue cases; parliamentary opponents were a more likely target. But Gladstone's behavior lay outside the accepted parliamentary norm in its degree of vehemence. Indeed, Gladstone himself recognized this after the event. An exchange of letters between Gladstone and Sir William Heathcote (a Derbyite supporter but a personal friend of Gladstone) reveals mutual puzzlement about Gladstone's behavior. Heathcote wondered how, after the budget debates, it would be possible for Gladstone to follow through on his avowed aim of rejoining the Conservatives once their protectionist policy was abandoned. In effect, Heathcote charged Gladstone with dysfunctional behavior: Gladstone's passionate denunciation and humiliation of Disraeli—and through him of the ministry as a whole—would make such a confederation unlikely. Indeed, Derby's resignation speech in the House of Lords a few days later was certainly delivered in an angry tone. Nor does it seem that Gladstone had won the hearts of the Conservative backbenchers: he was nearly assaulted in the Carlton Club by a group of disappointed if tipsy Conservatives. In spite of whatever psychological gain he had made in making Disraeli a scapegoat, political popularity had eluded him.[15]

Yet it is a testament to Gladstone's psychological flexibility and his capacity for rapid adaptation that out of the wreckage of the Derby ministry he gained a political advantage. If he could not reach his goal of high office under the Conservatives, then he must achieve this aim under some other arrangement of parties. Thus, he became a willing convert to a Peelite-Whig coalition government. This was a change of heart. In the past he had been much opposed to a union with the Whig-Liberals. In a long memo dated 18 December 1852, he justified his new views and advocated what he called a "mixed government" to be made up of the "most temperate portions of both the Conservative and the Liberal parties." Such a mixed government, as opposed to a "fusion of parties," would allow a greater independence of opinion among ministerial colleagues on such issues as parliamentary reform—the issue that most divided him from the Liberal leadership. In addition, Gladstone broadly hinted that in such a government he would like to be chancellor of the Exchequer in order, as he put it, to make a "vigorous and united effort to settle and secure the finances of the country."[16]

With the defeat of Disraeli's budget and the resignation of the Conservative ministry, the "fusion" that Gladstone had advocated was brought about by the formation of the Aberdeen Coalition. Composed of roughly equal parts of Whig and Peelite, the ministry had every prospect of success. Gladstone, appointed chancellor of the Exchequer, was bound to play a central role in the ministry. He thus began, in December 1852, the first term of many that made him the preeminent financial expert of modern times. Psychologically, the attainment of high office also came at a fortuitous time. It helped re-create a sense of order and purpose in his life that had been lost in the late 1840s.[17]

Of all the cabinet offices, that of the chancellor of the Exchequer allowed the greatest scope for independence in executive action. Having shown a flair for financial detail when at the Board of Control under Peel, Gladstone now extended his expertise to budget making. From the vantage point of the Exchequer, he could assert his control over other departments of the government. He could command not only the Treasury but the armed services under the Admiralty and the War Office as well.[18] From his office, he could manage his own world and then the wider political one. Without that office, or some other, he was rudderless. Indeed, when Gladstone resigned from the Aberdeen government in early 1855, he was plunged once again into misery.

Gladstone's managerial style and command of his subject were clearly in evidence during the preparation and presentation of his famous budget of 1853. He pitched himself into the making of the budget with the zest of one who had found a new purpose in life. His diary is filled with the details of the daily round of his work as he gathered and sifted information. He received visits from various interest groups. He corresponded and spoke with Treasury officials, financial experts, parliamentary colleagues, and even Prince

Albert. He read solidly in the relevant theoretical and practical literature: John Stuart Mill's *Principles of Political Economy;* J. R. McCulloch on taxation and the funding system; articles in the *Edinburgh Review, Quarterly Review,* and *Blackwood's;* and numerous additional pamphlets. Into the evenings, after a day's full labor, he worked through cabinet and Treasury papers. As the deadline for the budget neared, Gladstone's regular hour of retirement was well after midnight. Unavoidable ceremonial events could prolong his working day: after nearly six hours at the Lord Mayor of London's dinner on 28 March—"a lamentable hole in my evening"—he was up until four o'clock in the morning on budget matters. No budget could have been more thoroughly prepared.

Gladstone's presentation to the cabinet of his budget on 18 April 1853 was a masterful performance. That day was clearly remembered nearly half a century later by the duke of Argyll, a Whig-Peelite peer then serving as Lord Privy Seal in the cabinet.[19] As Argyll recorded the event, Gladstone entered the cabinet room carrying a shabby leather-bound box. He sat down with the cabinet in a circle around him. Opening the box on his knee so that the lid formed a rest for the pages of the budget, he drew out from time to time tables of detailed statistics, which he placed upon the lid. Apart from an occasional reference to these exact figures, no word of his presentation was read. For three hours, Gladstone held forth in an uninterrupted flow. "The order was perfect in its lucidity," Argyll recalled, "and the sentences as faultless as they were absolutely unhesitating. Never for a moment did he overrun himself on any point, or require to hark back in order to recover some forgotten or omitted matter. It was like the flow of some crystal stream—passing sometimes through narrows, and elsewhere spreading itself over broader channels, but everywhere glancing with light, full of lively movement. Not one of us could think for a moment of interrupting him, even to ask a question. It seemed not only to leave nothing obscure or incomplete, but to raise and to settle, as it went along, a thousand questions which had not occurred to any of us before." Throughout the presentation, Gladstone was perfectly composed, his face grave, showing no emotion—"except just a little of a satisfied smile." The only sign of nervousness was his habit of continually wadding up the feather of a quill pen into a ball, unrolling it, and beginning again.[20]

Argyll's opinion of Gladstone's budget has been confirmed by modern scholarship. He had fashioned a comprehensive budget that was a model of an evolving system of Victorian finance. The primary problem facing the chancellor had been the need to secure state revenues through the income tax—always an unpopular measure. Gladstone's principle of taxation was that every class should bear its fair share. Thus the major provisions of the budget revealed a countervailing strategy between various classes. He extended the income tax to more of the middle class (by lowering the exemption rate), for example, but balanced this by imposing a legacy duty on real property that applied largely to the landed classes. He also, like Disraeli, lowered to one hundred pounds the threshold of annual income above which income tax would be paid. Those who wanted to maintain the income tax in perpetuity—principally radical politicians and the liberal economic thinkers—he satisfied by extending the life of the tax for another seven years. For those who wanted the tax to end—principally the propertied classes—the very fact of its planned redundancy offered hope of its eventual repeal. He extended the income tax to Ireland, thus borrowing another leaf from Disraeli's book, but balanced this by remitting a debt of several million pounds owed Britain by Ireland. His reduction in the tea tax, again an echo of Disraeli, was generally regarded as a boon to the poor.

Gladstone's 1853 budget was well orchestrated, systematic, and supremely orderly—characteristics of his budgets in all the years to come.[21] From his vantage point as chancellor of the Exchequer, he had the power to shape the ministry by making the budget largely his own production and by employing secrecy to guard against criticism. He once advised a future chancellor in making budgets "to keep his own Counsel & let the Cabinet as a whole not know his plans till his mind was made up in the main, & the time close at hand."[22] In the great budget of 1853, and in subsequent ones, he followed his own advice.

Although the cabinet generally supported Gladstone's presentation, some members had specific, if slight, complaints. As Lord Palmerston (the home secretary), observed, the budget "opened too many points of attack."[23] But Gladstone stoutly defended the budget as it stood. He argued that it could only be carried "by dint of strong feeling"—that is, with a united front. Ostensibly willing to compromise on some issues, Gladstone in fact wanted the budget to go forward untouched by cabinet amendments. He even hinted of resignation on the first day of the debate, in response to some of the initial cabinet criticisms. He ultimately had his way. "I strongly adhered to my whole plan," he wrote of his role in the cabinet debates.

Gladstone robustly presented the budget to the House of Commons in a speech of nearly five hours' duration. Afterward, he celebrated quietly at home with a few friends, supping on soup and negus. He recorded that evening in his diary a subdued impression of his speech: "Many kind congratulations afterward," he wrote. The following day, he received "innumerable marks of kindness: enough to make me ashamed."[24] However modestly Gladstone may have portrayed himself and his speech, it was in fact a wholly triumphant performance. His speech had brought on a "tumult of applause" at its close. Old parliamentary hands thought that it was substantively the soundest and rhetorically the most persuasive budget speech since the great wartime speeches of Pitt in the 1790s. Others compared Gladstone to Peel. Even the petulant Greville praised it as "one of the grandest displays and most able financial statements that ever was heard in the H. of Commons; a great scheme, boldly, skillfully, and honestly devised."[25] Argyll, a friendlier critic, had more extravagant praise. He marveled at Gladstone's "pellucid clearness of exposition," which "made close listening a positive pleasure to the mind." Argyll's estimation of the wider significance of the speech was probably correct. It not only helped consolidate the coalition government in the eyes of Parliament, but it also revealed Gladstone to be more than a man of promise. He had "made a long and flying leap in his ascent to power."[26]

But the physical toll and nervous strain involved in his intensive work during the first months of the session at last caught up with him a few days after his budget speech. He recorded in his diary on 28 April: "I felt at length a good deal overset." That night he took a "blue pill." The following day he felt worse and took another pill: for the next two days he was in bed under doctor's orders. Illness continued to plague him in the months that followed. In early September, Gladstone fell ill once again, this time on a visit to Dunrobin, the seat of the dukes of Sutherland where he had gone directly after the end of the parliamentary session. The trouble was erysipelas and— one may suspect—the complications brought on by an overly rigorous schedule of work. This time he was laid up for nearly three weeks, the most lengthy illness since a childhood bout of scarlet fever.[27]

Illness aside, there seems little doubt that the coalition government was given direction and legitimacy by Gladstone's coming of age as a minister of the Crown. The government was now free to pursue its program of mild reform during the remainder of the session, including a restructuring of the governance of India, a series of legal reforms, and a number of measures that fell under the Home Office.[28] Gladstone himself had played a significant role in civil service reform and in modernizing antiquated financial practices and administration at Oxford University.

Gladstone's participation in the government's program of reform should not mislead; he was not an enthusiastic reformer. As Matthew has noted, Gladstone's policy of centralized management was characterized by a strict maintenance of executive authority and control. In this, he followed the precepts of Sir Robert Peel, his earliest guide in political life. Any necessary reform, Gladstone believed, should be initiated by responsible governments, rather than by parliamentary cliques or by extraparliamentary pressure groups. Thus governments—by recognizing the need for change, gathering information on the options available, and then devising a legislative packet—kept reform firmly in the hands of ministers. Because of these views, Gladstone was unsympathetic to extending the franchise at this time in his career. He was less interested in a wider political nation than he was in an efficient governance by the privileged classes.[29] It was not surprising that he opposed Lord John Russell's program for the extension of the franchise introduced in February 1854.

If Gladstone's place within the coalition was secure and his contributions to its reputation were widely recognized, the government itself was increasingly threatened by the onset of international tensions. By March 1854, Britain was embroiled with its ally France against Russia in the Crimean War. Gladstone's role in the decision to wage war was not significant. His attention was focused on his domestic program, and essentially he spoke for peace in the cabinet. But the war had a severe impact on his own department of state, and ultimately on the popularity of the government. With increased military expenses, Gladstone's fiscal expectations for the budget of 1854 were thrown out of kilter. Instead of reducing the income tax (one of the key provisions of the 1853 budget), he was forced to double it. He was driven to offering some six million pounds in Exchequer Bonds to the public, which conflicted with his expressed preference for financing war by taxation, rather than by borrowing.[30] Further expedients included an increase in the import duties of some consumer articles—such as spirits, malt, and sugar—thus contravening Gladstone's free trade convictions. His reputation for fiscal wizardry, earned so recently, was in some disarray by the end of the parliamentary session of 1854.

More fateful for the coalition's tenure was the mounting military indecision and incompetence at the battlefront. With the futile charge of the Light Brigade, the most fitting symbol of British fortunes in the Crimea, the coalition's prestige fell dangerously low. By January 1855, parliamentary opinion was unsettled enough to prompt the establishment of a Select Committee to look into the conduct of the war. Should such a committee be authorized—regardless of what its investigations might reveal—it would likely censure the government's conduct of the war. Gladstone was not the minister most responsible for the military failures; his friend and colleague the duke of Newcastle bore that burden as secretary of state for war. Nevertheless, Gladstone spoke out energetically against the committee before the House of Commons on 29 January. In a powerful justification of executive privilege, he argued for a centralized, executive style of management. Admitting that the government had encountered "many calamities" and was responsible for "many faults" in the Crimean campaign, he yet defended its general record. Members of the Commons who wished to censure the government for its actions, or to "put a period" to its work, should do so openly. Using the "disguised" device of a Select Committee was without precedent. Indeed, should the Commons vote to pursue that route, it would be abrogating its responsibilities by devolving its powers into the hands of the few who served on the committee. Gladstone's argument did not still the critical voices: the motion for a Select Committee was overwhelmingly passed by a vote of 304 to 148.[31]

Treating the issue as a vote of no confidence, the Aberdeen Coalition resigned the following day. An unusually prolonged search for a ministry ensued: Lord Derby, Lord John Russell, the Whig Lord Lansdowne, and even Aberdeen himself were scouted as heads of government before Lord Palmerston was successful in late February. Gladstone was naturally sought as a prize catch in any government. But he played a cautious game, entering into a continuous round of discussions with various party leaders. His first preference seems to have been Aberdeen's return to power, although the sense of his private memoranda was that his view was based more on personal loyalty than on any faith in Aberdeen's efficacy as a party leader. Consequently, Gladstone was not averse to a government led by Derby. "To a Derby government," he wrote reflectively years later, "now that the party had been *drubbed* out of protection, I did not in principle object; for old ties were with me more operatively strong than new opinions."[32] Derby would have the advantage of a united party at his back, whereas Aberdeen could only come forward, as before, with a coalition. The least attractive candidate to Gladstone was Lord Palmerston, whom he characterized as "in no way equal to the duties which fall upon a Prime Minister."[33] Within two days of this statement, however, Gladstone joined Palmerston's government, essentially the government of the Aberdeen Coalition without Lord John Russell—who had been sent abroad on a diplomatic mission—and without either Aberdeen or Newcastle, who had fallen as scapegoats to the critics of the Crimean War.

Gladstone appears curiously indecisive throughout these weeks of government making. His decision to accept Palmerston was reluctantly made. Perhaps Gladstone believed that once he was in office and serving again as chancellor, he could swallow his reservations about Palmerston. Or perhaps he hoped that Palmerston's government would soon fall (he predicted it would last a year at most), giving another ministry an opportunity. In any case, Gladstone very much wanted office—this much is clear. But he wanted it on his own terms. When the House of Commons repeated its demand for a Select Committee in the early days of the new Palmerston government, Gladstone again reacted angrily. He argued in cabinet meetings "at some length and vehemently" against the committee.[34] It was, he said, more than a committee of inquiry: it "was itself a Censure on the Govt."[35] Other members of the cabinet generally took a different view. Palmerston was willing to grant the committee, recognizing its inevitability. Argyll reported that Palmerston was "evidently much annoyed" at Gladstone's position. Argyll himself attributed Gladstone's "considerable irritation" to his tendency to "exaggeration"—to follow his own line of reasoning to the exclusion of other arguments.[36] Gladstone held his ground, and on 22 February he resigned from the government, taking with him Sidney Herbert and Sir James Graham. The departure of these three Peelite ministers brought the coalition experiment of Peelites and Whigs to an end. With the exception of a brief Conservative interlude, Palmerston was prime minister until his death ten years later.

Gladstone's resignation from Palmerston's government brought him once again into the political wilderness. At first, he reacted by plunging headlong into his books, especially classical studies. He chose a discrete topic for extended analysis—the life and work of the great epic poet Homer. Eventually, he published several articles and a substantial three-volume book on Homer. In this lengthy undertaking, Gladstone postulated that Homer had received divine revelation like the Jewish prophets; thus did Gladstone's classical studies buttress his religious beliefs.[37] Working on the ancient Greeks was no doubt all-absorbing and served as a way of usefully marking time. "It is so interesting that I can hardly bear it," he wrote to Lord Lyttelton in late 1855. A year later, his news was the same: "All my spare time goes to Homer. But I find myself obliged to write, re-write, & re-re-write upon the historical part: the field extends as I dig."[38]

His Homeric labors, however, could not mask Gladstone's political restlessness. The years 1855 to 1859 provide the clearest case yet of Gladstone's attempt to employ a variety of coping devices to deflect his continued political and psychological frustrations.[39] Both aggression and withdrawal characterize Gladstone's behavior in these years. Just as Disraeli had earlier served as a scapegoat, so now Palmerston played that role. Gladstone's resignation from the Palmerston cabinet may be understood as the employment of a strategy of withdrawal. Within a few months of his departure from the government, however, he initiated an aggressive strategy designed to discredit Palmerston. In May 1855, he launched a direct attack on the prime minister's Crimean policy. In so doing, Gladstone reversed his own views on the war. From favoring Britain's ally Turkey, he switched to favor Russia. When he learned that attempted peace negotiations with the Russians had broken down and that the Palmerston government was determined to prosecute the war, he "at once got up a high head of steam, and argued himself into a fever of antagonism and suspicion against Palmerston" as a warmonger. These were the observations of Argyll, who had remained in Palmerston's cabinet as postmaster general.[40] Argyll professed himself unsurprised at Gladstone's behavior. His actions often were so extreme, Argyll believed, that he did his own cause more harm than good. So it was in this case: his "violence" (as Argyll noted it) against the government alienated some of his parliamentary friends. Even the amiable Sidney Herbert parted company with Gladstone on this issue.

Gladstone may well have simply changed his mind about the conduct of the war.[41] But as a former member of the Aberdeen Coalition, he had at least implicitly supported the war. And he had entered the Palmerston government with the certain understanding that hostilities would continue. Further, Gladstone's resignation from Palmerston's ministry had not hinged on any difference of opinion on the war. In short, it would seem that Gladstone's change of mind came about only after his resignation from Palmerston's government. He justified this reversal by asserting that it was not so much that his opinions

had changed as that circumstances had altered. The czar was now more ame-
nable to British war aims. Why prolong the conflict?

Few accepted Gladstone's explanation. His "uncritical Russophilism"
opened him to the charge of political inconsistency. Some even called him a
traitor (as Morley dutifully notes). Indeed, his "tenacious hostility" to a peace
plan may have been counterproductive because it diminished the effectiveness
of the peace party.[42] This was certainly the opinion of Argyll, who remained
throughout this controversy an essentially friendly yet detached critic of Gladstone. In an interesting series of letters, Argyll suggested that Gladstone
"ought to consider very carefully" how he could "so guide the debate as to
promote really and effectively the cause of peace."[43] Given the assumptions
of the time, Argyll took a reasonable approach to the conclusion of the war.
It was not an "abominable doctrine," as Gladstone claimed; there were simply
different opinions about the war. No one wished it to continue indefinitely:
the problem was to find the appropriate diplomatic moment for peace. "You
define much too sharply, I think, the point—the exact point at which peace
ought to be made. I cannot so define it in my mind."[44] Argyll also gently
reminded Gladstone that he was once, not so long ago, a member of the
cabinet that had been responsible for entering the war.[45]

Even after the peace treaty had been signed with Russia in March 1856,
Gladstone's "continued animosity to Palmerston . . . on every question on
which opposition could possibly be raised, did not tend to rehabilitate him
in the public estimation."[46] His attacks on Palmerston were only part of a
wider complaint about the course of political development during the previous
ten years. In a long letter to Aberdeen, Gladstone set out his views in detail.
A disrupted party system, he believed, had greatly weakened the "strength of
the Executive." Any new peacetime ministry "ought to be a strong Government."[47] He elaborated his ideas in an anonymous article in the *Quarterly
Review*, published in late 1856. Ostensibly a commentary upon the weakening
of parliamentary efficiency, the article was in fact a thinly disguised attack on
Palmerston and his government.[48] Reviewing for his readers the previous
parliamentary session, Gladstone found little of cheer. Parliament was increasingly paralytic, he believed. Although the "forms and figures" of the
House of Commons had gone on much as before, legislative achievements
were few and far between. It all reminded him of the "tossing of a ship at
anchor" where there was "motion but no progress." Scandal and incompetence were multiplying. "For blunders, scandals, failures, and disgraces, official, political, constitutional, executive, and above all legislative," the session
of 1856 surpassed even that of 1855. He condemned the "scandalous inaction"
of the government and its "combination of levity with inertness of purpose."
Too often, legislation was either abandoned or defeated, resulting in "constant
defeat and disparagement to the Administration." Indeed, Gladstone believed
that "such legislative wreck and ruin never has been seen." In addition, Pal-

merston's diplomacy "has kept the country in perpetual hot water." Other lapses included blatant nepotism in the government's administration of patronage and "financial blundering and feebleness."

Gladstone's roundhouse condemnation was based on some widely recognized weaknesses in Palmerston's government. Some of these could be laid directly at the prime minister's door. But other issues lay outside Palmerston's responsibility: many items of domestic legislation had either been inherited from Aberdeen's fallen ministry or had been brought forward by political opponents. And, too, Palmerston's government, like others of that fluid political era, was at the mercy of unusually unstable parliamentary alliances.[49] Palmerston, in short, was no worse than his predecessors in the art of governing.

In criticizing Palmerston so extensively, Gladstone was doubtless attempting to position himself politically. Palmerston's ministry, he thought, was vulnerable and likely to give way to a more congenial Conservative one, led by Lord Derby. Gladstone made it known that he was once again willing to hear Conservative party overtures. Tentative moves were made in April 1856, when Heathcote served as an intermediary between Gladstone and Derby, but Derby was understandably cautious after earlier failures, and nothing came of it.[50] The tremulous dance of these two cautious partners over many months was public knowledge. As the Conservatives were without a leader and Gladstone was a man without a party, a match seemed desirable. "The Tories are in a necessitous plight," the *Daily News* noted in December 1856, "and so is Mr. Gladstone." Indeed, an apt analogy might be drawn, and the *News* drew it: Gladstone was "like the owner of a large amount of capital seeking profitable investment, and looking out for a high rate of interest."[51]

By the end of 1856, Gladstone was clearly banking on the Conservatives. In a letter to Graham in December, he declared that the country could best be served by a Derby ministry. Peace abroad, sound economic management, financial equilibrium, and the promotion of practical improvement were the specific issues that Gladstone believed lay closer to Derby's heart than to Palmerston's. But Graham, in reply, could not refrain from pointing out that these were the very issues on which Derby in the past had been more destructive to Gladstone's wishes than had Palmerston.[52]

Gladstone's equivocal political position also brought advice from Lord Aberdeen, who counseled "prudence and circumspection." It would hardly do, said Aberdeen, to work for the overthrow of Palmerston, of whose government Gladstone had so recently been a member, without a specific and sufficient reason. Merely opposing the general tenor of the government would not, in Aberdeen's opinion, constitute adequate grounds for opposition. Moreover, Gladstone could not act from a position of strength. "I fear," Aberdeen wrote, "that you do not really possess the sympathy of the House at large. . . . Your recent conduct in Parliament has not been fully understood, but it has been very unpopular." Stung by Aberdeen's candor, Gladstone excused his actions by attacking Palmerston. "He will do, say, undo, unsay anything," Gladstone wrote. "This he has already shown not once but twenty times." Closing a long letter of self-justification, Gladstone ended somewhat self-pityingly. Perhaps it was "much better to hide my head in a rabbit hole, than to remain a simple disturber and mischief maker, on the principal public questions in Parliament."[53] Unmoved by the tone of Gladstone's letter, Aberdeen's response unsparingly discouraged "any fatal entanglement" with Derby. Aberdeen also sounded a warning. Should Gladstone join Derby, he might find himself "in a painful state of isolation": his Peelite friends would not support him. In conclusion, Aberdeen emphasized, "Preserve your independence." Gladstone's reply in turn was simply to reiterate his distaste of Palmerston. "I despair of Lord Palmerston & look upon him as incurable. I despair of his colleagues and their party, as long as they have him at their head."[54]

Gladstone also turned to his old friend Newcastle, as he sought assurance in his feeling of resentment against Palmerston. "I think Ld Palmerston the worst and the most demoralizing Prime Minister for this country that our day has known," he wrote. "I do not know any one who could probably succeed him that I would not prefer to see in his place." By now, Gladstone's rage had reduced him to a state of impotence. As he confessed to Newcastle, he could see little beyond the evils of Palmerston and little beyond the "evident fact that my own political position . . . is bad and mischievous."[55] Newcastle was not helpful. Plagued by his own personal and financial problems and depressed by the public blame cast on him for his role in the Crimean War, he seemed indifferent to politics. But he had the heart to disagree with Gladstone: Palmerston was not as bad as depicted. Gladstone could not tamely accept this moderate response. He excused Newcastle's benign opinion on the grounds of his unfamiliarity with Palmerston. Sitting in the House of Lords, Newcastle could not see as readily as Gladstone what was really happening. "Nothing but the daily observation of the manner in which Lord Palmerston conducts public affairs would I think fully have opened my eyes to the . . . political evils attendant upon his sway. Never have I seen such an abundance of false schemes & such an absence of true: never have I seen the resort to expedients of so low an order."[56]

By the time he had written to Newcastle, Gladstone had already begun another approach to Lord Derby. He had sent the Reverend Whitwell Elwin, editor of the *Quarterly Review,* on a mission to Derby, who agreed that a "frank interchange of opinions may lead to an improved political understanding."[57] On 4 February, Gladstone and Derby spoke confidentially for more than three hours. Gladstone's account of the meeting is surprisingly (and unintentionally) revealing of his mental state. He began, as usual, by castigating Palmerston, declaring that he so thoroughly disapproved of the prime minister that he was prepared to "aid in any proper measures" to depose him. He also stated that the "isolated position" in which he stood tended to "prolong & aggravate" the existing parliamentary fragmentation, which in turn contributed to governmental weakness. And then in a remarkable phrase, he denounced himself "as a public nuisance" and suggested "that it would be an advantage if my doctor sent me abroad for the Session."[58] What Derby made of this is unknown, but he cannot have neglected to observe the strained quality of Gladstone's remarks.

Nothing was settled at the meeting, but during the ensuing fortnight, Gladstone was in frequent contact with Derby. An attempt to strike an accord on the basis of fiscal measures was in the making. Gladstone insisted on steady budget surpluses, lowered indirect taxes, and the temporary character of the income tax. He prepared for a full onslaught on Palmerston's budget, to be introduced later in February by his chancellor of the Exchequer, Sir George Cornewall Lewis. He had been especially incensed by a rumored deficit of five to six million pounds that Lewis would propose.

On 20 February, Gladstone launched in the House of Commons a ferocious attack on the budget and on Lewis personally. Gladstone rebuked Lewis for proposing import duties on certain consumer articles and claimed that the chancellor of the Exchequer "has completely . . . thrown overboard, condemned, repudiated" the sound principles of financial policy that had been successfully worked out over the past fifteen years. He warned that the budget promoted an "improvident expenditure and a reckless system of finance": it would additionally inculcate a "habit of extravagance." He charged Lewis with patronizing the House of Commons, of "trifling with the House, and . . . using us like children." Time and again, he compared Lewis' budget unfavorably to his own of 1853.[59]

His angry rhetoric seemed a repetition of his behavior against Disraeli four years earlier. The consensus of the House, according to Argyll, was that Gladstone—once again—went far beyond the bounds of parliamentary propriety. His speech had been "very overstrained, and unfair in argument to the highest degree."[60] The diarist Greville reported a few days after the speech that Gladstone was "so inflamed by spite and ill-humour that all prudence and discretion forsook him . . . it is not easy to discover the cause of his bitterness." He concluded: "Everybody detests Gladstone."[61] Gladstone's parliamentary outburst was fresh in the minds of observers even years afterward. Stanley remembered the attack on Lewis as spoken "with bitterness rarely equalled in parliament." Indeed, Stanley thought that throughout the parliamentary session Gladstone had behaved with a "peculiar vehemence, like that of a man under personal provocation."[62] Nearly a decade after the event, an article in *Blackwood's* recalled Gladstone's behavior at that time as expressing a spirit that "seemed to prey upon itself." With his attack on Lewis, his banked fires burst forth. "Mr. Gladstone was *very* angry. He struck out right and left ... exhibiting not one spark of generosity towards either friend or foe."[63]

The whole affair was particularly surprising because Gladstone and Lewis were friends and correspondents. Gladstone had even coached Lewis on fiscal matters. Additionally, Lewis was widely regarded as a sound, sensible, fair-minded man. Lewis himself, as Argyll reports it, "was quite amazed" at Gladstone's "personally bitter" speech.[64] Perhaps political considerations were involved in Gladstone's attack on Lewis. By such action he could convince the Conservatives that he was determined to bring down Palmerston's government. But the inappropriate ferocity of his attack suggests that Lewis—like Palmerston himself, and before him Disraeli—was a focus for Gladstone's frustrations, both private and (now largely) public.

In the weeks that followed, Gladstone seemed more subdued but still peevish. Writing to Aberdeen on 4 April, he took exception to a recent statement of Aberdeen's that the Peelites no longer existed and had effectively been absorbed into the Liberal Party—which was, of course, under the leadership of Lord Palmerston. This was too much for Gladstone to bear. If this were true, said Gladstone, then he had been "deceiving both the world and my constituents." His closing remarks conveyed his unhappiness: "In pain & distress I shall endeavour to keep quiet: bow the knee I cannot, but I shall leave the management of public affairs to others who may be better satisfied with their own conduct & path before them." Aberdeen's response was tinged with some asperity. "I am very sorry," he wrote, "to find that you still continue in a state of great doubt and perplexity respecting the course to be pursued by you. ... After all, it must probably be more a matter of feeling and impression than of argument or reasoning." In any case, concluded Aberdeen, "I do not propose to follow up the discussion in any detail."[65]

Gladstone's hint of retirement to Aberdeen was no doubt prompted by the result of a general election just concluded. Lord Palmerston had called it with an apt sense of timing in order to consolidate his hold in the House of Commons against the pesky opposition led chiefly by Gladstone. The results were satisfactory. Palmerston's government gained fifty seats, thus repudiating his critics.[66] The election also dampened the prospective alliance between Gladstone and the Conservatives. Palmerston, now preeminent in the House of Commons, was far less vulnerable to political overthrow. In addition, Gladstone's hand was weakened by the loss of personal support in the House, as several Peelites had failed at the polls. In doleful letters to Sidney Herbert, Gladstone reviewed this latest blow. The "prolonged pain" of "political suspense" made him feel like a man who was roasting at a slow fire.[67] "For the past eleven years," he wrote, "with the exception of two among them, the pains of political strife have not for us found their usual and proper compensation ... while suspicion, mistrust, and criticism have flanked us on both sides and in unusual measure." The only compensation had been the personal friendship and political camaraderie of the Peelite connection, but even this was jeopardized. "The loss of this one comfort I have no strength to face." His only recourse was to seek his duty "by absconding from what may be termed general politics, and secondly, by appearing, wherever I must appear, only in the ranks."[68] True to his word, Gladstone began to absent himself from the House of Commons. When he attended, he rarely opened his lips, as Greville reported.[69]

This pattern had become common with Gladstone. When one coping strategy failed, he attempted another. In this case, a failed aggressive strategy was followed by a more passive one. Palmerston, the focus of his anger and frustrations, was triumphant. Gladstone had little choice but to avoid his enemy by absenting himself from parliamentary duties. In only one parliamentary topic did he involve himself during the remainder of the session of 1857, but this proved a disheartening effort. Toward the end of the session, a divorce bill was introduced in the House of Lords and was quickly passed. Supported by the archbishop of Canterbury and a fair number of the bishops, it was designed to secularize and simplify divorce proceedings by transferring cases from ecclesiastical to secular courts. Gladstone opposed the bill strongly during its passage through the House of Commons.

In preparing his arguments, Gladstone had characteristically read much of the pamphlet literature on marriage and divorce, including Milton's famous defense of divorce. He drew the substance of his own opinion into an orotund article for the *Quarterly Review*. His main objection was the tendency of the bill to treat marriage as a "purely civil contract between individuals." Arguing on narrowly religious grounds against the secularization of divorce, he briefly sketched out the entire history of the "greatest, oldest, and most universal of all social institutions, the great institution of marriage." Illustrations from Hebrew law, Christian morals, and English history he used freely. It was not his most successful exercise, which Gladstone himself realized when he offered to "release the reader from this wearisome but necessary inquiry."[70]

The main force of his argument he reserved for the House of Commons. Here he displayed flashes of anger—especially in the committee stage of the bill—that even Morley was forced to acknowledge. Gladstone's "holy wrath" against the bill was particularly noticeable in his altercations with the sarcastic Richard Bethel, the attorney general, against whom Gladstone argued "with a vivacity very like downright anger."[71] Their mutual insults were particularly pointed and personal. Gladstone once called down Bethel on the floor of the House for talking with a colleague on the Treasury Bench and not paying attention to his speech.[72] Bethel himself had clearly been agitated by Gladstone's *Quarterly Review* article, which was highly critical of Palmerston's ministry and of Bethel in particular.[73] All in all, Gladstone intervened seventy-three times in the three weeks of the bill's consideration, fighting it clause by clause in his attempt to delay its legislative progress.[74] His lack of success led to a despairing note to Catherine during the latter days of the debate: never during a parliamentary battle, he wrote, had he felt a "deeper anxiety."[75]

Gladstone's vehement opposition to the bill can be attributed in part to his religious belief on the indissolubility of marriage. But this had not prevented him, as a member of the Aberdeen Coalition, from supporting a divorce bill that was substantially the same as that brought forward by the Palmerston government. Indeed, Bethel reminded Gladstone of this fact during their celebrated debates. Gladstone's response to this charge was weak: he had not had sufficient time when chancellor of the Exchequer to make a proper investigation of that original bill.[76] It should also be remembered that Gladstone had acted several years earlier in the Lincoln divorce case in precisely the way the proposed bill would allow—that is, proceeding with the legal right of taking depositions and gathering evidence. He was ultimately forced to make a personal statement in the House of Commons about his contradictory behavior.[77] Overall, Gladstone's actions during the divorce bill debates must be placed in the context of his political isolation, exacerbated by his continuing antagonism to Palmerston. His behavior was expressive of a loss of control—an attempt to struggle toward a sense of coherence and orderliness through political affiliation.

Gladstone's prospects, however, had not advanced an inch during 1857. His virtual retirement from active parliamentary affairs was both symptom and cause of his continuing political malaise. As he confessed to Samuel Wilberforce, then bishop of Oxford, that summer: "I greatly felt being turned out of office, I saw great things to do. I longed to do them. I am losing the best years of my life out of my natural service, yet I have never ceased to rejoice that I am not in office with Palmerston, when I have seen the tricks, the shufflings, the frauds he daily has recourse to as to his business. I rejoice not to sit on the Treasury bench with him."[78]

Then, startlingly and from an unexpected quarter, early in the new year came an event that altered Gladstone's prospects: the attempted assassination of the Emperor Napoleon III of France. On the evening of 14 January 1858, as Napoleon and his wife rode up the rue Lepelletier to the Opera House, four Italian exiles hurled bombs at the royal carriage.[79] Missing the targets, the bombs exploded randomly in the crowd gathered outside the Opera: 10 bystanders were killed and 156 wounded. Further investigations revealed that the plotters were Italian refugees who had laid their plans in London and used bombs manufactured in Birmingham. Felice Orsini, leader of the conspirators, was tried in Paris in February and was executed the following month. The French government, backed by a rising Anglophobia, brought pressure to bear on Palmerston's government for at least a token apology. In response to French allegations that England harbored empericides, Palmerston decided to enact new legislation against conspiracy by making that crime a felony instead of a misdemeanor. This was a mistake: Palmerston's chief strength in the country had been his image as a patriot; his Conspiracy to Murder Bill seemed to truckle. An ensuing outburst of patriotic fervor in Britain was directed against both France and Palmerston. The prime minister was even jeered at in the streets. Not surprisingly, Gladstone took a lead in opposing the conspiracy bill, arguing the case—unusual for him—of national honor. His "vehement and eloquent" speech helped turn some of Palmerston's Liberal supporters against him.[80] Eighty Liberals deserted Palmerston at the count; he resigned on 20 February.[81]

Lord Derby, summoned to form an administration, turned to Gladstone in gratitude with an offer of a cabinet post. But once again Gladstone declined. It was a puzzling refusal. His desire for office had presumably not lessened. Acceptance would satisfy his ambition, and he knew himself well enough to understand that office would also—as it had in 1853—give him a sense of purpose and control in his political life. His public reason was his reluctance to join the Conservative cabinet without some of his Peelite friends. But he also recognized his continuing unpopularity with the protectionist backbenchers. Should they fail to support Derby because of Gladstone, the ministry could fail, further isolating Gladstone. These political arguments no doubt had some weight with him. Other reasons may have been involved as well. Shannon suggests that Gladstone was in the process of shedding conservative principles on his way toward a new identity.[82] Equally plausible, however, was the fact that Palmerston's fall would not remove Disraeli in any new Conservative ministry. Still leader of the Conservative Party in the House of Commons, Disraeli remained as effective a bar to Gladstone's goal as Palmerston had recently been. And there seemed little chance of displacing Disraeli.[83]

In spite of Gladstone's refusal to take office in February 1858, the Conservatives persisted in their attempt to land him. When a vacancy appeared in the cabinet in May, Derby renewed the offer of a cabinet post. This time, definite offices were named: he might either have the Board of Control or the Colonial Office. The offer was not only a testament to Conservative weakness in Parliament but even more a testament to Gladstone's intelligence, superlative oratorical talents, and unmatched power of application—however enigmatic and eccentric his political judgments were. Gladstone, as was his habit, sounded out his closest colleagues. In a memo circulated to Aberdeen and Graham for their approval, he seemed cautious.[84] His argument was similar to that of several months earlier: he could not act alone. Room must be made in the Conservative leadership for his Peelite friends. Nor was he certain that his adherence to Derby would be popular. Gladstone, while acknowledging the "personal misfortune and public inconvenience" of being without a party, noted that a "man at the bottom of the well must not try to get out, however disagreeable his position, until a rope or a ladder is put down to him." Graham repudiated Gladstone's argument by observing that in fact "Derby tenders this ladder."

Gladstone could "with perfect honor" ally with Derby. Perhaps most important—and here Graham spoke for all Gladstone's friends—was that he not waste himself "in fruitless controversy." "I think," Graham continued, "that fixed party ties and active official duties would conduce to your present happiness and future fame." In accepting office Gladstone thus would have had the sanction of one of his oldest political mentors, and one who had drifted increasingly into the Liberal camp. Graham's advice was in the best sense disinterested. Yet Gladstone chose to read it as "indecisive," as he put it in a letter to Derby confirming his refusal of office.[85]

Gladstone's continuing tentative behavior must be seen as a failure of strategy. He had attempted a series of contrasting aggressive and avoidant behaviors. Nothing had worked. He lacked a clear avenue to the reassertion of the kind of authority he once carried as chancellor of the Exchequer in the Aberdeen Coalition. He remained a political outsider. Caught within a web of rejection and ambivalence, Gladstone slid into self-pity. Such a condition, as one might expect, could lead to more serious aberrant behaviors. And, indeed, in late 1858, Gladstone entered into one of the strangest episodes of his career.

The background for this circumstance lay in the Treaty of Vienna, which concluded the Napoleonic Wars in 1815. According to its terms, Britain was granted a protectorate over the Ionian Islands, off the coast of Greece. In the following decades, the residents sought freedom from colonial rule under Britain and desired a union with Greece.[86] Matters came to a head in the late 1850s. The Derby government was determined to settle the issue and invited Gladstone to serve as a special commissioner to the islands. He would report on conditions and recommend a course of action. As Edward Bulwer-Lytton, the colonial secretary, put it, Gladstone would go "to reconcile a race that speaks the Greek language to the science of practical liberty."[87] Why the Conservatives should have chosen a man of Gladstone's parliamentary stature for this essentially trivial task was not at first clear. A more appropriate official would have been a middle-rank civil servant. Perhaps they hoped that by removing Gladstone from the parliamentary scene for a time, they would remove a power for mischief. Or they may have felt that if he succeeded, he might at last be sufficiently grateful to accept office in the Conservative cabinet; conversely, if he should fail, he might be sufficiently damaged so that his influence in Parliament would be diminished. Evidence for this reasoning occurs in the recollections of Lord Carnarvon, who was at that time an undersecretary at the Colonial Office. When Bulwer-Lytton asked Carnarvon's advice, he recommended Gladstone because of his abilities and because he was unconnected with any major party at that time. Disraeli agreed: "The place with its classical aestheticism suits him [Gladstone] very well." But as Disraeli also added, in a remark closer to the truth, "Now that we have got him down, let us keep him down."[88]

Even more surprising than the ministry's invitation to Gladstone was his interest in the project. Historians have since tried to puzzle it out. Morley emphasizes the decline of Catherine Gladstone's health since the death of her sister Mary Lyttelton.[89] Matthew believes that Gladstone understood the strategic importance of the islands within the context of the traditional European rivalries in the eastern Mediterranean and thus saw his role as a significant one.[90] Pointon thinks Gladstone was intellectually intrigued with the visit to offshore classical Greece: he could continue his researches on the Homeric age in a most congenial atmosphere.[91] Shannon, however, sees Gladstone as "frustrated, impatient, and restless"; Ionia offered an "opportunity for escape."[92] It may be that all these reasons played a part in his decision to go. But above all, the Ionian mission represented for Gladstone the ladder lowered to the bottom of his well. Ionia might provide a resolution to his political isolation, or it could become a kind of restful limbo. In any case, taking the position would be a revival of the strategy of avoidance—to the extent of removing himself entirely from the sources of stress in England.

Gladstone did not make up his mind precipitately. As in months past, he consulted his friends. They were not enthusiastic. Aberdeen was skeptical. "I scarcely see how you could undertake the proposed work," he replied, "with credit or safety to yourself."[93] Graham considered the events in the islands a "storm in a Tea Pot" and unworthy of Gladstone's talents. "You are destined for better work," he wrote.[94] Newcastle took the same line: using Gladstone for this task was not unlike, he said, employing a steam engine to untie a shoestring. Mixed metaphor aside, however, Newcastle thought the "change of scene, thought & interest" would be good for his friend.[95] Later, when he realized the possible negative implications of the mission for Gladstone's career, he changed his mind.

Ignoring his friends' advice, Gladstone went forward on what one historian has called "his comic-opera adventure."[96] From an advisory capacity, Gladstone quickly went on center stage in Ionia, and by January 1859 he had become high commissioner. This post made him solely responsible for the successes, and—as seemed more likely to his friends—the failures, of his mission. Once again, Gladstone's undeniable talents seemed threatened by a fatal lapse of judgment. "What is Gladstone about?" asked Graham querulously of Sidney Herbert. In reply Herbert spoke plainly: he was "annoyed" with Gladstone, whose course was "unintelligible." Indeed, Herbert was more than annoyed. "What an infernal position he has placed himself in," he wrote. Gladstone was "not safe to go . . . out of Lord Aberdeen's room. It is heartbreaking to see him throwing so much away."[97] Newcastle sent along his second thoughts. Gladstone's presence in Ionia was a "serious mistake." Absence from his parliamentary duties was an "act of self-immolation without any compensating good to the Public."[98]

The soundness of this advice was finally brought home to Gladstone when he learned that his acceptance of the office of high commissioner automatically forfeited his parliamentary seat. What mischief might develop in contentious Oxford during his absence was not beyond Gladstone's imagining. He resigned on 1 February 1859 and immediately made plans for his return to England. In the meantime, he had outlined a policy for the Ionians, who, he discovered, were overwhelmingly in favor of reunion with Greece. This Gladstone refused to promise, advocating instead a liberalized constitution providing greater self-government while maintaining the link to Britain.[99] The Ionian assembly promptly rejected this idea. Unperturbed by this action, Gladstone set sail for England shortly afterward, arriving in London on 8 March 1859.

If unsuccessful in a political sense, the Ionian venture seems to have benefited him in other ways. Accompanied by his family en route to Ionia, Gladstone spent time in Brunswick, Berlin, and Dresden, and in Prague and Vienna, visiting museums and sight-seeing. A high priority was shopping for china to add to Gladstone's new collection. When not involved in official business in Ionia, the Gladstones went on picnics, visited Homeric sites, and paid two visits to the mainland. In Athens, Gladstone was properly impressed with the Acropolis. He even had time to engage in several rescue cases in Corfu—although presumably his classical Greek made communication with these women of the street more difficult than in London. All in all, Gladstone managed to turn the mission into a refreshing family vacation. It was a welcome relief from the strains of political isolationism.

Upon his return, Gladstone was quickly reelected for Oxford. He then plunged into issues of domestic reform and foreign affairs, especially the growing importance of the Italian unification movement. The question of Gladstone's position within the structure of the political party system at Westminster seemed no nearer an answer, however. Weary of the uncertainties in his political life, Gladstone was for the first time in several years strongly tempted by a rescue case. His rescue work had continued into the late 1850s, but with less emotional intensity than in the early years of the decade. He used the scourge rarely in the years 1855–60. In late July 1859, a few months after his return from Ionia, Gladstone met an artist's model and courtesan named Maria Summerhayes. She was, in Gladstone's words, "full in the highest degree both of interest and of beauty."[100] In less than a week, Gladstone arranged to have her portrait painted by his friend William Dyce.[101] For the next several months, Gladstone was intensely involved with Summerhayes. On 4 August, he recorded in his diary that he "saw Summerhayes long." He was again with her late on the night of 15 August. Three days later, he sought her out before leaving London for Hawarden. By 1 September, he seemed on the verge of reinstating his method of physical discipline: "My thoughts of S," he wrote, "require to be limited and purged." On 16 September, returning from Hawarden, he arrived in London at half past ten in the evening. He went straightaway to Summerhayes, with whom he spent the next four and a half hours, reading Tennyson's "Princess" with her. Gladstone described himself afterward as "much & variously moved." Similar entries attest to Gladstone's attraction. The following year, Summerhayes changed her name to Mrs. Dale; she was either conforming to the Victorian convention of the marriage form of address for women of a certain age, or she had in fact married. Although the two had intermittent contact for the next several years, Gladstone's feeling for Summerhayes never again attained the intensity of that summer.

The need for the sublimated sexual expression that Gladstone found in Summerhayes may well have lessened as his political prospects at last changed for the better. Only weeks before he met Summerhayes, he had once again gained political office. The circumstances of his acceptance followed a familiar pattern. The opportunity had come with the defeat of Derby's Conservative ministry on a vote of no confidence in the House of Commons on 7 June 1859. Throughout the debate on the motion, Gladstone remained uncharacteristically silent. At the division on 10 June, Gladstone voted for the Conservatives. This was not surprising, as he had been indulgent to the Conservatives throughout their brief ministry. His acceptance of the Ionian mission at their request was taken as an indication of his real political sympathies.

What was astonishing about his behavior was his acceptance only days afterward of office under Lord Palmerston. Gladstone even had the temerity to ask for the office of chancellor of the Exchequer. His eagerness to enter Palmerston's government—the government of his archenemy for the past four years—was a matter of general comment. Even at a time of commonly accepted shifting party allegiances, his action came as a thunderbolt. Lady Clarendon, wife of the Liberal foreign secretary from 1853 to 1858, was shocked that a man who had "voted in the last division with the Derby ministry should not only be asked to join this one, but allowed *to choose his office*." The long-suffering Lord Aberdeen believed Gladstone to be the "most ... abandoned of English politicians." John Bright thought Gladstone "wholly unjustifiable" in his decision to take office.[102]

Palmerston's reasons for seeking out Gladstone are obvious enough. In spite of Gladstone's unpopularity and growing reputation for eccentricity, his oratory and debating power made up for many faults. Palmerston certainly feared the damage that Gladstone might do in opposition. "They want his tongue to help, and they dread it in opposition," was Lady Clarendon's opinion.[103] But Gladstone's motives for such a turnabout are less obvious. Had ambition triumphed over principle? Had he become merely (in the language of the time) a factious politician? Or had the political views of Gladstone and Palmerston converged somewhat? Each of these questions has been answered affirmatively by one or another of Gladstone's contemporaries and later historians. Gladstone himself realized that his action would raise suspicion in many minds. He explained his reasons to Sir William Heathcote, his fellow M.P. for Oxford, on two grounds. The first was his political isolation. "In thirteen years," he wrote, "the middle space of life, I have been cast out of party connection, severed from my old party," and essentially "left alone by every political friend in association with whom I had grown up." Should he continue the "one remaining Ishmael of the House of Commons?" Second, Gladstone claimed that he now found himself "in real and close harmony" on issues of the day with Palmerston.[104] These issues were reform, which he now desired to have settled, and, most particularly, Palmerston's growing commitment to the self-determination of Italy. This accorded with his own pro-Italian sentiment—a sentiment first formed in Naples in 1851 and confirmed during his brief Italian tour undertaken on his return from Ionia in March 1859. There may indeed be something to Gladstone's fellow feeling with Palmerston on the Italian question. Bright reported Aberdeen's opinion that Gladstone "so long hostile to Palmerston was full of Italian sentimentality and would serve under him."[105]

This reasoning, however, is not wholly convincing and has the ring of self-justification.[106] So sudden a conversion to Palmerston's policies must be suspect. A deeper reason for Gladstone's change of heart is not hard to find. Gladstone had clearly determined by 1859 that he soon must accept office. His various strategies to gain authority and control had failed. How long must he wait? An added spur to his decision was the sense of his own mortality. Death had touched Gladstone often in the 1850s. His daughter Jessy, his father, and his political mentor, Peel, had all died during the decade. In these years, his year-end diary entries often reflected an elegiac mood. "In looking back over the stained course of my life," he wrote in 1854, "I have cause to feel yet more keenly my need to escape before long from a sphere of so much temptation so sorely oppressing me." "How long a time for me to cumber the ground," he wrote two years later, "and still not to know *where* to work out the purpose of my life."[107] A sense of renewal and hope was within his grasp, however. Accepting office under Palmerston would give him both the opportunity to make his mark from a position of power and authority, and a means of controlling the political and personal course of his life. Seven months into the Palmerston government, he entered into the diary his altered mood. "I think in a wondrous matter it has pleased the Lord whose eye slumbereth not to bring me in His own way towards a place of safety." He felt within himself a quickening pace of triumph over, if not age and death, at least the fear of their inhibiting his achievement: "There is in me a resistance to the passage of Time as if I could lay hands on it & stop it: as if youth were yet in me & life & youth were one."[108]

6

Prelude to Power

By the 1850s, Hawarden had become increasingly a center for Gladstone's repose. In the seclusion of north Wales, surrounded by his wife and children, he could relax. Typically for Gladstone this often took the form of vigorous physical activity: long walks, swimming off the coast at Penmaenmawr, and his most celebrated hobby, the cutting and "kibbling" of the trees on the estate. Tree cutting was especially beneficial. He once explained how it rested his brain: in chopping down a tree, there was time to think only of "where your next stroke will fall."[1] More sedentary pursuits at Hawarden included arranging his voluminous papers and numerous books, putting his china collection in order, and keeping to his extraordinary schedule of omnivorous reading.[2]

It was well understood within the family that Gladstone was a person of privilege and that his needs were paramount. His daughter Mary, reflecting in later years on her father's role, remembered him as a "portentous potentate" whose "time, health and convenience had to be considered first."[3] Mary's brother Herbert corroborated her account. For the most part, as Herbert recorded in his own memoir, the children were allowed access to their father only at regulated intervals: Catherine was the guardian of his time. "We grew to understand that he was much occupied and must not be disturbed. We accepted that, and it was soon supported by the evidence of our senses. There were countless books, heaps of papers, much writing, and a constant incursion of impressive visitors." In an unwittingly revealing passage, Herbert assures us: "We were like little dogs who never resent exclusion but are overjoyed when they are allowed in. . . . Our affection was secured."[4]

Gladstone was not a modern, liberated father. His expectations were firmly within Victorian conventions. As the children grew, they followed unexceptional paths in their education and later careers. The four Gladstone boys entered manhood with every advantage, but the strong paternal hand was in evidence. Willy, the eldest, who attended Eton and Christ Church, was designated to carry on the political tradition of his father. Gladstone, in effect, managed Willy's reluctant candidacy for the parliamentary seat for Chester in 1865. Never a popular representative, Willy feared for his seat at the general election of 1868 and sought another at Whitby. There, too, Willy was a luckless M.P. He seldom spoke in Parliament, rarely visited the town, and frequently squabbled with his constituents.[5] Stephen, the next eldest son, had wished from his earliest years to enter the church and was ordained deacon in 1868. He eventually became rector of Hawarden. Henry, a merchant, seems to have orbited early out of the family influence. Herbert, the youngest boy, was the only child to achieve political eminence, initially as M.P. for Leeds, then as his father's personal secretary and political agent. He eventually became the first governor-general of the Union of South Africa and was created Viscount Gladstone in his own right. The hold of the family upon its sons was attested to by their tardy marriages: Willy at thirty-five, Henry at thirty-eight, Stephen at forty-one, and Herbert at forty-seven—late even by Victorian standards.

The Gladstone daughters also had a conventional Victorian upbringing.[6] None of them were formally educated as were the boys, nor were they given special training. Like their brothers, they were tied closely to the family until late in their lives. Agnes, the eldest daughter, married at the age of thirty-one, Mary was nearly forty when she married, and Helen, the youngest, ended her life a spinster. Both Mary and Helen were representative of the large number of British women in the second half of the nineteenth century who remained unmarried or married late. They were obligated to devote their lives to their parents, just as had Gladstone's sisters. Their vocational ambitions were not encouraged. Agnes had, like Florence Nightingale, wanted training as a nurse; unlike Nightingale, Agnes did not brave parental displeasure for her ambitions. Helen began a promising career as an academic administrator. She attended Newnham College, Cambridge; became secretary and assistant to the vice-principal; and in 1882 was appointed vice-principal of Newnham. Four years later, she was invited to become the first principal of the newly created Royal Holloway College, London. Unfortunately, this offer coincided with Mary's engagement. At her sister's marriage, Helen was summoned home to assume the primary role of managing her parents' household.

Mary had demonstrated unusual talent before her marriage and, in a later age, would no doubt have risen high in political life. Serving as her father's unpaid private secretary during his second ministry of 1880–85, she was given special responsibility as secretary for ecclesiastical patronage. Because she was at the center of political life and the sharer of her father's secrets, her tact was also useful in soothing wounded egos. She provided additional invaluable service as organizer and hostess for Downing Street social functions. In addition, Mary was well read, an excellent conversationalist, knowledgeable in music, and had an extensive correspondence with some of the leading figures of the day. Yet as a woman and as her father's daughter, she had little scope for an independent life or for the recognition that her ability deserved. Even after her marriage to Harry Drew, a clergyman nine years her junior, she and her husband lived for twelve years with the Gladstones at Hawarden Castle when Harry was curate of Hawarden Church.

Gladstone's relations to his wife and children were as one would expect in that era. His aloofness, sovereignty over the family, and executive benevolence were characteristic of a strong pater familias who assumed by right a dominant place in the household. Yet mutual affection on the part of children and parents was also the norm in the Gladstone family. If Mary remembered her father as a privileged being, she also remembered her family as lively and without pretension.[7] There was room for growth and development of relations between family members. Most particularly, the relationship between husband and wife altered over time. Tensions between the two seemed diminished after the early years of adjustment. His letters to her were increasingly tolerant of her foibles, less didactic about her behavior. He grew fond of her company and was more willing to break away from political responsibilities, if need be, to join her for a holiday—a distinct change from his earlier practice. "I shall have to work desperately hard to get away on Wednesday morning," he wrote in August 1853, "but I have refused the Cabinet Dinner which *Lord Aberdeen* gives on that day and I fully intend to flit."[8] True to his word, he caught the express train that morning, got off at Stafford, and waited for Catherine (who had been at Hagley) for the next train north to Glasgow.[9] All in all, he made genuine efforts at accommodating Catherine within the framework of his busy life.

Catherine's letters to Gladstone, too, had changed. They were more assured: "wifie" had been dropped. She had gained confidence and an air of independence. Her urgent wishes for Gladstone's company were now relegated to special occasions, misfortunes, or emergencies. Her own routines were better established. Her travels to favorite coastal towns and visits to her sister's home at Hagley were a source of increasing pleasure. She was adept at making new friends. While at Brighton in 1852 for a long convalescence after the birth of their third son, Catherine met a Mrs. Talbot, who became a close friend and confidant.[10] "You can have no idea how Mrs. Talbot waits upon me," Catherine wrote to her husband. She "feeds me, dresses me, & has such tenderness I am sure you will be pleased."[11] After her eleventh pregnancy, Catherine's sister Mary went to Brighton as a convalescent and there formed a trio of friendship with Catherine and Mrs. Talbot. Catherine had thus begun to create an independent persona within the constraints of the Victorian tradition.

Catherine even became confident enough in the early 1850s to proffer political ideas and advice to her husband.[12] She well knew that his growing political isolation—whatever personal benefits it brought her—could not fail to be discouraging. "I wish you had a nice party assembled around you," she wrote from Hagley. "Colonial matters would be the stand [*sic*] & I see numbers flocking in under yr standard!" Catching herself somewhat, she admitted, "What *crude remarks* but I have some larger ideas!"[13] During the Conservative ministerial crisis of 1852, she urged him to "shew d'Isy well up" in his forthcoming budget speech, for "if the Conservative body see that you cd. make a safe budget they wd. not stick to their present unfit leader & really it is unfit he should be permitted to gull them." Cheering him on, Catherine concluded, "I want a *good stirring unanswerable conservative* speech."[14]

But in the summer of 1857, Catherine's evolving sense of self was badly shaken. Her sister Mary sickened in childbirth and died shortly afterward. On her deathbed, Mary had asked to see Gladstone, who rushed to Hagley during a break in the divorce bill debates. "She spoke to me a good deal & had wished to see me, that she might give me her dying charge," he recorded in his diary. "I wish to say one thing to you," Mary continued, "take care of *her* (C): for it will be a great change for her and she will feel it more & more after a time."[15] Mary's dying prophecy was fully borne out in the following months. In late October, Catherine was "not very well." In November, a portrait of Mary that arrived at Hawarden "quite overset" her. A week later she was afflicted with severe influenza. Gladstone noted in January 1858 that the past twelve months for Catherine had been a "year of tears & of somewhat broken health." In mid-January began a series of "bad nights" for Catherine: a local physician reported "her whole system much deranged." Gladstone promptly made arrangements for her care. In early February, after additional difficult nights, she was sent to rest with friends near Wrexham for a few days.[16] By late winter, although she was improving, she remained melancholic.

In the spring, Catherine went to Brighton to recuperate. At first the associations of the town with her dead sister were overwhelming. "All looked so beautiful so exactly the same as last year when we were watching my darling Mary. . . . You know we were here so often together each petting the other as we needed—how she cherished and comforted me after little Jessy—

and when I was ill."[17] Within a few days, Catherine felt more at ease: "I breakfast in bed, am up & dressed *before ten*—walk on very gently to church for by taking my time it only does me good, & then I end up on the pier."[18] Because she was benefiting from the sea air, she decided to stay on for a time at Brighton, but she hoped to have her husband with her. "It would be a horrid blow if really you don't appear at all here," she wrote on 26 March. "Surely you can write *here*, oh *dear dear*! I shall have been here three weeks alone if I stay till Sat. week. I think you won't be quite as bad as this." She suggested that he arrive after a late dinner. And his trip would not increase expenses, for, she hinted broadly, "you will come into *my bed*."[19]

Gladstone was not to be moved; he had again become the preoccupied politician he had been in the early 1840s. The Palmerston ministry had fallen, bringing in the Conservatives under Derby. Political opportunity and high office could be around the corner. In addition, he was revising *Treatises on Homer,* as well as having undertaken to write an article for the *Quarterly Review.* Until he finished his article, he could not visit her: he needed the references close at hand. It was not an article he had solicited, he assured her. "You know how it came upon me & how little I desired it," he wrote. After several exchanges about his schedule, he finally relented. "By not coming till Saturday I hope that I may finish at least in rough my intended Article. You complain of my going straight to it after Homer: and *so do I*."[20]

Recurring bouts of Catherine's illness lasted into the autumn of 1858. In late October, she wrote of another bad night—serious enough to want the family doctor. "I cannot at all account for these odd unearthly feelings after the lovely air, but I try to be patient."[21] Catherine's inability to recover completely from her sister's death probably contributed to Gladstone's decision to accept the Ionian Islands Commission that winter. Judging from the correspondence, Catherine seems to have profited from the Ionian interlude. By the time the Gladstones had returned and Gladstone had entered Palmerston's government, she had fully recovered.

In the meantime, Gladstone had made one of the most important social and political friendships of his life. Harriett, the duchess of Sutherland, was a granddaughter of Georgiana, duchess of Devonshire, one of the Whig grande dames of the eighteenth century. In her younger days Harriett had been a great beauty, but in later life (she was fifty-four in 1860) she had become corpulent. It is unlikely, therefore, that Gladstone—who had a keen eye for the feminine form—was drawn to her physical beauty. Rather, the duchess provided something that he had lacked to this point in his political career: the capacity to manage a salon for his benefit. Catherine Gladstone could not perform this service. She did not have a sophisticated knowledge of the political world in which Gladstone moved, judging from her naive and hortative political remarks to her husband. This characteristic probably suited Gladstone well. Hawarden had become for him a place of repose from the uncertainties of a chaotic world. His library and working room at Hawarden was christened the Temple of Peace in 1860—more than a symbolic title. In contrast to Hawarden, the duchess's residences—Cliveden, near London, and Stafford House, near the Green Park in town—were ideal places from which to see and be seen. The duchess, too, was an ideal patron.[22] She was superbly well connected. As a daughter of the earl of Carlisle, she linked the Howards to the Sutherlands. Her stepson was Lord Acton, the historian, and her son-in-law was the duke of Argyll, Gladstone's loyal supporter until the 1880s. The duchess had been mistress of the robes in various administrations since Victoria's accession and remained a close friend of the queen. The Sutherlands were among the most influential and wealthiest of the Whig families: they owned five great houses and estates in both England and Scotland. Gladstone was drawn to the duchess in part because she was obviously quite taken with him and because she offered him certain political advantages. He also found it a genuine pleasure to discuss important issues of the day with an intelligent and high-minded woman. She was well informed and had astute opinions on such topics as Italian unification, the Abolitionist movement in the United States, and various humane causes at home.[23] She was a lover of books and ideas, a representative of virtue, purity, and simplicity— qualities that would attract a man like Gladstone.

The duchess was the first woman since Gladstone's marriage with whom he had a long-standing, open, equal, and respectable intimacy. In the spring and summer of 1860, he was often at Cliveden or Stafford House. During the autumn of 1861, he was with the duchess frequently enough to lend the appearance of courting her (although this was more likely an effort on his part to be consolatory: the duke had died in February). Catherine was not unaware of Gladstone's admiration and affection for the duchess. His letters to Catherine in the 1860s are often sprinkled with news of the duchess, announcing her birthday, say, or his plans for a forthcoming weekend at Cliveden. Even when Catherine was with Gladstone in London, he usually went alone to the duchess. He realized that on those occasions at least, he slighted his wife. After spending a weekend at Cliveden in May 1861, he returned again the following week, "leaving C. which seems but selfish," as he noted in his diary.[24] Only rarely, it seems, did Catherine protest. Her attitude was forgiving: she knew well enough that his friendship with the duchess was based on her range of experience and knowledge of subjects that far exceeded Catherine's own. Still, Gladstone's time with the duchess was time away from Catherine. Her attempts to be with Gladstone now had to take into account the duchess.

Clearly Gladstone's independence from his wife and his desire for the company of sympathetic women as a comfort to his frenetic public life were becoming well entrenched. Perhaps it was Gladstone's friendship with the duchess that finally revealed to Catherine the necessity of finding a satisfying commitment outside her home and family. The resources were at hand. As an affluent woman of leisure, connected to the highest political circles in the country, she could wield some influence. With the advance of the railway system, Catherine's abundant energies no longer had to be limited to local projects; she could operate on a national level. In addition, she had already developed a strong interest in philanthropy, a traditional field of endeavor for energetic Victorian women.[25] No doubt her own generous impulses led her to charitable causes, but philanthropy primarily offered her the opportunity to develop a sense of her own competence, to have a sphere of influence and responsibility that would be separate from her husband.

The most active phase of Catherine's charity work was an indirect outcome of the American Civil War. In 1861, the disruption of the cotton trade with the Confederate states had begun to affect Lancashire textile workers. In the autumn of that year, she visited the cotton towns of Lancashire, noting the effects of unemployment. Under her sponsorship was created the Hawarden Charities, an orphanage and an asylum for elderly women affected by the Cotton Famine. In later years, Catherine became increasingly involved in other charitable organizations. During the cholera epidemic of 1866, she spent many hours visiting patients at the London Hospital. In those days of philanthropic laissez-faire, epidemics commonly prompted a spate of new charitable institutions. Catherine responded by sponsoring the Catherine Gladstone Home in Woodford, Essex—at that time the only free home for convalescents in the kingdom. She also branched out into other philanthropic fields. She helped found the Newport Market Refuge, became interested in the House of Charity for Distressed Persons, worked for the Institution for the Blind, and aided her husband in establishing the Mary Magdalen Rescue Home, designed to shelter illegitimate babies as well as their mothers. She also performed innumerable acts of individual charity. During the Cattle Plague of 1866, for example, she brought to Hawarden Castle the family of a distressed gentleman farmer. On another occasion, she brought home to Wales from the House of Charity in Soho a parson ill with scarlet fever.[26]

As philanthropic work took more and more of her time, Catherine discovered in herself an unexpected capacity to organize public sympathy for important causes. She also discovered the delights of public life. Her travels were less and less for private pleasure and holiday visits; she was now summoned for the good she could do. No longer was she merely an appendage of her husband. Her public achievements were real and, for her, psychologically significant. As she became more deeply involved in her charities, her letters to Gladstone gradually lost their plaintive tone—just as they had before her sister Mary's death. Her duties were so pressing that sometimes it was difficult for her to find the time to write. "I have plenty to do here so much that you were cheated yesterday of any letter," she wrote in the spring of 1863. Before one of her charity visits in 1865, she wrote, "It provoked me sadly that I did not get in a few lines before leaving Hawarden." Or, more colorfully, in the autumn of 1867, "I grieve that this letter was not sent yesterday, but I was run off my legs."[27]

Gladstone's response to his wife's new responsibilities was at first a manifest concern about the cost of such extensive traveling. He took the occasion of a niece's marriage in October 1870 to chastise her: "You are I think a little extravagant in bringing 2 daughters all the way to the marriage—I wish we could have an account of our traveling expenses in the year; I think they would alarm you." Perhaps knowing that Catherine kept only the sketchiest of books, he concluded more kindly, "But it is not possible, things must take care of themselves."[28] Catherine shot back an answer immediately: "I can show you that we have *not* been extravagant as to journeys." Nevertheless, she was "very ready to keep a *careful journey* expense separate," which would be, she concluded diplomatically, "very useful & very good for me."[29] The tone of Catherine's letter suggests the sense of confidence engendered by her new philanthropic vocation.

Catherine's public life did not always please Gladstone. She rocketed around the country with an independence that must have been somewhat unnerving. Her letters began to look like railway timetables. Even then, it was not easy to know her whereabouts. A few days after his niece's wedding in Wiltshire in 1870, Gladstone lost track of her: "Yesterday I knew nothing of your address," he wrote, "so I write at a venture to Lady Charlotte's."[30] The following month, when he arrived at Hawarden for a fortnight's stay, Catherine was away. His letter had a plaintive note: "I hope you will come soon. There is all the difference between this place & London. There the absorption is continual, here only periodical." In a surprising reversal of roles, he expressed loneliness: "The white room seemed too odd without you. . . . I am not sure that I have even slept there alone, since the year 1835!"[31] A few days later, he wrote again: "I was in hopes of an announcement from you this morning of a speedy arrival: but none arrived."[32] During Christmas of that year, Catherine was again away from Hawarden. "The severance during this Christmas time is a sad trial," Gladstone wrote. "It is almost the only time of year when I can at all reckon on seeing or being with you. I scarcely know what to do."[33]

Throughout Gladstone's first ministry of 1868–74, Catherine's obligations to her charitable work remained strong.[34] Her work was unceasing even after his ministry fell in 1874. "I hope my going . . . is not pure selfishness," she wrote in the summer of that year, but "I find it is most important I go to London upon urgent matters connected with these poor girls."[35] In December 1874, his first ministry well behind him, Gladstone felt no less desirous of his wife's companionship: "It will be a great disappointment if you do not come on Saty. but of course it is best you should finish what you have to do."[36] Happily for him, Catherine arrived two days later.

If the decade of the 1860s saw Catherine making her way toward a separate identity, Gladstone found his way out of political isolation with less ease. The new Palmerston government, which included Gladstone as chancellor of the Exchequer, was contentious from the first. Gladstone and Palmerston were ill suited for a working partnership. Conflict over policy was compounded by personal animosity.[37] Palmerston's eighteenth-century aristocratic insouciance was foreign to the earnest striving of a descendant of the Scots and Liverpudlian commercial mind. Palmerston seemed at ease in his surroundings, wherever they might be. He was as accepted in elite circles as he was popular in the countryside. He probably had more political experience than any other living politician. Under ten prime ministers, Palmerston had held cabinet posts at the Admiralty, War Office, Foreign Office, and the Home Office before becoming prime minister himself in 1855. He had been secretary at war during the whole of Lord Liverpool's fifteen-year term as premier. It was his expertise in foreign affairs that seemed especially attractive to the electorate in the 1850s and early 1860s. Ever since the Don Pacifico debate of 1850 when Palmerston struck a patriotic (or, in Gladstone's eyes, chauvinistic) note, he was the voice of British nationalism. He had a swagger to his public utterances and a bounce to his step that belied his seventy-odd years. His speeches—although they could not match Gladstone's—were "racy, buoyant & facetious," and it was said that in Parliament, he slept "like a duck—with one eye open."[38]

Palmerston spoke to a patriotic and emerging imperial population. His anti-French prejudices during his premiership were shared by the country as a whole. The government of the Emperor Louis Napoleon was too reminiscent of his great-uncle to be comfortable to the British. Palmerston's enmity toward France led naturally to a policy emphasizing military preparedness: expenditures for ships, men, and guns rose significantly. Although rattling swords was his specialty, Palmerston managed somehow to retain his composure: he gave the paradoxical impression of a belligerent yet calming influence. Gladstone, in contrast, projected a contentious image in Parliament—one of passion and even anger, often directed inappropriately.

The initial clash between the two men began over Palmerston's defense policy, which was designed to meet the perceived threat from France. His proposals included modernizing the antiquated wooden-hulled British fleet by introducing iron-clads, and constructing a series of naval fortifications along England's southern coast. Gladstone did not oppose military spending in principle, but he believed that Palmerston's plan was unnecessarily expensive. He also wished to establish the primacy of the Treasury over the traditional spending departments, such as the Admiralty and the War Office, thus imposing a degree of order on them. It was this development in his financial thinking that increasingly made him, as Matthew notes, an "executive politician."[39]

Gladstone's need for control and order not only undergirded his fiscal thinking but also characterized his behavior in general as a minister under Palmerston. Indeed, Gladstone sometimes followed an essentially independent position, acting outside the sanction of the cabinet. This was clearly demonstrated in the French Commercial Treaty of 1860. At this time, French protectionism was particularly harmful to British manufacturing interests. Such basic British industries as iron, cutlery, and various cotton, wool, and leather goods—as well as many other manufactured products—were entirely prohibited. Other commodities allowed into France came burdened with erratically levied duties ranging from 2 percent to 268 percent. Trade between the two countries had naturally diminished in recent years.[40]

Gladstone, determined to pursue the policies of his mentor, Sir Robert Peel, established a connection with the like-minded radical free trader Richard Cobden. Cobden, invited to Hawarden in September 1859, worked with Gladstone in devising the framework of a proposed trade treaty with France. According to the proposed treaty, British goods were allowed entry into France with duties no higher than thirty percent, with the prospect of further reductions in later years. On the British side, all import duties on French manufactured goods were abolished. Important, too, were the reductions of duty on French brandy and wine (the so-called Gladstone claret). Neither Palmerston nor the Foreign Office was fully informed of the details.[41]

Once the treaty had been signed in Paris in January 1860, its terms had to be ratified. On 10 February 1860, Gladstone presented the details of the treaty to the House of Commons in one of his most admired parliamentary speeches.[42] Arguing that the treaty was to be the capstone of Peelite free trade policy, Gladstone proposed to abolish, with two or three exceptions, all duties on manufactured goods. He then reviewed, item by item, those articles mutually agreed upon by Britain and France whose duties would be significantly reduced. Unknown to his parliamentary audience, however—and possibly even to Gladstone himself at that time—there lay embedded within the tariff proposal a hidden political and constitutional issue. Among the duties to be abolished were those affecting paper. Gladstone made a strong case against paper duties, pointing out that they obstructed "general skill and enterprise" in no less than sixty-nine trades that used paper for one reason or another: anatomical machinists who made artificial limbs, telescope makers, cap manufacturers, coach makers, comb makers, and dollmakers. Paper was also used in pictures and mirrors, in portmanteaux, and in teapots. The working class especially would receive special benefits, "not only because they will get cheaper paper, which must be of advantage to every man who furnishes a cottage and desires to give some of his rooms an appearance of comfort and neatness," but also because cheaper paper promotes the "extension of cheap literature."

Palmerston, who supported the Commercial Treaty in general, was strongly opposed to paper duty repeal, claiming that its revenues were needed for his defense program. In late April 1860, he urged Gladstone to postpone for a year the abolition of paper duties. Gladstone refused. The cabinet as a whole supported Palmerston. As the cabinet continued its debate on paper duty repeal throughout April, Gladstone hinted freely of resignation.[43] The issue was still unresolved at the cabinet level when it came before Parliament for a vote in early May. Because a divided ministry could not present an effective front in the House of Commons, the paper duties bill barely passed its first parliamentary test (by a vote of 219 to 210). Gladstone's own speech in favor of the bill was "to a very adverse House."[44] Weak support for the bill in the Commons foretold trouble in the House of Lords, whose negative sentiments were encouraged by Palmerston himself when he told the queen that the Lords ought to vote it down.

By his forceful and concerted actions over the paper duties, Gladstone had begun to alienate some of his colleagues. There was a legitimate feeling in the House of Commons that, as the French Commercial Treaty had already surrendered considerable revenue, the loss of additional revenues from the repeal of the paper duties would be too great for a single year. (The loss was indeed substantial: £1,737,000 from the treaty and another £1,000,000 from the paper duties.) Gladstone's inflexible attitude and unwillingness to compromise provoked wide comment. He was chastised by the Whig hostess Lady Waldegrave.[45] He resigned from the Carlton Club. He began to brood on the likely actions of the House of Lords on the paper duties bill. "The meditated aggression of the Lords presses more & more upon my mind," he wrote in his diary on 15 May. To escape the rising political tension, he spent nearly every other weekend at Cliveden. On one of these visits, he apparently poured out his frustrations to the duchess of Sutherland, who advised him "about sensitiveness in the H of C."[46] On 21 May came the expected verdict of the House of Lords: the paper duties bill was rejected by a vote of 193 to 104.

Gladstone was placed in a difficult position. Increasingly unpopular among his colleagues, stymied in the cabinet, and defeated on paper duties, he fell back on an old stratagem: he moved from vague hints to an explicit threat of resignation. This was apparently discussed at the cabinet meeting of 2 June. "My resignation *all but* settled," he recorded that day. Palmerston attempted to dissuade him on the grounds that he would be thought irresponsible, which could be his ruination as a public man.[47] Gladstone, who was well aware of the dangers of resignation both personally and politically, was losing his ability to cope with political realities. He began to grasp at straws. On 9 June he suggested that the entire ministry should resign, on the curious grounds that because the ministry had entered office on a pledge of reform and had not yet carried it out, it was thus shirking its responsibility. Quite simply, Gladstone was attempting to bring down the entire government to provide a smokescreen for his own inclination toward resignation. Or so thought Palmerston: "Gladstone's motive evidently was, to cover under a general Resignation his own failure as to Budget, & to escape from being a Party to Fortification Loan."[48] A few days after the failure of Gladstone's suggestion of mass resignation, the earl of Clarendon reported to Sir George Cornewall Lewis that Lord Aberdeen had recently told him (Clarendon) that Gladstone had become "rabid."[49]

Gladstone's staunchest friend during these difficult days was the duke of Argyll. On 16 June, Argyll wrote Gladstone to discourage his talk of resignation, praising his talents as "invaluable to the ministry." He also warned Gladstone on the fortification issue: "If you ride a high horse—objecting to the whole principle of making the great dockyards into strong places, I am satisfied you will not be supported by public feeling."[50] Argyll also tried to mediate between Palmerston and Gladstone, suggesting a compromise—fortifying, say, only one or two ports at first, which could be financed either by taxes or by a loan, depending on the state of the revenue. But Gladstone held firm against fortifications.

Not only did Gladstone continue to oppose Palmerston on the fortifications plan, but he was also determined to revive paper duty repeal, which had been recently quashed in the House of Lords. To overrule the action of the Lords, he raised the stakes by claiming that their action was unconstitutional. On 30 June, during an "ugly" cabinet meeting, Gladstone read a long memo that joined the rejection of the paper duties bill to the broader issue of the House of Lords' intrusion on the taxing power of the House of Commons. He interpreted the Lords' rejection of the bill as a violation of the constitutional prohibition against the Lords' amending a money bill. The argument ran thus: by rejecting a remission of import duties on paper (as voted by the Commons), the House of Lords was in effect reimposing a kind of tax. In a private memo reviewing the Lords' action, Gladstone concluded, "I see no way of ultimate hope or safety except some plan of action founded on the principle that the Lords are not to tax the people without their consent."[51] Gladstone had some support for this view. Ancient Whiggery was stirred in Lord John Russell, who believed that although the Lords had the right to throw out the bill, it was the kind of right "which has lain dormant since the Revolution" and, if persisted in, "must give a great shake to the constitution."[52]

While the fate of the paper duties bill hung in the balance, fortifications remained a major issue. On 4 July 1860, after a two-and-a-half-hour cabinet meeting, Gladstone wrote in his diary, "Fortifications discussed: my knell." More discussion in the cabinet a few days later brought this remark from Palmerston: "Settled arrangements of Bill for fortifications. Impossible to say whether Gladstone will go or stay."[53] On 16 July, Gladstone drew up a thirty-eight-point rebuttal to the fortifications scheme—"the last shot in the locker," as he characterized it. Two days later, after another cabinet meeting, a surprised Gladstone confided to his diary: "And still I am not dead."[54] The crucial breakthrough to compromise occurred on 21 July. Gladstone left the cabinet meeting early so that, as he put it, "the discussion might be free." But in fact, Gladstone had arranged for Argyll to read a letter from him to the cabinet, agreeing in principle to the fortifications bill. In short, unable to discuss a compromise face to face with the cabinet (and especially Palmerston), he had used a mediator. By allowing Argyll to act as his agent, Gladstone could safely absent himself. This was very much in the mold of his strategy of avoidance used on earlier occasions in his political past. In this instance, however, it was a more successful strategy than it had been earlier. By removing his own contentious presence, Gladstone not only saved face but also permitted a compromise—though one weighted in Palmerston's favor. Because Gladstone's objection to the fortifications had been primarily financial, Palmerston did not insist on an increase in taxes or a short-term loan to build the fortifications. Rather, he suggested a two-million-pound loan raised by thirty-year annuities. In this way, the fortifications issue was put to rest for 1860.

Palmerston was understandably uncharitable in his judgment of Gladstone's tactics: "He evidently has throughout been playing a game of Brag & trying to bully the Cabinet & finding he has failed, he has given in."[55] But this was only partially true. Gladstone was not simply attempting to bully the cabinet or to place the government in an awkward position for political gain. In fact, Gladstone isolated himself: he made his own job more difficult. His behavior in the cabinet and Parliament was less calculated politically than it was designed to extricate himself from an untenable psychological position. His need for control—that is, his need to be thought undeviatingly correct in his ideas and to be unopposed—was critical to his psychological well-being. When he was opposed, when he sensed a loss of control, he put into play a series of strategies to regain his equilibrium. Over the years, these strategies varied considerably. Sometimes he avoided conflict, sometimes he courted it.

In sum, it is readily apparent from the example of paper duties repeal that Gladstone was impelled less by a moral force in pursuing his policy than he was by his determination for psychological reasons to impose a sense of order on his immediate political environment. Yet in this year, his first as Palmerston's chancellor of the Exchequer, his behavior demonstrates a subtle change in his strategy. Although he threatened resignation, he did not resign. By calling upon a mediator (Argyll) who was able to smooth over the issue, Gladstone demonstrated a new flexibility in his coping strategy. No longer, it would seem, was he willing to put his office at risk. He did not cross the line that would have made retreat impossible.

Not only would it appear that Gladstone was becoming more flexible in his coping strategy (although this strategy still had some political cost), but he was also beginning to turn his own needs to advantage. In pushing for an ordered and dominant Treasury, he gave a strong impetus to a methodical administrative system based on thrift of public money, resolute resistance to waste, and efficient use of time.[56] He fought constantly against what he called the "spirit of expenditure." In a public speech, he once stated that "it is the mark of a chicken-hearted chancellor when he shrinks from upholding economy in detail, when because it is a question of only two or three thousand pounds, he says that is no matter."[57]

Following the July compromise on the fortifications bill—and fortunately for the life of the ministry—the holidays were soon at hand. Gladstone left London on 1 September for a month-long family vacation at Penmaenmawr. Alternating trips to Hawarden and London followed before winter settled in, bringing with it the prospect of more parliamentary battles on paper duties and fortifications. On paper duty repeal, Gladstone had come to the conclusion that the best solution would be to bring forward the bill again, but not as a single article of tariff reform. Because the programmatic mind of Gladstone always saw his financial measures as part of a larger whole, it was natural for him to consider combining all the financial measures into a single bill, although this was a novel practice. The House of Lords would then be forced to vote for or against the entire budget for the year. Not only would this guarantee the success of the paper duties repeal, he believed, but it would make it crystal clear that the Lords—should they reject the bill—were overstepping their authority on matters of supply.

On 10 April 1861, Gladstone met with Palmerston at his house to explain his budget plan. Gladstone announced a surplus of more than £1.5 million for the forthcoming fiscal year, which would permit the revival of the paper duties repeal scheme. But this "did not meet" with Palmerston's views. It was for Gladstone a "laborious & anxious day." The next two days of cabinet meetings were dispiriting. On the eleventh, it was "chaos!"; on the twelfth, "very stiff."[58] Negotiations behind the scenes later that day, however, reduced the stiffness on both sides. On 13 April, Gladstone's mood was "entirely altered," even "bland and conciliatory." Palmerston, too, had yielded "gracefully."[59] On 15 April, Gladstone spoke for three hours in the House of Commons about his plan of a single financial bill. Within three weeks, the bill had passed both the Commons and the House of Lords. Gladstone's persistence in the face of opposition had won the day. He had not only reversed the House of Lords' rejection of a part of his financial scheme, but he had also justified his own actions. He had additionally reversed the dangerous "gigantic innovation" of the Lords' assuming an unwarrantable role in matters of supply.

Near the end of the session, Argyll wrote to Gladstone in a retrospective frame of mind. Admitting that public expenditure, especially on defense, was "*enormous,*" he also doubted that any policy of financial reduction would be popular. "After all, *Palmerstonianism* is the strongest element in favour of the present govt—and the idea most essentially connected with Palmerston's popularity is the Front he shows to France in Military [and] Naval preparation." Argyll gently suggested that it was a popular policy: "I think you somewhat underrate the strength of this feeling."[60] Argyll's views were likely correct. Perhaps he had written in order to reduce the wrangling that had become common in the cabinet and Parliament. Perhaps Gladstone took his friend's advice to heart. In any case, the intense struggles between Gladstone and Palmerston eased midway through the ministry. The likeliest reason is that the rationale for Palmerstonianism had ebbed by 1863. France seemed less diplomatically active, Italy was well on the road to unity, Europe as a whole offered no surprises, and British colonies were at rest. Domestically, trade was sound, harvests were abundant, and even Lancashire, once starved of American cotton, had slowly improved. Gladstone's path was ultimately smoothed by Palmerston's death in October 1865. On the day of his death, Gladstone sent an unsolicited letter to Lord John Russell acknowledging him as the inevitable choice to succeed Palmerston as prime minister. Perhaps more to the point was Gladstone's expressed willingness to serve as chancellor under Russell. This was agreed: in addition, Gladstone was made leader of the House of Commons for the ministry, an action not universally praised. His "dictatorial manner and want of tact" had long been a matter of comment. Some doubted his judgment; others his temper and habit of rash speaking. One critic admitted his talents but was fearful he would not "perceive the difference between leading and driving."[61]

At first, things went well for the new ministry. If Gladstone's diary is any guide, the budget process of 1866 was far easier than his earlier attempts. Palmerston's death probably made the greatest difference; Lord John was a less formidable opponent in fiscal matters. In addition, a revived sentiment for franchise reform had taken up much of the cabinet's energy formerly given to budget questions. And Gladstone's grasp of the Treasury was by this time unmatched. The cabinet was more willing to defer to his judgment; Gladstone was making a mark on the office of chancellor of the Exchequer as no other chancellor had in his century. He had worked unswervingly in establishing his control over the budget-making process. He had followed without deviation recognizable lines of policy: avoidance of military expenses, remission of existing tariff duties, reduction of taxes, and the creation of annual surpluses. His budgets had become a high point of the parliamentary year. Even political enemies admitted his financial supremacy.[62] Above all was his supremacy in oratory and debate. Sir John Trelawny's observations of Gladstone's parliamentary performance during the debates on the budget of 1860 must stand for many. Praising Gladstone's "extraordinary brilliancy," Trelawny was struck by the resources of his "inexhaustible" brain. "At the end of every sentence one said 'now that will do—you may spoil it.' Not so. The next sentence was better still & so the speech went on to the last word." "To immense memory," Trelawny went on, "marvellous facility in applying principles & facts—& close logic—this extraordinary man adds genius & first class powers of declamation. It appears to me that he has now taken his place as facile printemps among the orators of his time." So powerful a persuader was Gladstone on the floor of the House of Commons, it was said that he could sway twenty-five votes with a single speech.[63]

Gladstone's reputation as a scrupulous manager of the nation's finances extended far beyond cabinet and parliamentary circles. His speeches reached the commercial middle classes through the daily columns of the national and provincial newspapers, while the literate working class could follow his career in the penny press. As Biagini has observed, the working class were particularly supportive of Gladstone's free trade budgets. His paper duty repeal, the reduction of duties on numerous items of consumption, and his emphasis on balanced budgets were popular among laboring families, who understood and approved of living within the constraints of a fixed income.[64]

A more novel way of disseminating political information directly to the electorate was through extraparliamentary speeches in the countryside. Speeches to constituents were standard practice at election times. But to address assembled crowds on issues of national importance in off-election years was rare. Gladstone himself had pioneered this experiment during the early years of the Palmerston ministry. At these rhetorical fetes, Gladstone's booming baritone inevitably made a sensation, just as it had in Parliament. To hear him speak was an unforgettable experience. He had the gift of involving his audience in alternating moods of enthusiasm or indignation.[65] For Gladstone, too, such performances had benefits. He realized that he could use mass meetings to drum up support for his parliamentary programs—a far less common notion then than now. Gladstone's cultivation of opinion "out of doors" may at first seem paradoxical. One would expect that a man so concerned with order in his own life and an upholder of Burkean ideas would be loath to stir up seemingly disconnected groups who lay well beyond the direct governing process. But Gladstone found in public meetings a restorative and refreshing quality lacking in Parliament. The crowds he addressed were compliant, supportive, even (although he would think it blasphemous to say so) worshipful; his interactions with crowds were completely unlike the contentious verbal conflicts that were waged across the floor of the House of Commons. Crowds were a tonic to Gladstone.[66] Nor did he consider these occasions dangerous to the body politic. He preached restraint, moderation, and loyalty to the existing order in the state. Thus he could address thousands of respectable middle-class or working-class listeners without fear of disturbance.

In this way, Gladstone created a different image of himself in the public eye than that which existed in Parliament. In the Commons, he could be moody and angry: outside it, he was the "people's William," a man who spoke for both the entrepreneurial middle class and the striving working class. In time, Gladstone capitalized on his new image, using it as the basis of his political power, for he had surprisingly little power in the traditional ways of politicians. The details of political wire pulling he avoided, nor did he cultivate a following or encourage a political clique. He was, in short, never a strong party man. Thus, one may argue that he did not surrender his sense of control by establishing himself as a political force outside Parliament. On the contrary, he strengthened his sense of control. He could manipulate the electorate in open meetings more easily than he could manage Parliament.[67]

The first significant public meeting that Gladstone addressed as a member of Palmerston's government was at Tyneside in the autumn of 1862. He had been invited by prominent northern Liberals in honor of his free trade policies. His reception can only be described as fervent. Arriving at Newcastle on 7 October, he spoke to a "crowded & enthusiastic dinner of near 500."[68] The next day Gladstone (along with Catherine) went down the Tyne at the head of a flotilla of steamers, with the banks of the river lined with people and saluting guns for more than twenty miles. Before entering his steamboat, Gladstone shook the hands of a few of the thousands of miners who had emerged from their pits in Durham and Northumberland to see him.[69] In his diary, Gladstone described the scene by invoking a painterly image: "The spectacle was really one for Turner, no one else."[70] He was at Sunderland, Darlington, and Middlesbrough the next day, spending fifteen hours in traveling, receptions, and speeches. One can only imagine the impact on Gladstone as thousands of cheering working men raised their voices and shouted his name. With pardonable exaggeration, Morley wrote that Tynesiders "gave him the reception of a king."[71]

Of more importance as a clue to the later development of Gladstone's political behavior was his praise in the Newcastle speech for the solidity and good sense of the working class, who had borne much during the trade disruptions following the American Civil War. Gladstone was clearly moved by the adulation of the northern coal miners and by the evidence of working-class accomplishment in the Tyneside improvement scheme. The benefits of British commerce, he said, must not find the working class in arrears: their reward for steadfastness under adversity would come soon. Whenever the subject of franchise reform "shall again come under the consideration of the Executive Government and of Parliament the conduct of the men of Lancashire in the year 1862 may be favorably remembered . . . by all who . . . have a share of political power."[72]

Gladstone's views on franchise reform had clearly changed. From the first days of his parliamentary career, Gladstone had been a reluctant reformer. As a young Tory, he had strongly opposed the 1832 reform bill on the grounds that it was revolutionary rather than merely reformative.[73] In the years that followed, there was some modification of this view, although he was never sorry to see the various attempts at franchise reform fail. He was quite willing to delay the issue for what he considered more important matters, such as commercial treaties and budgetary reductions. This was the view he held when he joined the Palmerston government in 1859—a view not far distant from the Palmerstonian position on reform. He placed himself among those cabinet members who favored what they called modest reform. Claiming they had "no fear of the working class," modest reformers believed "that something *real* though limited should be done towards their enfranchisement."[74] Sometime during the early 1860s, however, Gladstone became convinced that the timetable for reform should be shortened. It is tempting to think that his pilgrimages through the countryside had shown him that a liberal, moderate working-class opinion could complement the commercial middle classes as guarantors of responsible budgets and as bulwarks against any further incursions by the House of Lords in the budget-making process.[75]

At ease in his new popular role, Gladstone became a qualified champion of the electoral rights of the respectable working man. This was first publicly known in May 1864, when Gladstone spoke in the Commons in support of a private member's bill to lower the franchise requirements. Noting that only one out of every fifty working men had the vote—an "almost infinitesimal" number—he argued that the "best-conducted and most enlightened working men" should be enfranchised. Then in a startling statement, long remembered, he declared, "I venture to say that every man who is not presumably incapacitated by some consideration of personal unfitness or of political danger is morally entitled to come within the pale of the Constitution."[76] He hastened to add that there should be no "sudden, or violent, or excessive, or intoxicating change" and that only men with certain additional qualities should be brought within the political nation—men who had "self-command, self-control, respect for order, patience under suffering, confidence in the law, regard for superiors." Palmerston deplored the speech and drew the inescapable logical conclusion: Gladstone had laid down "broadly the doctrine of universal suffrage."[77] The *Times,* in its leader column, agreed: "Surely this is the language of sweeping and levelling democracy."[78] Sir John Trelawny thought that Gladstone had made a "Chartist speech": it was a "historical event." Trelawny mused further, "Rousseau is, apparently, in communication with our Chancellor of exchequer thro' some medium."[79]

Gladstone's increasing affinity with a wider electorate was further demonstrated in the general election of 1865. He was unexpectedly defeated for his seat at Oxford: his opinions were no longer sufficiently sound for the strong clerical element of the university. Oxford's rejection of Gladstone freed him to unite his policies and future political career with the voters of South Lancashire, where he had recently enjoyed a triumphant tour and where he had been selected as a parliamentary candidate. Directly upon his defeat at Ox-

Mr. W. E. Gladstone in 1839.

1. An early, doubtless idealized portrait of Gladstone, which nevertheless shows his earnest good looks.

2. Gladstone in 1857, showing the cares of a decade of crisis.

3. Early in his first ministry, Gladstone manifests an air of quiet determination.

THE END OF THE "TEMPEST."

Prospero. "BE FREE, AND FARE THOU WELL!"—*Shakspeare.*

4. The journal *Punch* often portrayed Gladstone sympathetically, as in this cartoon by John Tenniel depicting the prime minister as Prospero, magically transforming the Church of Ireland into a purer Protestantism.

THE MARTYR CHURCH.

5. In contrast, the conservative graphic journal *Judy*, in a cartoon by William Bowcher, represents Gladstone at the head of a band of vandals, sacking the Church of Ireland.

6. Gladstone (left) at rest after a bout of tree cutting with his eldest son, William Henry Gladstone (right), at Hawarden in 1877.

7. Gladstone in the late 1880s in the Temple of Peace at Hawarden.

8. *Judy*'s comment on Gladstone's oratorical tricksterism of the Midlothian Campaign in 1879.

9. At the beginning of his second ministry, Gladstone assumes a tranquil pose.

10. A saturnine Gladstone at Hawarden with Catherine in about 1880.

REAPPEARANCE OF THE POPULAR FAVOURITE.

["Mr. GLADSTONE at the Music Hall, Edinburgh, Nov. 11th; West Calder, 17th; Dalkeith, 21st."—*See Advertisement in Daily Papers.*]

11. The Old Stager during the election campaign of 1885: Gladstone's axe (a common symbol among cartoonists of the time) is at rest.

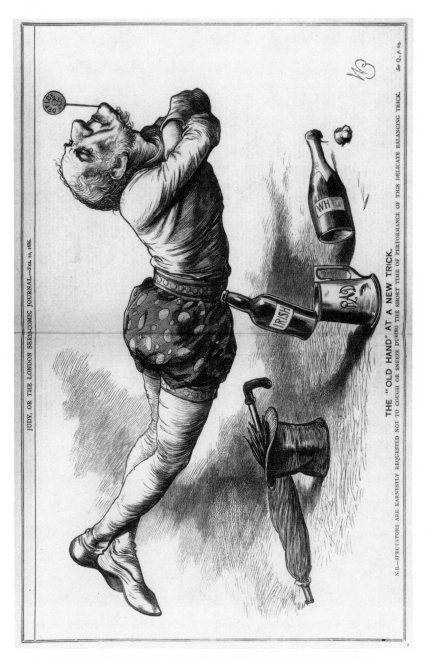

12. *Judy*'s accurate prediction of a short-lived third Gladstonian ministry.

13. Here holding his granddaughter, Dorothy Drew, Gladstone gives evidence of his intensity in his domestic scenes even in old age.

14. At other times, Gladstone fell into a ready repose, perhaps here with one of his famous "five-minute" books.

15. Gladstone again among the wood chips, about 1890.

ALL-ROUND POLITICIANS.   No. 1.—THE G. O. M. VARIETY ENTERTAINER.

16. Inspired by Gladstone's axemanship, Harry Furniss of *Punch* characterized Gladstone in a flurry of activity.

17. A glum Gladstone in the final months of his last ministry.

ford, he set out by train to Manchester. There at the Free Trade Hall in front of an audience of six thousand, Gladstone began his speech of acceptance with the famous line: "I come among you 'unmuzzled.' " In a whirlwind campaign of four days, he was returned for South Lancashire, a far different constituency from his first at Newark and his second at Oxford.

With Palmerston's death in October 1865 came the opportunity to put into legislative form the desires of a mass constituency. The new premier, Lord John Russell, had been associated with reform movements since 1819 and was determined to open the parliamentary session of 1866 with a franchise reform bill. Gladstone was less eager, but as Liberal leader of the House of Commons, he would necessarily play an important role in its passage. Cabinet meetings in the early months of 1866 indicate the long hours taken up with the issue. The idea was not to draft a radical bill but rather to contrive a "safe, limited, tranquillizing extension" of the suffrage.[80] By early spring the government was ready: the bill was introduced on 12 March. The heart of the proposal would permit borough residents who occupied premises worth more than seven pounds' annual rent to vote: this reduced the old ten-pound requirement set in 1832. Thus some three hundred thousand town artisans would enter the political nation. By similarly reducing requirements in the counties—from fifty-pound tenancies to fourteen-pound ones—and by giving votes to certain other property holders, another hundred thousand new voters would be created.

When Gladstone introduced the measure in the House, he emphasized its conservative nature. But it was clear from the outset that the government's bill would not be supported by a substantial number of its own Liberal allies. Conservative Liberals like Robert Lowe were fearful that the "working men of England, finding themselves in a full majority of the whole constituency, will awake to a full sense of their power."[81] Countering these arguments, Gladstone brought public opinion to bear on the deliberations in the Commons. On 6 April, he advocated franchise reform to a crowd of three or four thousand "full of enthusiasm" at the Liverpool Amphitheatre. It was an unprecedented action for a sitting cabinet member to appeal for public support for legislation then in progress through Parliament.[82]

Gladstone's actions in Parliament, however, were less effective. He was unwilling to deviate from the cabinet plan, nor was he willing to countenance compromise. On a motion from Lord Grosvenor that the House not proceed with the debate on the franchise until the government's intent upon redistribution of seats be known, Gladstone stated that the motion would be treated as a question of confidence. On occasion Gladstone also acted impulsively. In a debate on an amendment by the Irish Liberal M.P. Lord Dunkellin that would have reduced the numbers enfranchised, Gladstone intimated—apparently without cabinet sanction—that the vote would be one of confidence.[83] The vote nevertheless went against the government; the majority included forty-four Liberal M.P.s. This signaled the end of the ministry, which resigned on 26 June 1866, bringing to power Lord Derby's Conservative ministry.

Post mortems after the fall of the government were not kind to Gladstone. John Evelyn Denison, then speaker of the House of Commons, faulted Gladstone's leadership during the reform debates. Denison claimed that Gladstone so misunderstood the views of his own followers that his actions produced "much collision and ill will," ultimately breaking up the government.[84] Lord Clarendon, then foreign secretary, was more strongly critical of Gladstone's leadership. To Lord John Russell, he wrote that Gladstone wanted "to humiliate the H. o. C. or is unprepared to make such reasonable concessions as are necessary where compromise & conciliation are honestly desired, . . . he wants a triumph over them to wh. they will not submit . . . & wh. he knows men as honourable as himself cannot accept."[85] Modern historians have tended to agree. F. B. Smith has called Gladstone's management of the bill "confused and inflexible," criticizing him for his "implacable high-mindedness" and "intransigence" that alienated his own backbenchers.[86] Maurice Cowling presents abundant evidence of contemporary criticism: Gladstone appeared "even to old friends and members of the government, to be unapproachable and uncompromising, and to be attempting to bully the House," which he inflamed by "his arrogant ill-temper."[87]

Shortly after the government's defeat, Gladstone made plans for an extended stay in Italy. As he explained to his brother, "The truth is that after having been from circumstances so prominent during the Session it is well I should be in the shade for a while now."[88] In the opinion of his friend Sir Robert Phillimore, the journey to Italy "was really a measure of self-defense, to escape the incessant persecution of correspondence, suggestions, and solicitations."[89] From October 1866 to January 1867, Gladstone was abroad, accompanied by Catherine and his daughters Agnes and Mary (and later joined by his three eldest sons). His departure from England is not surprising. Facing divisions within his own party and an ascendant Disraeli in the opposition, Gladstone knew that his political prospects had once again dimmed. His characteristic response was to withdraw.

This Italian holiday proved quite different from his trip to Naples in 1850–51. Most of his time was spent in Rome, where he played the tourist with enthusiasm and energy. In the early morning, he read Dante in the original with his daughters. Later in the day, he spent much time "in book and curiosity shops."[90] Lord Clarendon, by chance also in Rome, was amused by the diversions of Gladstone, who ran about "all day to shops, galleries, and persons."[91] Visits to the Sistine Chapel, a viewing of the Vatican sculptures, an audience with Pope Pius IX, and a day trip to Monte Cassino gave much of his touring a satisfactorily religious tone.

In Gladstone's absence, the Conservatives had begun to debate among themselves the very question that had brought down the Liberal government—reform of the franchise. Taking the initiative on reform was a sensible political tactic for the Conservatives: it would perpetuate the division within Liberal ranks and keep them off balance.[92] Given their past performance, perhaps some disenchanted Liberals could be attracted to Conservative ranks. Political reasons, however, were not the only considerations for a reform bill. Radical M.P.s within the Commons, allied with some moderates, believed that the time had come to settle the question after twenty years of abortive reform bills. It should also be remembered that the Conservatives were a party with some sympathy for progressive legislation. They were not opposed in principle to franchise reform; they had themselves introduced a limited measure in 1859. With care, the Conservatives believed they could broaden the basis of support for their party in the countryside and perhaps even—in spite of reservations by a few die-hard members of their own party—make a direct appeal to urban working men, a class of rising importance.

The curious course of the bill through Parliament is well known. As Lord Blake has noted, the launching of the reform bill of 1867 constituted "one of the oddest histories of confusion, cross-purpose and muddle in British political history."[93] It was a bill for which the "juggler-hearted"[94] Disraeli performed extraordinary feats of political manipulation and casuistry equal to Gladstone, revealing Disraeli's "almost endless source of plausible equivocation"[95] and thus showing up the bill as essentially "an improvisation."[96] The bill followed such a tortuous path through Parliament that it prompted one backbencher to cry out in exasperation that it was "quite impossible to know what was going on."[97] It was paradoxically a bill that elicited powerful arguments against democracy, yet John Stuart Mill's motion for women's suffrage won seventy-three votes in the House of Commons. It was, finally, a bill that owed much to the swings of party fortune and to the desire of the Conservative leadership to embarrass its Liberal opponents, especially the Liberal leadership and, most particularly, Gladstone.

From the first, considerable delay and perplexity hampered the process of setting out the principles of the bill. Even after it was under way in the Commons, the bill suffered from an apparent lack of direction and firm management. Because Disraeli was driven by tactical motives rather than by any principle of reform as a political or social good in itself, it is not surprising that he vacillated. His high-wire act, during which he teetered between broad and restrictive electoral requirements, was a natural consequence of his desire to reform only as much as was necessary to satisfy the reformers without alienating the antireformers. Thus, as the debate on the bill intensified during the spring of 1867, Disraeli (occasionally acting without cabinet authority) was often pushed into increasingly progressive positions. The most important surrender by Disraeli to a wider electorate was his acceptance of household suffrage, which enfranchised every householder who personally paid borough rates, that is, local taxes. This was a proposal detested by the right-wing Conservatives but much favored by radicals, and it had long been a topic of interest especially to John Bright.

Disraeli's ability to maintain the political initiative while gathering support across the political spectrum at first prevented Gladstone—fresh from his Italian holiday—from finding an effective parliamentary footing. As the shape of the bill increasingly tended toward a wider electorate, Gladstone was forced into a curious position. Disraeli appeared to be the Liberal, Gladstone the Conservative. Disraeli's ability to hold center stage during the parliamentary debates, and his willingness to surrender quickly, almost eagerly, to the progressive elements in the Commons, allowed him to capture Gladstone's natural constituency. As the *Times* noted, the country was treated to the strange sight of "an attempt made by the Liberal party to repress the enfranchising zeal of a Conservative Administration."[98]

Gladstone, trapped into an awkward political position, did not respond well. At first, he attacked. When Disraeli introduced the reform bill on 18 March 1867, Gladstone "sat fidgeting through the speech" and then rose in a fury to strike at Disraeli. Gladstone's niece, Caroline Lyttelton, who was present in the strangers' gallery during the debate, commented in some surprise on the tenor of her uncle's "bitter onslaught" against Disraeli. "Never shall I forget the fire and scorn and vehemence of Uncle W.'s speech," she wrote in her diary. "He glared from one side to the other, gesticulated with both arms, often spoke with a kind of bitter laugh, [and] stumbled over the formal phraseology of the house, in his violent feeling."[99] The Irish M.P. Chichester Fortesque agreed: Gladstone had been "over-excited" during his attack. A more judicial tone "wd. have better suited the occasion."[100]

Within a fortnight, Gladstone was active in attempting other strategies. Concerned that Disraeli's surrender of restrictive franchises might go too far, he devised a formula (Coleridge's Instruction) that would impose a rate threshold of five pounds' annual rental for household occupiers: below that level none could vote; above it, all could. The instruction, designed to formalize opposition to the second reading of the bill, was pressed upon a reluctant gathering of Liberal Party members at Gladstone's house on 5 April.[101] To the more reformist minded, this was an inadequate response to the needs of the country. Three days later, some fifty radical M.P.s met in the Tea Room at the House of Commons, where they voted to oppose the instruction and to demand household suffrage without restrictions. From this "conventicle,"[102] a deputation called on Gladstone, forcing him to retreat. Four days afterward, Gladstone tried an evasive tactic: by amendment he reintroduced to the Commons in a milder form the embattled five-pound franchise threshold clause. Disraeli, however, turned the trick against the Liberal leader. Castigating Gladstone's amendments as motivated purely by an attempt to regain power, Disraeli charged that they constituted a "party attack." Indeed, these were not amendments at all but "counter-propositions." Gladstone, he said, had his chance to pass a reform bill "very recently" and had failed.[103] It was now the turn of the Conservative party.

The Commons agreed with Disraeli. In a crowded House, Gladstone's amendment was beaten back with the aid of forty-seven Liberals who deserted their party leader. Gladstone admitted that this was "a smash perhaps without example."[104] Indeed, as Cowling points out, the two revolts against Gladstone's leadership on 8 April and 12 April were significant not only in numbers but because they represented two very different kinds of Liberals: radicals largely composed the first, and Whig-Liberals the second. In short, more than one hundred Liberal backbenchers of diverse opinions had revolted against Gladstone on a critical legislative matter.

The rejection by so many Liberals of his leadership filled Gladstone with "*disgust* and *deep mortification*," as his friend Phillimore noted in his journal.[105] Not surprisingly, the failure of Gladstone's attack on Disraeli and the reform bill turned him to thoughts of resignation from the Liberal leadership.[106] His closest colleagues rallied around him and urged circumspection. His old friend Sir Thomas Dyke Acland hoped he would rise above any wounded feelings he may have: "Your position as leader of a large & important party . . . imposes on you very distressing conditions of self-restraint." Neither Disraeli's insolence nor the "defection of the Sneaks" should alter his relation with his "real followers." Acland revealed his main concern in a final word of advice: "It is absolutely necessary to your great future . . . that you should not show a disposition like Achilles & return to your tent in the sulks."[107]

Fortunately, the Easter recess intervened. At Hawarden for the holidays, Gladstone channeled his frustration into an ordering of his books and papers in the Temple of Peace. He also pursued more strenuous activity among the trees of Hawarden.[108] These restful occupations may have done their work. Shortly after his return to Parliament, Gladstone issued what he called "a quasi-manifesto" in which he gave up the five-pound threshold for household occupiers.[109] He had freed himself from his former moderate reformist position; he could now embrace more liberal views.[110] His withdrawal had given him a needed respite. But the Liberal revolt against his leadership had wounded him deeply, and its memory was to shape his conduct at another crucial time in his political life.

Disraeli had predicted after Gladstone's failure to derail the bill that "we ought to carry our Reform now in a canter,"[111] and so it occurred. Amendment after amendment was brought forward in May and early summer as private members added to and extended the franchise. The same was true of the redistribution bill that followed. But Disraeli gained a significant victory in keeping the county electorate relatively untainted by the newly enfranchised borough voters. Throughout this final stage of the bill, Disraeli faced more difficulty from Conservatives than from Gladstone, who took a back seat in the debates. Once the bill reached the House of Lords, Lord Derby's leadership assured it a smooth passage. By mid-August it had become law.

The years 1866 and 1867 had been unkind to Gladstone's reputation as a leader of his party. He had been severely tried and had been found wanting as a manager of men. Lady Waldegrave, a repository of political gossip, made it plain. She "reported to me," as Gladstone dutifully noted in his diary, "from friends the errors & defects they notice in me."[112] The summer of 1867 was particularly uncomfortable to Gladstone. He remained suspicious of his party and wary of the Commons. To Fortesque he revealed his state of mind: "The H. of Commons is no better than a dead dog in a ditch—nothing to be got out of them."[113] To regain stature among his colleagues in Parliament, Gladstone needed an issue which he could so thoroughly dominate that none could challenge his authority. It had to be an issue that could rally the divided Liberal ranks and convince them of timely action. It also had to be an issue that played on the weakness of the Conservatives, especially the weakness of Disraeli, who became prime minister at long last with the retirement of Lord Derby in February 1868. For Gladstone, the natural topic would be finance, but this was difficult to manage from the opposition benches. A second issue was at hand, however, which perfectly played to Gladstone's strength: the future role of the established Anglican Church in Ireland. This was not an issue of narrow religious impact but one that involved the life and culture, and the political fortunes, of England's nearest colony, Ireland.

7

"My Mission Is to Pacify Ireland"

Gladstone, it is said, when summoned to form his first ministry in December 1868, intoned, "My mission is to pacify Ireland." Whether or not this story is true, it is symbolic of the greatest achievement—and the greatest failure—of his political career. For Gladstone considered Ireland above all other issues as a cause to be championed. Reflecting on his first ministry in his later days, Gladstone recalled that it was Ireland "which mainly and almost entirely filled the political horizon."[1] How Gladstone was drawn into Ireland and how he sought to extricate himself have a significant psychological dimension.

Gladstone was initially attracted to Irish matters because of his own religious concerns, especially the role of the Anglican Church of Ireland. As a novice in the House of Commons, he had strongly opposed the Whig reforming ministry of the 1830s in its attempt to diminish the privileges of the Church of Ireland. In the early 1840s, he had argued against permanent state aid to Maynooth, eventually resigning his office in protest when Peel's government refused to countenance his views. Two decades later, however, he had changed his mind.[2] The public first learned of this in March 1865, when he spoke in the House of Commons in support of the principle of a private member's motion that the

Irish Church establishment was unsatisfactory. Gladstone believed that the difficulties of the Church of Ireland were directly related to its "false position."[3] He claimed that his reversal of opinion was neither recent nor lightly undertaken.[4] Indeed, since the episode of Maynooth twenty years earlier, he had realized that the cause of an established Protestant church in Ireland was hopeless. If Parliament could endow a religious establishment such as Maynooth that was *not* Anglican, then it certainly had the right to disestablish an Anglican institution such as the Church of Ireland. Gladstone could comfortably argue that his policy was conservative. Unlike the Church of England, in which the "religious life throbs more and more powerfully within her," the Church of Ireland had not become a prominent part of the religious life of Ireland—nor was it ever likely to be.[5]

In this opinion, Gladstone was not alone. To the overwhelmingly Roman Catholic Irish, the Church of Ireland was an alien institution, imposed on Ireland and shorn up over the centuries by an oppressive foreign government. Its numbers were only a fraction of the dominant Roman Catholic faith; its wealth was far in excess of its needs. Protestantism was merely a tiny island in the wider sea of Catholicism. By disestablishing the Church of Ireland and thus removing state aid, a significant Irish grievance would be addressed. Additional political advantages would come from dealing with the question of the Irish Church. Tactically speaking, this issue offered the best hope of unifying the Liberal Party after its recent political defeat at the hands of the reforming Conservatives. If played well, the Irish Church question could even bring down the Conservative government.[6] Disestablishment would also likely prove popular among Nonconformists in England, whose emergence as a cohesive political block was soon to be recognized in the election of 1868. Disestablishment in Ireland might well set a precedent for a similar measure in Britain, freeing Nonconformity from remaining restrictions imposed by the Erastian Anglican establishment.[7]

For Gladstone personally, the Irish question provided an opportunity for overseeing an issue that he was uniquely qualified to address. His knowledge of religious matters and clerical politics was unsurpassed. Gladstone was also profoundly concerned about the potential for disorder in Ireland should Irish grievances deepen. His preparation for a specific Irish policy may be traced in his diaries. After the bruising battles over the Reform Act of 1867, Gladstone had retreated to Wales. Leisure activities soon gave way, however, to lengthening reflections on the forthcoming parliamentary session. By the winter of 1867, he turned his attention fully toward Ireland. The quickening pace of Gladstone's relevant reading was the strongest indication of his line of thought. He read the *Quarterly Review* on Ireland, A. G. Stapleton's "Origin of Fenianism," John Bright's sympathetic views on Ireland, and numerous other papers and tracts over which he "ruminated."[8] He spoke to his neighbor and fellow parliamentarian Sir John Hanmer on Irish matters. Most impor-

tant of all, he delivered a speech on Irish affairs to his constituents at Southport in December, outlining his legislative plan and signaling his intentions
to the nation at large.

The Southport speech was one of his most stirring, and its sympathy for
Ireland was unusual for a British politician of that day. In it, Gladstone
expressed his "utmost sadness" that after hundreds of years of political connection between England and Ireland the "union of heart and spirit which
is absolutely necessary for the welfare of the country has not yet been brought
about." Ireland shall "for years to come," Gladstone predicted, provide "for
the Governments . . . and for the people of England the most difficult and
the most anxious portion of their political employment." He cautioned his
constituents against confusing the cause of Fenianism with the cause of Ireland and urged them to "preserve an equal temper and perfect self-command"
as they pondered the fate of Ireland. What England must do, Gladstone
urged, was to ensure that "those sympathies in Ireland which now hang and
float bewildered between law and lawlessness shall be brought into active
alliance" with the law and its legal procedures. This could happen only if
inequities were removed and wrongs were righted, especially in the areas of
Irish education, land, and religion. His final peroration was a call to action:
"Ireland is at your doors, Providence has placed her there, law and Legislature
have made a compact between you; you must face these obligations, you must
deal with them and discharge them."[9]

Emboldened by an issue that had a chance of raising Liberal hopes for a
significant political victory, Gladstone entered the parliamentary session of
1868 in far better fettle than he had ended the session of 1867. As Fortesque
noted in his diary, Gladstone had been "demoralized and cowed" by "his
Reform fiasco." But now he was "very cordial, & cheerful in manner—greatly
changed for the better by improved relations with his party."[10] Eagerly, he
convened "Conclaves" and planning sessions with his political colleagues in
the early days of the new parliamentary session in order to consolidate Liberal
opinion. By March, the Liberals were ready.

The timing was natural enough. The Irish question was brought dramatically into the public consciousness by Fenian organizers who had become
increasingly active in both North America and Ireland in the late 1860s. They
had devised grandiose plans for an invasion of Canada, and closer to home,
they hatched a plot against the military arsenal at Chester, only a few miles
from Hawarden. Insurrectionary actions were to be followed by an armed
expedition to Dublin and a general uprising in Ireland in March 1867. All
these schemes, however, came to a bad end. Poor organization and lack of
promised support from abroad doomed a Fenian revolution. More alarming
to English opinion were Fenian incidents on British soil that affected up-
holders of the law and innocent bystanders alike. At Manchester, in September 1867, thirty armed Fenians bungled an attempt to rescue two Fenian

prisoners from a police van. In the ensuing confusion, a policeman was shot dead. Two months later, three Fenians were hanged for complicity in the murder. In December 1867, in an attempt to free other Fenian prisoners implicated in the Manchester murder, an explosive device was set against an outside wall at Clerkenwell prison in London. Dozens of inhabitants nearby were killed or injured.[11] These incidents not only outraged the English population at large but also brought home to the politicians the deadly seriousness of Irish nationalism.

This heightened sense of danger was the background for a notable speech by Gladstone in the Commons on 16 March 1868. Expressing a sense of urgency, he was far more explicit than he had been at Southport three months earlier. A sure way to Irish hearts, Gladstone believed, was the creation of religious equality to its "fullest extent" in Ireland. Only disestablishment (that "very grave word," as Gladstone put it) of the Church of Ireland could bring it about.[12] In the weeks and months of the session that followed, he carried against Disraeli's government a series of parliamentary resolutions that advocated disestablishment. Faced with the continued prospect of Gladstone's governing from the opposition benches, Disraeli was forced to call a general election in November.

The tactical ploy of raising the flag of Irish disestablishment proved its worth: the Liberals won a majority of 112 over the Conservatives. Gladstone himself, however, was ousted from his seat in South-West Lancashire as its conservative traditions were reasserted.[13] Well aware of his tenuous hold on the constituency, Gladstone had arranged as a fallback his candidacy for the safe Liberal constituency of Greenwich. As expected, Greenwich returned him handily. With this victory, and armed with the nationwide Liberal triumph, Gladstone at last attained as prime minister the complete authority and power he desired in political life.

Gladstone's choice of a cabinet was reassuring to critics who had a tendency to fault him for impetuous behavior. It suggested no sudden departure from past policies. More than half his choices were Whigs or Peelites, with a few straightforward Liberals. Only John Bright had radical pretensions. Bright, as a Quaker, was also the only non-Anglican in the cabinet. As a whole, the cabinet has been characterized as "remarkably unambitious"[14]— that is, no cabinet member served as a consistent source of opposition to Gladstone's leadership. It was a cabinet, as Gladstone himself once wrote, "easily handled."[15] He dominated its deliberations in the same way that he had begun to dominate the debates in the House of Commons—through his mastery of detail, his habit of logical thought, and the sheer force of his personality. He directly shaped not only policy but also the course of cabinet proceedings. Indeed, his innovative practice of keeping systematic records of cabinet meetings suggests that he brought to his ministry formal principles of organization.[16] Morley is surely right in maintaining that Gladstone "created, guided, controlled and inspired" his cabinet.[17]

The most congenial of Gladstone's colleagues proved to be Lord Granville. Although Granville was not known for efficient administrative habits and was uninterested in details, he was in his element as leader of the House of Lords, where his sagacity and tact were put to good use in smoothing party conflicts. Granville's talents served him well when dealing with Gladstone. He rarely contradicted Gladstone; if he differed with his chief, it was deftly done, with a light diplomatic touch—quite unlike the more waspish Argyll, for example, or the blunt Clarendon. The ease and informality between them gave at times an almost playful tone to their correspondence. With Granville, Gladstone was far more revealing and candid about political tactics than with any other cabinet colleague.

Gladstone, with Granville's crucial help in later stages, wasted no time in the pursuit of his legislative plan for Ireland. Within a week of his acceptance of office, he set before Queen Victoria the "case of the Irish Ch." The following day, he wrote "some queries & some heads on Irish Church." He consulted with members of the government and other officials on the Church of Ireland, wrote memoranda, and read "on Ireland." On Christmas Eve, he set out "to work on draft of Irish Church measure, feeling the impulse." Working through Christmas Day, he finished his draft that night. On Boxing Day he entered into his diary, "Revised Irish Ch. draft and sent it to be copied: with Notes."[18] In the weeks that followed, Gladstone worked around the clock, meeting with colleagues, courting the clergy, and listening to advice, warnings, and veiled threats. Somehow he also found time to continue his reading on every possible item of relevance—including a study of disestablishment in the Bahamas.[19]

In late January 1869, Gladstone placed before the queen a long memo outlining his plan for disestablishment. Gladstone explained to her the complicated measure, which, he commented later, "appeared to be well taken."[20] But the queen was not able either to understand the memo or to follow Gladstone's arguments. She had wanted to retain some connection between the Crown and the Church of Ireland—at least the appointment power of its bishops. When she was forced to give way, she signaled her disapproval by refusing to open Parliament in person. Thus began a long history of strained relations between Gladstone and his sovereign.

Gladstone well knew that his most intransigent opponents would be clerics of the established churches in both Ireland and England. He had to exercise special care in orchestrating his appeal to them. He encouraged potential clerical allies to be active in the cause. As he put it to Bishop Wilberforce, "The bill must be framed with ref. to those who support it & not to those who oppose it. . . . Those who *act* . . . become our practical supporters."[21] Suspect prelates, in contrast, might be given a different message. A letter from the new Lord-Lieutenant of Ireland, Earl Spencer, to the bishop of Peterborough had an edge to it. "If . . . the Church party carry on the principle of 'no surrender.' . . . , the disposition of the Liberal party now calm and in favour of dealing tenderly with the Interests of the Church, will be altered, and they will carry out a slashing policy of cutting down everything on which the state has a legal claim."[22] Gladstone let it be known that compromise was out of the question on the main points of the bill. "We must proceed on the principles we have declared," he wrote to Spencer.[23]

On 8 and 9 February 1869, the cabinet devoted seven hours to the major heads of the bill—"to my great satisfaction" as Gladstone recorded in his diary.[24] The remainder of that month was taken up with preparations for the first reading in the Commons. Gladstone saw the queen again, spoke to the archbishop of Canterbury, held numerous conclaves, and chaired additional cabinet meetings. Throughout these crucial weeks, his energy remained undiminished. His management of the bill at this stage seemed flawless. His labors drew high praise from an admiring cabinet member, John Bright: "Mr. Gladstone's activity wonderful, and his knowledge extraordinary."[25]

On 1 March, Gladstone introduced the bill to the House of Commons. It had two distinct parts. The first, disestablishment proper, would completely sever the Church of Ireland from its counterpart, the Church of England, and from the British government. No Irish bishop or archbishop would thereafter sit in the House of Lords. All Irish ecclesiastical courts would be abolished. In effect, the former church would become a private corporation, no longer sustained by a system of legally enforceable tithes; it would subsist on its remaining endowments.

Disestablishment proved to be relatively uncontroversial. But the second part of the bill, disendowment, was a different story. The difficulty was that disendowment was primarily an economic, not a religious, matter. The estates, lands, and other property of the Church of Ireland were worth approximately £16 million. How such an immense property should be divided and dispersed was a complicated question. The original bill proposed that clergymen be given lifetime annuities equal to their net annual income prior to disestablishment. They were to be further compensated for life interests in their glebe houses, rent-free dwellings traditionally granted to Church of Ireland clerics. What property remained would be held in trust by a newly created body called the Commissioners of Church Temporalities in Ireland. The commissioners were to have full authority to decide specific issues of compensation as they arose. Once compensation had been satisfactorily settled, the remaining monies were to be used not for religious purposes but for charitable relief in aid of the poor.

The proposed bill was a remarkable piece of legislation and deserves the praise that it received then and since. Although not radical in motive or intent, it dealt with the Church of Ireland in the most thoroughgoing fashion possible.[26] The legislative combination of removing a centuries-old religious anomaly while simultaneously contributing to the future social welfare of Irish poor was a notable coup de main. Politically, the bill was well timed and astutely managed by a series of subtle pressures brought to bear against potential opponents. Every question seems to have been anticipated, mainly by Gladstone himself. "I can truly say that no labour has been spared," Gladstone wrote to Lord Lyttelton. The bill had been his "almost incessant thought."[27]

For the first time, an opposition party experienced the concentrated force of Gladstone as chief political officer in the state. The Conservatives could not make headway against the bill. Indeed, it seems to have been a foregone conclusion that the bill would have smooth sailing in the House of Commons. The diary of Gathorne Hardy reflects a listlessness among high-ranking Conservatives. On 10 March, he noted, "A stupor has fallen on the Irish Chmen & their friends in England seem not much more alive." In the following weeks, Hardy complained about the "depressing work" in the Commons and the "long dreary nights"—presumably because the Church of Ireland Bill was so firmly hitched to the Liberal juggernaut.[28] Hardy's fears were well grounded. The bill won a majority of 114 on its third reading the last day of May.

Its reception in the House of Lords, where there was no assured Liberal majority, was far different. Opponents of the bill attacked it through a series of amendments designed to postpone the effective date of disestablishment and to win as large an endowment as possible for the newly independent church. Most important of all was a series of maneuvers that would establish the principle of concurrent endowment, that is, the endowment of all religious faiths in Ireland. Under this scheme, out of the surplus property of the Church of Ireland, glebe houses and lands were to be provided not only for Irish Church clerics but for Roman Catholic clergy and Presbyterian ministers as well (Methodist clergymen would not receive benefits). Concurrent endowment would cost nearly £3 million more than the endowment proposed by the original bill, and it would reduce substantially the amount of money intended for the poor of Ireland.

Action by the Lords encouraged flagging Conservative spirits. "What will be the end?" Gathorne Hardy queried expectantly on 13 July. "Gladstone will not accept."[29] This prediction proved accurate. Gladstone's initial response to the amendments was laconic. "Sad work in the Lords," he wrote in his diary.[30] Once he realized the full implications of the opposition's tactics, however, his attitude quickly hardened. After conceding a further small financial compensation to the new church, he was in no mood for compromise. As he wrote to Edward Cardwell, his secretary of war, "We have now made *every* concession for which we can discover even the rag of reason."[31] The crisis worsened in the third week of July. The Conservative Lord Carnarvon, knowing the drift of opinion in the Lords, posed a rhetorical question to his diary:

"Is it like the first shot fired on Fort Sumter?"[32] The following day, the House of Lords once again upheld concurrent endowment by a substantial vote.

The vote provoked an "emotional reaction" from Gladstone.[33] He was prepared to suspend the government's responsibility for the bill, leaving the opposition "to work their own will."[34] This notion he also communicated to the archbishop of Canterbury, one of the mediators in the crisis: "I have nothing further to communicate or propose," he wrote. "The matter now lies with the majority in the House of Lords."[35] It was clear to Gladstone's cabinet colleagues that this intransigent attitude jeopardized the entire bill. Gladstone's Lord Privy Seal, the earl of Kimberley, joined with every other cabinet member except Cardwell to dissuade Gladstone from his "rash determination."[36] Some sort of compromise, they believed, was possible.

The mastermind of the compromise as it evolved over the next three days was Lord Granville, the colonial secretary and Liberal leader in the House of Lords. At a cabinet meeting on 21 July, he insisted that the government go forward with the bill. Then, working behind the scenes, Granville hammered out an agreement with Lord Cairns, the Conservative leader in the Lords. Gladstone in the meantime had fallen ill. He spent the crucial day of negotiations (22 July) in bed, although Granville, the Liberal whip G. G. Glyn, and others kept him informed of events. Granville also urged moderation upon Gladstone: among members of Parliament, he said, "not one was for any course but a patient one." Furthermore, Granville confided, "we shall lose the confidence of some of the best and staunchest of our friends in the H of Commons if we were thought to be the persons who broke off the chance of a peaceable passage of the bill."[37] Late that Thursday afternoon came the good news of a compromise, brought to Gladstone on his sofa.

The details of Gladstone's management of the Church of Ireland Bill, and especially of the crisis of its passage in July 1869, demonstrate the workings of mid-Victorian parliamentary life and cabinet government. More relevant, however, is the light that these events shed on Gladstone himself. The days of July 1869 illustrate, as no other series of events had thus far in the life of Gladstone, the importance of the element of control in his psychological makeup, and the strategies of attack and withdrawal that he employed at times of stress. A review of the months of work that Gladstone put into the Church of Ireland Bill, and of the care that he lavished on its reception, reveal his tutelary genius. Until the very end of its parliamentary progress, Gladstone piloted the bill with remarkable facility. When he encountered difficulties at last, he lost his political dexterity and became less resilient. As he faltered, he fell back on the habit of command. He expected, indeed he demanded, obedience. When the opposition failed to relent, he began a two-stage process of withdrawal from challenges to his authority. First, Gladstone quite simply tried to wash his hands of the matter—to abrogate responsibility for his own bill. When this failed and he then encountered opposition from his cabinet, he retreated further into illness. It is quite possible, of course, that by this time Gladstone was simply suffering from "nervous exhaustion," as Matthew believes.[38] Gladstone was bound to have been fatigued, but his ill health on this occasion fits the pattern he had established in the past: once he had reached a critical stage in political negotiation, he could not carry on in the face of what seemed intractable opposition.

After disestablishment was out of the way, Gladstone turned to the other two planks of his Irish platform: Irish land and the reform of Irish higher education. Here again, it was Gladstone who engineered the legislation, developing his expertise through study and application. By maintaining control of these bills as they were shaped in the cabinet, he also hoped to ensure their ready acceptance in the houses of Parliament.

The central problem of the landholding system in Ireland during the late nineteenth century was the relationship of rights between landlord and tenant. The power of the (largely English and Protestant) landlord over the native Irish tenant farmer had increased over the generations, and inequities between landlord and tenant grew concomitantly. Landlords, for example, could raise rents arbitrarily. If tenants refused to pay increased rents, evictions could follow. These relatively straightforward economic tensions were exacerbated by a sense among the tenantry that landlords were often indifferent to the management of their own estates and were ultimately disinterested in their tenants' welfare. Thus, landlords became marginal economic and social partners in the management of rural life—and such management was crucial in pastoral Ireland.[39]

It is a testament to Gladstone's honesty that his study of the Irish land question led him in time to an understanding of the historical disadvantages of the Irish tenantry. Among the most important influences on his opinion was George Campbell's pamphlet *The Irish Land,* published in 1869.[40] Campbell, a member of the Indian civil service who had recently visited Ireland, was struck by the parallels between Irish and Indian tenantry. The Irish, no less than Indians, based their notions of landholding arrangements on customary rights. From their point of view, custom was as legitimate as the statutes and rulings of parliaments and courts. Thus when Irish tenants acted to protect their occupancy, they did so not because they were naturally contrary but because they believed they acted legally. Campbell saw the conflict in rural Ireland essentially as a clash of legal systems. The contractual, investment-oriented, and designed-for-profit English system of a landlord-dominated countryside was clearly at odds with views of the more communally minded and family-centered Irish smallholder.

As Gladstone worked up his brief, encouraging the cabinet to do the same, and as the idea of an Irish land bill became more developed, the inevitable focus of discussion became the question of "tenant right." This issue seemed to lie at the heart of the difficulties between landlord and tenant in

Ireland and symbolized the contrasting legal systems that Campbell had noted. In England, tenant right concerned compensation for improvements—such as repairs to drainage systems or additions to farm buildings—that tenants had made on the land they held. When the tenant left the occupancy for whatever reason, tenant right dictated that either the incoming tenant or the landlord fairly compensate the departing tenant for the improvements. Such a system acted as an investment incentive for occupying tenants. But in parts of Ireland, tenant right had a much broader meaning. In Ulster, especially, tenant right was widely recognized as a form of property; that is, tenants bought and sold their leases in what was known as free sale. In some cases, tenants even drew up testaments bequeathing their farms. With such a proprietary view, tenants would expect to have considerable say in the conditions of the renewal or termination of their leases, and they certainly would object to unilateral evictions.

Gladstone became increasingly convinced that some form of tenant right, based on the Ulster custom, must be central to any proposed land bill. Most simply, this would mean that Ulster tenant right should be extended to all Ireland. Gladstone saw this measure as conservative because it originated in custom—that is, it was a practice carried on from time immemorial. It was, in Burkean terms, a prescriptive right of the tenants. It had the additional attraction of applying an indigenously Irish solution to the land problem.

Gladstone's strongest cabinet ally for a substantial land reform scheme was the radical John Bright. The seven Whigs in the cabinet were less friendly to any notion of reform that might alter the exclusive property rights of landlords. Gladstone, well aware of the likely cabinet opposition to the extension of the Ulster tenant right, decided early on to withhold from the initial cabinet meeting a definitive bill. Sketchy proposals, he believed, would be a useful tactic to prevent alarm among the more conservative cabinet members. In spite of his careful maneuvering,[41] Gladstone found the cabinet in varying degrees of opposition throughout the autumn of 1869. The Whig duke of Argyll, who was concerned that the proposed bill might surrender too much to the tenantry, was among Gladstone's strongest opponents.[42] In his verbal battle with Argyll, Gladstone was not above intellectual intimidation. "For the last two months, I have worked daily, I think, upon the question, & so I shall continue to do," he wrote. "The literature of it is large, larger than I can master: but I feel the benefit of continual reading upon it." He asked Argyll pointedly, "Have you *read* much on Irish tenure & disturbances?"[43]

As discussions continued into the winter of 1869–70, other cabinet members became uneasy with Gladstone's increasingly strenuous arguments, based as they were on the historical wrongs visited on the Irish peasantry. Gladstone's elevation of the land bill to the status of a moral obligation was "bewildering as well as alarming" to his colleagues.[44] His behavior was typical of his desire to control the events around him, and especially to manage the legislative program he had begun. By lending that program moral authority, he could more readily justify it—if not to his unbelieving colleagues, then certainly to himself.

Gladstone's task did not ease as the deadline for submission of the bill to Parliament drew near. In fact, discussions on the land bill were increasingly complicated by the intrusion of a related issue: an increase of agrarian incidents, many of which were reputedly Fenian led. Gladstone's position on the disturbances, and on the Fenians generally, was from the first cautious. He believed that a generous land bill would settle agrarian grievances and draw the teeth of the Fenians; to act harshly would only make martyrs of the Fenian leaders. But he was strongly opposed in the cabinet by Fortesque and Earl Spencer, the chief officers of the Irish executive. They argued for coercion and gradually won the support of other members of the cabinet. Even Granville was persuaded. Thus opposed, Gladstone gave way. He agreed to a Peace Preservation Bill that granted local magistrates greater power to compel witnesses to testify and that created special military patrols to put down outbreaks of violence.[45]

In the meantime, Gladstone introduced the land bill to the House of Commons in a three-and-a-half-hour speech. The bill bore the marks of cabinet compromise. The legality of Ulster custom was granted in that province, for example, but it was legalized in the south only when tenants were evicted. Upon eviction, damages to the tenant were granted, including compensation for tenant improvements—although this compensation was hedged with certain qualifications. The "compensation for disturbance" clause was designed to limit evictions; in effect, landlords were taxed on every eviction and the proceeds were used to subsidize evicted tenants. Evictions for nonpayment of rent were exempt from the bill. All other kinds of evictions initiated by landlords, such as a desire to consolidate holdings, fell under the provisions of the bill. The bill thus moved at least partially toward Gladstone's main objective—"to prevent the landlord from using the terrible weapon of undue and unjust eviction."[46]

As the bill wound its way through the legislative process, opposition emerged. Ironically enough, the most dangerous opponent was a respected Liberal M.P., Roundell Palmer. Palmer was already recognized as one of the sharpest of legal minds and was soon to enter Gladstone's cabinet as Lord Chancellor. But he believed that the bill favored tenants excessively. In Palmer's opinion, compensation for disturbance amounted to "giving something to the tenant which does not belong to him, and taking away from the landlord something which belongs to him."[47] Thus he supported an amendment moved by William Fowler, a radical M.P., which would deny compensation to tenants of holdings rated at more than fifty pounds annually.

Gladstone was incensed with Palmer's behavior. He argued that to exclude from compensation the larger tenants—effectively the leaders of Irish tenant opinion—would undermine the principle of the bill. When Fowler's amendment lost by only thirty-two votes, far below the usual Liberal margin of victory of more than a hundred, Gladstone thought, with some exaggerated sense of danger, that Palmer brought the government "within an inch of shipwreck."[48] Gladstone even hinted—in a veiled threat of resignation—that if the government were brought down by Palmer's opposition, Palmer himself ought to bear the responsibility for forming a government.

Gladstone enlisted his colleagues to bring pressure to bear on Palmer. To Argyll, he wrote that he was engaged in an "arduous correspondence" with Palmer, who had "nearly been the death of the Land Bill."[49] Argyll took the hint and promptly wrote to the recalcitrant M.P. He reminded Palmer that Gladstone had recently made a great concession in the direction of free contract in favor of the landlords. Clause 10 of the land bill had originally allowed tenants rated annually at a hundred pounds or more to contract themselves out of the legislation; Gladstone agreed to reduce the ratable threshold for contracting out to fifty pounds. "I do not think Gladstone can safely do more," Argyll assured Palmer.[50]

Gladstone's fears about Palmer's opposition to some parts of the land bill seem overdrawn, and his response exaggerated. Clarendon, at least, thought that Gladstone's "quasi-menaces" had actually been harmful.[51] A hint of a self-defeating mechanism is at work in Gladstone's sudden rigidity. The episode is reminiscent of his threat to abandon the Church of Ireland Bill the previous year. As he felt control ebbing, the sense of strain no doubt rose, ultimately pushing him hard against his opponents. Palmer in any case was apologetic: "I have desired to help, and not to oppose you," he assured Gladstone.[52] Writing years later in his memoirs, Palmer reflected on his chief's behavior: "It was always one of his defects, to have no just sense of the proportion of things. This made him irritable under the most friendly criticism [and] disposed to exalt details into principles."[53] Palmer was slightly unfair, but he was identifying a trait that Gladstone exhibited under pressure. In this case, this episode passed off without harm. Palmer backed down, and the bill went forward to a relatively easier time in the House of Lords, passing Parliament essentially as introduced.

The Gladstone ministry had now dealt with two of three outstanding Irish issues: religion and land. Only university education in Ireland remained. This problem may at first glance seem potentially less difficult than disestablishment and land reform. But in fact, it proved one of the most unpopular of all the ministry's measures, for it combined the strands of religion and nationalism in a manner that brought out the dangerous opposition of the Irish clerical hierarchy.

The prevailing system of secular and denominational instruction in the schools called "mixed" had been created in the 1830s to the dismay of the

Roman Catholic leadership, who feared that it was only a matter of time before Britain would extend mixed education to the universities.[54] By the mid-1860s, the Catholic hierarchy decided to act. In December 1865, the four Irish archbishops traveled to London to meet a deputation of Lord John Russell's government to discuss the matter. On the English side were Gladstone and his future home secretary, H. A. Bruce, as well as the colonial expert Sir George Grey. The prelates demanded from the British government a charter for the Catholic University in Dublin. This would lend legitimacy to denominationalism and would allow Irish Catholics to attend an institution of higher learning without fear of Protestant taint.[55] They also advocated a division of the secular colleges of the Queen's Colleges along denominational lines: Cork and Galway Colleges should become Catholic, and Belfast College, Presbyterian. Trinity College would remain exclusively Anglican. As the archbishops pointed out, this distinction merely recognized a de facto arrangement. Agreeing in principle with the prelates, the government decided to bring forward legislation on the Irish university during the next parliamentary session. Before the government could act, however, the Conservatives under Derby came to power and were less enthusiastic for changes in Irish education. There the matter stood until Gladstone's ministry took it up once again in late 1872.

Cabinet meetings throughout the winter of 1872–73 saw the evolution of a plan that was eventually presented to the House of Commons in February 1873. Its progress through the cabinet was uneasy, however.[56] Hartington, now chief secretary of Ireland in place of Fortesque (who had moved to the Board of Trade), nearly resigned on the issue. Argyll effectively boycotted cabinet meetings because of his displeasure with the bill. Other members of the cabinet had reservations to varying degrees. Yet Gladstone, who once again was piloting an important Irish measure through the cabinet, remained optimistic about its chances. Nearly a fortnight after the bill's introduction to the House, Gladstone reported to his brother Robertson that the reception had been favorable "in almost all quarters" and that the bill seemed likely to pass.[57] Gladstone had also received significant encouragement from Cardinal Manning, who had been in frequent contact with the Irish hierarchy and who had urged them to accept the bill.[58] Perhaps Gladstone's optimism was based on the efforts he himself had made to anticipate every conceivable objection from all possible religious quarters. But his effort to satisfy diverse viewpoints gave the bill a cobbled look.[59]

At the heart of the bill was the establishment of an Irish national university. Federal in structure, the new university would be composed of affiliated colleges, such as Trinity, the Queen's Colleges of Belfast and Cork, the Catholic College in Dublin, and Magee College in Londonderry. (Galway Queen's was to be abolished because of low enrollments.) The advantage of such an organization from Gladstone's point of view was that it preserved the denominational character of the individual colleges. But Cardinal Cullen believed that the proposed bill perpetuated mixed education; that is, the abolition of religious tests meant that Catholics could now go to Protestant Trinity, whose rich endowment and consequent educational advantages "would act as a bait to poor Catholics to desert their Denominational Tutors."[60] From an Irish point of view, the bill lessened, but did not abolish, discrimination against Catholics who sought a first-class education on a par with Trinity. An equally well endowed Irish Catholic university was the solution. Cullen's opposition was made public in a Pastoral letter against the bill, which discouraged Irish M.P.s from supporting it.

Gladstone remained optimistic in spite of Cullen's hostility. The worst he anticipated was a "mutilation" of the bill in the House of Lords; he certainly saw in February no prospect of resignation. Among Gladstone's own Liberal followers, however, support for the bill was rapidly eroding; it seemed tilted too far toward Irish demands. One clause, for example, would allow even small denominational colleges (which were almost sure to be Catholic) a seat on the governing body of the national university. This spread fear among some Protestant Liberals that the university would ultimately become dominated by Catholics, with unhappy consequences for Trinity College. All in all, the bill had fallen between several stools, as the debates in the House made clear.

Faced with a growing opposition, the cabinet took stock. Meeting on 8 March, they decided that some compromise might be possible at the committee stage of the bill. Virtually no one in the cabinet defended the bill as it had been drawn up under Gladstone's guidance.[61] To judge from his diary, Gladstone took this news with apparent calm, noting merely of the cabinet meeting that it was "most harmonious, at this critical time."[62] But Gladstone's mood as noted by Fortesque was far different. He threatened the cabinet over a tactical matter. Should the government be defeated on the second reading of the bill, as then seemed likely, he proposed to dissolve and go to the country. If the cabinet decided to resign without recourse to an election, he in turn would resign the leadership of the party.[63] Gladstone substantiated Fortesque's observations in a letter to Cardinal Manning that same day. In it, he also hinted strongly at resignation should the bill fail in the Commons: "When this offer has been made, and every effort of patience employed to render it a reality, my contract with the country is fulfilled, and I am free to take my own course."[64]

On 11 March, the bill was defeated by three votes, after Gladstone had declared it a question of confidence. Most of the Irish Liberals, a smaller group of other Liberals, and virtually all the Conservatives made up the victorious voting list. Two days later, the cabinet met again to determine a course of action. As Fortesque recounts it, Gladstone retracted his earlier resignation threat: he would continue to act with the party after all, even in defeat. In fact, Gladstone now preferred resignation, rather than dissolution—in direct contrast to his previous statement. After the cabinet agreed collectively to resign, Gladstone made a farewell speech to the cabinet "in a very few and affecting & sincere words—wh. he cd. hardly get out, stopping two or three times."[65]

Later that same day, Gladstone met with Queen Victoria to resign office. During his conversation with the queen, he also intimated his desire to withdraw from public life—at least for a time.[66] Rumor had it that Gladstone had declared "nothing would make him come back" and that he planned to go abroad "for six months or a year."[67] Fatigue was doubtless in part responsible for his decision, but Gladstone, as in the past, seems to have opted to retreat in the face of political rejection. This time, however, he could not put his plan into action. Disraeli refused to accept the commission to form a government, and Gladstone returned to office. The ministry had begun, and had nearly ended, with Ireland. Nearly a year of the ministry's life remained, little of which had to do with Irish issues.

8

"Our Lease Is Out"

Gladstone's first administration is rightly considered one of the great reforming ministries of the century. Yet Gladstone was not equally interested in all areas of reform. Some issues captured only a modicum of his energy and determination: these included educational reform for schools and reform of the election laws. Indeed, it is interesting to note that Gladstone proved more enthusiastic about army reform than either educational or election issues. Army reform was, however, directly related to foreign affairs and diplomacy—areas in which Gladstone proved surprisingly eager to exercise authority and control.

Gladstone's role in educational reform was mainly to provide the opportunity for others to frame legislation that would satisfy a strong popular movement. It was widely recognized in the mid-Victorian era that greater numbers of school-aged children must be brought into the educational system. Even middle-class conservative thinkers understood this, as revealed by Robert Lowe's famous maxim uttered after the reform bill of 1867: "We must educate our future masters." If an illiterate and ill-informed populace could not enter fully into the entrepreneurial and self-reliant society prescribed by the Victorian middle class, they could become rebellious, perhaps even revolutionary. Articulate working-class artisans were no less eager for compulsory education for all children, if for different reasons. In part, better education was for them a social issue. They could easily make the connection between ignorance, crime, and poverty and between literacy, self-respect, and good citizenship. By the late 1860s, there was a general agreement among the reform-minded that certain educational goals were desirable. Among these were a recognition of the need for more state regulation of the schools, a determination to work within the preferences of various religious denominations insofar as possible, a willingness to build better schools and increase salaries of poorly paid teachers, and the need to create local boards with substantial power to administer their own schools.[1]

Gladstone had taken very little part in the expanding educational debate in the country. Nor did he give evidence of much interest in it during the formative stages of the government's education bill. Still, it was he who set in motion the government's educational policy, once Irish disestablishment was under way. In a letter to Earl de Grey (soon to become the marquess of Ripon), then president of the council, Gladstone arranged for a meeting with W. E. Forster "to lay the foundation stone of our Education measure in England."[2] Forster was then M.P. for Bradford and was serving under de Grey as vice-president of the council. That Forster was primed and ready to act is evident. In less than three weeks, he presented Gladstone with a memorandum drawn up to provide the legislative basis for a reform of elementary education.[3]

The bill was presented early in the forthcoming parliamentary session, on 17 February 1870. (Parliament had a full plate: only two days before, Gladstone had introduced the Irish land bill.) For the next two months and more, intense debate within and outside Parliament altered the shape of the bill. Roman Catholics and Anglicans preferred to retain the existing denominational character of schooling. Most Nonconformists, however, wanted an undenominational arrangement, that is, the absence of religious teaching, fearing that the dominant Anglicans would suborn their children. Gladstone himself favored denominational education and condemned an undenominational educational system as a "moral monster."[4] He believed that religious and secular education were inseparable and that some attention should be paid in the schools to religious teaching. This teaching need not necessarily be Anglican. Just as Gladstone believed that individual religious sects ought to be free to organize and propagate their messages, so he believed that all specifically religious teaching should be free. But eventually even he had to give way. As the bill proceeded through Parliament, it evolved that religious instruction in primary schools would be Christian but strictly undenominational—confined essentially to Bible reading without attendant glosses. The new school boards, directly elected by the taxpayers, would determine the details of school administration and financial arrangements. The bill also provided for two rival systems of schools: the old denominational schools were to be retained—to the chagrin of the Nonconformists—alongside the new board schools, established where there was a proven need for them. Thus was the "dual system" enshrined.

The consequences of the bill for Gladstone were unfortunate. Because it was hammered out in the fires of contending religious sects, its compromises satisfied few. Struggles between church and chapel erupted at every three-year election to the boards. Electoral contests were particularly embittered by the provision that every voter had as many votes as there were members on the local school board. Thus, each voter could cast all votes for a single member or could split them in a variety of ways, encouraging the emergence of religiously oriented local election machines. So divisive were the struggles for the local boards that the discouraged Nonconformists withdrew their support from Gladstone during the 1874 general election, thus contributing significantly to his defeat.[5]

Gladstone had better luck with a significant reform of electoral practice: the introduction of the secret ballot in national elections.[6] Yet this was an about-face for him. He had long supported open voting. As recently as December 1867, in his famous Southport speech, he had condemned the secret ballot. "I own to an attachment to what I view as the old English principle," he told his constituents, "that as far as possible all public duties and functions should be performed in the public eye."[7] Among politicians of standing, only John Bright was identified as a supporter of the secret ballot, a position he argued forcibly on the eve of the formation of Gladstone's ministry after the general election of 1868. Bright wrote to the new prime minister that open nominations and open voting should be abolished. A week after the despatch of his letter, Bright conferred with Gladstone in London. It may well be that at that meeting Bright and Gladstone struck a bargain: Bright would accept a cabinet post and the ministry would bring in a ballot bill.[8]

Other issues were also forcing a reconsideration of the election laws. Passage of the Reform Act of 1867 had raised hopes that a broadened electorate might bring order to the traditional riotous proceedings at polling times. But the general election of 1868 witnessed serious incidents of bribery and intimidation. So flagrant were they that a Select Committee was appointed in 1869 to examine the whole subject of parliamentary and municipal electioneering. Evidence indicated that Liberals and Conservatives had transgressed equally. The committee, reappointed in early 1870, met through the winter; by May, the cabinet had approved a ballot bill.

Included in the bill, however, was a controversial clause providing for an investigation of suspect elections. Through a system of numbered counterfoils, it would be possible—under scrutiny—to determine the identity of any elector. This provision was not popular among the more progressive Liberals, who believed that voter anonymity should be inviolate. Other complications arose during parliamentary debates. Some members espoused the traditional view that voting in secret was somehow un-English—that secrecy in voting was tantamount to deception, a trait unknown to manly and honest Englishmen (unlike the furtive and cunning French).[9] Others believed that the secret ballot in Ireland would fuel a dangerous Home Rule movement.

Because of these various threats to the bill, Gladstone was forced to step in with oratorical support. He defended the ballot as a natural extension of the Reform Act of 1867. The adoption of household suffrage in that act presumed the natural competency of an enlarged electorate to exercise a wise suffrage; the secret ballot would allow this to happen by reducing the opportunities for undue influence, whether exerted by landlord over tenant, factory owner over worker, or cleric over parishioner. The bill was nevertheless rejected by the House of Lords in August 1871. When it was reintroduced the next year, the Lords again seemed prepared to vote it down. Gladstone finally took a firm stand and rallied his clerical troops. To Bishops Moberley and Wilberforce he issued an appeal. He asked Moberley's support in persuading aristocratic opponents of the "very serious evil of a collision between the two Houses with the consequences it might entail."[10] He wrote similarly to Wilberforce and to the bishop of Bath and Wells: "Each individual vote will be of the utmost consequence either in causing or in averting very grave public mischief."[11] He sent a like message to G. G. Glyn, the Liberal chief whip: "Let the trumpet blow," he commanded, so that "the Lords may know before the time comes what the country thinks."[12] Perhaps these appeals had effect. The ministry also worked a compromise with the help of Lord Granville: the Liberals accepted a scrutiny clause and a limited duration of the act in return for Conservative support. These concessions were barely enough: the Liberals gained a victory of only 157 to 138. The Parliamentary and Municipal Bill received the royal assent on 18 July 1872. It was renewed annually from 1880 until 1918 when it became permanent under the Representation of the People Bill.

Gladstone's primary political interest had always been in domestic matters, with the single exception of Ireland. Foreign affairs and the practice of diplomacy were rarely his major concern. His stated view on diplomatic issues was that Britain should insofar as possible lead other nations in a kind of "moral empire" or "ecumenical council" that would sensibly solve international problems.[13] Perhaps he considered foreign affairs an area in which he could less clearly exert personal control. Foreign affairs were inherently ungovernable and always full of surprises, especially in Britain's far-flung empire. With the added difficulty of the unpredictable global ambitions of other countries in the late nineteenth century, an attempt to maintain control would likely be an exercise in futility. Nevertheless, Gladstone often took a surprisingly interventionist position in foreign affairs, and one that suggests that his need for control could indeed extend beyond the boundaries of Britain.

The earliest example of proactive diplomacy in Gladstone's first ministry occurred as a direct result of the American Civil War. The victorious

Northern states had pursued war claims against Britain since 1865 because of alleged British complicity in harboring Confederate commerce raiders in the waters of the Mersey, the Clyde, and the Thames. The most notorious example occurred in July 1862, when the shipbuilding firm of Laird Brothers in Birkenhead delivered to the Confederacy the steamer *Alabama.* Designed as a commercial raider, the *Alabama* became a legend on the high seas: it sank forty-eight Northern merchant ships in its first year of operation and delayed the voyages of dozens more. The *Alabama,* eventually sunk off Cherbourg in 1864 by a Northern warship, came to symbolize British sympathy with Southern aspirations.[14]

In the vengeful atmosphere after the Civil War, Northern politicians capitalized on a fervent Anglophobia. Speeches favoring the Fenians, promising them support and the use of American ports, soon exacerbated the bad feeling between the two countries. American threats against Canada became common. Americans talked of taking British Columbia in exchange for the damage done to Northern shipping by the *Alabama.* The American government, in addition to its claims related to the *Alabama,* soon demanded "indirect claims," that is, extensive reparations for increased insurance rates, the destruction of maritime tonnage, and the crippling of the American merchant fleet during the Civil War.

The British position throughout the controversy was straightforward. The construction and delivery of the *Alabama* had never been officially sanctioned; they had been carried out in secrecy and without the knowledge of the British government. Consequently, the government was not liable for the damages claimed by the Americans. Gladstone took an active role in orchestrating the British diplomatic position. He had at first hoped for an amiable round of negotiations, but continued American demands for indirect claims opened his eyes to the depth of American sentiment. When diplomatic tensions reached a critical level during 1872, Gladstone allied himself firmly against the indirect claims, terming them a "dishonoured carcass."[15] To Granville, too, he wrote in some asperity of "all the bunkum and irrelevant trash" of the American claims. He recommended a counterstroke: "We might retaliate a little, [and] show up their method of working foreign politics for home purposes."[16] In order to break the deadlock, Gladstone opened direct negotiations with the American minister, General Robert Cumming Shenck. As Matthew notes, this move allowed Gladstone more control and initiative during the most delicate phase of the negotiations.[17] Eventually the Americans dropped the indirect claims, and an agreement between the two sides was reached. The tribunal awarded the United States $15.5 million (or £3.2 million), an amount considerably less than they had asked for.

Before the negotiations had come to a reasonably satisfactory end, Britain was faced with a more important diplomatic event on the Continent, in which Gladstone also took an active role. In the summer of 1870, Europe as a whole was caught up in the quarrel between France and the newly emerging German power. The prospect of an imperial France at war in the heart of Europe was uncomfortably reminiscent of the great Napoleon during the French revolutionary wars. Once again, France seemed unstable, ambitious, dangerous. In spite of a simmering Francophobia in the country as a whole, the Gladstone ministry responded at first cautiously.[18] This was not surprising, given the recent succession of the conciliatory Lord Granville to the Foreign Office. What is surprising, however, is that Gladstone quickly became dominant in pushing forward his own diplomatic agenda.

On 14 July, Gladstone summoned the cabinet on an hour's notice after receiving word of the famous Ems despatch. The cabinet immediately decided in an evenhanded fashion to discourage both French and Prussian moves toward war. Two days later, during a four-hour cabinet meeting, a more detailed response to the European crisis was devised. The cabinet decided to frame a proclamation of watchful neutrality and to be prepared to act in accordance with that policy.[19] They ordered the sale of warships stopped, and belligerents were to be asked to respect the commerce of neutrals. The secretary of war, Cardwell, was to prepare a statement on the military preparedness of the forces. Most important, in its concern for the neutrality of Belgium, the government agreed to seek guarantees from both France and Prussia.[20]

In the weeks that followed, Gladstone followed up his sense of the cabinet's mood to pursue an active neutrality. His correspondence with Cardwell quickened; he wrote to Sir Thomas Erskine May, clerk of the House of Commons, inquiring about a possible emergency summons of Parliament; and he informed Disraeli of the government's plans to request an additional twenty thousand men for the army and an extra £2 million for military expenses. To ensure Belgium's territorial integrity, he urged Granville to proceed at "full gallop" toward a treaty with France.[21] Should all else fail, he suggested to Cardwell the possibility of sending as many as twenty-five thousand troops to Belgium without any parliamentary sanction.[22] He also found time to write to Count von Bernsdorff to request safe passage for his sister Helen, then in Cologne, should she need it.

Like most European observers, Gladstone thought that in any war, France would win. When the news of the French defeats of early August reached London, he professed himself "stunned" and surprised that the French had been "overmatched." But he indicated no unease at the Prussian victories. His view of the Prussians underwent a considerable change, however, once he learned of their demands for the annexation of Alsace and Lorraine. He immediately took steps to counter the Prussian plan.[23] He first proposed to the cabinet a remonstrance against Prussia's territorial ambitions, using if necessary a loose alliance of signatories from other nations. But the cabinet declined, believing that taking such action without the prospect of enforcing its demands would be futile and damaging to British diplomatic credibility. Gladstone, confessing that he had found the cabinet's rejection of his plan "rather indigestible,"[24] wrote several times to Granville in the following week to urge alternative strategies, including the creation of a demilitarized zone on the frontier between Germany and France as a way of preventing annexation. Granville, however, firmly opposed this idea, emphasizing the need to reserve "our full liberty of action."[25]

Having failed with the cabinet, Gladstone quickly moved to bring his ideas to the public at large. Without the knowledge of his colleagues, he wrote an anonymous article in the *Edinburgh Review* for October 1870.[26] Entitled "Germany, France, and England," it was ultimately a plea for a European community, or "moral empire," or "new law of nations," that could give voice to a "Public Right, as the governing idea of European policy." This publication could be seen as another way of putting forward his notion of using a concert of powers to block the annexation of Alsace and Lorraine— a notion that so recently had been rejected by his own cabinet. Gladstone's authorship of the article was readily disclosed through some unknown leak. Thus his opinions had the full, if unofficial, weight of his office and his government behind them. The effect he hoped to bring about is unclear. It is difficult to imagine that the tone of the article could have contributed in any positive way either to the peace process or to the issue of the annexation of Alsace-Lorraine. It was in any case an extraordinary exercise for a prime minister to bypass his own cabinet under the cloak of anonymity in discussing matters of vital national interest—especially when some of the ideas alluded to had been negatived in formal cabinet session.[27]

The real importance of the article lies in its revelations about Gladstone himself. The article, very much a Gladstonian production—moralistic, didactic, and self-justifying—may have been a form of release. He may have felt a kind of impotence in the face of European events over which he had no control. Britain had been forced to the sidelines during the Franco-Prussian war: there was little that he or the government could do. The only way he knew to reassert a form of authority was an appeal to a higher order. An appeal of this sort might somehow persuade the combatants to an orderly solution to their conflict. In this, he failed.

If Gladstone's efforts to influence the course of the war were unsuccessful, he nevertheless understood clearly the lessons that the war held for Britain's own military forces. The British army badly needed reform. To remake the British military into a more efficient organization, and one less costly to operate, appealed to his Peelite reforming instincts. But he was also attracted to army reform because of the superlative achievements, and particularly the orderliness, of the Prussian military machine. As he wrote in his *Edinburgh Review* article, "There is . . . something almost of miracle or of magic in the administrative perfection, to which the combined action of necessity and sagacity have worked up the Prussian system." Their army had been brought "to the highest mechanical perfection ever known in history." Other armies, Gladstone noted, "can destroy a railway; the Germans carry the means in men and tools, of making one." So prepared had the Prussian army become, Gladstone noted, that they even had a special corps for gravedigging.

Gladstone's admiration for the Prussian army's military and logistical feats led him to request of Cardwell the "fullest & most accurate accounts of the whole of the Prussian military system, both at rest & in action."[28] Gladstone's suggestion fell on receptive ears. From his first days in office, the Peelite Cardwell had initiated a programmatic scheme to modernize and centralize the army command. He had also instituted regular army discipline in the militia and volunteer corps, had raised army pay, and had begun to attack the demoralizing purchase system in the army.[29] Gladstone indicated that in any scheme of military reorganization, he would defer to Cardwell's judgment. Nevertheless, as was characteristic of him, he began to read widely on the subject: he consulted Barkley Britten on artillery, Sir A. Alison on army reorganization, and C. C. Chesney and H. Reeve on recent changes in the art of war.

Gladstone also helped pave the way in the autumn and winter of 1870–71 during Cardwell's preparations for a parliamentary bill. When Cardwell felt unable to bear the burden of the Commons debate on army reorganization, for example, Gladstone set about finding a parliamentary seat for General Sir Henry Storks, then surveyor-general of ordnance at the War Office. But a compliant parliamentary constituency and borough patron was not easy to come by, and the search provoked an angry letter from Gladstone to Lady Herbert, who held Wilton in her gift and refused Gladstone's request. A seat was finally found at Ripon, and Storks was returned on 15 February 1871, the day before Cardwell introduced his army reorganization bill.[30]

At the heart of the bill was the abolition of purchase, with compensation for all officers who held salable commissions. The bill's weakness was that it was not comprehensive: it left untouched specific details of military reorganization and the promised improvements in ordnance, training, and logistics. To those who criticized the narrowness of the bill were added the inevitable opponents of the abolition of purchase. Parliamentary debates were acrimonious. The bill dragged on throughout the spring and early summer, reaching its third reading only in July. The margin of victory for the government was 58, the vote dividing along party lines, with the exception of twelve Liberals (five of them army officers) who voted with the Conservatives.

Fierce opposition in the House of Commons was a bad omen for the progress of the bill through the House of Lords. Within a fortnight, the Lords had tabled it. Gladstone was unwilling to delay the passage of the bill, however, and within a few days of the Lords' action, he secured from the queen a royal warrant that declared the end of purchase. This legal but infrequent use of the royal prerogative raised a storm of protest. Predictable outcries arose immediately from the Conservative opposition. But those more sympathetic to the ministry also had reservations. Lord John Russell, who could be counted on to give a traditional Whig reading of contemporary events, had his doubts. The whole episode reminded him too much of the questionable dispensing power of the later Stuarts.[31]

Modern historians have agreed that Gladstone's action was high handed. Gallagher sees Gladstone's behavior during the whole of the debates on the purchase system as marked by a kind of ferocity: "He berated Lady Herbert over the nomination boroughs, he denounced the mental sloth of upper-class youth, he made fierce remarks in debate about the intellectual poverty of the public schools and the universities."[32] And indeed, opposition to Gladstone could elicit in him a disproportionately strong, even punitive response. But in this case, Gladstone's action had a beneficial effect in terms of the goals of the ministry and was in fact a shrewd political move. The warrant only abolished the purchase of army commissions; it did not offer compensation, as had the parliamentary bill. To save the compensations clause, the House of Lords now passed the bill. Gladstone's dislike of opposition and fear of loss of control thus meshed with the political exigencies of the moment and concluded with a victory for his ministry.

The army reorganization bill represents the high-water mark of reformist activity for the ministry. Thereafter the ministry seemed to be taking on more than it could manage. A general deterioration of parliamentary efficiency was brought about by a significant increase in private members' bills and a growth of independent action on the part of backbench M.P.s. The loss of Liberal Party cohesion initiated a period of marked decline in the government's prestige and influence. From normal majorities of more than one hundred, the ministry increasingly had to operate with majorities of half that number or less.[33] The disenchantment of Liberals with their party and their leader was plain. Sir John Trelawny's diaries are graphically candid.[34] He complained of Gladstone's want of "judgement & moderation"; he criticized the prime minister's "vehemence & excitability" and his "imprudent & fussy" leadership. Trelawny made unfavorable comparisons with Disraeli, whom he found "calm," and with Palmerston, who had "happy qualifications" as a leader. The ministry itself, Trelawny believed, was "weak" and "unfortunate." The defeat of Irish educational reform in March 1873 he attributed to "bad judgment and mismanagement."

Gladstone was not unaware of this shift in his political fortunes. In June 1873, he lamented the "deplorable" position of the ministry in the House of Commons: it was being undermined by an active opposition and by "enemies on our own side . . . thinking only of their electioneering interests."[35] Matters worsened during the summer when financial irregularities in the general post office implicated Robert Lowe, the chancellor of the Exchequer. Although no illegalities were involved, this episode was the final straw for the testy and tactless Lowe.

These events weighed heavily on Gladstone. His friend Sir Robert Phillimore, who was increasingly concerned about the premier's health, observed in late July 1873 that Gladstone had taken to walking with a stick and appeared worn and unwell.[36] Something had to be done to restore order among the parliamentary ranks and to regain some measure of popularity for the government. Gladstone decided that the ministry needed rejuvenation. In August 1873, he reshuffled the cabinet. He assumed the office of chancellor of the Exchequer (for the third time in his political life), moved Lowe to the Home Office, and made several other minor changes. Gladstone then sought to find an attractive rallying cry for the party and for the electorate. He fell back on the issue he knew best: finance. On 11 August, he wrote in his diary the outline of a scheme that initially he showed only to Cardwell at the War Office. He proposed nothing less than the abolition of the income tax and sugar duties, the shortfall in revenue to be partially made up by increases in spirit and death duties. It was a dramatic, even desperate plan. Gladstone believed it to be the only chance for the life of the government.[37]

The autumn and early winter of 1873, however, brought little change in the government's fortunes. Gladstone's pessimism grew. In November he hinted to Baron Robartes, a former Liberal M.P. for East Cornwall, that he would stand only reluctantly for Parliament at the next general election.[38] In December, he informed Cardwell of his admittedly "dark view" that unless matters improved soon, the government must be abandoned.[39] Early in the new year, he wrote a long letter to Granville, reviewing the options: he concluded that the country "has had enough of us, that our lease is out."[40]

Still, Gladstone retained some hope. If sufficient retrenchment in the military estimates could be made, in addition to the increase in spirit and death duties, the budget could be made respectable and possibly accepted by Parliament. But Cardwell, when sent a copy of Gladstone's letter, balked. He opposed further military reductions. Divisions within the cabinet were now added to the government's other woes. These difficulties turned Gladstone's mind toward dissolution and a consequent general election. He seems to have come to this decision on 18 January 1874. At a cabinet meeting the following week, he announced the dissolution. The cabinet members were surprised at Gladstone's decision. Kimberley wrote in his diary that most of the cabinet "had not heard a whisper previously of such an intention on his part." Certainly Fortesque had not.[41] Apart from informing Bright and Granville, Gladstone had in fact kept his intentions a secret.

By taking the life of the ministry into his own hands with little consultation, Gladstone had carried out "a coup d'etat!"—as Fortesque termed it in a letter to Spencer, who in turn gave a similar gloss on Gladstone's action, calling it a "thunder clap."[42] Newspaper comment of the time expressed varying degrees of shock. The last dissolution during a recess without prior public announcement had occurred nearly a hundred years before. The *Manchester Guardian* believed an immediate dissolution "so uncalled for" that Gladstone would need all his eloquence "to justify it to his party and to the country." The mass-circulation *Lloyd's Weekly* declared that Gladstone's swift dissolution did not provide enough "thinking hours" for the electorate. *Reynold's Newspaper* took the same line, condemning Gladstone's "blunder."[43]

Because Gladstone had not prepared the way, many Liberal candidates were caught on the hop. Indeed, the decision had been taken so quickly that Gladstone himself scarcely had time to determine whether he would stand again for one of the Greenwich seats. The Conservative opposition was no less taken aback. Disraeli, in London only by chance on a Friday evening, was awakened the following morning with a copy of the *Times*, handed him by his servant. After studying Gladstone's manifesto in that newspaper, Disraeli immediately summoned his political staff, who worked furiously all weekend preparing a reply to Gladstone's election manifesto for Monday morning's papers.[44]

Although Gladstone had long been concerned with the fate of the government, his decision to dissolve seems to have been reached quickly, perhaps even impulsively. This suggests that Gladstone, as in the past, had at least partly nonpolitical motives. A weakened government, divisions among his own cabinet, and the Conservative opposition's increasing strength with each passing by-election all posed insurmountable difficulties. To a man who operated best when he could control circumstances, this was a particularly difficult moment. For Gladstone, there seemed no option other than dissolution, and the sooner the better. The forthcoming parliamentary session—when a hard-riding Conservative opposition could hunt at will among the wounded Liberal pack—promised increased political difficulties and consequent additional personal stress. In short, Gladstone attacked in an attempt to surprise his political opponents. This preemptive electoral strike was intended not only to reverse his political fortunes but also to place himself on a better psychological footing.

His strategy failed. A Conservative reaction in England, Scotland, and Wales, and the loss of many Liberal seats in Ireland to the Home Rulers, gave the Conservative Party a majority of some fifty seats in the House of Commons. Gladstone himself had a narrow squeak in his Greenwich constituency, winning the second seat by a small margin. Like many another party leader, Gladstone was cast down by electoral defeat. "I am weary," he confessed to his brother Robertson, "of this life of contention." To spend the remainder of his days "in tranquility and at any rate in freedom from political strife" was his hope.[45] But unlike other party leaders, Gladstone came to a decision even more dramatic than his sudden call for a dissolution. The day following his letter to Robertson, he revealed his intention to his wife: "Conversation with C. G. on the probable changes in our position & consequent measures." Catherine was, he noted, "startled."[46] This cryptic reference he made plain in a cabinet meeting on 16 February: he had decided to resign from the leadership of the party.

If Catherine had been taken aback by this news, doubly so were his cabinet colleagues. Gladstone's professed reasons were largely personal. He wanted to avoid, as he told the cabinet, the "insults and outrages" of 1866–68. Furthermore, he had a "keen sense of the disloyalty of the party during the last three years." He would thereafter sit only as a private member, would not attend the House regularly, and would not serve in any function as a leader of the party. "He does this," Lord Aberdare quoted Gladstone, "not from temper or anger" but because the party must learn their obligations.[47] The evening following his cabinet announcement, Gladstone slept badly, lying awake for three hours—unusual for him—"with an overwrought brain."[48] The next day, he went to Windsor and resigned. Thus began the lengthy Conservative ministry of his political nemesis, Benjamin Disraeli.

Why had Gladstone taken such a step? Why had he, after surrendering the reins of government, followed with a resignation from the party leadership? For a politician to abdicate the leadership of his party when he remained the obvious and natural chief was virtually unknown to the traditions of the British party system.[49] No party members had called for his resignation; on the contrary, they pleaded with Gladstone to change his mind. Did he intend to teach the party a lesson, as Aberdare had implied? Was he simply angry? Had he made a calculated move to test the loyalty of his supporters or to lull the Conservatives into a false sense of security—perhaps to throw them off balance in some way? Had a "mood of depression," as Magnus believes, settled on Gladstone after the election?[50] Perhaps elements of each of these reasons were involved in his decision. Gladstone was certainly unsettled by the strains of office. As he wrote (in an echo of his letter to Robertson) to the chief whip, A. W. Peel, he did not intend to spend his final years "in the career of stress and contention which the House of Commons offers to me" as leader of the Liberals.[51] He clearly took the news of electoral defeat as a personal repudiation. But his reaction was far more significant than merely a display of personal pique. After the failure of his psychological strategy, when he had failed to win a snap election—in short, after the failure of attack—he had simply fallen back on his alternative strategy. He withdrew.

But Gladstone was forced to modify his decision. At the strenuous urging of his colleagues, he agreed to lead the Liberals for another session, until the beginning of 1875; he would then reevaluate his position. The reasons for his colleagues' insistence were apparent. Even more than in 1868, in 1874 Gladstone was indispensable to the cohesion of the Liberal Party. During the course of his ministry, he had increasingly settled into a central position. On the right were the diminishing band of Whig aristocrats such as Granville, Spencer, and Hartington. On the left were the spent force of John Bright and, more important, a younger generation of administratively skilled and politically ambitious politicians, such as Sir Charles Dilke and Joseph Chamberlain, who had newer radical visions. Thus Gladstone had become an attractive anomaly who paid high political dividends: he was a high-churchman who spoke the Evangelical tongue, a conservative who could appear to be radical, and a parliamentarian of high office who could also move the masses.

In spite of the gentlemen's agreement that had been made to retain Gladstone as head of the party, it became clear in the months following the Liberal defeat that his leadership was purely titular. He rarely attended Parliament. "The anti-parliamentary reaction has been stronger with me even than I anticipated," Gladstone wrote to his wife. "I am as far as possible from feeling the want of the House of Commons."[52] Indeed, only one topic caught his attention during the first parliamentary session of Disraeli's ministry, but it was significant as a clue to the cast of his mind. This was the controversy surrounding the Public Worship Regulation Bill. At issue was the growth of ritualism and high church practices within the Church of England. Such practices included the use of altar candles, ceremonial ablutions, facing east at Holy Communion, and eucharistic vestments. The younger clergy had instituted noticeable changes in clerical garb, such as long straight coats reaching to their heels (which proved a delight to critical cartoonists) and what Evangelicals called "Mark of the Beast" waistcoats—that is, solid waistcoats without dividing, all too similar to the garments of Roman Catholic priests.[53]

In April 1874, the archbishop of Canterbury brought forward the bill in the House of Lords. It would allow parishioners to appeal to their bishops if they thought their local clergyman used excessive ritual in his conduct of church services. If the defendant was recalcitrant, a lay judge could impose a prison term (five clergy were ultimately imprisoned under the terms of the act). Gladstone opposed the bill because he believed it would destroy the diversity that had grown up in the Church of England over the centuries. He also feared that it would ossify worship by restricting the free exercise of ritual expression. In its place, he offered a series of six resolutions that he thought would better guarantee congregations' rights and would safeguard against an errant bishop. Gladstone's insistence that the government's bill should be thrown out placed him beyond the pale of most Liberal members' views, many of whom supported it. Indeed, it appeared for a time that Gladstone would not receive an endorsement in the House of Commons from a single member of his own party. Bowing to the inevitable, he withdrew the resolutions without a division.[54] Thus, Gladstone's violent attack on the bill had the simultaneous effect of heightening the political stakes, placing himself in the minority, and dividing the Liberal party over the issue—all without the intervention of Disraeli, who remained in the background during the debates.[55]

But Gladstone was not finished with the topic of ritualism. Even before the parliamentary debates on the Public Worship Regulation Bill had run their course, he had set pen to paper to justify his views. "Ritualism and Ritual," published in the October 1874 issue of *Contemporary Review,* is a subtly argued plea for tolerance of the growth of ritual in the Church of England. Removed from the political battleground during the parliamentary debates on ritualism, his arguments have a strength of conviction, persuasion, and logic that clarify (and justify) his own position. In this sense, the article made a reasoned contribution to the national debate on the role of ritual within the church. Yet the article caused considerable furor among its readers. Opponents objected not to the general tenor of Gladstone's remarks but to a single aside, unrelated to his main point, in which he launched an attack on the Roman Catholic Church. In a direct reference to the recent Vatican Council decrees on papal infallibility, Gladstone charged that Rome had "refurbished and paraded anew every rusty tool she was fondly thought to have disused." Most important of all, "no one can become her convert without renouncing his moral and mental freedom, and placing his civil loyalty and duty at the mercy" of Rome.[56]

Gladstone's remark was a gratuitous insult to all Roman Catholics and was especially offensive to Irish sensibilities. His response to the outcry, however, was not designed to smooth ruffled feathers. As in the past, when he found himself at the center of controversy, he felt impelled to justify himself to the world. Within a month of the publication of "Ritual and Ritualism," he decided to expand his views on the "Papal question." Thus was launched the second controversial pamphlet of his retirement, the famous "Vatican Decrees in Their Bearing on Civil Allegiance."

It is difficult to discover a simple explanation for Gladstone's behavior after the fall of his government in 1874. He seemed to strike out simultaneously against the Liberal leadership, Roman Catholicism, and the Irish. Why had Gladstone acted in an apparently dysfunctional manner since his retirement? This question has two likely answers. The first takes into account the circumstances of Gladstone's political life during the previous eighteen months. Since March 1873, his political fortunes had declined precipitously, culminating in electoral defeat, resignation of his party leadership, and ignominious failure in the Commons over a subject dear to his heart, religion. This was especially galling because he had hoped to use religion to assuage his political wounds after the trials of his ministry.

Second, one of his major concerns since his first year in office had been the Vatican Council's preparation for the declaration of infallibility at the instigation of the reactionary Pope Pius IX.[57] When the decree was finally proclaimed in July 1870, Gladstone was profoundly alarmed. He believed that the papal decree established an ultramontanism that could become a powerful "anti-social" force.[58] The decree seemed to him presumptuous in the extreme, and an attempt to revive medieval papal authority. Indeed, Gladstone's anxiety about the threat of a growing papal authority had been strong enough to push him into an argument with his cabinet in its final meeting in January 1874: he had wanted to include in his dissolution address an unflattering reference to "ultramontane" aggression. But the cabinet objected, almost unanimously. Even the timorous Fortesque spoke against it.[59]

That the rise of a papal ultramontanism had become intermixed with Gladstone's residual feelings of suspicion toward religious apostates is borne out by the case of Lord Ripon, Gladstone's former cabinet minister and political colleague. Ripon, who had served as Gladstone's Lord President of the Council until the cabinet reshuffle of 1873, was one of the most prominent Catholic converts of the late nineteenth century. Born at Ten Downing Street when his father, Viscount Goderich, was prime minister in 1827, Ripon had served in a variety of important posts: he had been secretary of state for War in Palmerston's ministry and later Indian secretary before he joined Gladstone's cabinet. He had also successfully chaired the Anglo-American commission that settled the *Alabama* claims, earning for this service a marquessate. In 1870, he had been named grand master of English Freemasons.[60] With this background of solid political (and Protestant) achievement, Ripon's conversion, announced publicly in the summer of 1874, was a shock to the country and, it would seem, most especially to Gladstone.

Ripon knew well enough that Gladstone would receive the news badly and therefore alerted him before it was widely known. Ripon had his wife write first to Catherine Gladstone. This indirect approach did not soften the blow. Gladstone wrote immediately to Ripon that both he and Catherine were "stunned" by the news. How was it possible, he inquired of Ripon, that he could become a "sworn soldier in the army banded to destroy the church that had been his home?" He strongly implied that Ripon had not thought through his decision and hinted that he was acting irresponsibly. This unkind letter apparently went unanswered.[61] A few months later, however, Ripon wrote to Gladstone—as soon as he had read "Ritualism and Ritual." Ripon charged that Gladstone made it appear that no one could become a Catholic convert "without renouncing his moral and mental freedom, and placing his civil loyalty and duty at the mercy of another." Gladstone's remarks—which seemed to point directly at high political figures, and perhaps even specifically at Ripon—were a "very serious charge against those, to whom it refers, and of whom I am one. . . . I, who have so lately been one of the Queen's ministers, have no alternative, . . . but to remonstrate as strongly as I can against such an accusation." Ripon cleverly made his relationship as a Catholic citizen to the queen the focus of his argument. "I utterly deny," he wrote, "that by becoming a Catholic I have become one whit less loyal or dutiful as a subject of the Queen, and I have served Her Majesty too long . . . for me to allow you . . . to say or to imply . . . that I have done or am ever likely to do any thing inconsistent with perfect loyalty and duty to her."[62]

Gladstone claimed in his diary that he wrote a "stiff letter" in reply to Ripon.[63] But in fact Gladstone attempted (somewhat obliquely) to make a conciliatory statement. Still, he did not retract, and he reiterated his belief that Ripon was bound to believe what the pope decreed in matters of faith and morals, which Gladstone interpreted widely as covering most of human conduct.[64] The argument continued through an exchange of letters, with Ripon alternately fishing for an outright apology and denouncing Gladstone's views. Gladstone, for his part, tried to remain on friendly terms, while holding to his notion of the impossibility of simultaneous loyalty to both pope and civil state. "I do not think you 'likely to be wanting in civil loyalty & duty,'" he wrote to Ripon. "I think the very reverse, & am most ready to say so in the most formal and public manner." In the very next sentence, he hedged: "But I think loyalty & civil duty might make just calls upon you, which would require you to break with the principles of the system you have been led to embrace." Gladstone's final word attempted to square the circle of his friendship with Ripon while impugning Ripon's reasoning. "My opinion is that you will refuse consequences which you are logically bound to accept."[65]

Gladstone's reactions to apostasy were not grounded in fundamental anti-Catholic sentiments. He made a clear distinction between the body of the Roman Catholic Church and what he called Romanism—which included the exalted authority of the papacy, ultramontanism, and Mariolatry.[66] Papal pretensions to secular power were an especial anathema to Gladstone, in part because he believed that he had himself been a victim of them. The defeat of the Irish University bill, and the consequent decline of his ministry, could be laid directly at the door of the papacy. The pope had instructed the Irish bishops to defeat the bill. That Lord Ripon should have sided with the pope was too much to bear.

Undoubtedly Gladstone's behavior also reflected a deeper psychological reaction. As Colin Matthew has observed, Gladstone's earlier painful experiences with the apostasy of his sister, and of his friends Manning and Hope, had not been purgative. He bore the emotional scars still—scars that had now been opened by the events of the last months of his ministry. That mysterious mixture of religion and authority bound up in the pope, beyond Gladstone's control, prompted a recurring trauma he experienced at vulnerable times in his life. Following his typical pattern, Gladstone struck out against symbolic enemies on whom he could vent his rage. Ripon bore the brunt of Gladstone's hurt and anger because he had been a member of the very ministry that the pope had helped bring down. Indeed, Ripon's suspicion that his conversion had been the cause of Gladstone's insertion of the offending clause in "Ritual and Ritualism" was probably well founded.[67]

However personally helpful Gladstone's pursuit of a psychological strategy
of coherence may have been after January 1874, his behavior had been harmful
to his political fortunes. His pamphlet war against the pope and Catholic
converts had exacerbated the leadership difficulties of the Liberals. A general
murmur of complaint against Gladstone grew during the parliamentary session of 1874. His erratic—and, to some, irresponsible—behavior had to be
curbed. By the end of 1874, complaints against Gladstone had been voiced
by a wide spectrum of Liberals, from the radical Sir Charles Dilke (who
thought Gladstone was "in the sulks") to the Whiggish Argyll (who believed
that Gladstone had seduced and abandoned the Liberal Party).[68] That rising
Liberal star, expert on international law, and resolutely cantankerous parliamentarian Sir William Harcourt took a particularly strong anti-Gladstonian
tack. Harcourt declaimed widely against Gladstone's "temper and passion,"
his "wild proposals" and "flighty nature," and his "sudden impulses."[69]

Gladstone was aware of these developments. In January 1875, he resigned
his already tenuous hold on the party leadership. This had not been an easy
decision. Characteristically, he set down in a memorandum the arguments
for and against, as though to understand his own behavior. He had certainly
no physical reason to resign. A favorable medical examination "makes it impossible for me to plead health," he confided to Catherine. His wife was
genuinely puzzled by his decision and argued against it. He admitted that if
there had been special and temporary causes "pointing to some important
public purpose," he might have decided differently. Above all, he was glad
to be rid of "all the old taint of indiscipline and spurious independence"
among Liberal M.P.s.[70] In any case, the party accepted his resignation. His
replacement by two Whigs—a diffident Lord Hartington in the House of
Commons and an acquiescent Granville in the Lords—marked a perceptible
shift to the right. Their leadership also introduced a far less intrusive managerial style than had been the norm in the Gladstone years.

Some have argued that Gladstone's behavior during the leadership crisis
of 1874–75 was a calculated strategy. By appearing to withdraw from the party,
Gladstone could punish errant Liberal M.P.s for their disloyalty and could
later resume the leadership once the lesson had taken hold.[71] But Gladstone's
behavior was too thoroughly divisive and destructive of Liberal party fortunes
for it to have been a considered policy of reconstruction. His behavior can
more likely be accounted for as a psychological working through of the
stresses of his political life, and an attempt to reestablish a sense of control
and direction. After his retirement from the leadership, he steadily withdrew
from public life. Increasingly drawn toward religious reading and writing, he
spent the early weeks of 1875 preparing yet another pamphlet on Vaticanism—
this time a rebuttal of his critics. Rarely did he appear at the House of

Commons. When in attendance, he seldom spoke, and only then to denounce the Conservatives. Gladstone was "hot & angry & very verbose" on the budget, according to Gathorne Hardy, the Conservative secretary of state for War. Disraeli was more colorful in his description: Gladstone, he said, came down "like the Dragon of Wantley breathing fire and fury on some of our financial bills."[72]

Gladstone felt increasingly out of tune with politics of the day and with life in London. "I seem to feel as one who has passed through a death," he wrote in his diary, but, he added—perhaps wistfully—he also felt as though he had "emerged into a better life."[73] He went through a painful and difficult period of transition. He gave up the house at Carlton House Terrace, which he had held for nearly thirty years, and took a lease on a smaller house nearby. His household contents were largely dispersed. He sold his collection of china and Wedgewood. His books were packed—he did much of this work himself—for shipment to Hawarden. His decision brought distressing conversations with Catherine, who regarded the dissolution of their home "with discomfort & reluctance."[74] But Gladstone was undeterred. He was determined to continue "unwinding the coil of life." Much yet needed to be done before the "business of solemn recollection & preparation" was complete.[75] Gladstone little knew what form that preparation might take.

9

Gladstone Redivivus

Gladstone's pattern of withdrawal from political life was consistent over many years. But his withdrawals were never lulls in his thinking or writing or managing his own affairs. He remained active during the years of his retirement from the Liberal leadership in the late 1870s, as his diaries reveal. Keeping busy was his way of overcoming aversive circumstances. "The habit of my life," he wrote in 1875, "makes me turn my eyes off a disagreeable resolution when once adopted it [sic], and go to work on giving it effect as if taking physic."[1] These withdrawals were always temporary; from a distance, he invariably prepared for an eventual return to political life. Had his political colleagues understood this pattern, they would have been less puzzled by his swings of temperament and action, and they could have predicted with more accuracy his political behavior.

His contemporaries, however, were at a loss to explain his behavior. To some, his renewed enthusiasm for religious writing in his retirement made him a kind of lay ecclesiastic—the "hermit of Hawarden."[2] That he was fundamentally religiously minded is undoubtedly true, and Colin Matthew has made a strong case for the significance of Gladstone's theological preoccupations during his retirement. Yet it is important not to overplay his religious motivation. One can plausibly argue that his religious concerns, attaining dominance in his thought at this time of his career, acted as the most efficacious means of mastering uncomfortable political and personal problems. When the time was once again propitious, he would again step forward, refreshed by his absences from the stresses of political life.

When the opportunity for Gladstone to resume an active role in politics came during the 1870s, he was slow to recognize it, in part because the events germane to his reemergence to power were distant and unfamiliar. They began in the summer of 1875, when Serbian subjects revolted against the Turkish empire. Disorder spread throughout the Slavic populations in European Turkey. By May of 1876, anti-Turkish sentiment had stirred the Bulgarians in Eastern Rumelia. Thus provoked, the Turks indiscriminately slaughtered thousands of Bulgarian civilians, many of whom were women and children.[3] Persistent reports from independent newspaper correspondents provided proof of the atrocities. Lead stories in the *Daily News* and the *Times* gave details of arson, sodomy, rape, and torture. The Turks, with their infidel religion and dissolute harems, had not merely murdered the innocent; they had also committed unspeakable offenses against women. More to the point, these were Christian women. As the news reached Britain during the summer of 1876, the public spontaneously reacted in outrage against Disraeli's Turcophilic policy. Protest meetings at the grassroots level took place around the country. By the end of August, nearly five hundred demonstrations had been held.

As the fervor grew in the countryside, Gladstone at first remained aloof. His reasons for avoiding the agitation for so long, and for deciding at last to become an active participant, are not entirely clear. Shannon believes that Gladstone was simply slow in realizing that the agitation provided a renewed opportunity for a "moral rapport" between himself and the British masses, which had been broken in 1874. Matthew sees Gladstone's revived political activity as an indication of a "refurbished" interest in Evangelicalism; that is, he had received a specific call from God to act. Saab makes the case that Gladstone was uncomfortably ambivalent about Britain's traditional policy toward Turkey. On the one hand, he understood the need for a dominant British influence in the eastern Mediterranean; on the other hand, he believed that the Ottomans were corrupt and intolerant. Saab claims that Gladstone, unable to maintain these contradictory views, was finally shamed into taking a position by a request for action from a trade union member.[4]

One may also argue that Gladstone's need for control could never be fully satisfied in retirement. It would therefore be natural for him to turn to public oratory as the avenue for a reentry into political life, in order to hear once again the adulation from the massed thousands who would likely support any standard he might raise. Gladstone was also well aware that leading a popular movement could have beneficial consequences for the Liberals and for his own political career. "I really hope that on this Eastern matter the pot will be kept boiling," he wrote to Granville. "Good ends can rarely be attained in politics without passion: and there is now, the first time for a good many years, a virtuous passion."⁵ Gladstone's oratorical exercises in the countryside were fundamental to his strategy as it evolved during the following weeks. Speaking engagements were supplemented by a published pronouncement— one of the most dramatically stated of all his writings. "The Bulgarian Horrors and the Question of the East" was a runaway best-seller.

A few days after its publication, Gladstone addressed a crowd of ten thousand at Blackheath on the subject of the "Horrors." In an hour-long speech, he held the audience in rapt attention as he tolled the sins of the Turks: "So far as it is in our power to determine, never again shall the hand of violence be raised by you, never again shall the flood-gates of lust be open to you, never again shall the dire refinements of cruelty be devised by you for the sake of making mankind miserable."⁶ The following month, he went into friendly Cheshire and Lancashire, in part for a brief holiday but also to keep the pot boiling. He had, as he confessed to Granville, the greatest difficulty "avoiding strong manifestations." "I never saw such keen exhibitions of the popular feeling, appearing so to pervade all ranks and places." Granville hastened to advise caution: "If I were you, I should contrive to avoid further utterances for the present moment." But Gladstone was firm: "I must make a further utterance . . . notwithstanding your opinion."⁷

Gladstone's independent campaign clearly worried Liberal Party leaders. He had no official standing in the party and had often been an absentee backbencher during recent parliamentary sessions. What was he up to? Fearful of the consequences of Gladstone's unpredictable behavior, especially as it could develop during a national campaign, both Hartington and Granville tried to dampen Gladstone's revived enthusiasm for public life. They were apprehensive that his leadership of the Bulgarian agitation would bind the Liberal Party to unacceptable policies, thus further dividing it in the face of a united Conservative government. In fact, this had already begun to happen. Gladstone's demand that Turkey withdraw from Bulgaria and the other European provinces was thought impracticable by both Forster and Hartington. So firmly did Hartington object to Gladstone's unauthorized extraparliamentary campaign that he contemplated resignation as party leader.⁸ Although he denied his own ambitions and desire for party leadership, Gladstone's continuing attempts to goad his colleagues had a presumptuous and commanding air about them. Even after the initial flurry of atrocity meetings had died down during the autumn of 1876, he kept up the pressure. In January 1877, he wrote to Granville that public sentiment remained strongly anti-Turk, and "while my own course is in principle perfectly clear and plain, I think that you and Hartington will soon have to make up your mind on a great question, namely the attitude you are to assume with reference to this great popular conviction."⁹

The Bulgarian agitation, apart from drawing Gladstone out of retirement and ruffling the feathers of the official Liberal leadership, had little immediate influence on the Conservative government's policy. Disraeli largely ignored it and refused to call Parliament into emergency session. But in the spring of 1877, the Eastern question suddenly became a European-wide concern. Russia, motivated by an ancient animosity and a newer pan-Slavism, had watched with a heightened concern the events in the Balkans. The protection of Balkan Christians provided a perfect pretext for armed intervention. In April 1877, Russia declared war on Turkey. The Russian military threat posed a significant question for the Disraeli government. How far should Britain support Turkey against Russia? If Disraeli abandoned Turkey, Russia might well advance to the Bosporus, threatening Britain's vital interests in the Near East—perhaps endangering the route to India. If Britain held fast, war with Russia was even more likely. For the first time since the Crimean War, a major European conflict appeared likely.

Gladstone believed that the Russo-Turkish War provided an opportunity to coerce Turkey into more acceptable channels of international behavior. The British people had had their say in the recent campaign against the Turks; now it was the turn of their representatives. Parliament must take the lead. "Is not the moment now come for raising the rather stiff question whether a policy . . . is to be submitted to Parliament?" he asked of Granville.[10] In answer to his own question, Gladstone drafted the "Five Resolutions," which condemned Turkey and urged British support for a policy of emancipation of subject peoples in the Balkans.

Once the news of Gladstone's intention was made known, the Liberal leadership was up in arms. Hartington would not endorse the resolutions. Harcourt was reported to be "boiling over with rage," for he believed that Gladstone's resolutions could only consolidate Conservative support and thus strengthen Disraeli's hand. Granville (in his most polite tone) reported to Gladstone that the leadership, having met, decided that "it was not opportune" to move his resolutions.[11] The greatest danger of all was a fatal division in the Liberal ranks: the radical wing of the party, among whom Chamberlain and Dilke were emerging as the most prominent, favored the resolutions and, indeed, hoped for a split and the eventual weakening of the Whig-Liberals. As Dilke gleefully wrote in his diary on 3 May, "The Liberal party will next week cease to exist."[12]

This was a crisis of the first order for the Liberals. Even Gladstone believed that things had gone too far. "This is a dreadful mess," he acknowledged to Granville.[13] As the day approached for the resolutions to be debated in the House of Commons, a compromise was worked out whereby Gladstone would withdraw two of the resolutions and modify a third. Hartington then agreed to support the rump resolutions. So late was the compromise reached, however, that few parliamentarians knew of it. This led to considerable confusion during the debate of 7 May. Gladstone was queried, jostled, and harried, mostly by Liberals, as to his intentions. "For over two hours," as Gladstone recorded his experience, "I was assaulted from every quarter, except the Opposition [Front] Bench which was virtually silent. Such a sense of solitary struggle I never remember."[14] The vote at the conclusion of the debate went heavily against the Liberal resolutions (354 to 223). Some seventy M.P.s who accepted the Liberal whip either abstained or voted with the Conservatives. This was the lowest point for Liberal fortunes during Disraeli's ministry. The Conservatives were in the comfortable position of watching the Liberals tear themselves apart.

It is difficult not to fault Gladstone for his seminal role in Liberal misfortunes. By attempting to impose a solution on the leadership, he had divided the party. Adopting an independent line, he tried to establish personal dominance. He had exasperated the Liberal leadership by recognizing their legitimacy as leaders yet acting as though he owed no allegiance to them. He appeared rigid and uncompromising, and a restless and irresponsible member of the party. Wounded by his colleagues' antagonism and distressed by Disraeli's continuing triumphs, Gladstone again retreated. "Since taking bodily to the Eastern Question last September," he wrote in his diary after arriving at Hawarden, "I have not known order or peace." But he was determined to rectify matters. That very day, he set out to arrange his books and papers. "Attacked my Chaos," he recorded, "which is worse than ever."[15] "Worked five hours on searching and arranging letters," he entered the next week. The following day: "Four more hours enabled to make my personal selections &c. & give final order to my letters of 1871–6. This correspondence has more than doubled since I left office."[16] The relentless cutting and kibbling of trees and bringing order to the grounds of the estate provided additional diversions. Such local events as the Hawarden Flower Show, the Hawarden School Prize Day, and walks with Catherine were also soothing.

A surer source of pleasure for Gladstone was travel. In late October and early November, Gladstone undertook a journey to Ireland—the first of only two he ever made. The press speculated as to his reason for going, but the trip seems to have been prompted in part by curiosity about Irish conditions: "There is much to observe & learn," as Gladstone himself put it.[17] Indeed, the Bulgarian agitation may have sensitized him to Irish problems.[18] Ireland could easily be likened to a Balkan country whose nationality was suppressed by a superior power. Gladstone's timing may also have been governed by his desire to escape the painful scenes of Liberal disarray and Disraeli's dominance at home.

Where Gladstone went, politics were sure to follow. For him to enter Ireland at a time of increased Home Rule sentiment made Granville, for one, nervous. "I suppose you will either remain quite silent," he wrote Gladstone, "or speak only on some question affecting the material prosperity, or artistic development of the Irish." Religious issues especially, he cautioned, could be touchy.[19] To Granville's relief, Gladstone seemed to hold his tongue. From Powerscourt—now a mournful ruin set within magnificent gardens—Gladstone assured Granville that he would "get back with my design of privacy fully accomplished." Only when he returned to Hawarden in November did Gladstone expand his views on Irish politics. Had the Home Rulers a "real leader," he believed that some accommodation could be made. As for himself, Gladstone informed Granville, he was much more disposed than the average Liberal to give some countenance to the notion of local government to Ireland. "On this subject however my lips have been closed," he told Granville.[20]

This was not quite true. During the acceptance speech he made when presented with the freedom of the City of Dublin, Gladstone took the occasion to praise local government, and in that message was a ticking time bomb. "I am profoundly convinced," he stated to the assembled notables at the City Hall, "that local government . . . is fundamental to the greatness of the country and its institutions." After the applause had died away, Gladstone went on to say that the tendency toward central control, all too noticeable in recent years, was a movement in the wrong direction: "Instead of abridging the power of those local institutions we ought to seek to extend it."[21] These ideas were lost in the larger speech, but it was not difficult to connect Home Rule for Ireland with the notion of local government broadly conceived. Gladstone realized what a premonition his words could be: he confided to his diary that night that in his speech, he had been "treading upon eggs the whole time."[22] The germ of Gladstone's Home Rule policy as it developed during the next decade was evident on that Dublin day.

While Gladstone remained essentially in political and personal retreat, Disraeli went from triumph to triumph. In a series of dazzling diplomatic maneuvers during the spring and summer of 1877, the Conservative prime minister adroitly countered Russian military successes. When the Russians forced upon Turkey in March the punitive Treaty of San Stefano, effectively dismantling Turkey-in-Europe and erecting client Balkan states (including a significantly enlarged Bulgaria), Britain rejected the treaty, calling instead for a European conference to settle the terms of the peace. To place additional pressure on Russia, Disraeli called up reserve forces in England and summoned seven thousand Indian troops to Malta in a dramatic demonstration of British imperial power. Britain also entered into a direct dialogue with Russia. The Anglo-Russian Conventions, held in May, were largely successful in blunting the Russian advance. Simultaneous with the conventions, Britain entered into secret talks with Turkey—the Cyprus Convention—by which Turkey promised better safeguards for its Christian subjects and ceded Cyprus to Britain, which in turn promised a defensive alliance with Turkey. A climactic triumph at the Congress of Berlin in June and July earned Disraeli additional laurels. He returned home with his reputation at its highest, having gained, in his famous phrase, "Peace with Honour."

At every stage of Disraeli's diplomatic processional, Gladstone and the Liberals spoke out, but with diminishing effect. Their popularity steadily waned, as a wave of patriotic conservatism swept the country. In London, violence broke out as crowds demonstrated noisily at Trafalgar Square, stormed Liberal meetings, and cheered mightily in Downing Street. The so-called Jingoes made Gladstone their target. Posters denounced him as a traitor, and his effigy was burned at some gatherings. In February 1878, a hostile crowd surged into Harley Street up to Gladstone's house and broke windows. A fortnight later, Gladstone and his wife were forced into a neighboring house by the crowd, then spirited away in a hansom cab with constables as outriders.[23]

Yet all was not well with the Conservative government. Unknown to Gladstone and to the country at large, the Russo-Turkish War revealed serious divisions within the cabinet. Disraeli, who was probably exaggerating for effect, counted seven different factions, ranging from the war party led by Gathorne Hardy to a peace party led by the foreign secretary, Lord Derby.[24] These Conservative disagreements over policy were a sign of the misfortunes to come. Within eighteen months of the Congress of Berlin, the popularity of the Conservatives had declined precipitously. Wars in Afghanistan and South Africa showed the limitations of aggressive imperialism. Expected military drains on the budget meant that taxes would likely increase. Concurrently, a trade depression and a simultaneous slump in agricultural prices made 1879 one of the worst years in recent British economic history. Unemployment had more than doubled since 1877—from 4.7 percent to 11.4 percent.

The Liberals at last had electable issues. Heartened by the Disraelian disasters, they took the offensive. Gladstone, like his Liberal colleagues, hammered away at the Conservatives in Parliament. He drew together the various strands of Conservative policy and presented them coherently as a failed program of "Beaconsfieldism." His greatest contribution to the campaign was his extraparliamentary agitation, perfected over the years. In January 1879, Gladstone, having decided to surrender his Greenwich seat, began negotiating for another. He accepted Edinburghshire, a county constituency popularly known as Midlothian. By late 1879, Gladstone had decided to cultivate his new constituency in the event of a parliamentary dissolution. Thus began the most famous election campaign of the nineteenth century. His withdrawal from the parliamentary stage neared its end.

On the morning of 24 November 1879, Gladstone, with his wife and political entourage in tow, steamed out of Liverpool station. Their destination was the capital of Scotland, his ancestral land. Well before his special train had crossed the Scots border, Gladstone's trip had become a triumphal procession. At St. Helens, Wigan, and Preston in Lancashire, the train was cheered by assembled crowds as it rumbled through. At Carlisle, local luminaries crowded onto the station platform to escort him to the County Hotel, where he delivered a short speech to a Liberal gathering of five to six hundred. Back on the train, he crossed the border to Hawick for a few words to a large crowd around the station. Then on through St. Boswells and Melrose—where again crowds cheered his passage—to Galashiels, where an estimated eight thousand heard his brief speech. Not until evening did Gladstone pull into Edinburgh, where he was again met by an immense throng. He spent that night at Dalmeny House, the home of Lord Rosebery, a rising Scots politician and one of the engineers of the campaign.

The following day, he spoke at the Edinburgh Music Hall and the City Hall, thus beginning officially the campaign for Midlothian. In all, Gladstone spoke thirty times to more than eighty-five thousand people for a grand total of fifteen and a half hours during that fortnight.[25] Tens of thousands more read his speeches in the newspapers. By speaking day after day, often before substantial audiences (twenty thousand gathered at the Waverley Market in Edinburgh), he could control the political news of the national and provincial newspaper press.[26] Gladstone was first among Victorian politicians to use consistently a saturation effect in managing the media. His speeches, when read today, do not reveal the impact that Gladstone had on his Midlothian audiences. Indeed, their substance was often unexceptional, rarely laced with flashing metaphors or the vituperative outbursts that characterized his parliamentary performances. At West Calder, for example, he spoke about crop production, declining land values, and the intricacies of the malt tax. He did, however, effectively indict the Conservative government's foreign and imperial policy, both generally and in specific terms. He condemned a "deficiency of six millions in England, confusion of finance in India, war in South Africa, war in Afghanistan," as he put it to the crowd at the Dunfermline Railway Station.[27] He made imperial failures a special object of censure. England had no reason, he told a crowd of more than three thousand at Dalkeith, to "load itself with a multitude of needless and mischievous engagements."[28]

The sight of Gladstone dashing about the Scots hills, speaking to large crowds and small, often from the back of his train, caught the imagination of the country. Never had a politician of such stature thrown himself with so much energy into an election campaign. Where Gladstone shone was in his presentation: he was a "tremendous old trooper," always giving a good performance.[29] To see Gladstone in top form, to hear his voice, and to catch a glimpse of the famous eye were the supreme attraction for the crowds. Granville had once observed during the days of the Bulgarian agitation that it was sometimes difficult to determine whether a genuine popular sentiment existed in a Gladstone crowd: the excitement was often created by Gladstone himself.[30] Gladstone, in turn, fed on the enthusiasm of the crowds. He was naturally buoyed by a good response to his speeches; he found a cheering and

demonstrative crowd far more satisfying than a speech-hardened and politically sophisticated Parliament. From the first evening, when he was received
"with fireworks & torches" at Lord Rosebery's Dalmeny House, to the daily
enthusiasm he noted on the road, his diary reveals his pleasure during the
campaign. At the "wonderful" meeting in Waverley Market, the press of
people was so great that many fainted and "were continually handed out over
the heads" of the others. The high point of the campaign was probably Glasgow, where Gladstone described the torchlight procession welcoming him on
the evening of 4 December as a "subject for Turner" (always his highest
praise). The following day, he spoke at four separate occasions, including his
inaugural address as Lord Rector of the University of Glasgow. His departure
the next day from Glasgow "was *royal*."[31]

The reaction to the Midlothian Campaign, both then and later, was varied. Historians have not agreed on its influence. Morley, who was present
during Gladstone's whirlwind tour of Glasgow and who heard him at first
hand, is at his most lyrical: "The campaign," he wrote, "had a soul in it."
When the campaign was over, Morley concluded that Gladstone's "tremendous projectiles had pounded the ministerial citadel to the ground."[32] Shannon, who is less certain about the impact of the campaign, believes that
Disraeli's own errors were most at fault for the unpopularity of the government.[33] The opinions of contemporaries, as one would expect, varied enor-
mously, and they seem to have been dictated by party allegiances. Disraeli
dismissed the campaign as "wearisome rhetoric." Gathorne Hardy (now promoted to the Lords as Viscount Cranbrook) was also predictably harsh, calling Gladstone's speechifying "without novelty and disgracefully bitter." Lord
George Hamilton, vice-president of the council under Disraeli and brother-
in-law to Lord Dalkeith—whose seat Gladstone was contesting in Midlothian—was no less critical. In a speech to the Conservative Association of
the University of Edinburgh, Hamilton criticized Gladstone as a "man of
high-strung, nervous temperament" whose "verbosity" was "a positive danger"
to the country.[34] In contrast, the Liberal Lord Ripon—now on friendly terms
with Gladstone after the news of his apostasy had settled down—was complimentary. "Gladstone's speeches in Midlothian are good," he wrote in his
diary; "he is evidently in his best mood & is speaking cautiously."[35]

Whatever critics thought, the country was enthralled. None could match
Gladstone's energy. None could present the details of the Liberal program
with such force. The conclusion was obvious. Only Gladstone could lead the
party into the next general election. Hartington, as quick as any to recognize
the inevitable, offered to resign as party leader. He was eventually dissuaded,
and a compromise was reached whereby the Liberal leadership should remain
as it was until after an election.[36] Little doubt remains that Gladstone's sustained campaign against Disraeli—reminiscent of his earlier attacks on Lord

Palmerston—had not only been a successful personal strategy but had also restored his career.

Although Gladstone's public life was looking up during the late 1870s, his private life remained less open to scrutiny. Subterranean stories and rumors about his relationships with prostitutes continued to circulate. During the Bulgarian Agitation in 1876, a campaign of anonymous letters had charged, among other allegations, that Gladstone requested a prostitute to strip naked, sit on his knee, and relate the story of her seduction and fall. Through this means, Gladstone was aroused and could have sexual intercourse with the prostitute. Afterward, he prayed. Another rumor had it that when Gladstone visited his friend Pastor Dollinger at Tegernsee in the Tyrol, he took a fancy to a household servant. The informant was told the tale by the servant's older sister, who was in service at a villa nearby.[37]

Gladstone's persistent habit of walking the streets at night in the company of women who were obviously prostitutes certainly lent credibility to these stories. In one well-documented case in 1882, he was seen in the company of a woman dressed in black satin walking down the steps at the duke of York's column at half past eleven in the evening. One witness was the Tory M.P. for Leitrim, Arthur Loftus Tottenham, who made free with his observations at the Carlton Club. A second witness was W. W. Parkinson, master of a workhouse to Bermondsey, who was shocked enough to write directly to Gladstone. "Had I seen the Heavens open & an angel descend & said such a thing [as I saw], I should have asked the Earth to open & swallow that angel as a liar."[38]

None of these rumors contains any evidence of Gladstone's infatuation with or sexual interest in women other than his wife. But it was an entirely different matter with Laura Thistlethwayte, who exerted a strange fascination for Gladstone over many years.[39] Her story remains the most remarkable of all the tales of women who attracted Gladstone. He first met her sometime in 1864, perhaps while riding in Rotten Row. She was the daughter of a Captain Bell, from County Antrim. As a young woman, she came to London and drifted into a distinctly raffish set. Her beauty and lively personality made her widely known: it is said that her departure from the Opera one night in 1852 brought the whole house to its feet to watch her go. Her marriage that same year to Captain Augustus Frederick Thistlethwayte, a man of some means and respectability, brought an end to her career as a courtesan. Their union was not a happy one, however; the Captain seems to have had a violent streak, often summoning his servants by firing a pistol into the ceiling. Sometime after her marriage, probably in the early 1860s, she became a convert to an obscure religious sect, a kind of ethical Christianity, the doctrines of which she occasionally expounded in public lectures at the London Polytechnic. Here Gladstone once heard her, though without praise: the experience was one he did "not much wish to repeat."[40]

Not until the summer and autumn of 1869 did their relationship enter a distinctly intimate phase. Gladstone's diary records the stages of their attraction. After he had dined with the Thistlethwaytes one July evening, she promised to send him "some personal history."[41] The following month, she wrote Gladstone a letter praising his *Juventus Mundi,* a book of fantastic theories just off the press that purported to show classical Greek mythological heroes as progenitors to the development of Christianity: Christ, for example, had been foreshadowed by Apollo, the Trinity by a combination of Zeus, Poseidon, and Hades, and so on. She also sent him a gift of grouse.

In September, she began sending the promised autobiography, which arrived in twenty-three separate installments. Mrs. Thistlethwayte had learned the lesson of Victorian serial writing: Gladstone hung on every word until the next batch arrived. He was "spell bound," as he put it.[42] Responding sympathetically to the tale unfolding in the manuscript, he received in turn deep expressions of appreciation from Thistlethwayte. Their bond grew stronger. "I am sensible that you have shown me a *great* confidence," he wrote.[43] Because the autobiography has been lost, its contents are unknown, but it seems to have been a detailed story of childhood adventures and misfortunes. "It is like a story from the Arabian Nights, with much added to it," Gladstone believed.[44]

Clearly Thistlethwayte struck a responsive chord in Gladstone. Because she was practiced in the arts of seduction, she may have naturally enticed men. Or perhaps she told her story to Gladstone with the hope that, in some way, he would rescue her. Her unhappy marriage may have impelled her to seek someone who could validate her past and thus justify her life. Gladstone, supremely powerful in politics and relentlessly moral in outlook, was an answer to her prayers. From what we know of Gladstone, we can state more confidently the reasons for his attraction. Thistlethwayte had a unique combination of qualities that drew him to her. Matthew captures these perfectly: she was "educated enough to understand something of his mind, young enough to offer beauty, religious enough to seem redeemed, but exotic enough to stand outside the ring of society women" with whom he usually associated.[45] She was the perfect paradox of an "evangelical ex-courtesan."[46] In one of the few times Gladstone mentioned her to his wife, he described her as a "very singular person, with great beauty still, I thought about eyes brow & ears, and most thoroughly and entirely Irish but full of ardent good impulses with unbounded expression in words."[47] Her emergence as a female confidante was also timely. The duchess of Sutherland, Gladstone's great friend, had died less than a year earlier.[48]

In late October Gladstone, now fully enmeshed in Thistlethwayte's artful autobiographical narrative, confided to his diary, "Narrative and letters taken together I am indeed astonished, though interested, & bound in honour to do the best I can for her if she really needs it."[49] By then, the two had begun trading personal secrets and making the little confessions to one another that lovers do. For the biographer of Gladstone, these revelations are the most important part of the correspondence. "I have not a good opinion of myself!" exclaimed Gladstone in one letter.[50] In another revealing letter, he told her: "From morning to night, all my life is pressure, pressure to get on, to despatch the thing I have in hand, that I may go on to the next urgently waiting for me. Not for years past have I written except in haste a letter to my wife. As for my children they rarely get any. In honesty, can you *conceive* such a state of life?"[51]

Soon they were discussing a topic that Gladstone could not bring himself to write about explicitly but that he summarized as a "great, deep, weighty word." Presumably the word was love.[52] By now, their relationship was moving forward rapidly. He had begun to address her as "Dear Spirit," they had exchanged photographs, and he had accepted the gift of a ring from her. When state business allowed, he squeezed in brief visits to her. He was with her on Friday, 12 November 1869; sent her verses the next day; and saw her twice on the fifteenth and once on the following day just as he was leaving town to dine with the queen. On the seventeenth, after his return from Windsor, he saw her again. On the eighteenth, he visited her for an hour and a half in the early evening; they "talked of deep matters."[53] Interspersed with these visits were notes and letters. (Her letters to him were sent in specially marked envelopes to avoid prying official eyes.) Gladstone was well aware of the direction and danger of his relationship: "Duty and evil temptation are there before me," he wrote in his diary, both "on the right & left."[54]

On 1 November he wrote her—in his sententious way—his most explicit love letter. "You brought me," he assured her, "into the interior of a human life, and a human heart. You laid a heavy debt upon me, and though I may be unable to pay it, believe that I do not think lightly of it. . . . We are accumulating matters for those conversations which I hope will be long and unreserved. . . . To avoid the deep things would be difficult for me, since all nearly that has passed is deep." He concluded with a postscript: "I cannot forgive your photograph for not showing the eyes."[55]

Their chance for long and unreserved conversation came in December, when Gladstone, along with Arthur Kinnaird, an old friend and Whig M.P. for Perth, visited the Thistlethwayte country house at Boveridge, Dorset, for the weekend. These few days seem to have been the climax of their relationship. He was with her that Saturday, and on the Sabbath, they walked together and spoke at length. And, in the most intriguing entry in his diary, "Mrs Th. came to my rooms aft. & at night."[56] They found time again the next day to be much together: he accompanied her to a local "meet" at a neighboring house, and afterward she accompanied him and Kinnaird to the station for their return to London. "On the journey to London," Gladstone wrote, "I thought of you all the way."[57] He recalled a "little group of images" that dwelt within his memory: "L. driving, L. riding, L. in red, L. in red & black as she walked on Sunday."[58] To his diary, he confided, "How very far I was at first from understanding her history and also her character."[59]

Precisely what Gladstone intended by this last diary entry may never be known, but the entry contains a slight hint of coolness. However flattered he was by the attentions of a younger woman, his sense of reality intruded and prevented a loss of control that he had experienced in earlier similar cases with Elizabeth Collins and Maria Summerhayes. Maintaining control was doubtless a relatively easy task for a man of sixty. His infatuation was checked by a sense of his public obligations and checked, too, by the settled pattern of his domestic life. Within a few days after his return from Boveridge, he spoke both to his wife and to G. G. Glyn, the Liberal whip, about Thistlethwayte.[60] What he revealed is not known, but he seems to have limited further intimacy with her. Thereafter he was determined to "build up her married life into greater fullness and firmness not withstanding the agonies out of which it came & in which it grew."[61] In April, Gladstone wrote to her in a tone that is difficult to construe as other than circumspect: he urged in her "self-command."[62] Perhaps she had been too importunate. A diary entry in February 1870 hints as much. After he had been to see her at "15 G. S."—that is, 15 Grosvenor Square, the Thistlethwayte London residence—he entered in his diary, "This is a case with an extraordinary claim for sympathy arising from an unparalleled history: but it embarrasses."[63] Gladstone must have known that the frequency of his contact with her was a matter of public knowledge. Lord Derby, having heard the "strange story" of Gladstone and Mrs. Thistlethwayte, was scandalized to learn that he intended to visit her and her husband at Boveridge. As early as 1866, Lord Carnarvon had learned of Gladstone's "passion" from Northcote; Carnarvon thought Gladstone must be "going out of his mind."[64]

Gladstone had flown close to the fire, but he had veered in time. Yet he was tempted by Thistlethwayte well into the 1870s, as his diaries confirm. He continued to send and receive letters and notes from her, he advised her on personal matters, he dined with her, and he went to the theater with her. The diaries indicate their frequency of contact. In 1871, Gladstone either saw her or corresponded with her in some way no less than seventy-five times; the following year, seventy times—even though she was abroad from early February until late June. ("It is well for me that she goes," Gladstone noted upon her departure.)[65] She remained a source of perplexity and attraction for him. In April 1871, their intimacy of fifteen months earlier seems to have resumed. On 17 April, he wrote, "Saw Mrs Th—wonder." Three days later: "Mrs Th. late: more wonder." On 29 April, he wrote in his diary—no less tantalizingly—"Saw Mrs Th. . . . It was the climax of our communications."[66] More than a year later, strong affect between the two remained: he wrote in his diary in November 1872, "Saw Mrs Th. It was distressing: & left me much to ruminate upon: but it was good."[67] Sometimes, Thistlethwayte even served as a point of contact with important officials. It was at her house that several meetings during the Bulgarian agitation took place, including one with the Russian ambassador, Count Shuvalov, in December 1876.

Ultimately, Thistlethwayte was a source of potential scandal for Gladstone, not only because of her dubious past and lack of social standing but also because of the increasingly tangled Thistlethwayte finances. For a time it appeared that she would be summoned to debtor's court, and Gladstone forced to testify as a witness (he was actually issued a subpoena). The case was eventually settled out of court in 1879.[68] Thus, for Gladstone, the final episode of what could have been a damaging sexual intrigue was put to rest well before the general election of 1880.[69] He had been more fortunate than other Victorian politicians, such as Sir Charles Dilke and Charles Stewart Parnell, who were involved in sexual scandals. He was luckier, too, than the post-Victorian H. H. Asquith, who was also smitten with a younger, unavailable woman. Perhaps he was even luckier than Disraeli, who fell for the beautiful Lady Bradford in his old age.[70] Gladstone had retained his sense of dignity and his aloofness, and above all, he remained in control.

10

"The Host of Pharaoh"

In spite of Gladstone's Midlothian Campaign, two by-elections won by the Conservatives in early 1880 suggested that the electorate remained loyal to Disraeli's government. Seizing the opportunity, Disraeli called a general election in March 1880. But he had miscalculated: final returns were 351 for the Liberals, 239 for the Conservatives, and 62 for the Home Rulers. The Liberals dominated the election campaign, and Gladstone played the salient role in this, his twelfth general election. His catalogue of the failures of Beaconsfieldism, first enunciated during his Midlothian triumph of only a few months before, were drummed home to his own constituency and to the electorate at large.[1] Gladstone's strong showing posed a dilemma for the Liberals. Still officially in retirement as leader of the party, he was less popular among the Liberal elite than in the countryside, where he had consolidated his hold on the public imagination. Indeed, some Liberals—especially moderates and Whigs—were concerned that Gladstone's pattern of impulsive and erratic behavior since 1875 might continue. But as party leaders knew, Gladstone's mastery of the issues, unflagging energy, and financial expertise made him the natural choice for prime minister.[2]

From the first Gladstone was determined to control his government, as he had in the past. He became not only First Lord of the Treasury and leader of the House but also chancellor of the Exchequer. In addition, he took an active part in framing the most important legislation of the ministry. His diaries reveal his usual intensity and abundant preparation on parliamentary issues. He read widely, maintained an extensive correspondence, and kept track of the smallest details of governing. Even in the seating arrangement during cabinet meetings Gladstone insisted on maintaining regularity: he sat in the middle of the long side of the cabinet table, with Granville and Derby to his right. Argyll, and after Argyll's resignation Carlingford, sat on his left.[3] Chamberlain and Dilke sat together opposite him. Other cabinet members were placed at regular intervals around the table. But as the ministry drew on, Gladstone increasingly preferred to govern without convening the cabinet, relying instead on "quasi-cabinets," "conclaves," or cabinet committees.[4]

Although this energetic and dynamic impulse at the heart of government offered a distinct advantage, Gladstone's dominant role also had the effect of overpersonalizing the government. Involved as he was in the extensive daily details of governing, he sometimes could not take the broader view necessary to give the ministry its needed perspective. Gladstone, too, was no longer a young man, or even a middle-aged man, at the beginning of his second ministry. He was nearly seventy-one and prey to the chronic annoyances of old age: lumbago, diarrhea, and decaying teeth. Occasional insomnia and loss of voice were also not uncommon. More serious illnesses of his later years sapped his strength and reduced his stamina. His absences, which became more frequent as his physical debility increased, could throw awry administrative efficiency.[5] If Gladstone's autocratic method of governing were ever to falter, a political vacuum within the cabinet could endanger the development of sensible and consistent policy. Any weakening of an overly controlling chief could additionally encourage independent policies and actions taken by individual cabinet members without the knowledge of the whole cabinet.

In the beginning, however, Gladstone's position at the heart of his ministry made him indispensable to the various factions of the Liberal party and remained his most important political asset. Each faction found what it wished to see in his policies. The radical Nonconformist wing—small in the cabinet but large in the countryside—applauded his moral crusades, especially against Beaconsfieldism. To the Liberal centrists, Gladstone offered sound financial credentials. And to the more traditional Whigs, whose influence was declining, Gladstone offered a guarantee against something worse,[6] as well as a sensible and moderate foreign and imperial policy.

Reflecting his own political position, Gladstone's cabinet was centrist, with a slight bias to the right. Of twenty cabinet members who served in the second administration, nearly half could be counted in the Whig camp, another quarter were mainstream Liberals, two (including Gladstone) were Peelite, and three had radical tendencies. Lord Granville, in a culinary frame of mind, summarized the composition of the cabinet as "like bread sauce—made up of two substantial elements. The few peppercorns are very obvious . . . but do not affect the flavour of the food."[7] Perhaps Granville's portrayal of Gladstone as a master chef was accurate enough in the early days of the ministry. But time revealed that the cabinet was more often a mixed salad. In contrast to his first ministry, Gladstone's second was composed of hostile and disquieting elements. Conflicting aims in policy, procedural differences of opinion, and contrasting personalities contributed to the dysfunctional nature of the government. Hartington's dissatisfactions, Granville's quiescence, Harcourt's flippancy, Dilke's Machiavellianism, Derby's unpredictability, Argyll's waspishness, Chamberlain's ambition, Carlingford's depressions, and Rosebery's strangeness were much in evidence at one time or another. With a contentious cabinet at his back, Gladstone's style of government was repeatedly challenged. As the ministry continued, he was less in control and less managerially effective, and was often overruled or overwhelmed. He increasingly adopted a strategy of withdrawal—even of absenteeism.

The discordant character of this second ministry can best be seen in its foreign and imperial policy. Especially in imperial matters there was much confusion and indecision, as each cabinet member was buffeted by events rapidly unfolding far from Britain. Policy was particularly divided over the issue of Egypt. Gladstone's own policy was sometimes inconsistent. Although conventional wisdom has it that Disraeli's foreign policy was "muscular" in contrast to Gladstone's "pacific, cautious, mild-mannered" approach, sharp distinctions between the two are not always easy to make.[8] Certainly examples exist of a Gladstonian conciliatory policy, such as the prime minister's attempt to mediate the conflict between indigenous Zulus and trekking Boers in the early months of his ministry.[9] Gladstone also sought to reduce tension with the expanding Russian empire in Central Asia by withdrawing British troops while guaranteeing the integrity of the Afghan government. In so doing, Gladstone hoped to convince the Russians of British disinterest in securing additional territory in Central Asia.[10]

Yet examples also indicate a Gladstonian forward policy abroad. During his first ministry, for instance, Gladstone presided over the Ashanti Expedition of 1873–74, which resulted in the creation of a British protectorate over the Gold Coast (ultimately annexed into the empire in 1901).[11] And in the early months of his second ministry, Gladstone was far more interventionist in the case of Turkey than Disraeli, who had looked benignly on Turkish transgressions in the Balkans. Gladstone, who regarded the sultan as an evil force in international affairs, was determined to keep the Turks on a short leash.[12] When the sultan refused to implement certain provisions of the Treaty of Berlin, Gladstone helped organize and lead a multinational naval demonstration that threatened to seize the port of Izmir.[13]

As these examples of his foreign and imperial policy illustrate, Gladstone was neither a pacifist nor a noninterventionist. He was quite willing to use military force and diplomatic pressure to preserve order and to maintain stability in the empire and among the nations of the world. International order was his supreme goal. Thus he was not, strictly speaking, an anti-imperialist but, rather, a reluctant imperialist. He was willing enough to maintain, but not eager to expand, Britain's imperial responsibilities. From the point of view of the Treasury, Gladstone believed that colonies were too expensive; inevitably they would cost the taxpayers more than they were worth. He preferred a self-governing, self-supporting, and self-defending colony rather than one closely organized and tightly administered from Whitehall. Although his colonial policy may seem inconsistent with his usual tendency to administer with a firm hand, Gladstone had always been willing to withdraw from conditions over which he could not easily exercise control. If order and coherence could not be preserved, he would remove himself from the threat of disorder and incoherence. And so it was with colonies and the imperial mandate generally. The two examples that follow illustrate that Gladstone ultimately could not withstand the challenges posed by ambitious and ruthless imperial adventurers operating far from Britain.

In April 1883, the Queensland government of Australia, without authorization from the British government, sent an agent to claim as British territory all that part of New Guinea not under Dutch rule. This was the culmination of more than a decade of active campaigning by various Australian imperial interests.[14] But the annexation was protested by Arthur Gordon, high commissioner and consul-general of the Western Pacific, who objected to such unauthorized acts as one colony's annexing another. Gordon also suspected the motives of the Australians and doubted their ability to govern such an extensive colony. "In no case," he observed to Gladstone, "do I think the rule of a vast native population can be safely entrusted to a small and, for the most part, ignorant, and selfish oligarchy, of another race, having interests directly opposed to those of the natives themselves."[15]

The cabinet, perhaps swayed by Gordon's opinions, initially disallowed the annexation.[16] But an intercolonial conference in Australia in December passed resolutions that virtually laid down a Monroe Doctrine for the whole of the South Pacific. The colonial secretary, Lord Derby, condemned their extravagant and unenforceable claim as "mere raving."[17] Yet Derby also believed that it would probably be necessary at least to establish a British protectorate—if not to resort to outright annexation—over selected coastal regions in New Guinea. Such a mid-course measure might ease Australian fears of occupation by a foreign power. Gladstone bowed to the growing pressure. To Derby, he wrote, "I feel many scruples about this Protectorate, but I should pay due deference to your opinion."[18] By August 1884, the cabinet had decided to establish a protectorate over the south coast of non-Dutch New Guinea, a decision reaffirmed in January 1885.[19]

Cabinet debates on Australian claims to New Guinea had stretched over a period of eighteen months. During that time matters had become complicated by German claims on the northern coast of New Guinea. Germany's sudden appearance as a world power was a surprise to the more established colonial nations. Gladstone's government was clearly caught off guard by the rapidity of Germany's first colonial ventures, especially by Otto von Bismarck's special animus toward Britain. Bismarck indeed had come to believe that Britain was pursuing a systematic *Deutschfeindlichkeit* as a matter of global policy. Thus he set out to challenge quickly and decisively Britain's colonialism.[20] Gladstone did not oppose German colonial aims; in fact, he may be said to have welcomed them. German colonies near British-held territory would, he believed, have a moderating effect on the kind of kinetic imperialism that had surfaced in both South Africa and Australia. German colonies could hold in check overly eager British colonists who might be tempted to initiate rash imperial schemes of their own. When Germany raised claims on the north coast of New Guinea, therefore, Gladstone was willing to accede.

Few felt as Gladstone did. Germany's colonial ambitions struck fire among his colleagues and the public at large. German actions in New Guinea were merely the climax of a flurry of colonial acquisitions during the summer of 1884. In early July, Germany had established a protectorate over Togoland in west Africa; scarcely a week later, it proclaimed a protectorate over the Cameroons to the south. These two acquisitions effectively straddled the Niger delta, long an object of British colonial interest. In August 1884, the Germans leapfrogged further down the African coast to annex a region in southwestern Africa known as Angra Pequena (which later became Namibia). The cabinet therefore opposed Germany's intended annexations in New Guinea; they issued an expostulation and decided to "invite" an explanation from German officials.[21]

By the end of the year, Derby was singing the jingo song. The British public, he reported, was "just now in a very aggressive and acquisitive mood," and among British colonists especially the "feeling of disappointment at the German annexations is running high." To counter the German threat in southern Africa, Derby proposed on 26 December that unclaimed bits of African coast from Natal south to the Cape and from Natal north to St. Lucia Bay "(which is ours)" be secured. "If the Germans seize on either, I would not answer for the consequences." The following day, having slept on his harsh words, Derby had harsher ones. He sounded positively warlike. Condemning further the "predatory Germans," he was convinced that Bismarck intended "ill will to England." He now recommended annexing the entire South African coast, from the mouth of the Orange River in the west to the beginning of Portuguese territory in the east. Gladstone, after consulting a map sent over by the Colonial Office, was unconvinced that annexation north of Natal was justified merely on the grounds of keeping out the Germans. He agreed, however, to the more limited annexation of the coast south of Natal, and this took place at a cabinet meeting within the week.[22] Gladstone's willingness to annex in South Africa marks a surrender to pressure that had already been manifest in his acquiescence in establishing a protectorate in New Guinea. He had, in a sense, abrogated his responsibility to his own non-annexationist creed. This pattern was confirmed in his ministry's involvement in Egypt and the Sudan.

Gladstone was well aware of the danger of involvement in Egypt. In an often quoted passage, written originally in 1877 for the British periodical *Nineteenth Century,* Gladstone warned, "Our first site in Egypt, be it by larceny or be it by emption, will be the almost certain egg of a North African empire."[23] Morley noted this statement's irony in retrospect, for it was Gladstone himself, building on Disraeli's purchase of the Suez Canal shares in 1875, who consolidated the British presence in Egypt, thus joining the two countries to a common fate for decades to come. Undoubtedly, it was the importance of the canal that continued to lure British interests into that part of North Africa. Because it shortened the route to India by some seven thousand miles, its commercial advantages were obvious. No less significant was its strategic position: India was now tied more closely to Britain through its Egyptian link. British politicians tended to think of Egypt only in terms of the canal. Egypt as a country, with its own rich history and varied culture, was viewed as an intermediary, perhaps even an obstacle, between Britain and its great colony to the east.[24]

Even before Britain's active intervention, the tensions of modernization had begun their destabilizing work within Egypt. During the late 1870s a series of economic and political crises buffeted the economic infrastructure of this essentially agricultural country, forcing it to default on debts to foreign bankers. To reestablish financial integrity, the European powers coerced the ruling khedive into the creation of a European commission of inquiry. This was followed by the so-called Dual Control, a system of administrative responsibility over Egyptian affairs shared between France and Britain, with Britain's interest explicitly paramount.

The presence of the Europeans caused an inevitable reaction in Egypt. Financial dependence was an especial concern to the Egyptian professional classes. In the countryside, village sheikhs amplified emergent national feelings by blaming faults of government and excessive taxation on the growth of European influence. Most significant was a simmering discontent among younger officers of the Egyptian army over staff reductions and inequities in pay. On 1 February 1881, army colonels mutinied. The khedive met their demands, but the victory did not satisfy the colonels. In late summer, groups of army officers began touring the villages, winning the population to their side and urging action against European rule. On 9 September 1881, four army regiments under Colonel Arabi Bey besieged the khedival palace and, in a coup, effectively dismantled the khedive's government. Thereafter Arabi Bey became a shadowy but real governing presence.

An obstreperous nationalist movement was the last thing the British government wanted. To evaluate Arabi's intentions, Gladstone relied heavily on British administrators in Egypt. With near unanimity, such officials as Sir Edward Malet, the consul-general in Cairo, and Sir Auckland Colvin, the controller general, viewed Arabi and the nationalists as direct threats to British interests. They mounted an ultimately successful campaign to persuade the government to take active steps against the nationalists.[25]

On 11 June a xenophobic riot broke out in Alexandria, during which nearly fifty Europeans or European-protected individuals lost their lives. More to the point, a British consular official was badly wounded. These actions thoroughly damaged the reputation of the Egyptian government in the eyes of the British public. As for Gladstone and the cabinet, they were convinced that the riot had been planned and carried out by Arabi and the nationalists. Given that assumption, the ministry decided on a military response should conditions in Egypt deteriorate further.

Exactly one month later, on 11 July, a British squadron under Admiral Seymour bombarded Alexandria, resulting in a severe loss of civilian life and property. Four days later, eight hundred British soldiers marched into the city, Arabi's forces withdrawing before them. Within a fortnight, the ministry had asked and received from Parliament a large vote of credit for the conduct of military operations. An expeditionary force of thirty-five thousand men under Sir Garnet Wolseley, the hero of the Ashanti Wars, was promptly dispatched to Egypt. By mid-August, the canal was taken. On 13 September, Wolseley caught and defeated Arabi's force at Tel-el-Kebir. Two days later, Cairo was occupied, and Britain was effectively in control of Egypt.

Gladstone was as happy as any Disraelian jingo at the turn of events. Magnus noted that Gladstone received the news of Tel-el-Kebir with "boyish glee."[26] His own words confirm this judgment. He rejoiced in the "spirit stirring intelligence from Egypt." Praising Wolseley for his "masterly conduct" and "brilliant success," Gladstone telegraphed him the news of his barony in acknowledgment of his "splendid services." To another correspondent, he wrote, "We certainly ought to be in good humour, for we are pleased with our army, our navy, our admirals, our Generals, & our organization!" In jubilation, Gladstone ordered the church bells rung and had celebratory artillery rounds fired in the London parks. "I hope the guns will crash all the windows," he confided to Childers, his war secretary.[27]

Gladstone's actions were a shock to many of his supporters. John Bright promptly resigned from the cabinet. A peace movement sprang quickly to life in Britain, critical of Gladstone's abandonment of his election promises to roll back Beaconsfieldism. The Anti-Aggression League, the Liverpool Peace Society, the Workmen's Peace Association, and several other groups dedicated to international peace sent petitions to the government. A rough coalition of politicians, clergy, intellectuals, and some workers condemned British intervention in Egypt. Wilfrid Scawen Blunt, a wealthy Sussex squire, former diplomat, and amateur Arabist, was among the most vocal in denouncing Gladstone as "a fraud."[28]

It is difficult to refute Ramm's judgment that the bombardment of Alexandria, the seizure of the canal, and the pursuit, defeat, and capture of Arabi were nothing less than "undisguised aggrandizement."[29] How can these actions be explained? How did the moral Gladstone of Midlothian days become the imperialist of 1882? Historians since have suggested numerous reasons: decisions taken by the "men on the spot," conflicts within the cabinet, Gladstone's distractions over Ireland, and his lack of mastery of international affairs, especially those in Egypt.[30] Others have argued that Gladstone invaded Egypt in order to hold together the Liberal party during complex and divisive Irish legislation. By acting aggressively in Egypt, he could also take the wind out of Conservative imperial sails.[31]

To these reasons can be added another—one that will indicate the psychological context of Gladstone's decision. Just as Gladstone felt intense satisfaction in managing domestic matters to bring coherence to them, so he felt satisfaction in tidying up the loose ends of global governing.[32] A perceived threat to Egyptian stability might bring his well-established penchant for order into play. Arabi's national movement, his break from the khedival government, and his apparent moves toward Egyptian independence were an unacceptable threat to the status quo in that important part of the world. Gladstone's justification to the House of Commons for a military expedition suggests as much: "We should not fully discharge our duty if we did not endeavour to convert the present interior state of Egypt from anarchy and conflict to peace and order."[33]

Gladstone's attempt to maintain order in Egypt was paralleled by his determination to control his ministry. As the crisis in Egypt deepened in the spring and summer of 1882, Gladstone was forced into various strategies to extricate himself from the growing influence of the interventionists, the most outspoken of whom was the Indian secretary, Lord Hartington. Frequent full-dress debates in the cabinet, Hartington believed, were the most appropriate forum for discussing the crisis. But in the critical days before the bombardment of Alexandria, Gladstone tended to avoid cabinet meetings. When Gladstone reported on 4 July that he was summoning a cabinet only as a favor to Granville, Granville replied with a rare touch of asperity: "It is obvious that [where] there are pros & cons of great weight the calm discussion of them by 13 men who are presumed to be intelligent above the average ought to be of great use."[34] After the cabinet thus summoned had taken place on 5 July, Granville—the next morning—once again wrote to Gladstone: "Would it not be well to have a short Cabinet this morning?" Gladstone responded, somewhat grudgingly, "Of course I will summon the Cabinet if you desire it," but he thought a delay would be preferable. He concluded feebly by justifying his inaction thus: "Hurried and frequent Cabinets create much stir."[35]

Gladstone's loss of authority in the cabinet was not the only difficulty facing him. The Eastern question—with its crosscurrents of opinion and conflicting snatches of information—was baffling. As he confessed to Granville after an anxious hour-long quasi cabinet on 1 July, "It is hardly possible (I think) for the human brain, at least it is impossible for mine, to maintain the due order and sequence of ideas in such a case."[36] Carlingford reported that Gladstone seemed "harrassed and depressed" at the meeting. "He submitted to the opinion of the Cabinet, & said something about having little more fight or work in him."[37]

Adding to Gladstone's stress at this time was his immense workload in the House of Commons. He was always scrupulous in attending business in the Commons, and during July he was averaging seven hours a day, sometimes not leaving until one o'clock in the morning.[38] An unexpected defeat in the Commons on the evening of 7 July brought matters to a head. Gladstone had introduced an amendment that softened the coercionist tone of the search clause of the Irish crimes bill then being debated. The amendment, however, had been added against the opinion and advice of Harcourt, the home secretary. Gladstone had been insistent and was unwilling to bring the amendment to the cabinet because, as he stated to Harcourt, he had recently yielded too much to cabinet opinion. But Gladstone misjudged the mood of the House and of his own party: the amendment failed by thirteen votes. Several members on the Liberal side deserted the government in spite of Gladstone's warning that if the amendment were defeated, he would "reconsider his personal position"—a veiled threat of resignation. In a long and private conversation with John Bright immediately afterward, Gladstone apparently discussed resignation. Harcourt himself expected Gladstone to resign, as did Dilke and Chamberlain, both of whom understood that Egypt would be at least partly the reason for his action.[39]

Gladstone's parliamentary defeat was one more reminder of the loss of control of his governing authority and (one must presume) of his own personal authority. The pattern is all too familiar. Pushed to the limit by his cabinet, by his party, and by the House of Commons, Gladstone must have felt that his administration was becoming ungovernable; and he must have felt, too, that his own familiar, coherent world was threatened. To resign, retreat, and withdraw was his strongest impulse. "The occurrence of Friday," he wrote the day after his parliamentary defeat, "was so far as I know without precedent, and I entertained personally views with regard to it on which it is unnecessary to dwell but which I fear are out of date."[40]

Isolated, thrust aside by his own strong-minded cabinet, burdened by legislative crises, and without any other recourse after his resignation threat had failed on the floor of the House of Commons on 7 July, Gladstone capitulated. But he did so with a heavy heart. Advocating peace, he found himself at war. Supporting nonintervention in Egypt, he became a party to military action. How could he justify his actions to his colleagues and to the electorate? How could he explain that the basis of his foreign policy was no longer moral? The evidence suggests that Gladstone engaged in self-deception to justify his change of opinion, but this change was neither a conscious desire to deceive nor a hypocritical or opportunistic change of mind. Gladstone used a common strategy to alleviate the tension engendered by holding mutually contradictory beliefs. That is, he sought to reduce cognitive dissonance.[41] In addition, Gladstone may well have employed a complementary coping device known as cognitive bolstering, a process that uses over-simplification, distortions, and evasions in order to magnify the benefits of a new course of action over a previous policy.[42]

Gladstone could have reduced the tension by admitting that he had become a man of war, a jingo in the late nineteenth-century mode—as many of his colleagues in the cabinet had become. But this strategy would have been difficult for him, given his history and predisposition. Instead, he maintained that his warlike actions in Egypt were the means to peace. Gladstone developed these strategies at the time of the bombardment in a series of letters to John Bright, whose reputation as a man of peace he valued. If Bright could be convinced by his arguments, then Gladstone's justifications to himself must be correct. His first letter, on the eve of Admiral Seymour's action, asked Bright's forbearance "if Seymour is driven to bombard." For it may be that the bombardment itself, as Gladstone explained it to Bright, would lead not to war but to peace. Two days later, after the bombardment had taken place, Gladstone developed the theme he had introduced to Bright. "We have not got peace in Egypt," he admitted, "but we are I do believe nearer by a good deal to peace than we were 48 hours ago." The next day in a follow-up letter, Gladstone informed Bright that the Turkish, Italian, Spanish, and Greek ambassadors were united with him "in believing that the action at Alexandria had brought us materially nearer to peace order & legality in the East."[43]

Gladstone's final letter to Bright found other justifications for his theme that "war is peace." This lengthy letter expressed his regret for the "solemn & painful" act of Tuesday, when the bombardment took place, but it had been necessary because Egypt "was governed by sheer military violence." A situation "of *force*" had been created, which could only be met "by force." The British fleet, moreover, acted responsibly. It could not be blamed for the heavy casualties inflicted on the defenders of Alexandria, for Admiral Seymour was "lawfully present" in Alexandrine waters. Besides, Gladstone continued, no other power, large or small, had disapproved of British action. In addition, the bombardment taught other salutary lessons. It struck a heavy blow against unauthorized violence, it demonstrated the value of legitimate rule, and it showed to Eastern fanatics that the massacre of Europeans was "not likely to be perpetrated with impunity." "I feel that in being party to this work," he assured Bright, "I have been a labourer in the cause of peace."

Bright was unconvinced by these arguments. He recorded in his diary a conversation with Gladstone on the afternoon of 14 July while they walked together from the Athenaeum Club to Downing Street. Bright found Gladstone's views "strange and unexpected. He urged as if all that has been done in the Egyptian case was right, and even persuaded himself that he is fully justified in the interest of Peace.... He seems to have the power of convincing himself that what to me seems glaringly wrong is evidently right, and tho' he regrets that a crowd of men should be killed, he regards it almost as an occurrence which is not to be condemned, as it is one of the incidents of a policy out of which he hopes for a better order of things. He even spoke of our being able to justify our conduct in the great day of account."[44]

Having struggled through the tensions engendered by the Egyptian crisis, Gladstone boarded the imperial bandwagon. A palpable sense of relief suffuses Gladstone's behavior in the weeks immediately following the bombardment. Reducing the dissonance in his views to an acceptable level allowed him to accept the results that followed: increased military reinforcements, the landing of invasion troops in Egypt, the pursuit of Arabi and the defeat at Tel-el-Kebir, and, most startling of all, Gladstone's call for Arabi's execution—"he should be hanged," he told Granville.[45] Luckily for Gladstone's later reputation, this irresponsible recommendation was not carried out. Arabi instead was given a trial without a prejudged sentence and eventually was exiled in comfort to Ceylon.[46]

Ultimately, however, the intense physical and mental strain of the Egyptian crisis brought Gladstone down.[47] Thoughts of physical decline, loss of energy, and retirement crowded into his mind. In a letter to Spencer in late October (with copies to Granville and Hartington), he argued his case for retirement, giving age and infirmity as "commanding" reasons. He noted within himself an "increase of disinclination to my work, and disposition . . . to scamp it." It was a "sign of diminished power." That he "should remain on the stage like a half-exhausted singer, whose notes are flat, & everyone perceives it except himself would be of no good anyone."[48] To Granville, he wrote additionally, "My central and conclusive" reason for retirement is "inability of brain, to face the legislative work that must come on."[49] During that autumn, he also visited Lord Derby at Knowsley Hall, spending many hours in recreational and political conversation. Of the visit, Derby recorded, "For the first time a suspicion crossed my mind that there is something beyond what is quite healthy in this perpetual flow of words—a beginning perhaps of old age."[50]

By late December and early January of 1883, Gladstone was suffering from severe insomnia, sometimes sleeping as little as two hours a night; on 15 January he was entirely sleepless. His doctor prescribed rest, and Gladstone wisely accepted Lord Wolverton's offer of his villa at Cannes, where he and Catherine remained for nearly six weeks. The effect on Gladstone was immediate. "I am stunned by this wonderful place," he wrote in his diary, "& so vast a change at a moment's notice in the conditions of life."[51] He walked and conversed with Lord Acton; visited neighboring villages; went yachting along the coast, exploring such places as "that wicked" Monte Carlo; and played whist in the evening. Most important, he slept longer hours, keeping a "Sleep Register" that recorded his improvement over time.[52] Business, he reported to the chief Liberal whip, Lord Grosvenor, was "now for once kept at arm's length."[53] The rest cure at Cannes was entirely successful. "I part from Cannes with a heavy heart," he wrote on 26 February as the train took him first to Paris and then to London, where Parliament was already at work.[54]

The legislative session of 1883 provided mixed fortunes for Gladstone's ministry. The most notable success was the Corrupt Practices Act, which set specific limits on election expenses—limits that were needed after the bribery and corruption scandals during the general election.[55] More significant was the reemergence of an issue that the election itself had first brought to prominence in 1880. Among the new members of the House of Commons was Charles Bradlaugh, M.P. for Northampton. A reform-minded journalist, orator, and pamphleteer who defended republicanism, birth control, and Irish independence, Bradlaugh was also a professed atheist.[56] Refusing to take the oath at the swearing-in ceremony before the assembled House of Commons, he requested permission instead to affirm, thus omitting the phrase "So help me God" during the ceremony. The right of affirmation had previously been granted (in 1866) to Quakers and members of a few other religious sects, but not to atheists. Instead of granting permission, the Liberal leadership referred the matter to a Select Committee, which in a divided vote turned down Bradlaugh's request. From this point onward, delaying tactics and indignant speeches, maneuvers by the Conservative opposition, and procedural wrangling characterized the Bradlaugh affair throughout the remainder of Gladstone's ministry.

Gladstone believed that Parliament could not exclude any duly elected member. No matter that Bradlaugh had "loathsome & revolting opinions"; the House of Commons quite clearly lacked jurisdiction.[57] As he later explained it to his friend Sir Thomas Acland, *"We do not say Bradlaugh ought to sit*: but simply that his right or non-right to sit should be determined by law: by a dispassionate Court of Law, instead of by a House of Commons of which the majority have in dealing with this question imbibed a degree of ungovernable excitement rare even in the struggles of party."[58]

Attempts to settle the issue by legislation failed in both 1881 and 1882. This failure may be due in part to divisions within the cabinet. Gladstone often found himself in the minority in upholding the right of Bradlaugh to affirm.[59] By early 1883, however, the cabinet had decided to introduce an affirmation bill in the forthcoming parliamentary session. As drawn up, the bill would give the option of affirmation to any who wished it. By the time the bill came before Parliament in April 1883, opinion in the country had been polarized by the vocal opposition of Gladstone's frequent critic Cardinal Manning. Perhaps this threat gave a special edge and conviction to Gladstone's speech on the second reading of the bill, which was considered one of his most eloquent orations.[60] He argued that the imposition of an oath on an M.P. struck at the very foundations of religion that the House of Commons sought to uphold. "I have no fear of Atheism in this House," Gladstone assured his hearers. But he was fearful of the effect on the country at large of the denial of a civil freedom in the name of religion. "When they see the profession of religion and the interests of religion ostensibly associated with what they are deeply convinced is injustice, they are led to questions about religion itself, which they see to be associated with injustice."[61] Always at his best in oratory, Gladstone no doubt moved the House—but not far enough. The vote went against the affirmation bill by three votes. The Bradlaugh case dragged on for another five years until an affirmation bill was passed in 1888, allowing him to take his seat. He died three years later.

The Bradlaugh case was more than a mere incident of high Victorian drama. Morley interpreted it as an episode demonstrating how far Gladstone's mind "had traveled along one of the grand highroads of human progress" in furthering toleration.[62] But Gladstone was less motivated by a desire to seat an atheist, or by an interest in establishing a wholesome climate for the freedom of dissent, than he was to clear up the impediment to parliamentary business that the Bradlaugh case had become. His primary purpose was to create an orderly climate for the furtherance of the Liberal legislative program. A continuing barrage of unexpected, chronic, and contentious issues could throw the business of the session off track. This was at the heart of his urging that Bradlaugh's claims should be settled in a court of law.

Gladstone was clearly ready to quit the cares of the legislative life after Parliament was prorogued in late August 1883. "Good bye!" was his happy farewell to the final sitting of the Commons.[63] Within two days, he was at Hawarden, where he relaxed in his accustomed manner during the autumn recess. He performed woodcraft at Hawarden, worked on his books, arranged his papers, and studied Homeric vocatives. In early September, perhaps remembering Cannes and its pleasures, he accepted an invitation from Sir Donald Currie (the shipping magnate and M.P. for Perth) to join the maiden voyage of his new four-thousand-ton luxury liner, the *Pembroke Castle*. Accompanying him were Catherine, his daughter Mary, and son Herbert. Others of the party were a number of Liberals, including Algernon West, Sir William Harcourt, and Sir Arthur Gordon (then governor of New Zealand).[64] Clambering aboard at the last minute was Margot Tennant, who became the "heart and soul and glory of the whole party."[65] Also aboard, to Gladstone's delight, was the poet laureate Alfred Tennyson, with whom Gladstone had "much and free" conversation.[66] Tennyson also gave several readings from his works during the voyage, although in one instance he was much offended when he caught Gladstone asleep. The *Pembroke Castle* made its way from Barrow north to Tobermory on Mull, then through the Minch to Kirkwall in the Orkneys. At Tennyson's suggestion the ship steamed over the North Sea to Norway and Denmark, where the party spent two days walking around Copenhagen. Gladstone and several others also attended a reception given by the king of Denmark. Present were the king and queen of Greece and the czar and czarina of Russia. They in turn were feted the next day on the *Pembroke Castle*. For a special treat, they heard Tennyson read "Grandmother." By 20 September, the ship had returned to English waters. The party disembarked at Gravesend to a "rather triumphal landing" and a "special train provided (*free*) to London."[67]

Perhaps the mood created by his refreshing holiday gave Gladstone an unwonted optimism as he approached the work of the coming autumn. After an uncharacteristically calm and quiet cabinet meeting (pronounced "very good" by Gladstone) in late October, the premier wrote Catherine that his colleagues "seemed at once to be lost in one smooth even forward current of opinion & feeling." In fact, Gladstone thought that "matters general look tranquil and rather comfortable." But he could not help ending his letter with a query: "Is this a sign of *coming* storms?"[68]

Gladstone's premonition was accurate enough. The storm had already begun that summer with a minor squall. In June 1883, at a jubilee celebration in Birmingham honoring John Bright, Joseph Chamberlain spoke of the need for franchise extension. He stirred the assembled crowd of twenty thousand with a proposed reform program that was a restatement of Chartist electoral demands: manhood suffrage, equal electoral districts, and payment for members of Parliament. He also made some slighting remarks about royalty. This shot across the ministerial bow by an up-and-coming radical was clearly designed to force the reform agenda. Since 1867, reform sentiment had increased steadily in the countryside, especially among those still excluded from the franchise. Specific interest groups, such as agricultural laborers and northern miners, had joined hands with urban workers and middle-class radicals to forge a reform alliance.[69] Gladstone's ministry was not insensitive to these pressures but delayed a serious consideration of a reform bill. Chamberlain's prodding seems to have had the desired effect, however. On 3 October, Gladstone asked the attorney general, Sir Henry James, to draft legislation that would extend the county franchise not only to agricultural laborers in England

and Wales but to Ireland and Scotland as well—all in one bill. In addition, Gladstone proposed that a second legislative packet proceed with the redistribution of seats made necessary by shifts in population since the previous reform bill of 1867. He was adamant that these two issues—reform and redistribution—be kept separate. His reason was that he lacked the strength to "undertake great legislative labour in the H. of C." Should the cabinet insist on a simultaneous redistribution bill, he hinted at resignation.[70]

As had been true in 1867, a desire for party advantage and the consequent tactical maneuvering added almost impenetrable layers of complexity to the bill of 1884.[71] Nevertheless, Gladstone maintained a firm hand on the progress of the bill, steering it through the cabinet in the autumn of 1883. Its main points included full household suffrage in the boroughs and counties throughout Britain, including Ireland. By July 1884, the bill had been carried intact through the House of Commons.

Once the bill had passed the Commons, it faced the greater hurdle of the House of Lords. There the Conservative opposition was ably and forcibly led by Lord Salisbury, whose primary concern was the redistribution of seats.[72] Salisbury and his Conservative colleagues (like the Whig Hartington) feared the consequences of a redrawing of constituency boundaries; he was determined that Conservative minorities in any voting district should be fully represented and not swamped by a wash of new Liberal voters. Anticipating Conservative resistance, Gladstone rallied the troops in the Lords. To the bishop of Bath and Wells, he urged support on a subject "full of menace & of mischief." He was no less insistent to the bishop of Exeter, asking his help in order to avert the looming "constitutional crisis." He sent a stronger (if implied) threat to the archbishop of Canterbury, warning of a conflict that could affect the future of the House of Lords. To Gladstone's surprise, Lord Tennyson was unsound on the bill. Letters to the poet, his son, and wife were necessary to bring him around.[73] The tactic worked, but for a lost cause, as the bill was negatived. "What a suicidal act of the Lords!" was the premier's reaction.[74]

With the loss of the bill began a tortuous round of negotiations. Over the next several months, party intermediaries on both sides tried to come to an accommodation. Gladstone was among the most active. Ministers discussed several schemes, among them life peerages and the creation of a special congress of the two houses voting together.[75] At last, driven by the need for a Liberal success after defeats at home and abroad, Gladstone went for his opponents' constitutional jugular. In secret and confidential correspondence with the queen, he raised the possibility of dire consequences unless the Conservatives in the Lords came to their senses. Should the Lords reject the bill a second time, he warned, a most serious question would surely arise: "whether the hereditary or the representative majority is to prevail?"[76]

This theme Gladstone carried into the countryside as he drummed up support during a speaking tour in his Midlothian constituency in late August and September. This was Gladstone at his dramatic best. He arrived at Lord Rosebery's Edinburgh house, Dalmeny, on Thursday, 27 August. On Saturday, he began his campaign at the Edinburgh Corn Exchange, speaking to a crowd of five thousand. The exchange, normally bare of ornament, had been transformed in preparation for Gladstone's visit. Decorations of blue and white calico hung from the ceiling, while the walls and pillars were festooned with sprigs of evergreens. Coats of arms of Scotland and of the Gladstone family hung behind the speakers' platform. When the Grand Old Man mounted the platform to speak, the hall burst into cheering and a frenzy of hat and handkerchief waving. For a full five minutes he was cheered. "Mr. Gladstone's presence has completed the electric circuit," wrote the *Times* reporter, "and the Liberalism of Scotland is glowing at a white heat."[77] Once he began to speak, the audience was reverentially still. His first visit to that room, he said, had been seventy years before. Now he returned for a great cause—"to promote by every legitimate means in my power the speedy passage of the Reform Bill." It had passed the House of Commons by a substantial margin, but it had failed in the Lords. The rejection of the bill suggests, he said, that the "time has come when it will be necessary to study the means of introducing an organic change into the constitution of the House of Lords." This was met by loud and sustained cheers. For more than an hour and a half, Gladstone held his audience, threatening the House of Lords and justifying the Liberal program.

For the next three weeks, Gladstone carried his message throughout Midlothian. First, he went to Invercauld House, Braemar, the seat of James Ross Farquharson, a friend of the Prince of Wales; then to Balmoral to see the Queen; two days later to Mar Lodge, the home of the Earl of Fife, who was to marry the Princess Royal within a few years. Arriving at Haddo House, the seat of Lord Aberdeen, he heard a deputation of tenant farmers. Next he traveled to Lord Dalhousie's estate at Brechin Castle for a few days. Rounding out his tour with a brief stay at Lord Strathmore's Glamis Castle and a short visit to his physician, Sir Arthur Clark in Perthshire, he returned to Dalmeny on 24 September. From these well-connected Scots bastions of aristocratic power and royal influence, he never relented in his onslaught against the House of Lords. At every stop along the way, he campaigned for the bill.

During the autumn, closer combat took place between the opposing parties. The crucial month was November. Conferences between the leaders of the Conservatives and Liberals were arranged late that month at Lord Salisbury's where a final compromise was hammered out. Gladstone seems to have been the moving force behind the compromise.[78] If the Conservatives offered "adequate assurances" that the franchise bill would be passed without delay, the ministry in turn would introduce a redistribution bill. Within this framework, both bills passed. All together, more than 1.7 million new voters were added, including a large infusion of working-class voters and agricultural laborers. The entanglements of the bill and the months of negotiations had ended well. Gladstone had been tenacious and effective, if somewhat alarmist in his public statements. He had been instrumental, as Matthew points out, in bringing about the most significant legislative triumph of his ministry.[79]

There was little time to savor a victory, however. Even before the final reform votes in Parliament, impending imperial issues in Egypt returned to haunt the ministry. Since the defeat of Arabi, the debate about the future role of Britain in Egypt had continued inconclusively. Gladstone believed that Britain should retire once order was restored.[80] Others thought that a fixed-term protectorate leading to eventual withdrawal was the better course. Still others, including Hartington, wanted a return to dual control, sharing the responsibility of governing with France; if this was impossible, Britain should continue governing alone. Some wanted a more informal control over Egypt—enough to manage Egyptian finances and to make the canal secure. The logic of the British presence in Egypt was summarized in a popular phrase of the time: "We must govern or go."[81]

The imperial debate had become complicated by the emergence of a newly formed religious group of dervishes in the Egyptian-controlled Sudan to the south. Led by a Muslim, Muhammed Ahmed, who claimed to be Mahdi (or guide) and successor of the Prophet, the movement soon had thousands of militant adherents.[82] In 1880, he had proclaimed a holy war. Operating at first out of the western mountains in the Sudan, the Mahdi's guerrilla units rapidly gained in strength. Isolated Egyptian garrisons in the Sudan fell one by one, and each time the Mahdi's ranks swelled as the defeated solders were pressed into service. In this way, too, arms and ammunition were confiscated by the Mahdi's troops. The Mahdi's most startling victory was in November 1883 at Kashgal when a large Egyptian force commanded by a retired British army officer, Colonel William Hicks, was ambushed and destroyed. This event brought home to Gladstone's ministry the Mahdi's potential threat not only to the Sudan but to all Egypt.

The ministry's response was to help the Egyptian government remove their remaining garrisons from the Sudan. As a prelude to the evacuation scheme, a mission was sent to draw up a feasibility report. After some discussion, General Charles Gordon was appointed for this task. Gordon had been a charismatic military leader in the service of the Chinese emperor in the 1860s. More to the point, he had been in the Sudan from 1873 until 1880, serving the khedive, and had been governor-general during his last three years in that province. Gordon's organizational capacity and his previous experience made him a logical choice.

Gordon's charge was to report back to the cabinet the best means by which the isolated Egyptian soldiers and large numbers of civilians could be brought to safety, presumably down the Nile northward across the Sudanese-Egyptian border. But it was not clear whether Gordon should merely report on the feasibility of an evacuation or also arrange for it. Gordon's orders apparently contained a clause authorizing him to perform whatever duties might be desired by the Egyptian government and sanctioned by the newly appointed consul general in Egypt, Sir Evelyn Baring. Once in Egypt, Gordon looked to Cairo as his principal authority rather than to Westminster; and out of range of London's circle of authority, he operated with a much freer hand than the spirit of his original orders would have allowed. Impelled by his messianic religious impulse and by his activism in military matters, and emboldened by the confusion engendered in the imperial chain of command, Gordon acted on his own.

When he arrived in Khartoum, at the confluence of the two Niles more than fifteen hundred miles to the south of Cairo, Gordon immediately set about assuming the duties of a governor. He opened the prisons and summoned a council of notables. Abolishing the tax system, he had old tax records, along with whips and other official instruments of torture, brought to the public square for burning. All pretense of an advising mission was gone. Thus Gordon initiated a series of events as the Gladstone ministry attempted to play catch-up. As the goals of the intended official mission receded to be replaced by Gordon's imperial schemes, the cabinet was placed in an awkward position. To recall Gordon would be an unpopular move with the public at large, which had taken a fancy to the eccentric general. But Gordon was, if not a rebel, a rogue. Most worrisome was the continued success of the Mahdi-inspired Sudanese rebels. By the spring of 1884 they had taken half the Sudan and were beginning to press on Khartoum. Apprehension in the cabinet grew. The possibility that Khartoum could be surrounded and Gordon's exits completely blocked was very real. The evacuation of the Sudan was no longer the issue: the "Gordon problem," as Gladstone put it, was now uppermost.[83]

The cabinet, however, were not of one mind. Some members wanted an immediate recall; others urged a relief expedition to rescue Gordon. Gladstone seemed puzzled by Gordon's behavior. At first he favored a recall, then he delayed. This tactic was followed by a curiously avoidant and punitive response: Gladstone suggested that Gordon should be responsible for his own actions because he disobeyed his orders. In late March, the exasperated cabinet came to a decision that simply abrogated their responsibility: it instructed Gordon that he was "at liberty" either to stay in Khartoum or to escape. "It was a dreadful fix," Carlingford conceded.[84]

The ministry's inability to come to a decision about Gordon was made more difficult by the most recent of Gladstone's health problems. Throughout most of March 1884, he was absent from cabinet meetings and was not fully well until early April. His personal physician, Andrew Clark, diagnosed a heavy cold in his patient's chest and larynx. A rapid pulse and cough were particularly worrisome. Clark prescribed a regimen "of *silence,* inhalation, potash drafts, and lozenges."[85] Gladstone's absence tended to exacerbate the tensions and uncertainties in the cabinet as discussions rambled. Meetings became increasingly dysfunctional. After one meeting during which the voluble Harcourt "lectured & denounced & prophesied," Carlingford wrote that Gladstone "was much wanted."[86]

In the meantime Gordon had begun to issue unrealistic proclamations from Khartoum. One of these threatened the Mahdi with British troops that he claimed were already on their way to Khartoum—an "amazing lie," as Sir Charles Dilke put it.[87] In spite of his eccentric behavior, Gordon retained strong support in Parliament, with the public at large, and most vociferously with Queen Victoria. In a telegram to Hartington in March 1884, she came near to issuing an order: "Gordon is in danger: you are bound to try and save him." To Gladstone two days later, she was only slightly less imperious. "If not only for humanity's sake, for the honor of the Government and the nation, he must not be abandoned!"[88]

The cabinet, however, were reluctant to send a rescue mission to Gordon. The journey could become a logistical nightmare: one military estimate forecast the need for either a thousand boats to sail up the Nile or fifty thousand camels to travel the overland route. Gladstone was clearly unwilling to justify such an expense, and he fell back on his legalistic rendering of Gordon's position: having disobeyed his orders, Gordon was no longer the ministry's responsibility.[89] Because of his doubts about a rescue mission, Gladstone tried to dampen enthusiasm for the general. Displays of sympathy in the press were difficult to control, but Gladstone felt he had a stronger hand to play with officials of the church. When he learned that the archbishop of Canterbury planned a public prayer for Gordon's safety, Gladstone objected on the grounds that Gordon was not in danger and that consequently such a prayer "would be entirely misunderstood."[90] Parliamentary references to the "Gordon problem" were less easily dismissed. During a motion for censure sponsored by the Conservatives in May, Gladstone was forced to speak for an hour—not his best performance, ("far from good") as he himself admitted.[91] At the conclusion of the debate the following evening, the Liberal majority was only twenty-eight.

In spite of foot dragging, both the cabinet and Gladstone moved slowly in the direction of sanctioning an expedition. Gladstone's remarks in the late spring and summer of 1884 occasionally hinted at a conditional acceptance of some sort of relief for Gordon. But no firm decision was made, as cabinet members "went backwards and forwards in their opinion."[92] Hartington was exasperated by Gladstone's indecisiveness, revealing to Carlingford his fear that an expedition to Khartoum would never get off the ground "if Gladstone remains in office."[93] Hartington's hopes lay in more frequent cabinet meetings devoted specifically to the topic of Gordon. But Gladstone, as he had done previously in the ministry, delayed. When cabinet meetings were held, Hartington was no more satisfied: he believed he was systematically "put off," receiving only five minutes at the "fag end" of meetings. "I cannot be responsible for the military policy in Egypt under such conditions," he complained to Granville.[94]

A compromise devised by the earl of Northbrook, First Lord of the Admiralty, was eventually approved. It recommended a parliamentary vote of credit to fund the preparations for an expedition only as far as Dongola, just beyond the great bend of the Nile north of Khartoum. This allowed the hardliners to ready troops for the field, while comforting Gladstone with the notion that these initial stages need not necessarily develop into a full-scale operation. Not until Lord Wolseley's arrival in Cairo to take command in early September 1884 did the prime minister finally give the go-ahead for a military advance.

As a British public breathlessly awaited the outcome, Wolseley's column methodically worked its way up the Nile.[95] But he was forty-eight hours too late. On 26 January 1885, Khartoum fell. Dressed in his official white uniform and standing at the top of the palace stairway, Gordon faced the invading dervishes as they burst through the weakened ramparts. Offering no resistance, he was speared where he stood. His body, dragged to the bottom of the stairway, was mutilated and his head severed, to be taken later to the camp of the Mahdi.[96] Before this news reached England, just as the New Year began, Gladstone raised an anguished and prophetic cry: "The Egyptian flood comes on us again and again, like the sea on the host of Pharaoh, which had just as much business to pursue the Israelites as we have had to meddle in Egypt."[97]

11

"A Dark and Dreary Cloud"

The death of Gordon brought down upon the ministry a fierce outpouring of criticism. Queen Victoria and the Conservative opposition led the outcry. The ministry survived a parliamentary censure by a mere handful of votes. The public, too, was outraged by the abandonment of Gordon to the heathen fanatics. A stream of pro-Gordon and anti-Gladstonian artifacts—medals, bookmarks, mugs for schoolchildren, pictures of all sorts, Gordon sermons, Gordon birthday books, Gordon readers, and even a Gordon acrostic prayer—spread their message of a heroic martyr betrayed by an indifferent government.[1]

Gladstone fully understood that these events could be a lethal shaft to the heart of his ministry. He at first attempted to deflect public anger by maintaining that Gordon was betrayed by some of his own men. If this claim were believed, it would absolve the ministry from responsibility. This was not a successful tactic, however, as criticism mounted. Gladstone's attempt to maintain a detached public demeanor was soon undermined by nervous ill health: diarrhea, weakness, and an irritation of his hands repeatedly bothered him throughout February. His voice, too, gave him difficulty.[2] In late March, he left for a recuperative trip to Rosebery's home at the Durdans, near Epsom, where the earl had begun to develop a stud farm. Gladstone, less interested in horses than rest, greeted the trip with pleasure: "Escape from London at once sensibly improves my bodily condition."[3] From Epsom, he traveled to Brighton and took an apartment for a few days. Walking, reading, and "much quiet" provided added relaxation.[4] Afterward, he went to Holmbury House, near Dorking, in Surrey, the home of Edward Leveson-Gower, Granville's younger brother, where he spent the Easter holidays.

Gladstone had need of a respite. Although the ministry survived the Gordon disaster, it was soon faced with the worsening of that most intractable of problems—Ireland. Irish issues had been simmering since the beginning of the ministry in 1880. The persistence of this issue had come as a surprise to Gladstone himself; he believed that Irish legislation passed during his first ministry had effectively settled such outstanding Irish issues as the disestablishment of the Church of Ireland and landlord-tenant relations. When he returned to office in 1880, his main legislative objective had been to dismantle Beaconsfieldism, not to deal with Ireland. But the slow working of nature on the land had profound consequences on Gladstone's political career.

The first signs of trouble had occurred when large numbers of tenant farmers refused to pay their rents. This was not an infrequent event: strapped tenants from time to time withheld rents as a bargaining tool in negotiations with their landlords. During the early months of Gladstone's ministry, however, the action became persistent and widespread, especially in the west of Ireland and most particularly in County Mayo. The underlying cause was a depression in Irish agriculture paralleling that in England. Cold and rainy weather had dogged planting and harvest time for three years. In earlier times, farmers would have borne the economic setback with dumb resignation or with the traditional ways of rural violence. By the 1880s, however, both social and political consciousness among farmers had risen, fanned by the well-organized Land League, established in 1878.

The league's essential strategy was to prevent landlords from evicting their tenants. To that end, the league pursued two tactical approaches: rent strikes and intimidation. For the rent strike to work, tenants had to be virtually unanimous in withholding rent. If tenants held together, landlords would be unable to secure other tenants to work the land in place of those evicted. To discourage the use of substitute labor, or scab tenants, the league resorted to intimidation. Threats of physical violence were often successful. Direct intimidation of landlords was also employed, including property damage, cattle maiming, and, in extreme cases, murder.

By the summer of 1880, tension on the land in Ireland, and the widening circle of dispossession and violence, forced from Gladstone's ministry a response. To slow the evictions, a Compensation for Disturbance Bill was drawn up, which would compel landlords to compensate tenants when they were evicted for their inability to pay rents during times of depression. But Gladstone immediately encountered opposition to the bill, especially from Whigs both in Parliament and in his own ministry. They feared it as an assault on property. Gladstone was willing to compromise, limiting the bill to only one year and applying it only to certain districts. Thus did it pass the House of Commons. But the Lords rejected it outright, with the majority including a considerable number of Liberal peers. Gladstone's response to this defeat was curiously muted and can be accounted for in part by the first serious illness of his second ministry. Overwork and the attendant stresses of an exceptionally busy parliamentary schedule had incapacitated him. He had been forced to take on more legislative duties than he had anticipated in the early months of his administration. The sudden irruption of the Eastern question and the issue of Ireland, as well as persistent domestic crises, sapped his energy.

His increasingly strenuous parliamentary burden was a growing concern among his friends. Sir Robert Phillimore told Lord Carnarvon that Gladstone was "killing himself by excessive work especially by night."[5] Phillimore's apprehension was borne out by Gladstone's diary. In late July 1880, Gladstone began to complain of exhaustion. On 23 July, he wrote, "A severe week: rather overdone." The following day he canceled an appearance at a public dinner. On 30 July, he was seized with chills and nausea, and on the next day his diary becomes illegible for a time as his handwriting deteriorated.[6] This was the beginning of the acute phase of a medical crisis. Fever and chills ("not shivering but shaking as a house is shaken by an earthquake") drove Gladstone to bed. Thoughts of death—"coming nearer to it . . . than I had done before"—occupied him in his discomfort.[7]

Ill he undoubtedly was, yet Gladstone quickly showed his remarkable recuperative powers. Within a week he had improved through bed rest and the ministrations of his wife and medical specialists. On 14 August he was well enough to leave for Holmbury, where he relaxed for the next ten days. On 26 August, he boarded ship for the first of his voyages courtesy of Donald Currie. This round-the-island cruise on the *Grantully Castle* began with brief views of Falmouth, then a short and unannounced visit to Dublin where he went to Christ Church for Sunday service to find the congregation—not surprisingly—"all agog" at his presence.[8] Thence to Greenock and Skye, passing the Orkneys in the dark. After an anchoring in the Forth and a stop at Edinburgh, the party hove to at Gravesend.[9]

Gladstone returned home, however, to an inflamed Irish issue. The Land League had continued its campaign throughout the summer with increasing success. Hundreds of local league offices had been formed in central and western Ireland. The Land League not only brought into its ranks large and small farmers but also enlisted increasing numbers of townspeople, including small businessmen, publicans, artisans, shopworkers, teachers, newspaper editors, and other representatives of the general professional classes. A notable addition were women, who qualified for league membership if they were tenant farmers in possession of a family farm. From its humble origins as an agrarian-based organization, the Land League had become a national movement and had adopted the name Irish National Land League. Its stated aim to speak for all Ireland was attractive enough to win some support even among Ulster Protestant farmers.[10]

The most significant recruit to the Land League was Charles Stewart Parnell, who became president of the league in 1879 and whose importance as a member of Parliament had already begun to mark him as a coming man in the struggle for a more independent Ireland. Why a Protestant representative from the conservative landed gentry of County Wicklow should have become the most important leader of Irish nationalism in modern times remains a mystery.[11] There is no doubt, however, that his career in the 1880s was curiously linked to Gladstone's as both politicians attempted to solve the great issues of Ireland. For Gladstone, the primary question was whether Parnell was at heart a constitutionalist, a man of order, and a social conservative. Once that question had been resolved, Gladstone believed it possible to work through Parnell to establish a wider system of order in Ireland as a whole.

Parnell's political career made it difficult to evaluate his motives and policies. Frequently skirting constitutional practices and exploiting parliamentary traditions, Parnell continually kept Gladstone and his cabinet off guard. Did he break the law by heading the league and accepting its principles? Did he secretly favor Fenian aims? Was his obstructionism in the House of Commons constitutional? Did he preach subversion in his many speeches to the Irish countryside? Gladstone and his Irish executive were never certain. In any case, there was a tendency in England to hold Parnell responsible for the growing violence in Ireland during the winter of 1880–81. If it could be proven that the Land League was behind the agrarian outrages, then a case could be made for conspiracy and terrorism.[12]

Worsening conditions in Ireland induced a siege mentality among the Irish executives at Dublin Castle and convinced them to take a harder line against the Irish.[13] W. E. Forster, chief secretary of Ireland, advocated a coercion bill to counter the violence. Earl Cowper, the Lord Lieutenant of Ireland, favored stronger measures: the suspension of habeas corpus and a policy of internment.[14] Gladstone, however, was reluctant to tamper with habeas corpus, believing that it could lead to unlawful preventive detention. He was not only averse to its suspension on these general grounds, but he also doubted that Cowper's plan would prove effective. It was necessary to know precisely who the ringleaders of criminal acts were before they could be imprisoned. Otherwise, as he put it to Forster, all that would happen would be the arrest of a "knot of obscure fools, while the real instigators go free."[15]

Although he was sympathetic to Forster's immediate problem in restoring order, Gladstone continued to be skeptical about the number and severity of violent episodes. He believed that a "sheer panic" was taking place in Ireland.[16] He therefore postponed action for several weeks. Delay might allow time for the Whigs in the cabinet to moderate their coercive inclinations, and time for a conciliationist sentiment to increase. If it had been Gladstone's intention to encourage a policy of conciliation for Ireland, however, his plan failed. One by one the conciliationists joined the ranks of the hard-line Whigs. Even John Bright was persuaded by Forster "that by locking up a small number of the chiefs the rule of law might be restored."[17] Chamberlain, too, waffled. Harcourt also shifted rightward. As home secretary, he had begun secretly to open the correspondence of Irish M.P.s in collusion with Fawcett, the postmaster-general, and to have Parnell watched on his trips abroad.

Eventually even Gladstone began to follow the coercionist drift of the cabinet. Three reasons may be behind this important development. First, Gladstone probably hoped that by accepting some of the coercionist program, he could retain their support for other issues. Second, he had been discouraged by the phlegmatic response of Irish landlords.[18] Legislative vigor in the new parliamentary session, Gladstone had concluded, must be substituted for the landlords' weakness. A third possible reason may also account for Gladstone's growing coercionism: his own need for control. His views were not altered merely because the Land League had established an unofficial judiciary and thus threatened to undermine English authority in Ireland, or because the Parnellites threatened to obstruct parliamentary deliberations. Gladstone was personally determined to maintain orderly functions to conform to his strongly felt sense of unease in the face of disorder.

Yet a tension remained within Gladstone. His humanitarian instincts and Evangelical susceptibilities, and his wide knowledge and understanding of the historical developments in Ireland, often gave him a logic and clarity of thought denied to others. Thus his initial abhorrence of the suspension of habeas corpus in Ireland warred with his equal antipathy to disorder. Although he was a conciliator at heart, his needs drove him to become a coercionist in practice. The stress engendered by the exigencies of decision was well recorded by Morley at a dinner party on New Year's Eve 1880. Drawing Morley into a corner, Gladstone outlined his coercion scheme "much as a man might say (in confidence) that he found himself under the painful necessity of slaying his mother. It was downright piteous—his wrung features, his strained gesture, all the other signs of mental perturbation in an intense nature."[19] Later that night, Gladstone, alone with his diary, looked with a sense of foreboding toward the new year: the prospects of Ireland he could only envision as a "dark and dreary cloud on the horizon."[20]

After teetering between coercion and conciliation in the autumn of 1880, the cabinet began the parliamentary session of 1881 with a straightforward act of coercion. On 24 January, Chief Secretary Forster introduced in the House of Commons the Protection of Person and Property (Ireland) Bill, which suspended the law in disturbed districts and allowed arrest on reasonable suspicion and detention without trial. It was similar to the Westmeath Act passed by Gladstone's first ministry. But the intervening decade had brought a difference. Now a powerful Irish party sat in opposition. The Parnellites immediately responded to the bill by engaging in obstructionist tactics. They delayed parliamentary business by moving amendments and adjournments or by lengthy filibustering. On 25 January the House of Commons sat continuously for twenty-two hours. A week later, on the thirty-first, Parliament began a sitting that lasted for forty-one hours, the longest parliamentary sitting on record up to that time. It ended abruptly on 2 February when the Speaker refused to allow further debate and adjourned the sitting on his own authority.

Such an important—and constitutionally questionable—decision could not have been taken by the Speaker acting alone. Indeed, the cabinet had long anticipated an outbreak of obstructionism and had begun to prepare a countervailing strategy during the previous parliamentary session. In December, Gladstone wrote Speaker Brand to ascertain the "best means of expediting business" should the Parnellites attempt to follow obstructionist tactics.[21] Brand, after consultation with the constitutional expert Sir Thomas Erskine May, admitted that no precedent existed for stopping lengthy parliamentary debates, but he also believed that the circumstances themselves were unprecedented. Therefore, he suggested to Gladstone a House resolution "setting aside our ordinary modes of proceeding, for the purpose of passing a Bill or Bills essential to the Public Safety."[22]

This device was used on 3 February 1881. The Speaker's decision to adjourn the previous day had only angered the Parnellites, and they were determined to make common cause against the coercion bill. The occasion for their action on the floor of the Commons came when Harcourt admitted that a ticket-of-leave had been canceled for Michael Davitt (a founder of the Land League) and that he had been ordered returned to prison. After this announcement, John Dillon, Davitt's close friend and a Land Leaguer, refused to take his seat and remained standing, silent, with his arms folded, thus defying the authority of the Speaker. Brand then "named" Dillon, who was escorted from the House. As Gladstone rose to speak, Parnell immediately interrupted him and moved that Gladstone be no longer heard. Parnell, too, was "named" and escorted out—as were eventually thirty-three other Irish members. Only then was it possible for Gladstone to move his resolution designed to complement the Speaker's action of the previous evening: upon the notice given by a minister that public business was urgent, and if supported by forty M.P.s, debate should cease and a vote be taken. This was, as Gladstone admitted, a resolution for a "quasi Dictatorship."[23] With obstruction thus removed, the coercion bill could be assured of an expeditious passage in the House.

During the debate on the coercion bill, the cabinet simultaneously considered a second coercive measure: a proposed arms bill. The bill would restrict the sales of arms in Ireland, make illegal the possession of arms and ammunition in certain districts, and extend the right of search. As had been true of the coercion bill, Gladstone was at first strongly opposed to an arms bill and fought hard against it along with the radicals Bright and Chamberlain. Several stormy discussions took place among ministers.[24] During a cabinet meeting of 12 February, the coercionists seemed to have gained a majority for an arms bill. It was at this meeting that the corpulent Harcourt made his often quoted remark that "coercion was like caviare: unpleasant at first to the palate, it becomes agreeable with use."[25] Within a week, however, the conciliationists had regained the upper hand, and the arms bill was dropped on 19 February.

But the decision was not final. Four days later, Gladstone had an accident while returning home from dinner at Marlborough House: his foot slipped in newly fallen snow by the garden door at his London residence. Falling heavily backward against the stone step, he banged his head, which bled profusely. After a neighborhood doctor bound his wound, he spent a restless night "with very uncomfortable feelings *inside* the skull."[26] During his absence, the arms bill was reconsidered yet again in the cabinet. This time Gladstone removed himself from the controversy. From his sickbed, he released the cabinet from its previous decision: "I hope the Cabinet will decide freely on what it deems to be for the best," he wrote to Hartington, "and I shall adhere loyally to the decision."[27] Thus the frequently postponed arms bill at last went forward, partly because of Gladstone's accident and because of what appears to be a weary resignation and reversal of his previous opinion. The House of Commons accepted the measure in March.

With coercion in place, it was now time to bring into play the conciliationist side of government policy. Historians have credited Gladstone with a kind of prescience in promoting the land bill of 1881 as a transition from the dominant landlord system toward a peasant proprietorship. But in fact Gladstone was very conservative when it came to land reform: he was loath to alter the basic landlord-tenant system, whether in Ireland or in England.[28] He had hoped that the 1870 land bill would be a final measure. The reemergence of land reform he viewed "with regret, and perhaps with mortification."[29] He was initially opposed to the "three Fs"—fair rents, free sale, and especially fixity of tenure, all of which he believed threatened landlords' contractual property rights. He found himself at odds with his chief secretary over the matter. "I believe," Forster wrote Gladstone, "no bill will be a settlement . . . which does not meet the popular demand for what is called the three Fs."[30] When the government's own commission on agricultural distress, chaired by Lord Bessborough, reported with a strong minority opinion in favor of the three Fs, Gladstone was incredulous and thought them "somewhat wild."[31]

Gladstone's dislike of the three Fs may have been grounded in his reading of political realities. Whig members of the cabinet—Selborne, Spencer, Argyll, and to a lesser extent Hartington—were even more opposed than he to any legislative tampering with the landlord system. Their opposition, carried too far, could break up the government. (Indeed, Argyll was to resign in protest over the bill.) Yet Gladstone—as he worked through the complexities of the land question in Ireland, mastering the material and reading current opinion in such contemporary journals as *Nineteenth Century, Contemporary Review,* and *Macmillan's Magazine*—was prepared for a change. The three Fs began to seem less radical a social and economic measure than he had at first assumed. As Gladstone explained it to Argyll, "With a country under coercion, and only just escaped from anarchy, . . . it is a question of the peace of Ireland."[32] The preservation of order and stability in Ireland was more important than consistency of opinion.

The land bill, introduced by Gladstone on 7 April 1881, strongly favored the rights of the tenantry. It prohibited the eviction of annual tenants so long as they paid rent and did not sublet, subdivide, or construct buildings on the rental property unless sanctioned by the landlord. Every annual tenant was also granted the right of selling the accrued interest to the highest bidder so long as the landlord was informed of both the name of the purchaser and the purchase price. The most important part of the bill was the provision made for fair rents, which were to be set by newly created land courts and an Irish Land Commission. Fair rents thus became the firmest plank in the government's program for Ireland.

The bill nevertheless had limitations that revealed Gladstone's reluctance to alter the existing Irish land pattern. Most significantly, the land bill of 1881 was not comprehensive. Only annual or short-term tenants were covered under the terms of the bill; tenants on longer leaseholds were excluded. In Gladstone's mind, the longer leaseholders ought to be more tightly bound, contractually speaking, than those with shorter leases. In addition, all tenants who were in arrears of rents were excluded from the benefits of the bill. This again was consonant with Gladstone's notion of adherence to contract: tenants who had defaulted in their rents should not be rewarded by a legislative act.[33]

Gladstone spoke for the bill through fifty-eight parliamentary sittings and defended it strongly in some of his most sustained oratorical performances. This was a surprise to some of his colleagues. As Spencer noted to Lord Cowper, the more the bill was discussed, the more its perfections were proven in Gladstone's own mind.[34] We may well wonder how he became so enthusiastic a convert to a land bill based on the three Fs after initially harboring such firm reservations. The answer is plain. Gladstone had come to see the bill's utility in preserving the land and its social fabric. Most important, the bill could effectively counter the attractions of the Land League. "I have leaned all along as you know to legislation against the Land League as the main thing," he wrote to Forster on Christmas Day 1880.[35] By bringing tenants to the land courts, the ministry could win them from their allegiance to the league. Gladstone also hoped that the bill would split the league leadership. Thus, his perceived need for public order superseded his preference for nonintervention in the economic affairs of the nation and for freedom of contract.[36] Gladstone's unwavering support of the bill won the necessary votes against a divided Irish opposition—indeed, fourteen of Parnell's regular followers supported it. After amendments by the House of Lords, it received the royal assent on 22 August.

Parnell, loath to lose the initiative in the Land War, launched a speaking campaign in Ireland in which he seemed to demand a nationwide rent reduction. He also hinted in his speeches that Ireland should be joined to Britain only by the most tenuous of political ties. Thus the duel between Britain and Ireland had become personalized. When either Gladstone or Parnell spoke, the other responded. In early October, Gladstone raised the oratorical stakes in a famous speech at Leeds. He warned Parnell that he would be met by the full force of governmental authority should he attempt to subvert the Land Act: "The resources of civilization," Gladstone promised the country, "are not yet exhausted." The speech was a calculated effort: "You will see that I dealt with the Irish case at length," he wrote to Forster, "in order to lay the ground hard & broad for any measures however strong that may become necessary."[37] A few days later, the ministry—at its highest level, in cabinet discussion—decided to arrest Parnell and other leading members of the Land League.

The imprisonment of Parnell under the Coercion Act was the climax of this first phase of the Land War. It was followed by the suppression of the Land League as an illegal organization. In addition, Gladstone encouraged a secret mission in Rome to persuade the pope to curb Irish priests who were supporting the league. The pope, Gladstone believed, was responsible for the conduct of "these priests" and had the means of silencing them. The envoy was George Errington, Liberal M.P. for County Longford—an Irish landlord and a Catholic. Although Errington spoke with Vatican officials and had a private audience with Pope Leo XIII, it appears that nothing substantive emerged from his contacts. The pontiff, uninformed on Irish affairs, was somewhat suspicious and reluctant to take any strong steps for fear of complicating matters.[38] Given his views of the Catholic hierarchy, Gladstone may have taken some satisfaction in this additional example of papal obduracy.

Throughout the course of the struggle against the Land League, Gladstone had been in the forefront of ministerial policy, actively pursuing the destruction of the league and diminishing the influence of Parnell. By late 1881, his goal of order within Ireland seemed to have been attained. Although in some parts of Ireland one heard the "accents of despair," from other areas came "good & sanguine reports." To Harcourt he observed that Irish juries were now consistently returning verdicts against agrarian crime. On Boxing Day 1881, he wrote to Lord Acton that the "outrages tend to diminish: the Land League does not get its head lifted from the ground."[39] Gladstone was additionally encouraged in the months since Parnell's arrest that the Irish leader was increasingly disposed to compromise. Parnell understood as well as Gladstone that the ministry's legislative initiatives had demoralized the Land League. On the day of his arrest, he wrote to his mistress, Katherine O'Shea, that his imprisonment had been a blessing in disguise, for the movement was "breaking fast": it was time to lie low for a while. But Kilmainham Prison, across the Liffey and south of Phoenix Park in the western environs of Dublin, was no easy place of confinement, in spite of the special privileges allowed the Irish leader. Poor food, unsanitary conditions, and anxiety for Katherine and their infant child soon brought upon Parnell a series of illnesses. By early spring 1882, he was willing to negotiate with Gladstone. Through formal and informal contact, both sides reached an agreement. Parnell would promote law and order in Ireland, while the government would introduce an arrears bill that would bring under the protection of the Land Act of 1881 those tenants who had fallen behind in rental payments. This was the so-called Kilmainham Treaty; under its terms, Parnell was released on 2 May 1882.

Gladstone, it seemed, had experienced a significant triumph. In striking down the Hydra of the Land League, he had disabled the monster of lawlessness and disorder. But like the Hydra, discontent in Ireland was not so easily destroyed. The ministry's policy of coercion had unintended consequences. Bereft of a responsible leadership, the rural Irish became violent. The winter of 1881–82 had witnessed an upsurge of homicide and intimidation. No doubt some of this was a settling of old and private scores; some of it was, however, a manifest frustration at Britain's stifling of Irish political and economic aims. The most ominous development during that winter was the formation of the Irish National Invincibles, a small group of extreme nationalists who pledged themselves to a policy of assassination.

Forster, worn out by the endless round of Irish violence and British attempts to legislate past the economic and social differences between the two countries, resigned in May 1882. Gladstone now had the opportunity of bringing in new brooms for Ireland. Earl Spencer replaced Cowper as Lord Lieutenant. The chief secretary's position proved more difficult to fill. Gladstone first offered the vacant position to Andrew Marshall Porter, an Ulsterman and Irish solicitor-general; after his refusal, Gladstone asked Lord Frederick Cavendish, then in a minor position in the Treasury, to serve. Cavendish accepted. His qualifications were, however, questionable. Apart from a widely acknowledged amiability, he was not well known and doubtless owed something of his selection to his family connections: he was the younger brother to Hartington and husband to Catherine Gladstone's niece.

Within a few hours of Lord Frederick's arrival in Ireland, both he and his permanent undersecretary, Thomas Burke, were killed by a gang of knife-wielding Invincibles as they walked in Phoenix Park only a few hundred yards from the Viceroy's Lodge. The Invincibles had done their work well: the bodies of both men were punctured by numerous deep wounds. Burke's head was nearly severed from his torso. The killers were spirited away in a waiting horse-drawn car.[40]

For Gladstone the shock of the murders was both personal and political. Not only had he sent Cavendish to his death, but the assassination as an ultimate act of political terrorism was bound to inflame English opinion against conciliation, thus jeopardizing his new Irish policy. Gladstone, however, coped admirably with this extraordinary event. He never blamed himself for Freddie's death and sought immediately to turn it to political advantage. To his niece he promised that her husband's death would "not be in vain."[41] Gladstone was therefore not deflected from an arrears bill, already negotiated with Parnell under the Kilmainham Treaty. The bill was introduced on 15 May, less than two weeks after Parnell was released from prison and scarcely a week after Cavendish's assassination. What Gladstone could not prevent, however, was the introduction by Harcourt of a crimes bill on 11 May. Harcourt, as home secretary, had pushed hard in the cabinet for a forceful response to the assassination and had overcome the premier's objections.[42] The new bill, passed little more than a year after Forster's coercion measure, created a special tribunal to deal with the most serious crimes, thus obviating the uncertainties of a trial by an Irish jury. Other provisions of the bill included curfews, enhanced powers of arrest, and injunctions against intimidation and memberships in secret societies. This act was to be in force for three years.

The terms of the new crimes bill and the impact of the assassination conspired to calm Irish conditions for the next few years. Parnell himself had been brought low by the murders and had offered to resign his seat if Gladstone so requested; the prime minister refused. But Parnell's gesture was welcomed, and it ushered in a brief time of closer negotiations between Gladstone and Parnell. Katherine O'Shea, serving as an intermediary, facilitated communications between the two men. The impact of letters and meetings between Gladstone and O'Shea is difficult to gauge, but these encounters may have contributed to Gladstone's growing sense of Parnell as essentially a moderate.[43] Believing in Parnell as a man of order, Gladstone could accept far more readily than many of his contemporaries the prospect of the Irish leader as a responsible spokesman for Irish Home Rule. Similarities between the two men ultimately gave them a common ground in altering the political union between Ireland and the rest of Britain. Thus, the campaign for Home Rule evolved as a kind of partnership.

How Gladstone arrived at Home Rule for Ireland, and his reasons for doing so, remain a matter of debate. Some historians believe that the Irish question in 1885–86 was another of his moral crusades: Gladstone was thus "converted" to Home Rule.[44] Others believe that he was much more calculating in his decision to support Home Rule—that, in fact, he used it as a device for bringing together a divided Liberal party.[45] Home Rule could thus become an effective political battle cry against the Conservatives. In fact, Gladstone's support of Home Rule involved much less of a conversion experience than many might think, and however calculating he may have been, he was also psychologically predisposed to manage and control Ireland through Home Rule.

As early as 1877, when Gladstone had made his first trip to Ireland and had spoken briefly at Dublin City Hall about the virtues of local government, he had hinted of its application to Ireland.[46] This theme he repeated during his celebrated Midlothian Campaign two years later. Speaking at Dalkeith, he advocated local government as a way of alleviating an "over-weighted parliament" whose efficiency had been hindered not only by an increase in public business but also "by obstruction from Irish members." Therefore, "if Ireland or any other portion of the country" would assume some responsibility for local affairs, Gladstone would "give a zealous support to any such scheme."[47]

After 1880, his determination to implement some form of local government for Ireland was strengthened by the disruptive tactics of Irish M.P.s in the House of Commons. In October 1880, Gladstone wrote what he called a sketch entitled "Obstruction and Devolution." Although he had composed it for his own use, he later circulated it to selected cabinet members. In it, he condemned the "scandalous evil of obstruction" practiced by the Irish, which had created "manifold legislative disorder."[48] Rejecting the view that repression was the only response, he opted for "devolution" to other legislative bodies some portion of the "overwhelming tasks" of governing. If Ireland were granted its own Parliament, for example, and Irish M.P.s were thus excluded from Westminster, British legislation would become far more orderly and effective. Devolution would thus answer "another call"—that of Home Rule. The logic of his thought he expressed to Forster, his Irish secretary. "Do not suppose I dream of reviving the Irish Parliament; but I have been reading Union speeches & debates, & I am surprised at the narrowness of the case, upon which that Parliament was condemned."[49]

Gladstone's early intentions to devolve governmental responsibility upon local units never came to fruition in the years that followed the drafting of "Obstruction and Devolution."[50] Other legislative programs and the press of foreign affairs removed this plan from his list of priorities. Nevertheless, the germ of the idea of a separate Irish legislative body remained. From time to time, he continued to mention it in public. At his famous Guildhall speech in October 1881, he touched on the need for local government in Ireland. Parliament, he emphasized, was burdened "by too great a centralization of duties."[51] That being the case, Gladstone assured his audience that he would "hail with satisfaction and delight any measure of local government in Ireland . . . provided only that it conform to this one condition, that it shall not break down or impair the supremacy of the Imperial Parliament." His nod toward Home Rule was overlooked because of his more dramatic announcement during the same speech of Parnell's arrest.

The cabinet was not averse to considering a limited self-government for Ireland. The specific form it might take, however, was a matter for debate. Under Chamberlain's guidance, a scheme for a Central Board was brought forward for the cabinet's consideration in the spring of 1885.[52] It would provide for county boards chosen by the Irish electorate that would manage local affairs, while the Central Board would govern nationally—although still under British rule. In effect, the Central Board would abolish the traditional administrative machinery headed by Dublin Castle. But the cabinet eventually turned down the idea as too radical. Spencer, for example, feared that the Board could assume the powers of an Irish Convention, and Carlingford warned that a Central Board would be a "virtual acceptance of Home Rule."[53]

Gladstone's role throughout the arguments over the Central Board scheme was curiously passive. Although he was committed in principle to the board—as it fell within his prescribed notion of Irish local government reform—he did not vigorously support it.[54] Reasons for his relative inactivity are readily apparent: he was simply overwhelmed by a variety of pressing and important events. Egypt and the Sudan were on the boil, and a revived dispute with Russia over Afghanistan demanded constant attention from the prime minister. There is no doubt, too, that the disputes in his cabinet, and its subversion of his own authority, were galling. In the face of these adverse circumstances and the threat of a loss of control, Gladstone initiated a strategy of withdrawal. The contents of a suggestive letter to Chamberlain on 6 May reveal his state of mind.[55] On Irish issues pending before the cabinet, he declared himself merely an amicus curiae and a "free man" to do as he wished. The cabinet, too, could do as it wished. Three days later, after the cabinet had voted down the Central Board, he admitted to Spencer that the board was "dead as mutton." He also intimated resignation in the likelihood of an ensuing struggle over an Irish policy.[56]

Within a few short days, however, Gladstone had made an about face, and he plunged into the thick of the fight to regain authority. On 14 May, he recorded in his diary, "Most of the day was spent in anxious interviews and endeavours to bring or keep the members of the Cabinet together." Tense

cabinet meetings followed; that of Friday the fifteenth Gladstone characterized as "stiff." Gladstone himself was partly to blame. In a surprise move, he
suddenly brought forward drafts of both a coercion bill and a land purchase
bill, to the strong objection of Chamberlain and Dilke. He made no mention
of a revival of the Central Board, so important to the cabinet radicals. It
appeared that Gladstone was simply trying to appease Spencer, who was well
known to dislike the Central Board scheme, and to favor land purchase for
Ireland's tenantry as a means of alleviating both economic distress and the
cry for independence. Both Chamberlain and Dilke upstaged Gladstone by
threatening resignation. Only by circulating an apologetic Minute to the cabinet could Gladstone forestall a breakup of the government.[57]

The motivation for this curious incident is not entirely clear. It may be
that Gladstone was simply trying to outmaneuver the radicals.[58] He certainly
tended to undervalue his radical colleagues and to listen more attentively to
Spencer's advice. But the likeliest explanation is that Gladstone had blun-
dered, and this event was one more example of a dysfunctional cabinet. Not
only the radicals were sore: according to Harcourt, who played a mediator's
role throughout this crisis, Gladstone had offended in one way or another
most of his colleagues. "Each section of the Cabinet thinks it has been betrayed . . . by Gladstone," he confided to his journal. "Chamberlain and Dilke
say they have been tricked over the Land Purchase Bill; Childers thinks he
has been betrayed over his Budget; Spencer thinks he has been abandoned
on the Crimes Bill; and Northbrook and Selborne believe they have been
deceived on the Sudan policy."[59]

In the days that followed, the ministry could not shake its debility. Every
effort seemed to go awry. Gladstone continued to hint at resignation. On 8
June, the government was beaten on an apparently minor point in the budget.
The next day, the cabinet resigned. Summing up the fortunes of his second
ministry, Gladstone was not far wrong when he confided to Catherine that
it had been a "wild romance of politics with a continual succession of hair-
breadth escapes and strange accidents pressing upon one another."[60] The
ministry's defeat in the Commons had been especially humiliating. Massive
Liberal abstentions brought down the government, and the resulting
Conservative–Irish Nationalist alliance was an unmistakable repudiation of
Gladstone's Irish policy.

The short-lived Salisbury ministry tackled the Irish question directly by
dropping the crimes bill and passing a land purchase bill for Irish tenants.
But Parnell wanted more. He kept up the pressure, hammering out the theme
of an Irish Parliament and the necessity of Home Rule for Ireland. Because
the Conservatives were willing to give additional latitude to Parnell's demands, Parnell called on all Irish voters in Britain to vote against Liberal and
radical candidates in the forthcoming general election. His aim was to play
a double game as long as necessary to attain his objectives. The election

succeeded even beyond his imagining: the Liberals won 335 seats, the Conservatives 249, and the Parnellites 86. Simple math showed that if Parnell brought his parliamentary supporters to the Conservative side, their numbers would exactly equal the Liberals in the House of Commons. He had achieved, in Lyons' words, the fulcrum.[61]

Gladstone, forced from office by ministerial blunders and a disillusioned electorate, withdrew during the Conservative-Irish alliance in the last half of 1885 for crucial months of reflection. Without the distractions of power for the first time in five years, he could turn his full attention to Ireland. He read widely. He consulted his own experience and that of others. He followed closely the interplay of the alliance, which he estimated was purely opportunistic and would be short-lived. The inferences he drew merely substantiated a movement in his thought that had begun many years before. As he explained to a skeptical Queen Victoria on the eve of his ministry's fall, a centralized English administration in Ireland was an "enormous mischief."[62] Dublin Castle visibly symbolized to the Irish that their government was foreign and prevented the indigenous development of good government. He attempted to persuade the queen that some form of Irish self-government was "in the highest sense conservative." The Irish, once they were busily governing themselves, would happily remain a part of imperial Britain. By granting to Ireland a large measure of authority, he thus hoped to deflect the drive for Irish independence.

As Gladstone refined his ideas during the summer and autumn of 1885, he sought information and advice from prominent members of the party. He held private discussions with Lord Acton and his old friend Sir Thomas Acland. He hosted an important dinner party with Goschen. He wrote and spoke to Hartington, Childers, Dilke, and Derby, among many others. To Derby, he indicated his belief that Parnell was no longer interested in a Central Board; only an Irish Parliament would do.[63] To clarify Parnell's position, Gladstone wrote directly to Katherine O'Shea, requesting further information. She replied, it seems, by return post, confirming Gladstone's understanding. To reform Irish government by establishing county councils first, she wrote, would be "putting the cart before the horse"; what now was required for Ireland was a "Constitution of a similar nature to that of one of the larger Colonies." She promised to send a draft of proposals written by Parnell himself.[64]

Gladstone's two-pronged strategy of consulting with Liberal leaders and simultaneously attempting to come to an understanding with Parnell was not followed by any attempt to inform his party of his conclusions. His refusal to provide a definite policy on Home Rule left former cabinet members to make up their own minds. Thus Spencer began his curious odyssey from hard-line coercionist to Liberal Home Ruler.[65] Spencer's drift toward Home Rule drew from the young Scots M.P. and future prime minister Henry

Campbell-Bannerman the anguished confession that his own opinions on Ireland were "moving about like a quicksand!"[66] Campbell-Bannerman would eventually follow Spencer into the Home Rule camp. Harcourt was following a similarly tortuous path. Childers and Granville also joined the ranks of Home Rulers; indeed, from Childers came a surprisingly comprehensive plan for federal Home Rule, allowing both an Irish legislature and executive full powers, except on matters concerning imperial affairs.

Gladstone's silence made those cabinet members who were less sympathetic to Home Rule highly suspicious. Among them were Hartington, Derby, Selborne, and Northbrook. Hartington especially complained that Gladstone's state of mind on Ireland was either "extremely alarming" or "most alarming."[67] Mystified by Gladstone's intentions, Derby went directly to Hawarden. After a three-hour bout of book arranging, Gladstone was ready to discuss Ireland. In a lengthy monologue, he told Derby that the Union "was a mistake, and that no adequate justification had been shown for taking away the national life of Ireland. . . . One thing he saw plainly, that parliament could not go on as it had done; the Irish organisation had been perfected during the last few years, the Irish had never been united as they were now, there was very high ability among them, much higher than among the average of English members, whatever other faults they might have: and it would be impossible to avoid coming to terms with them, if they returned to the next parliament eighty or ninety strong."[68] Recording these remarks into his own diary, Derby drew a worried conclusion—that Gladstone had in fact decided on Home Rule.

Gladstone's withdrawn and tenuous role at this stage of the Home Rule discussions is further demonstrated in his relations with Parnell. Both leaders hoped for some kind of dialogue. Both understood the importance of Home Rule and its ramifications for Ireland and Britain. Both had reached a kind of intuitive understanding of the conservative nature of the other and of the intense desire of each for orderly transitions. When Parnell sent to Gladstone in October 1885 his proposed constitution for Ireland, Gladstone's opinion of Parnell as a constitutionalist was confirmed.[69] This was an important document, and Parnell's first explicit and detailed attempt to define what he meant by Home Rule.

Among the provisions of the proposed constitution were these: an Irish parliament would have complete control over domestic matters, including the courts and system of justice; Protestants would have a proportionate representation; Ireland's financial liability would be limited to a fixed annual sum payable to the imperial Treasury; the Lord Lieutenancy would be abolished; and the Crown would have the right of assent to every law passed. (Parnell did not address the issue of Irish representation in the British Parliament at Westminster.) Although these demands were unlikely to be acceptable to everyone on the Liberal side—not to mention the Conservatives—they did provide a basis for negotiation. Gladstone was doubtless relieved at the terms Parnell offered: he did not demand separation from Britain. Nevertheless, Gladstone refused to bite. Instead, he insisted that Parnell approach the government of the day—that is, Salisbury's Conservative ministry. By this device, Gladstone could refrain from making a final commitment to Parnell on Home Rule, just as he had avoided promises to his own Liberal colleagues. Thus did Gladstone and Parnell adopt curiously similar strategies: both were secretive and reclusive during the critical days as Home Rule approached some sort of legislative resolution.

However reticent he remained publicly, and however disengaged he was from the party, Gladstone in private was moving toward a firm decision on Home Rule. By mid-November 1885, he had decided on the approximate institutional structure of Home Rule: it was strikingly similar to Parnell's proposed constitution presented to him a fortnight previously. Provisions included an Irish chamber for Irish affairs, with an oath of allegiance and prerogatives of the Crown unchanged; protection of minorities; and Ireland's share of imperial expenditures. An Irish representation at Westminster would remain for imperial purposes only.[70] Only to his son Herbert did he reveal the turn of his thought.[71]

Contemporaries and historians since have tried to puzzle through Gladstone's motives and his tactics on Home Rule.[72] Hamer emphasizes Gladstone's use of Home Rule as an overarching issue to unify the disintegrating Liberal party. Jenkins sees Gladstone seizing upon Home Rule as a means of strengthening his own leadership of the Liberals, as he believed that only he could find a solution to Ireland. Loughlin thinks that Gladstone's empathy with Irish problems—gained through his reading of Ireland's unfortunate history—sustained his sense of moral righteousness that lay behind his campaign for Home Rule. Matthew believes that Gladstone was essentially reverting to an elitist Peelite mode of executive action: grievances would be redressed, but only through the narrow terms of legislative enactment, and only when the opportunity for legislation was near. These are plausible explanations. They have in common the centrality of Gladstone and his desire to manage circumstances. Gladstone's reticence and circumspection about Home Rule no doubt placed him effectively at the center of Liberal Party deliberations.

It must also be said that by his strategy of withdrawal, he gained relief from the immense difficulties that faced him as he tried to find a way through the maze of Home Rule complications. By declining to spell out his evolving ideas and by remaining aloof from public debate, Gladstone found time for the construction of a necessary sense of coherence and balance. He could also keep his opponents at bay, diminish their power as challengers, and thus fend off threats to his authority. This was as masterly a way of gaining control as he had ever managed—equal to his dominance of his first ministry. If this tactic gave Gladstone a certain psychological strength, it also unfortunately meant that he abrogated the responsibilities of active leadership at a crucial hour in British politics.

The critical month for Home Rule, as Morley notes, was December 1885. The general election, begun on 23 November, was concluded on 19 December. Although Ireland was not the central issue of the election campaign, the result of the election—a parliamentary dead heat—gave the Irish Nationalists the swing votes in the House of Commons.[73] The most dramatic event of December, however, in both its impact on public opinion and its influence on policy makers, was the so-called Hawarden Kite. On 17 December, the *Standard* newspaper printed the details of a Home Rule plan purportedly favored by Gladstone himself. Other papers quickly picked up the story and spread the idea nationwide that the Grand Old Man had at last decided to publicize his plan to settle the Irish question. The shock to the Liberal leadership was immediate. After months of equivocation, could Gladstone have revealed his plans to the press without advance warning to his own party? Derby was indignant: "It is scarcely credible that the leader of a party should pledge himself and then to such an extent on such a subject, without consultation."[74] Hartington believed that Gladstone was acting "in the most extraordinary manner" and that he was sure to "utterly smash up the party."[75] Chamberlain, too, was incensed: he condemned the plan to Dilke as "death and damnation: . . . we must try and stop it."[76] Spencer was in despair and deeply puzzled about the *Standard*'s story. "How could they have got this?" he asked Granville. "Is it a pure shot?"[77]

It was not in fact a pure shot. The information in the *Standard* had indeed been gleaned from an authoritative source, but not from Gladstone. His son Herbert had flown the Hawarden Kite in an attempt to prevent disaffected Whig and radical leaders within the Liberal party—particularly Chamberlain—from shelving Home Rule. By leaking information to selected members of the press, he could, he believed, give a lead to Liberal sympathizers of Home Rule. Whether or not he recognized it, Herbert had stepped into the political vacuum largely created by his father. Although Herbert no doubt conveyed the substance of his father's views on Home Rule, he was also acting on his own strongly held belief.[78]

Gladstone, "somewhat stunned" by the reverberations following the Kite, quickly issued a public disclaimer.[79] He denied that the report accurately represented his views and claimed that it had been published without his knowledge or authority. He then set about mending fences among the Liberal leaders. Insisting that he had not changed his views on Home Rule, Gladstone emphasized his long-standing policy of supporting the desires of Ireland for self-government in local affairs.[80] He thus affirmed his definition of Home Rule as merely a matter of local government reform; separation from the Union was far from his mind. He would regard a division between Ireland

and Britain "exactly as if it were a proposal to separate Devonshire and Cornwall."[81] He had otherwise no clear plan of action, however. The future was too uncertain. Everyone was "in too great a hurry as to determining what is to be done," he complained to Granville. "What will Parnell do? What will the Government do? How can we decide without knowing?"[82] The only recourse, he continued to believe, was to encourage the Conservative government to settle the issue, and to support their efforts.

Roiled waters were not soon stilled, however; the Kite had energized the Liberal leaders. They redoubled their efforts to force a consultation upon Gladstone at the highest level. Spencer believed it was "essential" that Gladstone call a meeting of the former cabinet soon.[83] Rosebery wrote Gladstone, also urging him to call a meeting: "It would nip in the bud jealousies and misunderstandings that might ripen into schism."[84] Harcourt, too, requested through Hartington to Granville, who still had the ear of the Grand Old Man, a meeting of former cabinet members. But Gladstone repulsed these overtures and was snippy in response: "A cabinet does not exist out of office, and no one in his senses could convenant to call *the late cabinet* together, I think, even if there were something on which it was ready to take counsel, which at this moment, there is not."[85] Hartington was especially assiduous in pressing Gladstone to recognize that he was making important policy—even when he denied it. Gladstone's unilateral decision to support the Conservative government if it brought forward a Home Rule bill was in Hartington's eyes an "action of enormous significance." It elevated Home Rule to the front rank of political discussion and indicated that Gladstone himself believed the time for action on Home Rule had come.

Harcourt, with Hartington's knowledge, tried another tack. He wrote directly to Eddy Hamilton, asking him to intercede. With some apparent reluctance—"you will understand that I am merely acting as the sieve," as he apologetically put it to Gladstone—Hamilton agreed. Hamilton did not mince words. The Liberal leadership wanted to know what was on Gladstone's mind; they were "somewhat sore at not having any intimation of your wishes and intentions at the present critical juncture." Gladstone's colleagues expected some "light and leading" on his part. They were dismayed by the indirect ways in which his ideas got about. They had heard that Gladstone had been in touch with Salisbury and that his son had written to Parnell. Did Gladstone have a plan, and if so, what was it? Without such information, Hamilton concluded, "they feel all agog and to be groping about in the dark."[86]

Alarmed and discouraged at the withdrawal of their leader, several influential Liberals resolved to find "some way of bringing Mr. Gladstone to book."[87] On New Year's Day 1886, Chamberlain, Dilke, Harcourt, and Hartington met at Devonshire House to ponder Gladstone's management of the Irish question. It was a significant meeting in that diverse shades of party opinion were represented. The Irish question, Home Rule, and the Hawarden Kite were discussed. Hartington was deputed to write to Gladstone to discover his intentions. This Hartington did, once again urging an early meeting of party leaders.[88] Gladstone, in reply, was less than gracious. He simply referred Hartington to his earlier letter and defended his actions. "I am indeed doing what little the pressure of correspondence permits to prepare myself by study & reflection. My object was to facilitate study by you and others—I cannot say it was wholly gained." He concluded by informing Hartington that he planned to arrive in London on 11 January, reserving that afternoon "for any who wish to see me."[89] Even then, he would see people only individually. As Chamberlain accurately saw it, Gladstone—still avoiding common consultation—proposed "to *'nobble' us in detail.*"[90]

In the days that followed, Liberal leaders were in disarray as Gladstone's lack of leadership and reticence continued to baffle them. Harcourt drew up a sixty-three-page memo of critical reflections on the "causes of the present discontents"; Chamberlain declared it "monstrous" that Gladstone continued to "pay not the slightest attention to the claims or wishes of his late colleagues"; Spencer sent a worried letter to Gladstone, confessing himself "troubled with what I ought to do"; and Lord Northbrook hosted a three-day meeting on Home Rule with Trevelyan and Campbell-Bannerman at his estate in Stratton, Hampshire.[91] Unperturbed by his colleagues' sense of unease, Gladstone held fast at Hawarden, postponing as long as he could the journey to London. In the final days before departure, he was forced to abandon more congenial work among his books and papers to make unhappy preparations for his return ("alack!").[92] As Gladstone traveled south from Hawarden on the morning of 11 January for the parliamentary session that was to determine the fate of Home Rule, there occurred one of those rare historical events, trivial in itself, that symbolized the larger issue of missed political opportunities. At Chester station, while Gladstone waited in his saloon car for the train to depart, Parnell was in the refreshment room, on his way to Dublin for a party conference. Neither man apparently saw the other.[93]

While Gladstone and his colleagues squabbled, the Conservatives were hashing out their Irish policy during cabinet meetings in January 1886. They decided to turn down Gladstone's offer of support for a Conservative-led Home Rule bill and to adopt a coercionist policy by introducing a crimes bill into Ireland, thus casting aside their seven months' alliance with the Irish Nationalists. The consequences were immediate. At the opening of Parliament, the government lost an amendment to the Queen's Address as the Parnell bloc voted with the Gladstonian Liberals to bring down the government. Thus it fell to Gladstone to lead the Liberals in settling the greatest question of the day.

Gladstone's most pressing problem was to form a government in the midst of a seismic shift in the Liberal party. Several former ministers—Hartington, Selborne, Northbrook, Derby, and Bright—convinced that Gladstone was determined to pass Home Rule, refused to join. (Carlingford was not asked to participate in the government.) Home Rule was, of course, not the only reason for refusal. Hartington, at least, had other reservations relating more directly to the fortunes of the Liberal party. He believed that Gladstone's stewardship of the party had been disastrous, and he would no longer work with his former chief.

Several former ministers did join the ministry, however, and thus Gladstone was able to fashion a solid and reasonably seasoned cabinet, although few were enthusiastic for Home Rule. These included Spencer, Rosebery, Childers, Granville, Kimberley, Ripon, and Trevelyan. Rising men of talent such as Henry Campbell-Bannerman and John Morley (chosen for the sensitive position of chief secretary for Ireland) were also brought on board. The lure of office proved helpful in overcoming potentially anti–Home Rule ministers such as Harcourt, who hoped for the woolsack and its attendant lifetime pension (he was purchasing a new house). Surprisingly, Chamberlain also agreed to serve, even though he had to accept a lower-ranking office than he desired: he had asked for the Colonies but was given the Local Government Board.[94]

How firmly the government held together depended on the details of Gladstone's Home Rule plan. His silence now had to be broken, as everyone knew. Yet even in the details of the final formulation of that most important issue, Gladstone did not draw his cabinet into active consultation. He merely pledged the government to *examine* the possibility of a Home Rule bill, rather than pledge the introduction of such a bill. Indeed, in a tactical flanking movement, Gladstone bypassed a bill concerning government for Ireland and brought forward instead a land purchase bill for the cabinet's consideration. In the meantime, he also began work on the proposed Home Rule bill, assisted by only a few trusted administrators and cabinet members.[95]

For a bill of such importance, the preparation was done "with breathtaking speed," in the words of one historian.[96] The bill was also drawn up with such secrecy and lack of political preparation that, in hindsight, its defeat was likely from the beginning. Little attention was paid either to the main body of the Liberal Party or to the cabinet itself. Gladstone never addressed the issue of the House of Lords as an ultimate threat to the success of Home Rule. Most surprisingly, he seems never to have taken into account the problem of Ulster.[97] Gladstone, while personally overmanaging the details of the bill, had neglected to cultivate public opinion.

On 8 April 1886, Gladstone presented to the House of Commons his ministry's plan for Home Rule. Months of speculation and mystery were now at an end for the citizens of two expectant countries. The speech itself was a stupendous set piece of Victorian politics. As Gladstone noted, "extraordinary scenes" took place both inside and outside the House of Commons as he arrived. Members of Parliament had come at daybreak to reserve their seats. In the lobbies were swarms of ambassadors, peers, and princes who hoped for a sight of the great man or, better yet, a seat in the visitors' gallery—reportedly going for as much as a thousand pounds apiece.[98] In a speech of three and a half hours, Gladstone set out the object and terms of the proposed Home Rule bill. The object, he told the House, was "social order in Ireland." Not that he was prompted, he assured the House, by incidents of agrarian crime; indeed, compared with earlier years of "extreme disorder," crime in Ireland was ebbing. Even so, there were too many examples of "great interference in Ireland with individual liberty in the shape of intimidation." There remained, too, a weakened respect for the authority because the law came to Ireland "with a foreign aspect, and in a foreign garb." Ireland could no longer be forced to respect the law imposed by another country. "Our ineffectual and spurious coercion is morally worn out," he warned the House. The solution was to invest the law with a "domestic character." Once the law was Irish, respect for the law in Ireland would return. This was his aim: not separation but rejuvenation.[99]

The terms of the Home Rule bill provided for an Irish Parliament, divided into two orders. The First Order would be composed of the twenty-eight representative Irish peers and seventy-five additional members elected for ten-year terms on a twenty-five-pound occupier franchise. These elected members were required to have either a capital of four thousand pounds annually, or to have an annual income of at least two hundred pounds, or to own property worth at least two hundred pounds annually. The Second Order would consist of 202 county and borough members, half of whom would be the Irish members recently elected, with an additional two or four university seats (depending on whether the Irish parliament endowed the Royal University of Ireland with two seats, giving it equal electoral status with the University of Dublin). Elections would be held every five years. The two orders would sit and vote together as a unicameral body but could also operate apart in certain circumstances, thus giving each order an effective veto on the other. The new body had the power to legislate on almost all domestic matters. Foreign affairs, defense, and international trade were excluded. Irish members were to be excluded from Westminster (as specified by the controversial Clause 24). The Royal Irish Constabulary were to remain for a time under imperial authority but would eventually be placed under the Irish Parliament. From its own revenues, Ireland was to contribute one-fifteenth of all imperial expenditures.[100]

A week later, Gladstone brought forward the second of his proposals for the settlement of Ireland. His land purchase bill was designed to reduce agrarian violence and promote social order by establishing a peasant ownership. He proposed a voluntary measure under which Irish landlords, should they wish to sell out, would be compensated from a fund initially set at fifty million pounds drawn upon the Treasury. The bill's immediate unpopularity in England, however, forced its withdrawal. The national debate was now to focus wholly on Home Rule.

Opposition to the bill was fierce. Conservatives rejected it out of hand. More important, a significant knot of Liberals expressed their reservations on Unionist and imperial grounds. These dissentient Liberals, led by Chamberlain, held the key to the bill's passage. Desperate efforts were made to heal the widening breach in Liberal ranks. Meetings for and against the bill were convened, adjourned, and reconvened. A climax to these countervailing meetings came on 27 May 1886, when a crowd of more than two hundred M.P.s heard Gladstone declare that the forthcoming vote on the second reading of the bill would be only for the principle of Home Rule. If this were granted by the House and the second reading passed, the bill would be withdrawn and reintroduced in the autumn session of Parliament, with a strong hint that in matters of detail much of the bill might be altered. Most specifically, said Gladstone, it may be possible to "reconstruct" Clause 24, which allowed Irish M.P.s to meet and vote in their own Parliament in Dublin. This was a startling offer of compromise extended toward the dissident Liberals, and especially toward Chamberlain. Liberals present at the meeting cheered loudly for Gladstone at adjournment. It seemed that the impending split in the party could be avoided.

In this volatile political environment, however, change was more frequent than constancy. The day after the Liberal meeting, Gladstone's response to an interrogation by the Conservative M.P. Michael Hicks Beach in the House of Commons cast doubt on his pledge for a new look at the bill. Asked if he intended to remodel the whole of the bill, Gladstone responded vehemently: "Never, never!" Only Clause 24, he seemed to say, would be reconstructed. Gladstone's statement renewed the opposition to the bill. The Conservative anti–Home Ruler Cranbrook entered eagerly into his diary that the episode "must have strengthened some of the weak kneed [among Liberal anti–Home Rulers] to be more steadfast, or ought to have done so."[101] Labouchere's impression was that Gladstone's remarks in the House closed the door, so recently opened, on compromise.[102] On 8 June, the government was beaten on the second reading of the Home Rule bill, with 341 against and 311 for in a very full house. More than ninety Liberals had voted against their government. The cabinet decided quickly on a dissolution; within a few days, the country was involved in its second general election in six months.

During the electoral contest that followed, Gladstone exuded a moral rectitude and crusading spirit that had characterized his earlier campaigns. Psychologically speaking, this was no doubt the fruit of his failed parliamentary attempt to pass the bill. Having failed, he now decidedly went on the attack. The hectic electioneering weeks that followed brought no hints of retirement. He was fully engaged in winning the election and in returning to office. The theme of his speeches was that the countryside was more deeply divided than mere party splits would suggest. This division was between the "classes" and the "masses." By classes he meant the powerful and traditional governing groups such as the established church, the army, the agricultural interest, and to some extent the aristocracy.[103] These influential groups, operating in unison, acted against the interests of the rest of the country. At Liverpool on 28 June, he gave his most cogent declaration to a crowd of several thousand. Maintaining that the Liberals were opposed "by a compact army" made up of vested interests, Gladstone reviewed the lessons of history. On every important issue in the past fifty years, the classes had been against the nation: on the abolition of slavery, on the removal of the Corn Laws, on the disestablishment of the Irish Church. On these, the "masses have been right and the classes have been wrong." Although this notion was not new to Gladstone, he voiced it more clearly than ever before during the campaign of 1886 and in the months that followed.

Gladstone carried his message to the public not only through speeches. In letter after letter, interspersed with numerous telegrams, he assailed his opponents, not only for their political opinions but for their misreading of history. To the Unionist editor of the *Spectator* he prescribed his common remedy for wrong thinking—a study of the "abominable" history of the Union, and a "Soak[ing] & drench[ing]" in the writings of Burke. He spurred on his supporters in language no less hortatory. To a Liberal candidate in Wales, Gladstone attacked the "violence and corruption" that attended the Act of Union. To Sir Robert Peel, the son of his old mentor, Gladstone damned the Toryism of the present day—"the Toryism of the worst type . . . the Toryism of George III & Lord North."[104]

Gladstone's strong language found natural critics among apostate supporters. Lord Selborne, his former Lord Chancellor, thought Gladstone "reckless."[105] The earl of Northbrook, former First Lord of the Chancellor, who had doubted Gladstone's judgment since the Gordon disaster at Khartoum, was particularly harsh in his condemnation. "Mr. Gladstone's decadence, in his hasty adoption of Home Rule," he wrote to Sir Mountstuart Grant Duff, "his hasty and ill-considered and impracticable Bills, his ambiguous utterances in the House of Commons and his deplorable endeavour to set class against class in the country, is most melancholy."[106] Gladstone had also unnerved some of his loyal followers. Sir Thomas Acland urged him to modify his remarks: "Pray don't anger moderate men by any more remarks on Class."[107] Eddy Hamilton, once Gladstone's private secretary and now principal clerk in the Treasury Office, was similarly perturbed. Gladstone, he thought, was "firing off too many letters and telegrams which are undignified and which give an appearance of impatience and even petulance."[108] Liberal backbenchers were no less concerned. Charles Robert Spencer, reelected to a Northamptonshire constituency with a reduced majority, wrote his step-brother that Gladstone's letters "have done a great deal of harm" and, indeed, "the nonsense he has written and telegraphed has been dreadful."[109]

Gladstone's strenuous electioneering could not overcome a widespread distrust of his Home Rule policy. The election results were a decisive rebuff: Gladstonian Liberals won only 196 seats. The breakaway Liberal Unionists polled 74. The Conservative total was 316—a significant increase since the 1885 election. Parnellites remained steady at 83. The election still awaits its historian, and until then some details must remain obscure. It has been claimed, for example, that the election was characterized by "all manner of intrigue" and was "conducted in a spirit of unrivaled bitterness and passion." But it has also been suggested that the election had a low intensity of inter-party conflict, which "revealed a decline in partisanship."[110] Whatever the case, Gladstone understood the significance of the polls: "The defeat is a smash."[111] He could take comfort only in certain predictable regional returns: Wales, eastern Scotland, and some northern English constituencies.

What would be Gladstone's strategy for coping with a defeat of this magnitude? Would he retire from the party leadership and withdraw from an official role to the opposition benches, as he had after 1874? Or would he continue his campaign of attack, finding a focus for his anger and loss of control, as he had so many years before during the ascendancy of Palmerston and then Disraeli? He gave at least a clue to his intentions on the final day of his shortest ministry. On 20 July 1886, the cabinet decided unanimously to resign before meeting Parliament. Gladstone then announced that "if it were deemed advisable" by the cabinet, he would be "willing to retain the responsibility of leadership, & to place himself at the disposal of his friends & take a part when they might call upon him." Most particularly, he concluded, he would give "special heed to the calls of the Irish question."[112] The cabinet, responding to fighting words in the hour of their defeat, broke into applause. As so often before, Gladstone was down, but not out.

12

"The Stone of Sisyphus"

In the months following the defeat of the Home Rule bill, Gladstone continued his campaign for Ireland. He wrote extensively and spoke frequently to friends, colleagues, and the nation at large. He advanced the argument that Home Rule was historically correct and imperially sound. In addition, he maintained it was constitutionally tenable. The campaign of education on Home Rule that he thus conducted from the opposition benches would have better served his cause had it been carried out while he was still in office, before the presentation of the bill.

Gladstone, operating from a position of moral suasion and historical certainty supplemented with wide reading and reflection, managed the Home Rule campaign of the late 1880s and early 1890s as no other political figure could have, with the single exception of Parnell. In addition, Home Rule was for Gladstone a perfect platform from which to lecture on the efficacy of liberalism as a way of promoting the general good in righting a great wrong. Liberalism so practiced, especially in the service of Home Rule for Ireland, could also exercise the priestly function of supplying discipline and order in political life,[1] and it could thus fulfill Gladstone's need for coherence.

Indeed, the Liberal Party was ideal for Gladstone: the Conservative Party was too quiescent—a party of repose—but the Liberal Party was, in Gladstone's own words, a party of "life and motion."² Liberalism postulated a programmatic approach to the general good, but problems of party discipline among the Liberals were often more pronounced than in the Conservative Party. To impose party discipline, Gladstone paradoxically did not work through organizational means. Rather, he stood above party, and from this superior position he established national party agendas and carried out political crusades. Great speeches in and out of Parliament, letters to recalcitrant colleagues, and tracts for the uninformed were his preferred means of creating order within the party; he wished not to engage in tedious wire pulling. The Liberal Party thus served Gladstone as a moral agency to put spine and backbone into the flaccid elements of the population. Hence the importance of the great causes to which he could ally the Liberal Party and the nation at large. A great cause could subsume all other, less important issues and could promote the coherence he sought both politically and personally. Hamer thus explains Gladstone's propensity for finding "missions": his "concentration, the intensity with which it was organized, and the rhetorical power with which he presented it to others" can be seen as a conflict between his "extremely emotional and excitable temperament" and his "ceaseless striving to organize, systematize, and order the diverse materials of his existence."³

Irish Home Rule fulfilled this need for a great cause. In his last intensive campaign for Home Rule, Gladstone—as he had in his third administration—took into his own hands the core of the campaign. Throughout much of January and February 1887, he vigorously attacked the Conservative government's record on Ireland. His speech in June 1888 in the House of Commons against the recently passed Crimes Act was emblematic of the thrust of his campaign. Gladstone, claiming that there had never been such a sharp division between the British government and the people of Ireland, laid this condition directly at the door of the Crimes Act. The act had neither reduced crime nor increased respect for the law. Indeed, Gladstone further asserted, the Crimes Act was designed not to put down crime but to deny the right of Irishmen to express their grievances. "Ireland is perhaps the most conspicuous country in the world," Gladstone concluded, "where law has been on one side and justice on the other."⁴

Gladstone returned to this theme in perhaps his most celebrated speech in the countryside on the Irish question. To an audience of nearly twenty thousand at Birmingham on 7 November 1888, he denounced the Conservative government in ringing terms. He supported the Irish, he said, because they could not acquiesce to a "Government which is against them, a Government of unequal laws." Whereas in England the law allowed the people to protest inequities, Ireland lacked that protection. A system of government "by perpetual Coercion" could not be defended. Nor could the historical Union between England and Ireland be upheld; it was a Union carried by the "foulest and wickedest" means "that were ever put in action."⁵

Gladstone's speeches were "inflammatory" and "infamous" to his political opponents, or even "dangerous" to the queen.[6] His former ally the duke of Argyll believed that Gladstone's "violence of language" constituted an "unequaled series of provocations."[7] Even Liberal Party loyalists thought that Gladstone should moderate his speeches. Harcourt complained to Morley of Gladstone's lack of a "sense of proportion."[8] Morley, in turn, complained to Spencer of Gladstone's lack of awareness of the "delicacy of the ground he was treading upon."[9] Spencer, for his part, confided in Hamilton: "There is indeed no necessity for strong language—the steam is well up."[10]

Gladstone's performance on the stump, however unappreciated in the rarefied air of the Liberal leadership, was red meat to the party faithful. Under the banner of their chieftain, Liberal activists worked hard in the constituencies throughout Great Britain to foster the "union of hearts." Perseverance paid off. From 1886 to 1890, the Liberals won twelve by-elections. More significantly, the government's majority in the House of Commons dropped from 118 in 1886 to 66 at the time of the dissolution of 1892.[11]

In the meantime, Parnell's reputation was enhanced in Britain by the failure of a campaign launched by the *Times* on the personal integrity of the Irish leader. Basing its charges on what proved to be forged documents, the *Times* claimed in the spring of 1887 that Parnell was deeply implicated in agrarian crime. An action for libel against the newspaper vindicated Parnell, and in February 1889 the *Times* withdrew its spurious charges. In partial recognition of Parnell's stature, Gladstone had met with Parnell in March 1888 in London, and in December 1889 at Hawarden. In both meetings, Gladstone was favorably impressed with the moderate and conservative tone of the Irish leader.

At the height of the Home Rule campaign, however, Parnell's private life became public knowledge. Within a week of Parnell's meeting with Gladstone at Hawarden on 18 and 19 December 1889, Captain O'Shea filed his fateful divorce suit against his wife, citing Parnell as co-respondent. This unexpected turn of events ushered in a period of uncertainty. Parnell continued to reassure his Liberal allies that the divorce would not affect his political stature and that the movement for Home Rule would be secure. But the brief uncontested trial (delayed until November 1890) that granted Captain O'Shea a decree nisi cast Parnell in a poor light, revealing his use of aliases, false beards, and exits by fire escape from Mrs. O'Shea's bedroom. Deceit in Parnell's private life was readily used by the Conservative and Unionist opponents to discredit his public behavior. Former Liberal allies were no less alarmed at the potential damage to Parnell's leadership of the Home Rule campaign. In the words of Morley—who was to play a central part in the Parnell divorce drama—a tornado had swept the political landscape.

Gladstone, who deplored in private the "awful matter of Parnell," was at first cautious.[12] Writing to Morley from Hawarden on 19 November, he declared that the Liberal leaders "must be passive, must wait and watch." For his own part, he would "maintain an extreme reserve in a position where I can do no good . . . , and might by indiscretion do much harm."[13] A few days later, however, Gladstone seems to have reached the decision that Parnell should retire as leader of his party. Gladstone had undoubtedly been swayed by the waves of correspondence reaching him at Hawarden—"all one way" against Parnell.[14]

On 24 November, with the crisis intensifying, Gladstone traveled to London to a conclave of Liberal leaders, including Granville, Harcourt, and Morley. Also in attendance was the Irish Home Rule M.P., Justin McCarthy. During the course of the meeting Gladstone authorized McCarthy (who waited in an adjoining room) to inform Parnell the next morning that he must resign. If he refused, Gladstone himself might be forced to resign. After McCarthy's departure, the Liberal conclave decided to strengthen their decision by having Gladstone write a letter to Morley, who would show it to Parnell. Thus, through the intercession of McCarthy and Morley, Parnell would be assured the utmost secrecy in receiving what was in effect an ultimatum from Gladstone and his former Liberal allies.

Unfortunately, McCarthy's interview with Parnell was brief and incomplete, possibly because Gladstone failed to convey strongly enough his point of view to McCarthy during the previous day's interview. Morley, too, had bad luck: he simply could not find Parnell—who was likely in deliberate seclusion—to show him Gladstone's letter. Only after Parnell's unanimous reelection as Irish party chief that afternoon did Morley spot Parnell in the lobby of the House of Commons. Quickly ushering him into Gladstone's room, Morley read the letter. During the ensuing interview, however, Parnell firmly maintained that the outcry over the divorce was a "storm in a teacup" and that he must hold to the leadership for the sake of Home Rule. Parnell was, in Morley's words, "obdurate."[15]

Within minutes of Parnell's departure, Gladstone breathlessly arrived, "eager and agitated." But Morley's report struck him "dumb for some instants." Then, suddenly, Gladstone burst out that the letter must immediately be published. Morley demurred on the grounds that the whole issue had to be considered carefully. But Gladstone prevailed, and the letter was made public in a special edition of the *Pall Mall Gazette*. Parnell immediately counterattacked, publishing a manifesto designed to rally Irish public opinion and to charge Gladstone with attempting to wreck Home Rule. Gladstone, calling Parnell's action "reckless and suicidal," responded with his second letter to the press, casting doubt on Parnell's statement of the facts.[16]

Thus, within a very few days, discreet diplomatic efforts designed to ease the path of both Liberals and Irish Nationalists in preserving the alliance for Home Rule had flared into open political warfare. In Gladstone's mind, the fault lay with Parnell, who had revealed himself as reckless and untrustworthy.

As Gladstone put it to Morley, he had come within an ace of rolling the Home Rule stone of Sisyphus up the hill, but Parnell had brought it down again.[17] The crucial event, however, was Gladstone's decision to publish his private letter to Parnell. Had the publication not occurred, cooler heads might have prevailed.[18] It may well be that Gladstone, subject to immense pressure on several sides, simply wished to shore up his shocked and dismayed Liberal allies. He was most concerned about his Nonconformist supporters, who were scandalized at the details of the divorce. He was also deeply disappointed in Parnell and his mismanagement of the public consequences of the divorce.[19] Yet the pattern of his behavior is too reminiscent of previous episodes to exclude a psychological dimension. Gladstone acted quickly and aggressively—indeed, even enthusiastically—against Parnell by publishing the letter.[20]

Gladstone's action must be understood in the light of the curious and comfortable relationship that had developed earlier between the younger Parnell and the elderly Liberal statesman. In spite of their political differences, Gladstone had a high opinion of Parnell particularly since the Phoenix Park murders of 1882, when he had offered to resign his seat in Parliament in support of Gladstone. As Home Rule emerged in the years following, both men were drawn into negotiations essentially friendly and respectful. Parnell's visits with Gladstone in 1888 in London and especially at Hawarden in late 1889 were a singular mark of Gladstone's favor. At Hawarden, not only had things gone smoothly in a political sense, but the old man was obviously quite taken with Parnell. According to Morley, his "good breeding and easy composure" impressed everyone.[21] Parnell appeared "well and cheerful" and even proposed "to accompany (without a gun)" Gladstone's sons who went out shooting.[22] Showing him the ruins of Hawarden Castle, Gladstone was pleased that Parnell seemed to "notice and appreciate everything." As for the political talks, nothing could have been more satisfactory: Parnell was full of "good sense from beginning to end." "He is certainly one of the very best people to deal with that I have ever known," Gladstone wrote in his diary at the conclusion of the visit.

Clearly, Parnell had treated Gladstone with a deference that the older man heartily welcomed. Just as clearly, Gladstone expected Parnell to play a subordinate role in the politics of Home Rule. He fully expected Parnell to resign upon the receipt of his messages from McCarthy and Morley. When Parnell refused, Gladstone—faced by a rapidly deteriorating political front and a loss of control—resorted to a tried-and-true coping mechanism: he leapt at the threatening object. As in the past, this strategy served its psychological goal; by striking quickly and aggressively, Gladstone repelled the threat. But in doing so, he acted dysfunctionally in a political sense.

Gladstone's new aversion to Parnell was evident in the aftermath of the November episode. Writing to Morley in December 1890, Gladstone praised the results of the recent Kilkenny by-election, in which the Parnellite candidate had been defeated by a two-to-one margin. As happy as this news was, Gladstone thought it sad that even one-third of the voters had been "either rogues or fools" enough to have voted for the Parnellite. He would, he wrote, "rather see Ireland disunited than see it Parnellite."[23] He expressed similar sentiments to Acton early in the new year, criticizing Parnell as being "even worse since the divorce court than he was in it." He considered the Parnell chapter "finally closed for us, the British liberals."[24] With the death of Parnell in October 1891, Gladstone had the leadership of Home Rule entirely in his hands.

The fall of Parnell curiously presaged the fall of the Conservative government. During their remaining eighteen months, the Conservatives lost a governing focus, while the Liberals continued to rally under Gladstone. By early 1892, Gladstone and the Liberal leadership had begun to expect that a general election would return a substantial Liberal majority to the House of Commons on the strength of which they could pass Home Rule by an overwhelming majority. Pressuring the House of Lords into acceptance might then be possible. The election of 1892 was, however, a disappointment for Liberals. A majority of only forty (353 Liberals and Home Rulers to 314 Conservatives and Unionists) weakened their Irish strategy.

Even before the election had been concluded, however, a dramatic incident revealed an issue that was soon to become dominant for the new government: the health of the prime minister. While driving through the streets of Chester on his way to the Liberal club on the eve of electioneering, Gladstone was struck in his left eye by a piece of hard gingerbread thrown by an old woman, who escaped into the crowd. Half blind and wearing dark spectacles for relief, Gladstone continued campaigning in Midlothian, but he did so with difficulty. The incident prompted introspection about his health and physical capacity for governing. He admitted to Spencer that his "greatest personal difficulty" had become the "gradual closing of the doors of sense."[25] He wondered whether the state of his health meant that he was "no longer fit for public life."[26] In the months that followed, reading became difficult for him. Official documents were a particular trial; Gladstone had to ask an undersecretary to use a darker ink so that he might better see his reports. Near the end of his ministry, he could no longer read "even the better print" of newspapers.[27] Deafness, too, began to intrude upon Gladstone's ability to function as a political leader. By early 1894, he complained that "much over half of what is said in the House of Commons" was inaudible to him.[28] His vaunted stamina was also failing. Once a great walker, he now found that a drive and a walk of only two miles "entirely knocked me up."[29] He was increasingly forced to nap and rest during the day—"a vegetating life," as he deprecated it.[30]

Gladstone's physical infirmities, however, must not be overemphasized.

In spite of continuing health problems, he manifested an unusual resiliency in the early days of his fourth and final administration. Acting with dispatch, he encouraged the brooding earl of Rosebery to accept cabinet office, planned strategy for proposed legislation, and delivered a seventy-minute speech to the House in spite of weakness induced by an attack of nausea the previous day. Always particular about cabinet sittings, he designed a plan that would promote orderly meetings and improve the chances of his hearing all comments: he placed himself at the center of a writing table, with Rosebery at his right and other cabinet members sitting as closely around him as possible.[31] Thus, for the most part, he managed and accommodated his physical impairments. Indeed, Henry Lucy—who had a keen eye for parliamentary performances—found Gladstone in sprightly form throughout much of the ministry. Gladstone was "brisk and buoyant" in the House, often appearing in dinner dress with a flower in his coat, putting his plainer colleagues in the shade. He dined out nearly every night, occasionally varying the routine by hosting a dinner on his own. Even in the midst of the lengthy Home Rule debates in the summer of 1893, Lucy marveled at Gladstone's energy: "In appearance he looks younger rather than older as the weeks pass. His voice has gained in richness and vigour, while his mind seems to have grown in activity and resource."[32]

Gladstone's ability to govern, even in his old age, was manifest in his leadership in devising the new Home Rule bill.[33] As his diaries attest, Gladstone was active in bringing together the various strands of the bill in its earliest stages. Meetings of a newly appointed cabinet committee, and of the whole cabinet, were the primary forums. When completed, the bill provided for an Irish legislature that would eventually be granted full powers. Further clauses provided for the retention of eighty Irish M.P.s at Westminster, but only for certain Irish and imperial questions. The final financial clauses (which emerged only in the committee stage of the bill) provided that one-third of the general revenue of Ireland would go to the imperial exchequer as Ireland's payment for defense, and two-thirds would be designated for Irish expenditures.

Introduced in February 1893, the Government of Ireland Bill took up eighty-two days of debate, most of it contentious, including a fistfight among forty M.P.s on the floor of the House during a heat wave in July. Overall, the government delivered 459 speeches, for a total of 57 hours, while the Conservative and Unionist opposition gave 938 speeches, taking 152 hours of debate time. Gladstone's role in the debates in the House was paramount. At a party meeting in late March 1893, an important decision had been reached to impose a strict discipline on Liberal M.P.s: backbenchers and Irish supporters would remain largely silent during the debates to allow Gladstone a free hand in managing the bill on the floor of the House. This suited

Gladstone; he was at his best when he was in control of the process of legislation.

Yet there were disquieting undertones. For all his work, the bill was overwhelmingly defeated in the House of Lords by a vote of 419 to 41 in an unusually large muster of the peers after only four days of debate. Although this outcome had been expected, the bill had a surprisingly speedy death. The government had planned a dissolution in the event of its defeat in the Lords, but this tactic was not resorted to. It was as if Gladstone had wearied of the topic. Gladstone's apparent inertia had been brought about neither by ill health nor by a lack of interest. In truth, his parliamentary struggle for the bill and his drive to control its fate had been sidetracked by the sudden intrusion of an unexpectedly serious and stressful issue, which activated a psychologically necessary, if politically unfortunate, coping response.

As so often in the past, the issue was related to imperial events. Under an agreement signed by the Salisbury government in 1890, Germany had ceded to Britain control over parts of East Africa later known as Uganda and Kenya, and a British protectorate had been established over Zanzibar. These lands were granted in return for the German possession of Heligoland in the North Sea, scarcely fifty miles from the mouth of the Elbe. For Britain, the importance of Uganda was its possession of the headwaters of the Nile with its eventual riverine connection to Egypt, Cairo, and the Suez Canal. Soon after the beginning of British control of Uganda, however, the East African Company, a quasi-government-chartered company, encountered financial difficulties and decided to withdraw. At this juncture, Gladstone's new foreign secretary, Rosebery, attempted to take full charge of the fate of Uganda.[34] Within weeks of attaining office, Rosebery set the wheels in motion to maintain British influence in East Africa.

Rosebery's decisive and clear-eyed imperialism was anathema to Gladstone. He was strongly opposed not only to the general outline of Rosebery's policy but also to his tenacity in holding to it. "I hope," he cautioned his foreign secretary, "that Uganda will not long continue to be part of your daily bill of fare."[35] Hampered by a lack of firsthand knowledge of Uganda, Gladstone nevertheless tried to rally his cabinet colleagues against Rosebery. To H. H. Asquith, his home secretary and a rising star in the cabinet, he drew an obvious parallel with the disastrous Gordon mission to the Sudan.[36] To Harcourt, he complained in late September that Uganda had "occupied eyes & hand for some hours almost every day for the last week." Confiding further to the sympathetic Harcourt, Gladstone wrote that he "had a tempest of hard words" in his mind on "this painful matter."[37] Sending Morley a copy of only one of his "scores of letters to R.", Gladstone lamented the "incessant & astounding" correspondence on Uganda.[38] He confessed to Spencer, the new First Lord of the Admiralty, that he had had of late "really a terrible time" over Rosebery's position on Uganda.[39] In private, he told West that he "was horrified and astonished to find how Rosebery had given way to the jingoism of the Foreign Office."[40] And to Lord Acton he condemned the "mad acts" proposed for Uganda.[41]

Gladstone's anger at Rosebery was not surprising. Nor was it surprising that Gladstone would attempt to prevent the issue from formally reaching the cabinet. When Rosebery pressed for a cabinet meeting to settle their differences, Gladstone equivocated, claiming it was in Rosebery's own interest not to have his "untenable and most dangerous" position exposed before the cabinet.[42] Behind the scenes, however, pressures were building for a cabinet meeting and for an accommodation between the two sides. In late September 1892, efforts were made to work out a compromise, which would essentially delay an evacuation in Uganda for several months. This was merely a postponement, as Rosebery well knew. Employing Captain Frederick Lugard, then a professional soldier and employee of the East African Company and in later years an important imperial governor, Rosebery orchestrated a public campaign for the retention of Uganda, arguing outright the case for annexation.

The Uganda episode witnessed the emergence of Rosebery as a threat to Gladstone's ministerial authority. From the earliest days of his ministry, Rosebery was a constant reminder of Gladstone's growing impotence within his own cabinet, as imperial issues began to dominate the concerns of the government. Gladstone reacted predictably against Rosebery, but his aggressive strategy failed. He had been unable either to persuade or to intimidate Rosebery, whose determination matched Gladstone's own. Secure in his place in the cabinet, Rosebery's adversarial role was not unlike that of Palmerston's three decades earlier.

Rosebery's independence regarding matters of policy was to discomfit Gladstone a second time during a brief flare-up of the perennial Egyptian question.[43] In January 1893, the new khedive dismissed his Anglophile prime minister, to the consternation of the consul-general at Cairo, Lord Cromer. Telegraphing London, Cromer made alarming suggestions, including the occupation of certain Egyptian ministerial offices and a reinforcement of the British garrison. Rosebery supported Cromer. Gladstone, however, was strongly opposed, maintaining that consultation with the great powers was essential and that Britain could not act unilaterally. Rosebery, he intimated, must resign. A compromise of sorts was devised whereby a battalion of British troops coincidentally passing through the Suez Canal on their return to Britain were diverted to Cairo. But hard feelings between Gladstone and Rosebery remained.

There is little doubt that Gladstone's perception of Rosebery as a personal threat was exacerbated by his general feelings of anxiety surfacing early in the new year. His diaries tell the tale. In a letter to Rosebery of 20 January 1893, Gladstone had asked the foreign secretary not to press the matter of

Egypt until the completion of the financial clauses of the Home Rule bill, the complexities of which were absorbing "nearly all" his time and attention.[44] The following day he recorded as one of "much and varied anxiety."[45] As the Egyptian crisis continued into the next week, Gladstone gloomily wrote that he was "much troubled & tossed about."[46] His mood had not lightened several days later when he confessed to "both depression and worry."[47]

As dissension within the cabinet grew and the press of business engendered additional stress, Gladstone was increasingly reluctant to convene cabinet meetings. Lack of cabinet consultation became especially problematic prior to the beginning of the parliamentary session of 1893. Morley and Asquith both strongly believed that Gladstone could not continue to put aside the collegial consideration of important matters.[48] Asquith in fact had written to Rosebery asking sarcastically if it were true that a Government of Ireland Bill was soon to be introduced to the House of Commons—he had not yet seen the bill in its entirety.[49] Sir William Harcourt, the chancellor of the Exchequer, was also incensed when he learned on the eve of Gladstone's introduction of the Home Rule bill that critical changes had been made in the financial clauses without his knowledge. Confronting Gladstone directly, Harcourt declared that he found "much uneasiness amongst all the members of the Cabinet at not having the opportunity of seeing the Bill in its final form before its introduction."[50]

These were legitimate complaints. Between the appointment of the cabinet committee on Home Rule in late November 1892 and the introduction of the bill to the House on 13 February 1893, only eight cabinets were held— all of them in January shortly after Gladstone had returned from a three-week vacation at Biarritz. Only fourteen cabinets (including three on the two days of 17 and 18 August) were called in the six and a half months from 14 February until 1 September 1893, when the Home Rule bill received its final reading. Gladstone, as we know, had behaved similarly in previous administrations. Contentious cabinets, led by such stubborn ministers as Hartington or Chamberlain in the third administration or Rosebery and Harcourt in the fourth, could threaten Gladstone's control over the development and progress of legislation, undermine his management of the government, and strike at his own need for order.

Gladstone's tendency to withdraw in the face of cabinet opposition had not lessened in his later years. Indeed, it seems to have become more firmly fixed, perhaps exacerbated by the increasingly itinerant quality of Gladstone's life. Less and less frequently was he found at Hawarden. He was, of course, often in London during parliamentary sessions, but because the Gladstones no longer kept a London house, they stayed with friends or relatives, such as the Aberdeens in Dollis Hill, or Lucy Cavendish in central London. As Gladstone's desire for rest and withdrawal grew, he craved travel: Biarritz, Paris, Cannes, and Italy were all attractive. Brighton would do in a pinch

("Pier & salt air in perfection").[51] On trips abroad, the Gladstones were well taken care of, most often by George Armistead or Stuart Rendel, both successful businessmen and former Liberal M.P.s, who arranged and paid for their trips. In addition, the Gladstone children were pressed into service throughout their adult lives. This small group formed a kind of Gladstonian court, which shepherded the aging couple from place to place.[52]

Gladstone's absences from Hawarden were a topic of comment. Algernon West, Gladstone's private secretary during the second administration and his unofficial secretary during the fourth, thought it "remarkable" that Gladstone, who was so methodical in his arrangement of books and papers, "could bear this absence of a settled home."[53] Eddy Hamilton also seemed puzzled that the Gladstones "don't mind living in a sort of hugger-mugger style."[54] During 1887, for example, Gladstone was at Hawarden less than half the year, about twenty-five weeks. The following year, he was at home scarcely eighteen weeks. In 1889, he spent approximately sixteen weeks—and in the following two years, only eighteen and nineteen weeks—at Hawarden. These years of opposition were merely a prelude to the longer absences during the nineteen months of his fourth ministry. In 1892, he spent sixteen weeks at Hawarden, and in the complete ministerial year of 1893, six weeks. In January and February 1894, the final two months of his ministry, he was not at Hawarden at all and, indeed, had not been there since November 1893.[55] The cloistered, cosseted, and nomadic character of Gladstone's life undoubtedly promoted in him a sense of repose and well-being that exacerbated his aloofness and strengthened his strategy of withdrawal.

It seems, then, that retreat or withdrawal and anger or attack remained very much a part of Gladstone's psychological armory into his later years. He continued to alternate these coping devices, as he had throughout his adult life. This would not surprise psychologists, who have found empirical evidence that "confrontive" coping is often complementary to "escape-avoidance" coping.[56] Confrontive coping (or problem-focused coping) seeks to alter the troubled environment that causes the stress. Gladstone's use of anger was precisely such an attempt. His earlier attacks on Palmerston and Disraeli, and on Lord Rosebery in his fourth administration, were designed to change a stressful political environment by removing the stressor. When anger and attack failed, Gladstone tended to employ escape-avoidance (or emotion-focused) coping by threatening resignation or absenting himself from official duties, or by distancing himself in some other way from the stressor, in order to alter the emotion itself. Psychologists have observed that individuals often alternate the use of these coping devices in a pattern of engagement, disengagement, and reengagement.

Perhaps the clearest example of the alternating strategies of attack and withdrawal in Gladstone's long political life was the supreme and final political crisis of his fourth administration. Once again, an imperial issue brought Gladstone his greatest psychological stress. Britain's senior service, the navy, had long been unrivaled on the oceans of the world, particularly in the Mediterranean. By the 1890s, however, other powers sought to challenge this supremacy. When the Russian fleet visited Toulon in September 1893, the signal was unmistakable: a Franco-Russian naval alliance could threaten the British Mediterranean fleet. The prospect of such a hostile union—combined with Germany's newly invigorated navy and recent French advances in high-speed torpedoes—fostered a naval scare in Britain.[57] By the autumn of 1893, the scare had reached such dimensions that the Board of Admiralty threatened resignation en masse unless naval expenditure was significantly increased to enable at least seven first-class battleships to be laid down, with an additional construction of eighty torpedo-boat destroyers.

When the naval estimates came to Gladstone's full attention in December 1893, the public, the press, and the cabinet were already clamoring for more ships. Gladstone, however, was adamant against an increased naval program, denouncing it as a dangerous escalation in European militarism. In a letter to Morley, he condemned the naval program as "irrational and discreditable"; to Rosebery he characterized it as "folly."[58] But railing against his cabinet colleagues had little effect. Even the mild-mannered Spencer, whose position in the cabinet made him most directly responsible for the presentation of the navy's case and whose unwavering support for Gladstone's Home Rule policy since the 1880s indicated his loyalty, was apologetic but firm in his belief that the estimates were not unreasonable.[59]

Isolated and out of sympathy with popular imperialism and navalism, Gladstone fell into a fury at the cabinet's recalcitrance. Morley's private diaries describe the old man's state of mind. On 8 January 1894, the day before a critical cabinet meeting, Gladstone looked "old and worn and anxious and . . . ready for anger."[60] Gladstone made it clear that he would not compromise on the naval estimates. During the cabinet meeting on the following day, Gladstone spoke for nearly an hour "against this mad & mischievous scheme."[61] Unless the naval estimates were reduced, he would resign. The threat—so often effective in the past—this time had little impact. Cabinet members discussed among themselves in front of the premier whether it would be best for him to resign immediately or at some later specified time. In the ensuing acrimony, Gladstone at one point wheeled around in his chair and turned his back on Harcourt.[62]

When the cabinet broke up, no decision had been reached. Adding to the difficulty was Gladstone's determination to take a month-long holiday in Biarritz. He refused to allow a cabinet meeting during his absence. Effectively immobilized, members of the government indulged in rumors and speculation about Gladstone's intentions.[63] Would he stay or would he go? West, delegated by the cabinet, went twice went to Biarritz in January to sound out Gladstone. He found Gladstone "very silent": a "black cloud" seemed to overhang everything.[64] Insofar as he could tell, Gladstone was firm on retirement. The government remained in limbo.

Gladstone's anger and withdrawal, combined with a strongly held position and threats of resignation, had so rattled the cabinet that they could not easily devise a response to their chief's behavior. His action had imposed a kind of order upon his cabinet and had rendered them, however temporarily, harmless. Psychologically useful as this may have been in the short run, it was politically harmful in the long term—a fact well understood by West. Although one of Gladstone's strongest supporters, West now began to have doubts about the premier. By retreating to Biarritz then resigning in February at the beginning of a new parliamentary session, Gladstone "throws over Ireland, his party, and everything." West was "bitterly disappointed" at this turn of events.[65] The faithful Eddy Hamilton, too, was wavering. "It is what I always feared," he wrote in his diary, "that senility would show itself in some form or other."[66] Lord Acton, another Gladstone loyalist who had visited Gladstone at Biarritz, was no less discouraged. He confided to Hamilton that Gladstone was "very excited and apparently had rather lost his balance, declining to listen to arguments and catching at straws."[67] In a letter to James Bryce, then serving in the cabinet as the chancellor of the Duchy, Acton was harsher, describing Gladstone as "wild, violent, inaccurate, sophistical, evidently governed by resentment."[68]

Matters were not improved when Gladstone, from the safety of Biarritz, began urging the cabinet to consider an immediate dissolution of Parliament. By campaigning against recent hostile amendments to the government's Employee Liability and Parish Councils bills in the House of Lords, Gladstone asserted, the Liberals could win an enhanced majority at the polls. Hamilton, who thought the amendments relatively innocuous, was convinced that Gladstone's suggestion was a "last desperate throw of the political dice."[69] Certainly no member of the cabinet supported Gladstone's proposal. Harcourt made short work of his chief's plan, labeling it the "act of a selfish lunatic."[70] Even the respected Liberal whip, Edward Marjoribanks, thought the idea "preposterous."[71] Visions of the unfortunate snap election of 1874 were doubtless present in every mind. Rosebery's opinion best summed up the consensus of the cabinet. Noting that the Lords had not materially damaged the bills, Rosebery concluded that there was not the remotest change of arousing popular feeling against them. In addition, the Liberal party as a whole would likely resent the trouble and expense of a general election so soon after the last.[72]

When Gladstone returned to London on 10 February, expectations ran high. Surely Gladstone would have reached some firm resolution either about resignation or about a compromise on the naval estimates. But at a cabinet meeting two days later, no mention was made of retirement, of naval estimates, or of Gladstone's larger intentions. Morley recorded in his diary that

Gladstone seemed "easy and cheerful." For the cabinet, however, it was a "scandalously humiliating" meeting. A new parliamentary session began within a week, and the ministry remained rudderless.[73] Five days later, Gladstone hosted a cabinet dinner at 10 Downing Street. Once again, cabinet members were on the edge of their seats about the prime minister's intentions, but he failed to bring up the subject. Rosebery remembered that Gladstone talked "almost entirely of trees."[74]

Tensions visibly increased as the day approached for the new parliamentary session. It seems that Gladstone was finally prompted to commit himself by a request from Kimberley for a cabinet meeting. In his letter to Kimberley, Gladstone hinted strongly that he would announce his resignation in the immediate future.[75] But during the cabinet meeting on 23 February, Gladstone made only a vague statement at the end of the meeting, which was not caught by all the departing ministers.[76] In the meantime, Gladstone was dropping the subtlest of hints to Sir Henry Ponsonby, the queen's secretary, that he had a matter of great importance to convey to the queen.[77] But neither Ponsonby nor the queen seems to have understood Gladstone's intent. At last, during a strained and short audience on 28 February, Gladstone informed the queen that he would bring to her within a few days a formal letter of resignation (which he did on 3 March). The final scene in this dance of retirement came on 1 March—the last cabinet of Gladstone's career. Morley's diary almost stings with its candor as he describes Kimberley's breakdown and Harcourt's overwhelming sentimentality ("grotesque, nauseous, almost obscene") as they directed their farewell remarks to Gladstone "amid profound stillness." Above it all was the marmoreal Gladstone—aloof, composed, still. "The emotion of the cabinet," Morley wrote, "did not gain him for an instant."[78]

Later that afternoon, Gladstone made his last appearance in the House of Commons. After more than sixty years of an active parliamentary life, he never again entered the House. For a few months longer, he continued making regular entries into the diary, but these had ceased by July 1894. Many of his entries were concerned with his health. Some entries contain an echo of his search for order in his books and papers ("Began faintly [to] struggle with my Chaos," he recorded on 30 April 1894). Two entries reveal visits to the ailing Mrs. Thistlethwayte, who died a fortnight after the final visit.[79] Autobiographical reveries and retrospection complete the final entries in Gladstone's seventy-year documentation of his life.

Reflecting on his diary keeping, and justifying its cessation on the grounds of age and loss of public position, Gladstone oddly enough seemed to disparage his daily habit of making a "commonly dry daily Journal, or ledger as it might almost be called."[80] The diary contained, he wrote, only the "chief details of his outward life."[81] It was, he added, "nearly impossible" to write "honestly . . . on interior matters."[82] Perhaps Gladstone was right; self-analysis remains notoriously elusive. Yet for the historian and the student of human motivation, Gladstone's diaries can yield much, certainly more than their author knew.

In Gladstone's own time, loyal friends and political foes alike, while acknowledging his intelligence, devotion to duty, and moral concerns, questioned his judgment, character, and mental stability. Historians and other scholars of the twentieth century have followed these cues. John Vincent believes that Gladstone had a "pathological lack of self-control."[83] Felix Post has discovered in Gladstone symptoms of marked psychopathology, akin to Mussolini and Stalin.[84] Magnus, so often generous with Gladstone, uncharacteristically echoed Eddy Hamilton's lament on Gladstone's behavior in January 1894: "Overstrain was making him senile."[85] Placing Gladstone within the fortunes of the Liberal Party, Jonathan Parry condemns Gladstone's "manic frustration" and "obsession with power." To Parry, Gladstone "seemed to lack the character, tact and temper necessary to lead a party responsibly." Had Gladstone been more flexible about Home Rule, the Liberal Party might have emerged intact from the controversies over Ireland.[86] Michael Winstanley, in more colorful terms, denounces Gladstone as an "incubus" who offered "nothing constructive" to the debate on the party's future. Especially harmful was (variously) Gladstone's "personal," "hopeless," and "destructive obsession" with Ireland.[87]

In contrast to these examples of psychological labeling, I have argued in this book that the apparent discords of Gladstone's outward life can best be seen as the manifestation of a consistent effort on Gladstone's part to maintain within himself a stable and coherent psychological state. His diaries reveal that struggle between his inward and outward lives—between the two Mr. Gladstones. To the end of his life he was engaged in this struggle, as he was repeatedly drawn back to the public arena and to a dominance over the events of that life. Even after his final retirement in 1894, he could not remain aloof. He was perturbed enough at Asquith's Welsh disestablishment bill, for example, to threaten a return to the House of Commons to speak against it, and he was prevented from doing so only by the fall of Rosebery's government in 1895. More important, he was active in the protest movement against the Turkish massacres of the Armenians in the mid-1890s. His notable speech at Liverpool in September 1896—the last of his career—demonstrated the continuing power of his rhetoric. In tones reminiscent of his campaign against the Bulgarian atrocities two decades earlier, Gladstone pummeled the Turks. He advocated a European crusade against them or, failing this, unilateral British action. Although Rosebery was in general agreement with Gladstone, he could not sanction a wholly British intervention. Within a few days of the speech, Rosebery resigned as Liberal Party leader. It was surely a sweet revenge for Gladstone to have forced out Rosebery with a tactic that had won him political and personal battles in the past. Rosebery's letter to Gladstone acknowledged Gladstone's victory: "I will not disguise that you have, by again coming forward and advocating a policy which I cannot support, innocently and unconsciously dealt the *coup de grace*; by enabling discontented Liberals to pelt me with your authority."[88]

Apart from his occasional political forays, Gladstone remained active socially after his retirement. His table talk with friends was nimble and informative, as both Lionel Tollemache and Lord Rendel attest.[89] His colleagues observed that Gladstone's health seemed generally sound. West reported in March 1896 that Gladstone looked "wonderfully well" and in July "very vigorous and well."[90] Eddy Hamilton's comments were much the same. Returning from a holiday abroad in March 1895, the Gladstones were "as wonderful as ever." A year later, Hamilton found Gladstone "full of vigor"; in early 1897, Gladstone was still "very vigorous."[91] Gladstone had nevertheless been forced to scale down some of his more strenuous activities—he no longer cut down trees, for example, but only lopped off branches here and there.[92]

In late November 1897, however, Hamilton reported after a visit with Gladstone that he seemed "very glum" and complained of neuralgia in his face.[93] In January of the new year, Gladstone reported to John Arthur Godley, his former private secretary, that he had been "really a sufferer" for the past few months. His "physical existence" was "one long course of alternation between discomfort and positive sometimes very acute pain. . . . It is indeed an experience new to a life of which God gave me 87 1/2 years singularly free from any grave physical trouble."[94] The facial complaint grew steadily, and in March 1898 Gladstone was diagnosed with incurable cancer of the cheekbone. The disease metastasized, eventually reaching his palate. In the weeks that remained, Gladstone visibly declined, suffering constant pain relieved only occasionally by morphia. By the late spring of 1898, Gladstone was bedridden, and as he told Rendel, he hoped for death. In the early morning of 19 May 1898, Gladstone died peacefully in his sleep.

Gladstone died neither senile nor mad. He had survived, and often triumphed, in the tough world of Victorian parliamentary politics and in the larger world of European and imperial diplomacy. If he was not the hero of myth, neither was he the bogy of his enemies. He accomplished much, but he was not above reproach. He was a man of anger and of moods—a man known for his "sulking" and his rigidity. Yet he enjoyed good company, and he was a convivial host and an accomplished raconteur.

Although this book may have seemed to emphasize the dysfunctional side of Gladstone in order to follow his psychological coping devices, it is important to remember that he was a statesman of unusual ability and significant achievement. Gladstone was four times prime minister and head of one of the greatest reforming governments of the century. His unquenchable appetite for work, his persistence in the face of defeat, and his ability to voice some of the most popular political themes of the age all suggest a politician of rare ability. He was also a man of intellect and conviction, whose policies were grounded in sustained reading, reflection, and incomparable political experience. He retained his dynamism and remarkable stamina well into his old age. Time after time, Gladstone was able to recapture the political momentum—a testament not only to his capacity for coping with adverse circumstances but also to his power to influence public life and his dedication to public causes.

Notes

Chapter 1: The Two Mr. Gladstones

1. W. T. Stead, "Mr. Gladstone at Eighty-Six," *McClure's Magazine* 7, no. 3 (August 1896), 196.
2. Albert H. Broadwell, "The Gladstone Family," *Strand Magazine* 10, 215–21. See also D. A. Hamer, "Gladstone: The Making of a Political Myth," *Victorian Studies* 22, no. 1 (Autumn 1978), 29–50.
3. Justin McCarthy, *The Story of Gladstone's Life* (London, 1898), 1; Herbert Woodfield Paul, *The Life of William Ewart Gladstone* (London, 1901), 323; George W. E. Russell, *The Right Honourable William Ewart Gladstone* (London, 1891), 270; John Morley, *The Life of William Ewart Gladstone* (London, 1912), 1:2; Philip Magnus, *Gladstone: A Biography* (London, 1954), viii; J. L. Hammond and M. R. D. Foot, *Gladstone and Liberalism* (New York, 1966), 164; E. J. Feuchtwanger, *Gladstone* (New York, 1975), 282. For a brief and suggestive analysis of biographical accounts of Gladstone see Michael Bentley, *The Climax of Liberal Politics: British Liberalism in Theory and Practice, 1868–1918* (London, 1987), 128–32.
4. Richard Shannon, *Gladstone: Volume I, 1809–1865* (London, 1982), 211, 51, 63, 230, 260.
5. H. C. G. Matthew, *Gladstone, 1809–1874* (Oxford, 1986), 49, 82, 86, 88, 92, 231, 60.
6. Henry W. Lucy, *A Diary of Two Parliaments* (London, 1886), 224.
7. Henry W. Lucy, *Memories of Eight Parliaments* (London, 1908); see chap. 1 for this and the following quotations.
8. Roundell Palmer (earl of Selborne), *Memorials, Part 2: Personal and Political, 1865–1895* (London, 1898), 2:350.
9. John Vincent, ed., *Disraeli, Derby and the Conservative Party: Journals and Memoirs of Edward Henry, Lord Stanley, 1849–1869* (New York, 1978). See, for example, 149, 216, 252, 267, and 312.
10. A. B. Cooke and John Vincent, *The Governing Passion: Cabinet Government and Party Politics in Britain, 1885–86* (New York, 1974), 66.
11. *Quarterly Review* 120 (July and October 1866), 260. This article was said to be written by Lord Salisbury: see Deryck Schreuder, "Gladstone and the Conscience of the Victorian State," in Peter Marsh, ed., *The Conscience of the Victorian State* (Syracuse, 1979), 83.

12. Walter Bagehot, "Mr Gladstone," in Norman St. John-Stevas, ed., *Bagehot's Historical Essays*, paperback ed. (New York, 1965).

13. F. A., "William Ewart Gladstone: A Study of Character," *London Society* 15, no. 86 (February 1869), 97.

14. John M. Robertson, "Gladstone: A Study," *Free Review*, 94.

15. Bagehot, "Mr Gladstone," 239 and 241–42.

16. G. T. Garratt, *The Two Mr. Gladstones* (London, 1936), 6.

17. George W. E. Russell, "Mr. Morley's Gladstone," *Independent Review* 1, no. 2 (November 1903), 329–42.

18. Morley, *Life of Gladstone*, 1:141.

19. For a comprehensive review and evaluation of psychohistorical works that deal with political figures, see Faye Crosby and Travis L. Crosby, "Psychobiography and Psychohistory," in Samuel Long, ed., *The Handbook of Political Behavior* (New York, 1981), 1:195–254. For a more recent analysis see Geoffrey Cocks, "Contributions of Psychohistory to Understanding Politics," in Margaret G. Hermann, ed., *Political Psychology: Contemporary Problems and Issues* (San Francisco, 1986), 139–66.

20. The concept of stress has been notoriously difficult to define: see Alan Monat and Richard S. Lazarus, "Stress and Coping—Some Current Issues and Controversies," in Alan Monat and Richard S. Lazarus, eds., *Stress and Coping: An Anthology*, 2d ed. (New York, 1985), 1–12.

21. The most authoritative sources of stress and coping theories are Richard S. Lazarus, *Psychological Stress and the Coping Process* (New York, 1966), and Richard S. Lazarus and Susan Folkman, *Stress, Appraisal and Coping* (New York, 1984). See also Jay A. Mattlin, Elaine Wetherington, and Ronald C. Kessler, "Situational Determinants of Coping and Coping Effectiveness," *Journal of Health and Social Behavior* 31 (March 1990), 103–22.

22. Claire Armon-Jones, "The Social Functions of Emotion," in Rom Harré, ed., *The Social Construction of Emotions* (Oxford, 1986), chap. 4. Harré's useful collection of essays explicates the most recent thinking on social constructivism. See also Carol Z. Malatesta and Carroll E. Izard, eds., *Emotion in Adult Development* (Beverly Hills, 1984).

23. These ideas are adapted from James R. Averill, "Studies on Anger and Aggression: Implications for Theories of Emotion," *American Psychologist* 38, no. 11 (November 1983), 1145–60.

24. Morley, *Life of Gladstone*, 1:141.

25. Anton Antonovsky, *Health, Stress, and Coping* (San Francisco, 1979).

26. See Albert Bandura, "Self-Efficacy Mechanism in Human Agency," *American Psychologist* 37, no. 2 (February 1982), 122–47; and Suzanne C. Kobasa, "Stressful Life Events, Personality, and Health: An Inquiry into Hardiness," in Alan Monat and Richard S. Lazarus, eds., *Stress and Coping: An Anthology*, 2d ed. (New York, 1985), 174–88.

27. See Ellen Langer, *The Psychology of Control* (Beverly Hills, 1983).

28. These ideas may be found in Mary M. Gergen and Kenneth J. Gergen, "The Social Construction of Narrative Accounts," in Kenneth J. Gergen and Mary M. Gergen, eds., *Historical Social Psychology* (Hillsdale, N.J., 1984), chap. 9. In Michael Sherwood's opinion, the essence of Freudian analysis is to weave together hitherto inexplicable events into a web of unified narrative so that patients understand their behavior as a comprehensible whole: see Sherwood, *The Logic of Explanation in Psychoanalysis* (New York, 1969), 190.

29. See Elisabeth Griffith, *In Her Own Right: The Life of Elizabeth Cady Stanton* (New York, 1984), especially "Methodological Note: Stanton in Psychological Perspective," 219–25. Also see works by Albert Bandura, particularly *Social Learning Theory* (Englewood Cliffs, N.J., 1977); "Self-Efficacy: Toward a Unifying Theory of Behavioral Change," *Psychological Review* 84 (1977), 191–215; and "The Psychology of Chance Encounters and Life Paths," *American Psychologist* 37, no. 7 (July 1982), 747–55.

30. Erik Erikson's "Eight Ages of Man" is most accessible as chapter 7 in his *Childhood and Society* (New York, 1963). Dan Levinson's *The Seasons of a Man's Life* (New York, 1978) is the subject of an informative review by Michael Basseches and Janet Kalinowski in *New Ideas in Psychology* 2, no. 3 (1985), 269–79. George Vaillant's *Adaptation to Life* was published in Boston in 1977.

31. Sir Weymss Reid, ed., *The Life of William Ewart Gladstone* (New York, 1899), 2:601.
32. See Glen H. Elder, Jr., "Family History and the Life Course," *Journal of Family History* 2 (1977), 279–304.
33. *The Gladstone Diaries* (Oxford, 1968–). Volumes 1 and 2 were edited by M. R. D. Foot; volumes 3 and 4 were edited by Foot and H. C. G. Matthew; successive volumes were edited by Matthew. Noted hereafter as *Diaries*.
34. For an analysis of *My Secret Life*, see Stephen Marcus, *The Other Victorians*, paperback ed. (New York, 1985). Derek Hudson, *Munby: Man of Two Worlds. The Life and Diaries of Arthur J. Munby, 1828–1910* (London, 1972); Liz Stanley, ed., *The Diaries of Hannah Cullwick, Victorian Maidservant* (New Brunswick, N.J., 1984); Peter Gay, *The Bourgeois Experience: Victoria to Freud*, vol. 1, *Education of the Senses* (New York, 1984), 71–108 and passim.
35. R. J. Olney has a useful description of Gladstone's papers in "The Gladstone Papers, 1822–1977," in John Brooke and Mary Sorensen, eds., *The Prime Ministers' Papers Series: W. E. Gladstone*, vol. 4, *Autobiographical Memoranda, 1868–1894* (London, 1981), 118–30. Hereafter cited as Brooke and Sorensen, *PMP*.
36. Morley, *Life of Gladstone*, 1:5.

Chapter 2: Willingly to School

1. See Peter J. Jagger, *Gladstone: The Making of a Christian Politician*, Princeton Theological Monograph Series, vol. 28 (Allison Park, Penn., 1991), 5–15.
2. David Bebbington is suggestive about the "doctrine of assurance." See his *Evangelicalism in Modern Britain: A History from the 1730s to the 1980s* (London, 1989). Jagger, however, believes that Gladstone, because of his strong sense of "utter sinfulness," may not have fully understood the doctrine of assurance (see Jagger, *Gladstone*, 12).
3. For the ideas in this paragraph, I have relied on Philip Greven, *The Protestant Temperament: Patterns of Child-Rearing, Religious Experience, and the Self in Early America*, paperback ed. (Chicago, 1988), especially 109–24 and 250–56. Although Greven's examples are largely drawn from colonial America, they are suggestive for the English experience. Complementary ideas may be found in Carol Zisowitz Stearns and Peter N. Stearns, *Anger: The Struggle for Emotional Control in America's History* (Chicago, 1986), which analyzes a campaign for the control of familial anger in American society during the early nineteenth century.
4. This line of reasoning is consistent with Bandura's theory of social learning. Bandura, critical of the notion that anger is an innate drive, cites evidence showing that aversive treatment of an individual is likely to produce a generalized state of arousal, which can lead to a number of behaviors, not merely angry ones. An individual may become angry in part to win expected rewards. Invoking anger against an opponent who holds a contrary religious view with the consequence that the opponent retreats or withdraws an aversive opinion could reinforce a pattern of angry behaviors toward other like-minded opponents, with the expectation that anger brings a sense of rectitude and an ultimate justification of one's own actions. As Bandura observes, anger "can be repeatedly regenerated on later occasions by ruminating on anger-provoking incidents." Given this "cognitive capacity," individuals may thus control anger (and other emotions) for specific purposes. See Albert Bandura, *Aggression: A Social Learning Analysis* (Englewood Cliffs, N.J., 1973), especially 53–59.
5. Shannon, *Gladstone*, 1:5.
6. Ibid., 1:7.
7. As Matthew, *Gladstone*, 10, has noted. Useful general works on the public school include Rupert Wilkinson, *Gentlemanly Power: British Leadership and the Public School Tradition* (London, 1964); John Wakeford, *The Cloistered Elite: A Sociological Analysis of the English Public Boarding School* (London, 1969); and John Chandos, *Boys Together: English Public Schools, 1800–1864* (New Haven, 1984).
8. This point was made by Matthew in *Gladstone*, 16–17.
9. Glynne-Gladstone Papers 222, WEG to JG, 17 February 1831, fols. 212–13. Hereafter cited as GGP, the Glynne-Gladstone Papers are held at St. Deiniol's Library, Hawarden, Wales.
10. Ibid., 637, JG to WEG, 10 May 1831 and 16 May 1831.

11. Ibid., 222, WEG to JG, 12 May 1831, fol. 230.

12. As recorded in Morley's *Life of Gladstone,* 1:54.

13. Ibid., 1:3; the letter is found in full in the appendix, 1:417–22.

14. See ibid., 1:422–23, for the letter.

15. GGP 223, 7 January 1832, fols. 1–12. The letter is reprinted in Brooke and Sorensen, *PMP,* 1: 220–29.

16. Newcastle was also doubtless swayed by the Gladstone family's wealth. A pact to share election expenses was agreed to by John Gladstone and Newcastle. See John Golby, "A Great Electioneer and His Motives: The Fourth Duke of Newcastle," *Historical Journal* 8, no. 2 (1965), 214. More about Newcastle may be found in a biography of his son: F. Darrell Munsell, *The Unfortunate Duke* (Columbia, Mo., 1985).

17. See GGP 223–25, passim, for the 1830s.

18. Quoted in Morley, *Life of Gladstone,* 1:75.

19. Shannon, *Gladstone,* 1:59 n. 2.

20. The quotation is from *Diaries,* vol. 2, 26 April 1833.

21. William's evaluations of Peel were confided to his father in GGP 224, 5 Mar 1835, fol. 61; 9 April 1835, fol. 80; and 25 January 1836, fol. 179.

22. Both Shannon's *Gladstone,* chap. 2, and Matthew's *Gladstone,* chap. 2, are essential reading for an understanding of Gladstonian conservatism. Although I do not discard their arguments (in fact, I draw frequently on them), my emphasis is different from theirs.

23. *Diaries,* vol. 2, 2 August and 5 August 1834.

24. See William's complaints about his election committee's actions during the election of 1832 in Jagger, *Gladstone,* 253. This was apparently still an issue years later. See GGP 225, WEG to JG, 3 February 1837, fols. 20–22; *Diaries,* vol. 3, 2 June 1841.

25. GGP 223, WEG to JG, 13 December 1834, fol. 252.

26. See *Diaries,* vol. 2, 3 March and 6 March 1835.

27. GGP 223, WEG to JG, 11 March 1835, fols. 62–63.

28. This was the first of many threats of resignation throughout his long career, as M. R. D. Foot notes in *Diaries,* vol. 2, 156 n. 11. Gladstone, however, informed neither Aberdeen nor Peel of his intentions before this short-lived ministry fell.

29. *Diaries,* vol. 2, 22 August 1835.

30. Entitled "Thoughts by WEG," the paper may be found in GGP 1383.

31. *Diaries,* vol. 2, 25 August 1835.

32. Ibid., 4 September 1835.

33. Ibid., 13 February 1836. All translations into English are those of the editors of the Gladstone *Diaries.*

34. Ibid., 15 February 1836.

35. GGP 224, WEG to JG, 18 February 1836, fol. 204.

36. *Diaries,* vol. 2, 4 August 1836.

37. Ibid., 2 October 1835.

38. Shannon, *Gladstone,* 1:63.

39. See the account in Magnus, *Gladstone,* 29–30.

40. D. C. Lathbury, ed., *Correspondence on Church and Religion of William Ewart Gladstone* (London, 1910), 2:232. The quotation is taken from a letter dated 30 November 1835 to his father, the original of which is in GGP 224, fol. 152. Lathbury edits the letter to remove any reference to his brother's marriage.

41. *Diaries,* vol. 2, 18 November 1835.

42. Ibid., 28 January 1836.

43. Ibid., 14 November 1837.

44. Ibid., 15 November 1837.

45. Ibid., 30 March 1838.

46. Ibid., 23 May 1838.

47. Ibid., 4 June 1838.

48. Ibid.
49. As Feuchtwanger, *Gladstone*, 33, notes, working on the book was for him a kind of catharsis at a time of inner doubt and tribulation.
50. Works of the late twentieth century discussing Gladstone's purpose in writing *State and Church* include Richard J. Helmstadter, "Conscience and Politics: Gladstone's First Book," in Bruce L. Kinzer, ed., *The Gladstonian Turn of Mind: Essays Presented to J. B. Conacher* (Toronto, 1985); Perry Butler's comprehensive *Gladstone: Church, State, and Tractarianism: A Study of His Religious Ideas and Attitudes, 1809–1859* (Oxford, 1982); and Deryck Schreuder, "Gladstone and the Conscience of the State," in Peter Marsh, ed., *The Conscience of the Victorian State* (Syracuse, 1979), 73–134. Alec R. Vidler's earlier study, *The Orb and the Cross* (London, 1945), remains valuable, although it should be noted that Vidler used the fourth (and greatly expanded) edition of *State and Church*, published in 1841.
51. A useful review of contemporary responses may be found in Alfred F. Robbins, *The Early Public Life of William Ewart Gladstone* (New York, 1894), chap. 14. Opinions ranged from the *Times*'s condemnation of its "popish biases" to Arnold of Rugby's qualified approval.
52. T. W. Reid, *Life of Lord Houghton* (1890), 1:316; quoted in Shannon's *Gladstone*, 1:81.
53. For a brief life of Glynne, see A. Geoffrey Veysey, "Sir Stephen Glynne," *Journal of the Flintshire Historical Society* 30 (1981–82), 151–70.
54. The letter may be found in Magnus, *Gladstone*, 38–39.
55. *Diaries*, vol. 2, 6 February 1839, 576.

Chapter 3: The Need for Control

1. The poem may be found in Robbins, *Early Public Life of Gladstone*, 367–68.
2. For these quotations, see Edwin A. Pratt, *Catherine Gladstone: Life, Good Works, and Political Efforts* (London, 1898), 30–32.
3. Stead, "Mr. Gladstone at Eighty-Six," 199–200.
4. Broadwell, "The Gladstone Family," 216.
5. Although A. Tilney Bassett's edition of their letters, *Gladstone to His Wife* (London, 1936), remains a useful source, it perpetuates the myth of an unruffled domesticity. The unpublished Glynne-Gladstone papers at Hawarden disclose the rougher edges of their marriage.
6. Drafts of house rules for 1840 and 1841 may be found in GGP 1542–1544.
7. A. H. D. Acland, *Memoir and Letters of the Right Honourable Sir Thomas Dyke Acland* (London, 1902), Acland to his sister, 31 January 1840, 114. Acland was one of Gladstone's oldest friends: they first met at Christ Church.
8. GGP 769, WEG to CG, 18 January 1840, fol. 30.
9. Ibid., 20 January 1840, fols. 34–35.
10. Ibid., 17 December 1841, fol. 120.
11. Ibid., 22 June 1841, fol. 68; 25 June 1841, fols. 73–74.
12. Ibid., 609, CG to WEG, 9 December 1841. Catherine's letters to William are unfoliated.
13. Ibid., CG to WEG, 16 June 1841.
14. Ibid., 1840, undated, but probably late in the year.
15. Bassett, *Gladstone to His Wife*, 10 December 1841, 10.
16. GGP 610, CG to WEG, 8 April 1842.
17. Ibid., 769, WEG to CG, 9 April 1842, fol. 134.
18. Ibid., 21 April 1842, fol. 157.
19. Ibid., 610, CG to WEG, 22 April 1842.
20. Ibid., 769, WEG to CG, 19 January 1843, fols. 201–2.
21. Ibid., 1 August 1843, fol. 235.
22. Ibid., 3 August 1843, fol. 241.
23. Ibid., CG to WEG, 21 December 1845.
24. Ibid., 24 December 1845.
25. *Diaries*, vol. 3, 24 and 25 December 1845.

26. Joyce Marlow, *Mr and Mrs Gladstone: An Intimate Biography* (London, 1977), 40–41. The "growing family" ultimately included eight children: William Henry (1840–91), Agnes (1842–1931), Stephen Edward (1844–1920), Catherine Jessy (1845–50), Mary (1847–1927), Helen (1849–1925), Henry Neville (1852–1935), and Herbert John (1854–1930).

27. Georgina Battiscombe, *Mrs. Gladstone: The Portrait of a Marriage* (London, 1954), ix.

28. Essential for the details of Peel's ministry is the second volume of Norman Gash's biography, *Sir Robert Peel: The Life of Sir Robert Peel after 1830* (London, 1972). A shorter analysis of the ministry may be found in Travis L. Crosby, *Sir Robert Peel's Administration, 1841–1846* (Newton Abbot, Devon, 1976).

29. For a history of the agricultural protectionist movement see Travis L. Crosby, *English Farmers and the Politics of Protection, 1815–1852* (Hassocks, Sussex, 1977).

30. Morley, *Life of Gladstone*, 1:189.

31. See Shannon's account of Gladstone's work at the Board of Trade in his *Gladstone*, 1:115–30. F. E. Hyde's *Mr Gladstone at the Board of Trade* (1934) remains valuable for details.

32. Morley, *Life of Gladstone*, 1:143.

33. William E. Gladstone, "Course of Commercial Policy at Home and Abroad," *Foreign and Colonial Quarterly Review* (January 1843), 222–73.

34. *Diaries*, vol. 3, 174.

35. Ibid., 178.

36. Two accounts of this incident are published in his *Autobiographica*: see Brooke and Sorensen, *PMP*, 1:44–46 (dated 1892); and 1:74 (dated 1894). The quotation is from 1:45.

37. Gladstone's apology to Peel is found in ibid., 1:234–35 (in an appendix to *PMP*).

38. *Diaries*, vol. 3, 279–80.

39. For the importance of Maynooth to the Peel ministry see E. R. Norman, "The Maynooth Question of 1845," *Irish Historical Studies* 15 (1967), 407–37.

40. *Diaries*, vol. 3, 355. See Gladstone's detailed entries in ibid., 12, 13, 28 February 1844, and 2, 4 March 1844.

41. Ibid., 388.

42. Morley calls it a "truly singular" and "startling" offer. Gladstone himself in reflecting on this episode near the end of his life could not imagine how he came to believe that "this was a rational or in any way excusable proposal." See Morley's *Life of Gladstone*, 1:201.

43. Ibid., 1:202, 23 November 1844.

44. *Diaries*, vol. 3, 429.

45. *Hansard's Parliamentary Debates*, 3d ser., vol. 77, 77–81, 4 February 1845. (Hereafter cited as *Hansard*.)

46. Quoted by Morley, *Life of Gladstone*, 1:206.

47. *Diaries*, vol. 3, 3 April 1845.

48. *Hansard*, 3d ser., vol. 79, 550, 11 April 1845.

49. Matthew, *Gladstone*, 69.

50. As Matthew believes: see ibid., 69 and 72.

51. See David Newsome's readable discussion of the attractions of the Oxford Movement in *The Parting of Friends: A Study of the Wilberforces and Henry Manning* (London, 1966).

52. A division of opinion exists among scholars about Gladstone's adherence to the Oxford Movement. Agatha Ramm believes he was not wholly in sympathy with either Evangelicalism or the Oxford Movement: see her thoughtful article "Gladstone's Religion," *Historical Journal* 28, no. 2 (1985), 327–40. Matthew, *Gladstone*, 54, 71, 90, 93, seems firm that Gladstone was a Tractarian. The strongest case for Gladstone as an active Tractarian has been made by M. J. Lynch, "Was Gladstone a Tractarian? W. E. Gladstone and the Oxford Movement, 1833–45," *Journal of Religious History* (Australia) 8, no. 4 (1975), 364–89.

53. Perry Butler believes that Gladstone's trip to Rome in 1832 was important to his break with Evangelical religion: see his *Gladstone, Church, State, and Tractarianism: A Study of His Religious Ideas and Attitudes* (Oxford, 1982).

54. Peter Jagger has labeled Gladstone's new theological position Catholic Evangelicalism. Jagger's *Gladstone* has informed the following paragraphs.
55. See Christopher G. Ellison, "Religious Involvement and Subjective Well-Being," *Journal of Health and Social Behavior* 32 (March 1991), 80–99.
56. Ramm, "Gladstone's Religion," 330–31. Ramm's argument is far richer than I make it out here, but this seems to me representative of her analysis—that Gladstone in his religious quest acted as a pilgrim on an intellectual journey. I am suggesting that although Gladstone's religious decisions doubtless included intentional and reasoned elements, they had additional elements not wholly known to Gladstone himself.
57. GGP 751, 11 October 1829, fols. 45–50, passim.
58. Ibid., 18 October 1829.
59. Shannon believes that Helen's conversion had something about it of an "unconscious mode of revenge" against her family's treatment of her: see his *Gladstone*, 6.
60. GGP 751, 10 January 1841, fols. 146–47, passim.
61. Ibid., 30 May 1842, fols. 154–59, passim.
62. Ibid., 226, WEG to JG, 17 June 1842, fol. 178.
63. *Diaries*, vol. 3, 31 June 1842.
64. Ibid., 205.
65. GGP 226, 11 July 1842, fols. 188–89.
66. Ibid., 751, 28 June 1847, fols. 173–76, passim.
67. Matthew's recounting of this episode is in *Diaries*, vol. 9, "Introduction," xcvi.
68. Shannon, *Gladstone*, 44. Shannon also notes Hope's invaluable service to Gladstone as a painstaking editor of his *State and Church:* Hope virtually rewrote Gladstone's "rather tortured text" (ibid., 70).
69. Gladstone Papers, British Library (hereafter cited as GPBL), Add MSS 44214, 15 May 1845, fols. 267–69. The letter is printed in full in Lathbury, *Correspondence on Church and Religion of Gladstone*, 1:335–42.
70. Shannon terms this a ploy on Gladstone's part: see his *Gladstone*, 188.
71. For these entries, see *Diaries*, vol. 3, 6 March 1851, 29 March 1851, 6 April 1851, and 7 April 1851.
72. Morley, *Life of Gladstone*, 1:287. Gladstone's letter was to Robert Issac Wilberforce, then archdeacon of East Riding and Manning's Anglican confessor for many years. In 1854, Wilberforce himself entered the Roman Catholic Church.
73. *Diaries*, vol. 4, 30 March 1851, 11 May 1851, 19 August 1851. His remembrance of these tortured months remained fresh years later. Reviewing the galley proofs of Ornsby's *Memoirs of Hope-Scott* (Hope changed his name to Hope-Scott in 1853 after marrying Sir Walter Scott's granddaughter), Gladstone admitted to a revival of a "profoundly anxious past" (*Diaries*, vol. 9, 24 November 1883).

Chapter 4: "In Respect of Things of a Certain Kind"

1. For information on Oak Farm see Matthew, *Gladstone*, 88–89; Shannon, *Gladstone*, 202–5; S. G. Checkland, *The Gladstones: A Family Biography, 1764–1851* (Cambridge, England, 1971), 314–15, 353, 359; and Veysey, "Sir Stephen Glynne," 159–61.
2. Morley noted that Gladstone wrote 140 letters to Freshfield concerning Oak Farm (Morley's *Life of Gladstone*, 1:251).
3. *Diaries*, vol. 4, 21 February 1848.
4. GGP 228, WEG to JG, 23 February 1848, fol. 261.
5. *Diaries*, vol. 3, 5 May 1849.
6. Gladstone to Lord Lyttelton, 29 July 1874, quoted in Veysey, "Sir Stephen Glynne," 160.
7. For a general background see Checkland, *The Gladstones*, chap. 30, "The Ancient Baronet, 1846–51."
8. GGP 771, WEG to CG, 1 April 1847, fols. 3–6; and WEG to CG, 9 April 1847, fol. 21.

9. See *Diaries*, vol. 3, 29 March–15 April 1847, for the details of this visit to Fasque.

10. GGP 228, WEG to JG, 23 January 1847, fol. 13.

11. Ibid., 229, WEG to JG, 11 June 1849, fols. 111–14.

12. Ibid., 771, WEG to CG, 25 September 1850, fols. 275–76.

13. Ibid., 772, WEG to CG, 3 May 1851, fol. 39.

14. See *Diaries*, vol. 4, especially 29 November–14 December 1851.

15. Ibid., 7 December 1851.

16. The quotations in this paragraph are from *Diaries*, vol. 4, 13 December and 26 December 1851.

17. For these quotations see Bassett, *Gladstone to His Wife*, 145; Magnus, *Gladstone*, 107; and Derek Beales, "Gladstone and His Diary: 'Myself, the Worst of All Interlocutors,'" *Historical Journal* 25, no, 2 (1982), 468.

18. This follows Matthew's argument in his *Gladstone*, 90–95.

19. *Diaries*, vol. 1, 5 and 6 August 1828.

20. Ibid., 24 October 1829.

21. Ibid., 22 July 1831 and 7 September 1831.

22. Arthur J. Engel, "'Immoral Intentions': The University of Oxford and the Problem of Prostitution, 1827–1914," *Victorian Studies* 23, no. 1 (Autumn 1979), 79–107.

23. *Diaries*, vol. 2, 25 February 1837.

24. Ibid., vol. 3, 31 October 1842, 3 November 1842, 5 October 1844, 5 November 1844, 27 November 1844, 2 December 1844, 3 December 1844, 4 March 1845. Happier news about Ayscough came some time later, however. A letter from Catherine Gladstone to WEG mentioned her marriage, and that she was now Rebecca Daly (GGP 612, 21 April 1851, unfoliated). This was probably one of the few rescue cases known to Catherine. Some of Gladstone's early encounters with prostitutes may have gone unrecorded; see *Diaries*, vol. 3, "Introduction," xlv n. 1.

25. Matthew, *Gladstone*, 90–91; Shannon, *Gladstone*, 171–72.

26. The letter is dated 24 November 1844 and is reprinted in its entirety in Shannon, *Gladstone*, 160. The Engagement included such prominent men as Frederic Rogers, Roundell Palmer, and T. D. Acland. It lasted until about 1852. See Matthew, *Gladstone*, 90; *Diaries*, vol. 3, 436 n. 1; and Shannon, *Gladstone*, 171–72.

27. *Diaries*, vol. 3, 26 October 1845, and "Introduction," xlvi.

28. Ibid., vol. 4, 13 May 1848, 15 May 1848, 18 May 1848. See also 35 n. 9.

29. Ibid., 19 July 1848, 54.

30. Ibid., 51.

31. Ibid., 29 December 1848.

32. Ibid., vol. 3, "Introduction," xlvii. Matthew also hints that Gladstone may have been attracted to pain in some way. See Gladstone's diary entry of 4 January 1843 in vol. 3 where he speculates on "how far pain may become the ground of enjoyment." Gladstone wondered if a "joy in the justice and in the beneficial effects of that chastisement" might not "more than compensate and counteract even at the moment the suffering of the punishment itself?"

33. Ibid., vol. 4, 22 April 1849. The quotations that follow are taken from this diary entry.

34. Information on the Lincoln divorce scandal and Gladstone's part in it may be found in the following: *Diaries*, vol. 4, especially the entries from 13 July 1849 through 9 August 1849; C. C. Eldridge, "The Lincoln Divorce Case: A Study in Victorian Morality," *Trivium* 11 (1975), 21–39; and Munsell, *The Unfortunate Duke*, chap. 6.

35. *Diaries*, vol. 4, 7 July 1849.

36. As Shannon observes in his *Gladstone*, 215.

37. *Diaries*, vol. 2, 23 February 1833 and 20 January 1837.

38. Ibid., vol. 4, 5 August 1849.

39. Ibid., 2 April 1850.

40. This recollection may be found in Brooke and Sorensen, *PMP*, 3:50–66.

41. Lord Kilbracken, *Reminiscences of Lord Kilbracken* (London, 1931), 126–27.

42. Written in 1896 and quoted in Morley, *Life of Gladstone*, 1:282. In an earlier retrospective view, Gladstone recalled, "Suddenly plunged into a vortex of complicated controversies on the relations

of Church and State, I was a good deal tossed about: and in 1850 family cares and sorrow wrought me (for I was a kind of spoilt child of Providence) into an unusual susceptibility" (*Diaries*, vol. 7, WEG to Manning, 16 November 1869, 171–72).

43. *Diaries*, vol. 4, 15 August 1850.

44. Ibid., 5 October 1850.

45. Ibid., 25 October 1850, 248. Shannon implies that this was an excuse: the real reason for the trip was Gladstone's own restlessness. See his *Gladstone*, 226 and 228.

46. *Diaries*, vol. 4, 22 October 1850.

47. Shannon notes as much in his account of Gladstone's Neapolitan expedition: see his *Gladstone*, 228–33.

48. The tone of this important trip can best be gauged by reading the *Diaries*, vol. 4, from 18 October 1850 to 26 February 1851, 245–310.

49. Quotations in this paragraph may be found passim in *Letters to the Earl of Aberdeen*, republished in W. E. Gladstone, *Gleanings of Past Years, 1851–77* (London, 1879), 4:1–69.

50. Selections from the *Correspondence of George, Earl of Aberdeen, K.G., K.T., 1850–52*, ed. Arthur H. Gordon, Baron Stanmore (n.p., n.d.), Aberdeen to Prince Schwarzenberg (the Austrian chancellor), 15 August 1851, 125. For an additional account of this affair see Muriel Chamberlain's *Lord Aberdeen: A Political Biography* (London, 1983), 404–6.

51. See Shannon's suggestive interpretation of the circumstances behind the publication of the *Letters* in his *Gladstone*, 238–42. Shannon, unlike Morley (*Life of Gladstone*, 1:289), does not believe that the *Letters* are a sign of an emerging liberalism in Gladstone.

52. For Gladstone's essentially conservative position as it related to political change in Italy see D. M. Schreuder, "Gladstone and Italian Unification, 1848–70: The Making of a Liberal?" *English Historical Review* 85, no. 336 (July 1970), 475–501. Keith A. P. Sandiford extends this argument to other nationalist movements in his "W. E. Gladstone and Liberal-Nationalist Movements," *Albion* 13, no. 1 (Spring 1981), 27–42.

53. *Diaries*, vol. 4, 28 February 1851, 1 March 1851, 4 March 1851, 7 March 1851, 28 March 1851, 30 March 1851, 31 March 1851.

54. Ibid., 1 July 1852.

55. Ibid., 23 July 1852.

56. Ibid., 22 May 1852, 13 October 1852, 21 October 1852, 19 November 1852.

57. See the report in *The Greville Memoirs*, ed. Lytton Strachey and Roger Fulford (London, 1938), 6:422. Greville reported that the editor of the *Morning Herald* sent a letter to Gladstone assuring him "of their confidence in his purity and innocence" and that the *Herald* would play down the incident. The gossipy Greville reported that there was a general disposition to believe that Gladstone "had no improper motive or purpose." Nevertheless, Greville thought it a "very strange affair" not yet satisfactorily explained. Gladstone has a brief account in his *Diaries*, vol. 4, 10 May 1853.

58. See Matthew's comments in *Diaries*, vol. 3, "Introduction," xliv.

59. Ibid., vol. 4, 31 January 1854.

60. Bernard C. Meyer, "Some Observations on the Rescue of Fallen Women," *Psychoanalytic Quarterly* 53, no. 2 (1984), 208–39.

61. Eric Trudgill, *Madonnas and Magdalens: The Origins and Development of Victorian Sexual Attitudes* (New York, 1976), especially chap. 5, "The Welcome Social Outcast."

62. Gay, *Education of the Senses*, 248.

63. Ibid., 10.

64. Jeffrey Weeks, *Sex, Politics, and Society* (London, 1981), chap. 1, "Sexuality and the Historian," 2.

65. The discussion that follows is based on an essay by Leonore Davidoff, "Class and Gender in Victorian England: The Diaries of Arthur J. Munby and Hannah Cullwick," *Feminist Studies* 5, no. 1 (Spring 1979), 86–141.

66. Useful information on Victorian prostitution may be found in Frances Finnegan, *Poverty and Prostitution: A Study of Victorian Prostitutes in York* (Cambridge, England, 1979); and Judith R.

Walkowitz, *Prostitution and Victorian Society: Women, Class, and the State* (Cambridge, England, 1980).

67. Judith R. Walkowitz, *City of Dreadful Delight: Narratives of Sexual Danger in Late-Victorian London* (Chicago, 1992), esp. "Introduction" and chap. 1, "Urban Spectatorship."

68. Some notable Victorian "urban explorers" include Frederick Engels, Charles Dickens, and Henry Mayhew.

Chapter 5: *"The Stained Course of My Life"*

1. M. F. Lowenthal and D. Chiriboga, "Social Stress and Adaptations: Toward a Life Course Perspective," in C. Eisdorfer and M. P. Lawton, eds., *The Psychology of Adult Development and Aging* (Washington, D.C., 1973), 292.

2. Quotations are from Shannon, *Gladstone*, 211; Matthew, *Gladstone*, 88; G. M. Young in his Romanes Lecture, published as "Mr. Gladstone" (Oxford, 1944); and Brooke and Sorensen, *PMP*, 4:vii.

3. This is J. B. Conacher's judgment in his *Peelites and the Party System, 1846–52* (Newton Abbot, Devon, 1972), 62.

4. The most useful direct source of information comes from Gladstone himself: his memos are conveniently gathered together in Brooke and Sorensen, *PMP*, 3:103–30. See also Shannon's account in his *Gladstone*, 249–52.

5. For this incident, see Brooke and Sorensen, *PMP*, 3:121–22 and 125–26.

6. Shannon believes that Gladstone needed "some kind of demon or devil-figure" for his "footloose aggressiveness" (Shannon, *Gladstone*, 244). Thus Gladstone began to see Disraeli "as a symbol and symptom of something he could persuade himself was fundamentally and morally objectionable" (254).

7. Robert Blake, *Disraeli* (New York, 1967), chap. 15. P. R. Ghosh, in "Disraelian Conservatism: A Financial Approach," *English Historical Review* 99, no. 391 (April 1984), 268–96, finds more to praise in the 1852 budget.

8. Morley, *Life of Gladstone*, 1:324–26; and Bassett, *Gladstone to His Wife*, 91–95.

9. The speech may be most conveniently found in Arthur Tilney Basset's *Gladstone's Speeches* (London, 1916), 155–81. Quotations from it in the following paragraph are from 156, 172, 174, 176, and 179–80. Minor typographical errors have been corrected.

10. GGP 772, 6 December 1852, fol. 189; and 8 December 1852, fol. 191.

11. John Vincent, ed., *Disraeli, Derby and the Conservative Party: Journals and Memoirs of Edward Henry, Lord Stanley, 1849–1869* (New York, 1978), 89–90. Without detracting unduly from the accuracy of this report, I should note that Stanley's observation was unlikely to be friendly: he was the son of the prime minister and Disraeli's political pupil.

12. Letter dated 18 December 1852 in Basset, *Gladstone to His Wife*, 94.

13. *Diaries*, vol. 4, 17 December 1852.

14. Brooke and Sorensen, *PMP*, 1:81.

15. See Shannon, *Gladstone*, 262–63; and J. B. Conacher, *The Aberdeen Coalition, 1852–1855: A Study in Mid-Nineteenth Century Party Politics* (Cambridge, England, 1968), 47–48.

16. The memo may be found in *Diaries*, vol. 4, 18 December 1852, 477–79.

17. As Colin Matthew notes, "The Aberdeen coalition rescued Gladstone." His "private torments . . . largely fell away" during his term of office (Matthew, *Gladstone*, 86). For the maneuvering that lay behind the construction of the coalition see C. H. Stuart, "The Formation of the Coalition Cabinet of 1852," *Transactions of the Royal Historical Society*, 5th ser., 4 (1954), 45–68. See also Chamberlain, *Aberdeen*, chap. 26, "The Formation of the Aberdeen Coalition."

18. See Matthew, *Gladstone*, 110–20, for an important analysis of Gladstone's management of the Treasury.

19. Argyll's description of Gladstone's cabinet presentation may be found in Argyll, eighth duke of, George Douglas, *Autobiography and Memoirs*, ed. the dowager duchess of Argyll (New York, 1906), 1:420–29.

20. Ibid., 422–23.
21. Matthew suggests that Gladstone used his financial policy "to stabilize and check" his own feeling of drift in the 1850s and 1860s (*Gladstone,* 166).
22. *Diaries,* vol. 5, 3 March 1855, 34: Gladstone's summary of a talk with Sir George Cornewall Lewis.
23. The quotations in this paragraph are taken from Gladstone's cabinet minutes: these are printed in the *Diaries* following each day's diary entry. For the cabinet meetings of 11–15 April, see vol. 4, 513–18.
24. *Diaries,* vol. 4, 18 and 19 April 1854.
25. *Greville Memoirs,* vol. 6, 21 April 1853, 419.
26. Argyll, *Autobiography and Memoirs,* 429–30.
27. See *Diaries,* vol. 4, 4–23 September 1853, passim.
28. Conacher's *Aberdeen Coalition* remains the authoritative account of the government.
29. Matthew, *Gladstone,* 117.
30. See Olive Anderson, "Loans versus Taxes: British Financial Policy in the Crimean War," *Economic History Review,* 2d ser., 16, no. 1 (1963), 314–27; and chap. 6, "War Finance," in her *A Liberal State at War: English Politics and Economics during the Crimean War* (New York, 1967).
31. See Shannon, *Gladstone,* 298–300, for a discussion of Gladstone's reaction to the proposal for a Select Committee. Morley, *Life of Gladstone,* 1:390–91 describes the speech. Direct quotations are from *Hansard,* 3d ser., vol. 136, 1178–1206, 29 January 1855, passim.
32. Morley, *Life of Gladstone,* 1:392–93. Because of Gladstone's high church views and free trade beliefs, however, Derby was reluctant to make a place for him. See the research note by J. R. Jones, "The Conservatives and Gladstone in 1855," *English Historical Review* 77, no. 302 (January 1962), 95–98.
33. *Diaries,* vol. 5, 16. For Gladstone's memos during this ministerial crisis see ibid., 24 January–3 March 1855, passim.
34. *Diaries,* vol. 5, 24. For a thorough account of the early days of Palmerston's government see J. B. Conacher, *Britain and the Crimea, 1855–56: Problems of War and Peace* (New York, 1987), chap. 1, "The Palmerston Coalition, February 1855."
35. *Diaries,* vol. 5, 27.
36. Argyll, *Autobiography and Memoirs,* 537, 538.
37. As Matthew points out: see his discussion of Gladstone's Homeric studies in *Gladstone,* 152–54.
38. For these two letters see GGP 35, 4 September 1855, fol. 167; and 11 August 1856, fol. 171.
39. The following argument follows closely that found in Travis L. Crosby, "Gladstone's Decade of Crisis: Biography and the Life-Course Approach," *Journal of Political and Military Sociology* 12, no. 1 (Spring 1984), 12–17.
40. For Argyll's comments in this paragraph see his *Autobiography and Memoirs,* 1:556–7 and 561–62.
41. Morley's view: see his *Life of Gladstone,* 1:405–6.
42. As Shannon believes, in his *Gladstone,* 315.
43. GPBL, Add Mss 44098, 17 May 1855, fol. 99.
44. Ibid., 9 October 1855, fol. 127.
45. Ibid., 17 May 1855, fol. 94; and 1 November 1855, fol. 137. Parts of these (and additional) letters between Argyll and Gladstone have been printed in chap. 28, vol. 2 of Argyll's *Autobiography and Memoirs.*
46. Argyll's opinion in *Autobiography and Memoirs,* vol. 2, 51. Another Peelite, Henry Goulburn, regretted Gladstone's "perverseness" when it came to matters Palmerstonian. His unfavorable opinion of Gladstone, further elaborated, may be found in Lord Stanmore, *Sidney Herbert, Lord Herbert of Lea: A Memoir* (London, 1906), 1:459–60.
47. See *Diaries,* vol. 5, 13 March 1855, 112–14, for the letter.
48. *Quarterly Review* 99 (June and September 1856), 521–70, from which the following quotations are taken. This article was one of several in the late 1850s during Gladstone's "new phase of aggressive journalism." (Shannon, *Gladstone,* 313).

49. See Angus Hawkins, *Parliament, Party and the Art of Politics in Britain, 1855–59* (Stanford, 1987), chap. 1, "Palmerstonian Politics."
50. Gladstone's account may be found in his memo in *Diaries*, vol. 5, 103–26, dated 17 April 1856.
51. GPBL, Add Mss 44152, 11 December 1856, fols. 32–33.
52. Ibid., Add Mss 44164, 2 December 1856, fol. 66; 3 December 1856, fol. 70.
53. Ibid., Add Mss 44089, 2 December 1856, fols. 210–13; 8 December 1856, fols. 214–19.
54. Ibid., 11 December 1856, fols. 220–23; Aberdeen Papers, British Library, Add Mss 43071, 20 December 1856, fols. 349–50; 23 December 1856, fol. 351.
55. Ibid., Add Mss 44263, 30 January 1857, fols. 1–3.
56. Ibid., 10 February 1857, fols. 4–9; and 12 February 1857, fols. 10–13.
57. Brooke and Sorensen, *PMP*, 3:211. In an attempt to cloak his eagerness for an accommodation, Gladstone claimed that Elwin had acted without his knowledge. See the interesting exchange of letters between Gladstone and Derby, ibid., 210–13. Derby was not taken in: he well understood that Gladstone was *"very hungry"* (quoted in Hawkins, *Parliament, Party and Politics*, 42).
58. See Gladstone's memo in *Diaries*, vol. 5, 193–94.
59. *Hansard*, 3d ser., vol. 144, 985–1018 passim, 20 February 1857.
60. Argyll, *Autobiography and Memoirs*, 2:73. Olive Anderson points out that Lewis was simply following the principles of Gladstone's budgetary compromise of 1854 (Anderson, *Liberal State at War*, 205–6).
61. *Greville Memoirs*, 7:273 and 275.
62. Vincent, *Journals of Stanley*, 216 and 149.
63. "The Right Honourable William Gladstone, M.P.," *Blackwood's Edinburgh Magazine* 97, part 1, no. 592 (1865), 267.
64. Argyll, *Autobiography and Memoirs*, 2:73.
65. GPBL, Add Mss 44089, 4 April 1857, fols. 257–58; Aberdeen Papers, British Library, Add Mss 43071, 8 April 1857, fols. 368–69.
66. Hawkins cautions against seeing the election as a successful Palmerstonian plebiscite (*Parliament, Party and Politics*, 64–65). For Gladstone, however, the fact that Palmerston remained prime minister was the significant factor.
67. GPBL, Add Mss 44210, 17 April 1857, fols. 320–23.
68. Morley, *Life of Gladstone*, 1:421–22, letter dated 22 March 1857. He wrote similarly to Lord Aberdeen, concluding that although the recent election had once again placed him in the House of Commons, he could not, having arrived there, "find ground for the sole of my foot to rest upon" (*Diaries*, vol. 5, 211).
69. *Greville Memoirs*, 8:288.
70. "The Bill for Divorce," reprinted in Gladstone, *Gleanings of Past Years, 1851–75* (London, 1879), 6:47–106. The bill raised a number of broader issues that related to equal rights of men and women in the marriage union, as Victorian feminists pointed out. See Mary Lyndon Shanley, " 'One Must Ride Behind': Married Women's Rights and the Divorce Act of 1857," *Victorian Studies* 25 (Spring 1982), 255–76, for the parliamentary developments. Shanley's *Feminism, Marriage, and the Law in Victorian England, 1850–1895* (Princeton, 1989), chap. 1, emphasizes the feminist background. Margaret Woodhouse, "The Marriage and Divorce Bill of 1857," *American Journal of Legal History* 3 (1959), 260–75, analyzes the legal history of the bill.
71. Morley, *Life of Gladstone*, 1:425.
72. *Hansard*, 3d ser., vol. 147, 836, 31 July 1857.
73. "Prospects Political and Financial," *Quarterly Review* 101 (January 1857), 243–84. Although anonymous, the article was easily attributable—and Bethel did name Gladstone as the author publicly on the floor of the Commons.
74. As Shannon, *Gladstone*, 343 notes. Argyll also recorded that Gladstone was "in particular a violent opponent" to the bill (in his *Autobiography and Memoirs*, 2:79).
75. Bassett, *Gladstone to His Wife*, 8 August 1857, 117.
76. *Hansard*, 3d ser., vol. 147, 1052, 4 August 1857.

77. Matthew kindly observes that Gladstone's statement "gave great elasticity to truth" (*Diaries*, vol. 5, 245 n. 3).

78. A. R. Ashwell and Reginald G. Wilberforce, *Life of The Right Reverend Samuel Wilberforce, D.D.* (New York, 1883), 277.

79. The event and its implications are described in detail by Robert Woodall, "Orsini and the Fall of Palmerston," *History Today* (October 1976), 636–43.

80. Hawkins, *Parliament, Party and Politics*, 104, quoting from the diary (19 February 1858) of the Liberal backbencher Edward Knatchbull-Hugessen, M.P. for Sandwich.

81. "He is down: I must now cease to denounce him." So recorded Gladstone in his *Diaries*, vol. 5, 20 February 1858. This was a resolution soon (and often) broken.

82. Shannon, *Gladstone*, 348.

83. See Hawkins, *Parliament, Party and Politics*, 109–10.

84. See Brooke and Sorensen, *PMP*, 3:221–27, from which the following quotations are taken.

85. For the letter see Morley, *Life of Gladstone*, 1:439–40. For this latest episode of abortive office-seeking see Hawkins, *Parliament, Party and Politics*, 146–47.

86. For a summary of the historical background see Bruce Knox, "British Policy and the Ionian Islands, 1847–1864: Nationalism and Imperial Administration," *English Historical Review* 99, no. 392 (July 1984), 503–29.

87. GPBL, Add Mss 44241, 5 October 1858, fols. 5–9 for Lytton's letter.

88. These words were repeated to Gladstone, which infuriated him, and he returned to England with feelings of anger against the Conservative party. This was, Carnarvon believed, a turning point in Gladstone's relations with the Conservatives. See Carnarvon Papers, British Library, Add Mss 60992, Diary, 9 January 1884, fol. 6.

89. Morley, *Life of Gladstone*, 1:444.

90. Matthew, *Gladstone*, 163.

91. Marcia Pointon, "W. E. Gladstone as an Art Patron and Collector," *Victorian Studies* 19 (1975), 73–98.

92. Shannon, *Gladstone*, 365. Graham corroborates this view: a few months before the Ionian invitation, he had observed in Gladstone a "restless anxiety for a change of position. I cannot wonder at his hankering for power at his age and with his abilities" (in a letter to Aberdeen, 14 August 1858, quoted in Hawkins, *Parliament, Party and Politics*, 183).

93. GPBL, Add Mss 44089, 8 Oct 1858, fols. 275–76. Aberdeen was more candid to others. He wondered aloud to John Bright that Bulwer-Lytton had not asked Gladstone "to black his boots for him," and he feared that Gladstone "must be damaged" by the mission (Walling, *Diaries of Bright*, 1 March 1858, 235).

94. GPBL, Add Mss 44164, 19 October 1858, fol. 190.

95. Ibid., Add Mss 44263, 24 October 1858, fols. 38–39.

96. J. B. Conacher, "Party Politics in the Age of Palmerston," in Philip Appleman, ed., *1859: Entering an Age of Crisis* (Bloomington, 1959), 175.

97. Stanmore, *Herbert*, Graham to Herbert, 17 January 1859, 2:166; Herbert to Graham, 19 January 1859, 2:167–68.

98. GPBL, Add Mss 44263, 22 January 1859, fol. 79.

99. Keith A. P. Sandiford points out that Ionia was only one example of Gladstone's preference for sound and orderly government over the principle of self-determination: see Sandiford's article "W. E. Gladstone and Liberal-Nationalist Movements," *Albion* 13, no. 1 (Spring 1981), 27–42.

100. *Diaries*, vol. 5, 30 July 1859. See also Matthew's brief description of Gladstone's relationship with Summerhayes in ibid., lx–lxi.

101. In a slightly disingenuous letter to Dyce, Gladstone—after first praising Dyce for an earlier commissioned work—asked if he would be willing to paint another. "But how to find a subject?" Gladstone asked rhetorically. "Now this want I think I am able to supply," he answered. See GPBL, Add Mss 44392, 4 August 1859, fol. 111. The Summerhayes portrait is reproduced in *Diaries*, vol. 5, between 328 and 329.

102. Sir Herbert Maxwell, *Life and Letters of George William Frederick Fourth Earl of Clarendon* (London, 1913), 2:183. Remarks by Aberdeen and Bright are taken from Shannon, *Gladstone*, 384.
103. Maxwell, *Clarendon*, 2:186.
104. GPBL, Add Mss 44209, 16 June 1859, fols. 38–40. This letter was also printed in Morley, *Life of Gladstone*, 1:468.
105. Walling, *Diaries of Bright*, 3 June 1859.
106. Derek Beales has suggested as much in his *England and Italy, 1859–60* (London, 1961), 87.
107. *Diaries*, vol. 4, 29 December 1854; and ibid., vol. 5, 29 December 1857.
108. Ibid., vol. 5, 29 December 1859.

Chapter 6: Prelude to Power

1. Cited in M. R. D. Foot, "Introduction" to *Diaries*, vol. 1, xlvi n. 1. Also in Shannon, *Gladstone*, 249 n. 4. Gladstone seems, however, to have brought to tree felling the same intensity as to his political work: Reid reports that he chopped trees "as if his very livelihood depended upon it" (Reid, *Life of Gladstone*, 596).
2. See Matthew, *Gladstone*, 150–52 for a discussion of Hawarden's importance to Gladstone's escape from stress.
3. Lucy Masterman, ed., *Mary Gladstone (Mrs. Drew): Her Diaries and Letters*, 2d ed. (London, 1930), 4.
4. Viscount Gladstone, *After Thirty Years* (London, 1928), 6–7.
5. Michael Bentley, "Gladstonian Liberals and Provincial Notables: Whitby Politics, 1868–80," *Historical Research* 64, no. 154 (June 1991), 172–85.
6. See Patricia Jalland, "Mr Gladstone's Daughters: The Domestic Price of Victorian Politics," in Kinzer, *Gladstonian Turn of Mind.*
7. Mary Drew, *Mrs. Gladstone* (New York, 1920), 259–60.
8. GGP 772, WEG to CG, 15 August 1853, fol. 265.
9. *Diaries*, vol. 4, 16 and 17 August 1853.
10. Possibly Caroline Jane, wife of John Chetwynd Talbot, Q.C.
11. GGP 613, CG to WEG, 4 September 1852.
12. Although not to the extent claimed by Esther Simon Shkolnik's "Petticoat Power: The Political Influence of Mrs. Gladstone," *Historian* 42, no. 4 (1980), 631–47. Catherine's advice was more a sign of her increasing comfort within the marriage than it was an indication of either her political shrewdness or of Gladstone's reliance on it.
13. GGP 612, CG to WEG, 21 February 1850.
14. Ibid., December 1852 (partially undated).
15. *Diaries*, vol. 5, 16 August 1857.
16. See ibid., October 1857–February 1858, passim, for Catherine's condition.
17. GGP 615, CG to WEG, 17 March 1858.
18. Ibid., 20 March 1858.
19. Ibid., 26 March 1858.
20. Ibid., 774, WEG to CG, 23 March 1858, fol. 25; 25 March 1858, fol. 29; 27 March 1858, fol. 35; 31 March 1858, fol. 41.
21. Ibid., 615, CG to WEG, 21 October 1858. *Unearthly* was a word in Glynnese—the family patois—for something strange or mysterious.
22. Matthew analyzes the Duchess' influence in his *Gladstone*, 149–50.
23. See Morley, *Life of Gladstone*, 2:139.
24. *Diaries*, vol. 6, 18 May 1861.
25. David Owen's *English Philanthropy, 1660–1960* (Cambridge, Mass., 1964), remains the standard work, although it largely omits the role of women. This is rectified by F. K. Prochaska, *Women and Philanthropy in Nineteenth-Century England* (Oxford, 1980). Jessica Gerard, in "Lady Bountiful: Women of the Landed Classes and Rural Philanthropy," *Victorian Studies* (Winter 1987),

183–210, makes the case for women's charitable work operating as a kind of social control to perpetuate traditional ties of authority.

26. Sources for Catherine Gladstone's charitable work may be found in her charity correspondence, GGP 816–20; Mary Drew, *Mrs. Gladstone* (New York, 1920), 96–98 and chap. 7; Prochaska, *Women and Philanthropy*, 160–61; and Pratt, *Catherine Gladstone*, passim.

27. GGP 617, CG to WEG, 3 April 1863, 21 January 1865; ibid., 618, 27 October 1867.

28. Ibid. 777, WEG to CG, 22 October 1870, fol. 206. His niece, Katherine, was the daughter of his deceased brother, John Neilson Gladstone. The marriage was at John Neilson's home, Bowden Park, Wiltshire. See *Diaries*, vol. 7, 26 October 1870.

29. Ibid., 619, CG to WEG, 22 October 1870.

30. Ibid., 777, WEG to CG, 29 October 1870, fol. 211.

31. Ibid., 13 November 1870, fol. 214.

32. Ibid., 16 November 1870, fol. 216.

33. Ibid., 26 December 1870, fol. 256.

34. Marlow, *Mr and Mrs Gladstone*, 140.

35. GGP 620, CG to WEG, 2 July 1874.

36. Ibid., 778, WEG to CG, 10 December 1874, fol. 295.

37. This animosity was clearly revealed in their argumentative correspondence: see Philip Guedalla's edition of *Gladstone and Palmerston: Being the Correspondence of Lord Palmerston with Mr Gladstone, 1851–1865* (New York, 1928).

38. *The Parliamentary Diaries of Sir John Trelawny, 1858–1865*, ed. T. A. Jenkins, Camden Fourth Series 40 (London, 1990), 187 and 297. Sir John, M.P. for Tavistock, was a keen observer of parliamentary styles.

39. Matthew, *Gladstone*, 106. See chap. 5 in Matthew for the discussion that follows.

40. See Sidney Buxton's *Finance and Politics: An Historical Study, 1789–1885* (London, 1888), reprinted in the Reprints of Economic Classics series (New York, 1966), chap. 9, "The Commercial Treaty, 1860." Buxton's detailed and readable work remains useful.

41. Gladstone's justification for his independent action may be found in Morley, *Life of Gladstone*, 2:17. His account is in substantial agreement with A. A. Iliasu, "The Cobden-Chevalier Commercial Treaty of 1860," *Historical Journal* 14, no. 1 (1971), 67–98.

42. See Bassett, *Gladstone's Speeches*, 253–311. The stress of preparing the budget was probably instrumental in postponing his presentation before the House: he had been scheduled for several days earlier but fell ill on 5 February. The earl of Clarendon, later a cabinet member in Gladstone's first ministry, could not resist a knowing remark on his future's chief's illness. To the Duchess of Manchester, he wrote on 6 February: "You will see in the newspapers that our Jesuit has got his throat sore (perhaps in some benevolent nocturnal ramble) & can't perform today" (A. L. Kennedy, ed., *"My Dear Duchess": Social and Political Letters to the Duchess of Manchester, 1858–1869* [London, 1956], 89–90).

43. As reported by Sir George Cornewall Lewis, the home secretary in the ministry: see Maxwell, *Clarendon*, Lewis to Clarendon, 2:213–14.

44. *Diaries*, vol. 5, 8 May 1860.

45. She "told me her mind about myself," as Gladstone put it (*Diaries*, vol. 5, 19 May 1860). Gladstone's reputation at this time was puzzling to Morley: "For reasons not easy to trace, a general atmosphere of doubt and unpopularity seemed suddenly to surround his name" (*Life of Gladstone*, 2:23).

46. *Diaries*, vol. 5, 14 May 1860.

47. Ibid., 6 June 1860 and n. 1.

48. Ibid., 496 n. 9. Matthew quotes from Palmerston's diary (Broadlands MS D 20, at the National Registry of Archives).

49. Maxwell, *Clarendon*, 2:215. Clarendon also reported to Lewis a fortnight earlier that Aberdeen had news from Gladstone's Peelite colleagues in the cabinet (Sidney Herbert and the duke of Newcastle) that they "would not submit any longer to his dictation" (ibid., 2 June 1860).

50. GPBL, Add Mss 44098, Argyll to WEG, 16 June 1860, fols. 283–84 and 286.

51. *Diaries*, vol. 5, 501, 1 July 1860.

52. Brooke and Sorensen, *PMP*, Russell to Palmerston, 20 May 1860, 3:231. See also letters from Palmerston and Gladstone, 3:230–33.

53. *Diaries*, vol. 5, 503 n. 5, quoting from Palmerston's diary (Broadlands MS D 20).

54. Ibid., 18 July 1860. It is worth noting Morley's opinion about Gladstone's role during the cabinet debate on fortifications. "Mr. Gladstone was the least quarrelsome of the human race," he observed, yet the "controversy between him and his colleagues . . . raged at white heat over the whole ground of military estimates" (*Life of Gladstone*, 33 and 35).

55. *Diaries*, vol. 5, 506 n. 8, from Palmerston's diary (Broadlands MS D 20).

56. Morley, *Life of Gladstone*, 2:47.

57. Ibid., 49.

58. *Diaries*, vol. 6, 10–12 April 1861; see also the memo in ibid., 23–24.

59. See E. D. Steele's account of the compromise in *Palmerston and Liberalism, 1855–1865* (Cambridge, England, 1991), 104–5. Gladstone accepted a one-penny reduction of the income tax in return for ministerial approval of paper duty abolition.

60. GPBL, Add Mss 44099, Argyll to WEG, 23 August 1861, fols. 65–66.

61. See Morley, *Life of Gladstone*, 2:118; and Vincent, *Memoirs of Stanley*, 16 July 1863, 199, for these reservations about his leadership. Palmerston had once cautioned Gladstone in similar words: "The House of Commons allows itself to be led, but does not like to be driven and is apt to turn upon those who attempt to drive it" (Guedalla, *Gladstone and Palmerston*, 16 May 1861, 169).

62. Gladstone won appreciation even from the deepest part of the backbenches. Endorsing Gladstone's tax reduction plan, the Conservative Sir William Hardman opined, "I begin to think that Gladstone is not such a bad fellow after all." But he could not help adding, "I don't like him somehow" (S. M. Ellis, *A Mid-Victorian Pepys: The Letters and Memoirs of Sir William Hardman* [New York, 1923], diary entry of 12 April 1863, 302).

63. *Trelawny Diaries*, 10 February 1860, 98; 20 February 1860, 103; and 5 May 1863, 247. But Trelawny also noted those habits of arrogance that worked against Gladstone. He faulted Gladstone's habit of leaning back when not speaking in the Commons "with his eyes upturned & with a certain expression of wearied impatience." At times, "a smile of pity, or contempt, or derision" would play upon his face, as if to say, " 'What a hopeless task it is to battle with stupidity!' " (ibid., 27 March 1865, 316).

64. Eugenio F. Biagini, *Liberty, Retrenchment and Reform: Popular Liberalism in the Age of Gladstone, 1860–1880* (Cambridge, England, 1992), esp. 103–6 and 379–85.

65. M. R. D. Foot, "Introduction" to W. E. Gladstone, *Midlothian Speeches, 1879* (Leicester, 1971), 12.

66. Biagini only hints at the psychological utility of crowds for Gladstone. "If, politically, he needed the votes of the artisans, psychologically Gladstone needed the support of the masses that enabled him to go his own way" (Biagini, *Liberty, Retrenchment and Reform*, 381).

67. For a discussion of Gladstone's deepening understanding of public opinion out of doors see H. C. G. Matthew, "Rhetoric and Politics in Britain, 1860–1950," in P. J. Waller, ed., *Politics and Social Change in Modern Britain: Essays Presented to A. F. Thompson* (Hassocks, Sussex, 1987), 34–58. Gladstone also became adept at managing the news. Once, when shouted down by antagonistic Tories at a public meeting, Gladstone simply turned to the reporters who sat below him and gave them his speech. It was duly reported in the press the following day (ibid., 43).

68. *Diaries*, vol. 6, 7 October 1862.

69. See Shannon, *Gladstone*, 469–70, for the description.

70. *Diaries*, vol. 6, 8 October 1862.

71. Morley, *Life of Gladstone*, 2:60.

72. *Times*, 9 October 1862, 7.

73. This follows Matthew's argument in *Gladstone*, 27.

74. Brooke and Sorensen, *PMP*, memo dated 30 May 1860, 3:233.

75. See Matthew, *Gladstone*, 133; and Shannon, *Gladstone*, 455, who notes that the paper duties crisis had given a "decisive impulse" toward a more active movement for reform on Gladstone's part.
76. The whole of his short speech is contained in *Hansard*, 3d ser., vol. 175, 312–27, 11 May 1864.
77. Palmerston, of course, meant universal *manhood* suffrage: see Morley, *Life of Gladstone*, 2:98–99.
78. *Times*, 12 May 1864, 10.
79. *Trelawny Diaries*, 11 and 12 May 1864, 278–79.
80. The phrase is from F. B. Smith, *The Making of the Second Reform Bill* (Cambridge, England, 1966), 51. I have drawn on this indispensable work for the following discussion, as well as on Maurice Cowling's *1867: Disraeli, Gladstone, and Revolution: The Passing of the Second Reform Bill* (Cambridge, England, 1967).
81. *Hansard*, 3d ser., vol. 182, 149, 13 March 1866.
82. *Diaries*, vol. 6, 6 April 1866 and 429 n. 2.
83. For these critical comments of Gladstone see Smith, *Second Reform Bill*, 110.
84. John Evelyn Denison (Lord Ossington), *Notes from My Journal When Speaker of the House of Commons* (London, 1900), 201.
85. Letter quoted by Smith, *Second Reform Bill*, 119. Clarendon concluded his letter by observing of Gladstone that his abilities should one day make him prime minister, if, that is, "his arrogant ill temper did not repel the sympathies upon which a leader must rely for support" (ibid., 120).
86. Smith, *Second Reform Bill*, 49, 103, and 107.
87. Cowling, *1867*, 102 and 105.
88. GGP 573, WEG to Robertson Gladstone, 3 September 1866.
89. Quoted in Morley, *Life of Gladstone*, 2:162.
90. *Diaries*, vol. 6, 18 October 1866.
91. As he reported it to Lady Salisbury: see Maxwell, *Clarendon*, 24 November 1866, 2:328.
92. For the Conservative reform bill of 1867 see Smith, *Second Reform Bill*, and Cowling, *1867*. See additionally Blake's *Disraeli*, chap. 21, and Paul Smith, *Disraelian Conservatism and Social Reform* (London, 1967), intro., chaps. 1 and 2. Gertrude Himmelfarb, "The Politics of Democracy: The English Reform Act of 1867," *Journal of British Studies* 6, no. 1 (1966), 97–138, takes issue with the liberal historiography of the bill in making a case for the genuine democratic sentiments of the Tory party under Disraeli. A useful summary of the various interpretations of the origins of the bill may be found in Thomas F. Gallagher, "The Second Reform Movement, 1848–1867," *Albion* 12, no. 2 (Summer 1980), 147–63.
93. Blake, *Disraeli*, 456.
94. Disraeli was described as "juggler-hearted" in a satirical newspaper of the 1860s, the *Owl* (quoted in Reginald Lucas, *Lord Glenesk and the Morning Post* [London, 1910], 204).
95. Smith, *Second Reform Bill*, 198.
96. Monypenny and Buckle, *Disraeli*, 4:513.
97. Smith, *Second Reform Bill*, 201.
98. *Times*, 6 April 1867; quoted in Joseph H. Park, *The English Reform Bill of 1867* (New York, 1920), 206.
99. *The Diary of Lady Frederick Cavendish*, ed. John Bailey (London, 1927), 18 March 1867, 2:27. Gladstone admitted only to a milder version of his behavior, recording in his diary that he "spoke strongly" against the bill (*Diaries*, vol. 6, 18 March 1867).
100. Carlingford Diary, British Library, Add Mss 63678, 18 March 1867, fol. 27 (hereafter designated as CDBL). Fortesque's diary is not only an important source for Gladstone's affective behavior but is also a catalogue of his own severely depressive episodes, which hindered his career as a politician. He was created Baron Carlingford in 1874 after service in Gladstone's first administration. A brief summary of his life may be found in A. B. Cooke and J. R. Vincent, eds., *Lord Carlingford's Journal* (Oxford, 1971), "Introduction," 1–40.
101. Cowling, *1867*, cites evidence of Gladstone managing the meeting "dictatorially" (195).
102. *Diaries*, vol. 6, 8 April 1867. Cowling believes that Disraeli may have had a hand in fomenting the Tea Room Revolt (*1867*, 197).

103. *Hansard,* 3d ser., vol. 186, 1678–88, 12 April 1867, for Disraeli's speech.
104. *Diaries,* vol. 6, 12 April 1867.
105. Quoted in Morley, *Life of Gladstone,* 2:175.
106. Matthew, *Gladstone,* 141. Fortesque confirms the humiliation of Gladstone in these ill-starred April days. Gladstone—"low and mortified"—told Lady Waldegrave that he was in "the crisis of his life" and that if the Liberal party failed him now, "he wd. give up the leadership" (CDBL, Add Mss 63678, 13 April 1867, fol. 34; 10 April 1867, fol. 33; 8 April 1867, fol. 32).
107. GPBL, Add Mss 44092, Acland to WEG, 14 April 1867, fols. 65–68; and 16 April 1867, fols. 69–74.
108. "Attacked Tree-cutting," as he put it in his diary (*Diaries,* vol. 6, 25 April 1867).
109. The quotation is from *Diaries,* vol. 6, 11 May 1867.
110. Cowling, *1867,* notes Gladstone's "leftward shift in May" (292).
111. Monypenny and Buckle, *Disraeli,* Disraeli to Stanley, 22 April 1867, 4:535.
112. *Diaries,* vol. 6, 7 July 1867.
113. CDBL, Add Mss 63678, 15 June 1867, fol. 52.

Chapter 7: *"My Mission Is to Pacify Ireland"*

1. Brooke and Sorensen, *PMP,* 1:97.
2. See the discussion in Matthew, *Gladstone,* 144–48.
3. See *Hansard,* 3d ser., vol. 178, 422–34, 28 March 1865.
4. In a letter dated 9 April 1865 to his brother-in-law Lord Lyttelton: Morley, *Life of Gladstone,* 2: 179–80. Two years later, he wrote to John Bright, claiming that he had reserved a free hand with regard to the fate of the Church of Ireland as early as 1847. He had not spoken before because "in Ireland itself the question slept" but also because it was "well to ponder much upon a subject" that could "lead the Liberal party to martyrdom" (GPBL, Add Mss 44112, 10 December 1867, fols. 65–66).
5. W. E. Gladstone, *A Chapter of Autobiography* (London, 1868), 55.
6. As argued in J. H. Parry's *Democracy and Religion: Gladstone and the Liberal Party, 1867–1875* (Cambridge, England, 1986). I have drawn heavily on Parry's work in this chapter.
7. See D. W. Bebbington, "Gladstone and the Nonconformists: A Religious Affinity in Politics," in Derek Baker, ed., *Studies in Church History,* vol. 12, *Church, Society, and Politics* (Oxford, 1975), 369–82; and S. E. Ingham, "The Disestablishment Movement in England, 1868–74," *Journal of Religious History* 3, no. 1 (June 1964), 38–60.
8. *Diaries,* vol. 6, 16 December 1867.
9. For the complete speech see the *Times,* 20 December 1867.
10. CDBL, Add Mss 63679A, 21 February 1868, fol. 21.
11. For a summary of Fenian activity see R. V. Comerford, *The Fenians in Context: Irish Politics and Society, 1848–82* (Dublin, 1985), chap. 5.
12. *Hansard,* 3d ser., vol. 190, 1740–71, 16 March 1868.
13. For a description of South-West Lancashire and Gladstone's campaign in 1868 see H. J. Hanham, *Elections and Party Management: Politics in the Time of Disraeli and Gladstone,* 2d ed. (Hassocks, Sussex, 1978), chap. 14, especially 289–96; and P. Searby, "Gladstone in West Derby Hundred: The Liberal Campaign in South-West Lancashire in 1868," *Transactions of the Historical Society of Lancashire and Cheshire* (1959–60), 139–66.
14. The phrase is Matthew's; see his *Gladstone,* 174–80, for a discussion of the cabinet.
15. This phrase is from an autobiographical fragment written in 1897 and printed in Brooke and Sorensen, *PMP,* 1:96–99.
16. These minutes serve as rough guides to the topics discussed in the cabinet and are printed with the *Diaries,* beginning with vol. 7. See Matthew's discussion of cabinet records in *Diaries,* vol. 7, "Introduction," xxxiii–xxxv. A more abbreviated discussion is in Matthew's *Gladstone,* 176–77.
17. Morley, *Life of Gladstone,* 2:193.

18. Quotations in this paragraph are taken from *Diaries*, vol. 6, 13 December 1868, 14 December 1868, 19 and 22 December 1868, 24 December 1868, 26 December 1868.

19. Ibid., vol. 7, 3 January 1869.

20. Ibid., 23 January 1869; see also J. C. Beckett, "Gladstone, Queen Victoria, and the Disestablishment of the Irish Church," *Irish Historical Studies* 13 (1962–63), 38–47.

21. GPBL, Add Mss 44345, WEG to Wilberforce, 21 January 1869, fol. 62. The entire letter is printed in *Diaries*, vol. 7, 14–15.

22. Peter Gordon, *The Red Earl: The Papers of the Fifth Earl Spencer, 1835–1910* (Northampton, 1981), Spencer to Dr. William Conor Magee, 19 January 1869, 1:74–75. Magee, bishop of Peterborough, was reputed to have much influence in Anglican circles and was thought to be a moderate, but Spencer's appeal failed as Magee strongly attacked the bill in the House of Lords.

23. GPBL, Add Mss 44306, WEG to Spencer, 2 March 1869, fol. 84.

24. *Diaries*, vol. 7, 9 February 1869.

25. Walling, *Diaries of Bright*, 27 February 1869, 339. P. M. H. Bell, in *Disestablishment in Ireland and Wales* (London, 1969), concurs: the preparation of the bill was characterized by "vigor, speed, and efficiency" (123).

26. As Matthew notes, it was an "assault on the formal structure of the Establishment as dramatic in principle as anything achieved between 1689 and the present day" (*Gladstone*, 192).

27. GGP 35, 3 March 1869, fol. 312.

28. Nancy E. Johnson, ed., *The Diary of Gathorne Hardy, later Lord Cranbrook, 1866–1892: Political Selections* (Oxford, 1981), 10 March 1869, 91 and passim. Gathorne Hardy, first elected to the House of Commons in 1856, defeated Gladstone at Oxford University in 1865; he later became one of Gladstone's principal tormentors in the House of Commons. He served as home secretary under Derby and Disraeli from 1867 to 1868 and was thereafter often in Conservative cabinets. He was created Viscount Cranbrook in 1878 and earl in 1892.

29. Ibid., 13 July 1869, 100.

30. *Diaries*, vol. 7, 6 July 1869. See ibid., vol. 7, 92–108, for Gladstone's diary entries and memos on the Lords' stratagems against the Church of Ireland Bill. See also Morley, *Life of Gladstone*, 2: 202–12.

31. *Diaries*, 19 July 1869, 101.

32. Carnarvon Papers, British Library, Add Mss 60901, Diary, 20 July 1869, fol. 104.

33. Parry, *Democracy and Religion*, 286.

34. *Diaries*, vol. 7, 103.

35. Ibid., 104. Archbishop Tait's mediation is discussed by Bell, *Disestablishment in Ireland and Wales*, chap. 4.

36. E. Drus, ed., *A Journal of Events During the Gladstone Ministry, 1868–1874, by John, first Earl of Kimberley*, Camden Miscellany 21 (1957), 20 July 1869, 7. Kimberley noted further that "unfortunately with all his genius, cool judgement is a quality which Gladstone does not possess" (ibid.). Kimberley did not write from hostile political motives; he supported Gladstone throughout most of his political career and was one of the few Liberal leaders who followed him into Home Rule for Ireland in the 1880s.

37. Agatha Ramm, ed., *The Political Correspondence of Mr. Gladstone and Lord Granville, 1868–1876* (London, 1952), Camden Third Series 81, Granville to WEG, 22 July 1869, 1:38.

38. Matthew, *Gladstone*, 194.

39. A significant economic literature on landlords and tenants in Ireland has emerged. A good sample is: Cormac ÓGráda, "The Investment Behavior of Irish Landlords, 1850–75: Some Preliminary Findings," *Agricultural History Review* 23 (1975), 153; and ÓGráda's "Irish Agricultural Output Before and After the Famine," *Journal of European Economic History* 13, no. 1 (Spring 1984), 149–65. See also L. P. Curtis, Jr., "Encumbered Wealth: Landed Indebtedness in Post-Famine Ireland," *American Historical Review* 85, no. 2 (April 1980), 332–67; Lindsay Proudfoot, "The Management of a Great Estate: Patronage, Income and Expenditure on the Duke of Devonshire's Irish Property, c. 1816 to 1891," *Irish Economic and Social History* 13 (1986), 32–55; and W. E. Vaughan, "An Assessment of the Economic Performance of Irish Landlords, 1851–

81," in F. S. L. Lyons and R. A. J. Hawkins, eds., *Ireland Under the Union: Varieties of Tension* (Oxford, 1980).

40. *Diaries*, vol. 7, 12 Aug 1869; and ibid., WEG to Lambert, 24 August 1869, 120. E. D. Steele, *Irish Land and British Politics: Tenant-Right and Nationality, 1865–1870* (Cambridge, 1974), 104–8, discusses the influence of Campbell's ideas on Gladstone.

41. Steele, *Irish Land and British Politics*, 138–48.

42. John W. Mason, "The Duke of Argyll and the Land Question in Late Nineteenth-Century Britain," *Victorian Studies* 21, no. 2 (Winter 1978), 149–70.

43. *Diaries*, vol. 7, WEG to Argyll, 29 November 1869, 182; and GPBL, Add Mss 44101, WEG to Argyll, 1 December 1869, fol. 105.

44. Steele, *Irish Land and British Politics*, 200.

45. See Charles Townshend's discussion in his *Political Violence in Ireland: Government and Resistance since 1848*, paperback ed. (Oxford, 1983), 60–62.

46. Written in a letter to Manning, in Morley, *Life of Gladstone*, 2:223.

47. Quoted in Steele, *Irish Land and British Politics*, 303.

48. *Diaries*, vol. 7, WEG to Cardwell, 8 April 1870, 272–73. Gathorne Hardy reported that Gladstone made a "threatening" speech before the division on Fowler's amendment in the House (Johnson, *Diary of Gathorne Hardy*, 8 April 1870, 111). Gladstone admitted that he had "been obliged to resort to something like menace: the strain thus far has been extreme" (*Diaries*, vol. 7, WEG to Manning, 16 April 1870, 278).

49. GPBL, Add Mss 44538, WEG to Argyll, 21 April 1870, fol. 133.

50. The letter may be found in Argyll, *Autobiography and Memoirs*, Argyll to Palmer, 23 April 1870, 2:262–66.

51. *Diaries*, vol. 7, Clarendon to WEG, 21 April 1870, 282 n. 1.

52. GPBL, Add Mss 44296, Palmer to WEG, [Easter Day?] 1870, fol. 172.

53. Roundell Palmer, (earl of Selborne), *Memorials, Part 2: Personal and Political, 1865–1895* (London, 1898), 1:146.

54. For a brief background see T. W. Moody, "The Irish University Question of the Nineteenth Century," *History* 43, no. 148 (June 1958), 90–109; and Bruce L. Kinzer's "John Stuart Mill and the Irish University Question," *Victorian Studies* 31, no. 1 (Autumn 1987), 59–77.

55. The critical work for this topic is E. R. Norman's *The Catholic Church and Ireland in the Age of Rebellion, 1859–1873* (London, 1965), especially chaps. 5, 6, and 9.

56. See Parry, *Democracy & Religion*, 353–68, for a discussion of the framing of the bill and its parliamentary reception.

57. *Diaries*, vol. 8, WEG to Robertson Gladstone, 22 February 1873, 290.

58. GPBL, Add Mss 44250, Manning to WEG, 15 February 1873.

59. Derek Beales, in "Gladstone and his First Ministry," *Historical Journal* 26, no. 4 (1983), 996–97, has called the Irish University bill "this monster of a plan," filled with "inherent absurdities."

60. Gordon, *Red Earl*, Spencer's "Memorandum of Conversation with Cardinal Cullen," 1:104–6. See also a fragment of a letter from Cullen to Manning, quoted in Norman, *Catholic Church and Ireland*, 450.

61. Parry, *Democracy and Religion*, 364.

62. *Diaries*, vol. 8, 8 March 1873.

63. CDBL, Add Mss 63682, 8 March 1873, fol. 23.

64. *Diaries*, vol. 8, WEG to Manning, 8 March 1873, 297–98.

65. CDBL, Add Mss 63682, 14 March 1873, fol. 25.

66. Brooke and Sorensen, *PMP*, memorandum by the queen, 13 March 1873, 4:31.

67. As reported by Gathorne Hardy in Johnson, *Diary of Gathorne Hardy*, 16 March 1873, 175.

Chapter 8: "Our Lease Is Out"

1. Among the relevant sources for understanding the education question are G. F. A. Best, "The Religious Difficulties of National Education in England, 1800–70," *Cambridge Historical Journal*

12, no. 2 (1956), 155–73; Marjorie Cruickshank, *Church and State in English Education: 1870 to the Present Day* (London, 1963), introduction and chaps. 1–2; W. P. McCann, "Trade Unionists, Artisans and the 1870 Educational Act," *British Journal of Educational Studies* 18, no. 2 (June 1970), 134–50; Gillian Sutherland, *Policy-Making in Elementary Education, 1870–1895* (London, 1973); and Henry Roper, "Toward an Elementary Education Act for England and Wales, 1865–1868," *British Journal of Educational Studies* 23, no. 2 (June 1975). A later treatment is chap. 3 in Peter Marsh's *Joseph Chamberlain: Entrepreneur in Politics* (New Haven, 1994).

2. *Diaries*, vol. 7, WEG to De Grey, 2 October 1869, 140–41.
3. Henry Roper, "W. E. Forster's Memorandum of 21 October 1869: A Re-examination," *British Journal of Educational Studies* 21, no. 1 (February 1973), 64–75.
4. Parry, *Democracy and Religion*, 165. This paragraph is based on Parry's discussion, 164–67.
5. For the post-1870 working of the Education Act see N. J. Richards, "Religious Controversy and the School Boards, 1870–1902," *British Journal of Educational Studies* 18, no. 2 (June 1970), 180–96.
6. For the following paragraphs I have followed Cornelius O'Leary, *The Elimination of Corrupt Practices in British Elections, 1868–1911* (Oxford, 1962), especially chap. 3, "The Ballot Act"; and Bruce L. Kinzer's *The Ballot Question in Nineteenth-Century English Politics* (New York, 1972).
7. *Times*, 20 December 1867.
8. So Kinzer, in his *Ballot Question*, 100–101, believes, although he admits that the evidence for his conclusion is circumstantial.
9. Bruce L. Kinzer, "The Un-Englishness of the Secret Ballot," *Albion* 10, no. 3 (Spring 1979), 237–56.
10. *Diaries*, vol. 8, WEG to G. Moberley, bishop of Salisbury, 1 July 1872, 172.
11. Cited in Kinzer, *Ballot Question*, 237.
12. *Diaries*, vol. 8, WEG to G. G. Glyn, 3 July 1872, 173.
13. As Matthew notes in his discussion of Gladstone's foreign policy: *Gladstone*, 180–88.
14. I have drawn on Adrian Cook's *The Alabama Claims: American Politics and Anglo-American Relations, 1865–1872* (Ithaca, N.Y., 1975) for the following. Cook, as the title of his book indicates, emphasizes the American side of the question.
15. *Diaries*, vol. 8, 17 June 1872, WEG to Goschen.
16. Ramm, *Correspondence of Gladstone and Granville, 1868–1876*, WEG to Granville, 14 January 1872, 2:299. This volume is an important source for the progress of the negotiation.
17. Matthew, *Gladstone*, 187.
18. Essential reading for this topic is Richard Millman's *British Foreign Policy and the Coming of the Franco-Prussian War* (Oxford, 1965). See also C. J. Bartlett, "Clarendon, the Foreign Office, and the Hohenzollern Candidature, 1868–1870," *English Historical Review* 75, no. 295 (April 1960), 276–84.
19. The term "watchful neutrality" is Deryck Schreuder's in his useful "Gladstone as 'Troublemaker': Liberal Foreign Policy and the German Annexation of Alsace-Lorraine, 1870–1871," *Journal of British Studies* 17, no. 2 (Spring 1978), 106–35. For the two cabinet meetings see Gladstone's memos in *Diaries*, vol. 7, 325–26.
20. Throughout the crisis, Millman believes, Gladstone had to firm up Granville, urging him, for example, to use less diplomatic language with the French (*British Foreign Policy*, 192). The government's responses to the threat of war can easily be followed in the memos, letters, and diary entries in *Diaries*, vol. 7, 14 July 1870, 325 ff. See also Ramm, *Correspondence of Gladstone and Granville, 1868–1876*, 1:103 ff., passim.
21. WEG to Granville, 2 August 1870, quoted in Millman, *British Foreign Policy*, 204.
22. *Diaries*, vol. 7, WEG to Cardwell, 22 July 1870, 329 n. 4.
23. See Schreuder's "Gladstone as 'Troublemaker'" for Gladstone's campaign.
24. Ramm, *Correspondence of Gladstone and Granville, 1868–1876*, 1:137.
25. Ibid., 139.

26. Reprinted in Gladstone's *Gleanings of Past Years (1848–1878)* (London, 1879), 4:197–257. Quotations that follow are taken passim from this source.

27. Colin Matthew notes as much in his *Gladstone*, 181. Although Morley is kinder—terming Gladstone's article a "rather curious step"—he also notes that it was not a good precedent for a prime minister to volunteer an anonymous comment on affairs for which his responsibility "was both heavy and direct" (*Life of Gladstone*, 2:262).

28. *Diaries*, vol. 7, 21 Sept 1870, 365.

29. The most detailed modern discussion of Cardwell's reforms is found in Arvel B. Erickson's brief biography, "Edward T. Cardwell: Peelite," *Transactions of the American Philosophical Society*, new ser., 49, part 2 (1959), 67–95. See also Albert V. Tucker, "Army and Society in England, 1870–1900: A Reassessment of the Cardwell Reforms," *Journal of British Studies* 2, no. 2 (May 1963), 110–41.

30. The story is told in Thomas F. Gallagher, " 'Cardwellian Mysteries': The Fate of the British Army Regulation Bill, 1871," *Historical Journal* 18, no. 2 (June 1975), 335. Gladstone's letter to Lady Herbert included the following passage: "I must add that I know not what is to be said for small boroughs in these days if the last argument is to be abandoned of their returning occasionally eminent men who cannot get seats elsewhere" (GPBL, Add Mss 44539, WEG to Lady Herbert, 13 December 1870, fol. 100).

31. For the episode of the royal warrants see Erickson, *Cardwell*, 83; Johnson, *Diary of Gathorne Hardy*, 21 July 1871, 141; Russell's letter to William Harcourt in A. G. Gardiner, *The Life of Sir William Harcourt* (London, 1923), 1:228; Matthew, *Gladstone*, 209.

32. Gallagher, " 'Cardwellian Mysteries,' " 348.

33. Agatha Ramm, "The Parliamentary Context of Cabinet Government, 1868–1874," *English Historical Review* 99, no. 393 (October 1984), 739–69.

34. Trelawny, who had previously sat for Tavistock, was now M.P. for East Cornwall. He had evolved in his political ideas from a Benthamite ultra-radical in the 1840s to a moderate Whig-Liberal in Gladstone's first administration. The quotations that follow are taken passim from T. A. Jenkins, ed., "The Parliamentary Diaries of Sir John Trelawny, 1868–73," *Camden Miscellany*, Camden Fifth Series 3 (London, 1994), 329–513.

35. CDBL, Add Mss 63682, 15 June 1873, fol. 52.

36. Morley, *Life of Gladstone*, 2:351. Trelawny confirmed the state of Gladstone's health, noting on two occasions in May 1873 how pale and ill he looked.

37. *Diaries*, vol. 8, 11 Aug 1873, 368. See Matthew's discussion of the proposed plan in his *Gladstone*, 220–25.

38. *Diaries*, vol. 8, 24 November 1873, 416.

39. Ibid., 18 December 1873, 427.

40. Ramm, *Correspondence of Gladstone and Granville, 1868–1876*, 2:438–41. The letter is partially quoted in Morley, *Life of Gladstone*, 2:364–66.

41. Drus, "Journal of Kimberley," 23 January 1874, 43; CDBL, Add Mss 63683, 23 January 1874, fols. 11–12.

42. Sir Erskine May, clerk of the House of Commons, first used the term "coup d'etat" in reference to Gladstone's actions in his journal, quoted by Robert Rhodes James, "Gladstone and the Greenwich Seat: The Dissolution of January 26th 1874," *History Today* 9, no. 5 (May 1959), 350. For the other reactions see Gordon, *Red Earl*, Fortesque to Spencer, 23 January 1874, 1:114; GPBL, Add Mss 44307, Spencer to WEG, 26 January 1874, fol. 214. Modern historians have held similar views. Kitson Clark believes that Gladstone's dissolution was "reckless and ill-considered," brought on in part by his increasing "tendency to be impetuous and masterful" (see Kitson Clark's "Introduction" to Shannon's *Gladstone and the Bulgarian Agitation*, xxiii). See also Matthew, *Gladstone*, 227.

43. For newspaper comment see Biagini, *Liberty, Retrenchment, and Reform*, 113–17; and William Henry Maehl, "Gladstone, the Liberals, and the Election of 1874," *Bulletin of the Institute of Historical Research* 36, no. 93 (May 1963), 53.

44. Monypenny and Buckle, *Life of Disraeli*, 5:273. Gathorne Hardy, summoned by telegraph to

Disraeli's side, echoed the general surprise by commenting on Gladstone's "extraordinary proceeding in dissolving the Parliament about to meet" (Johnson, *Diary of Gathorne Hardy*, 26 January 1874, 193).

45. GGP 574, 6 February 1874, fols. 92–94.

46. *Diaries*, vol. 8, 7 February 1874, 456.

47. *Letters of the Rt. Hon. Henry Austin Bruce, Lord Aberdare of Duffryn*, (Oxford, 1902), 17 February 1874, 1:361. Aberdare was the former H. A. Bruce who had been moved from the Home Office to be president of the Council and who was given a barony during the previous year's cabinet reshuffle.

48. *Diaries*, vol. 8, 16 February 1874, 462. Gladstone reported of the cabinet meeting that he "did something toward snapping the ties, and winding out of the coil" (ibid., 461).

49. As Richard Shannon has observed in his *Gladstone and the Bulgarian Agitation, 1876* (London, 1963), 1–3.

50. Magnus, *Gladstone*, 229.

51. *Diaries*, vol. 8, WEG to Peel, 19 February 1874, 463.

52. Quoted in Morley, *Life of Gladstone*, 2:379; also partially printed in Bassett, *Gladstone to His Wife*, 201, where it is dated 6 April 1874.

53. See James Bentley, *Ritualism and Politics in Victorian Britain: The Attempt to Legislate for Belief* (Oxford, 1978), especially chap. 2. For the background to anti-Catholic sentiment of the time, especially as expressed in Parliament, see Walter L. Arnstein's *Protestant versus Catholic in Mid-Victorian England* (Columbia, Mo., 1982). For a more general view of the first year of Gladstone's opposition tactics see Matthew R. Temmel's discussion in his "Gladstone's Resignation of the Liberal Leadership, 1874–1875," *Journal of British Studies* 16, no. 1 (1976), 153–75.

54. This delighted Disraeli immensely: "*Gladstone ran away!*" he reported to Lady Chesterfield. See *The Letters of Disraeli to Lady Chesterfield and Lady Bradford*, ed. the marquess of Zetland (New York, 1929), 14 July 1874, 1:146.

55. Gladstone's parliamentary behavior has been commented on by Bentley in *Ritualism and Politics*, 63. Matthew concurs: "His ill-temper shows even through the flatness of the columns of Hansard" (Matthew's *Gladstone*, 246). See also the synopsis of Gladstone's role during the debates in Parry's *Democracy and Religion*, 413–17.

56. Quotations are taken from the reprinted article in Gladstone, *Gleanings*, 6:127.

57. Matthew, *Gladstone*, 182. Matthew believes that ultramontanism was the "obsession of his quasi-retirement" (ibid., 183).

58. As he expressed it in a letter to Acton on 8 January 1870, in John Neville Figgis and Reginald Vere Laurence, eds., *Selections from the Correspondence of the First Lord Acton* (London, 1917), 97.

59. CDBL, Add MSS 63683, 23 January 1874, fols. 11–12.

60. Arnstein, *Protestant versus Catholic*, 184. Anthony F. Denholm's "The Conversion of Lord Ripon in 1874," *Recusant History* 10 (April 1969), 111–18, is informative, although it makes exaggerated claims for Ripon. See also Denholm's longer work, *Lord Ripon, 1827–1909: A Political Biography* (London, 1982).

61. GPBL, Add Mss 44444, WEG to Lady Ripon, 21 Aug 1874, fols. 222–23. The letter is a copy. Apparently Ripon burned the original because of its offensive nature. Lucien Wolf, Ripon's first biographer, notes that all other letters to Ripon, including those from Aberdare, Granville, and Kimberley, were friendly and supportive, if regretful, of his decision (see Wolf, *Life of the First Marquess of Ripon* [London, 1921], 1:295 and 323–55).

62. GPBL, Add Mss 44286, Ripon to WEG, 1 October 1874, fols. 196, 197–98.

63. *Diaries*, vol. 8, 4 October 1874.

64. The original letter may be found in Ripon Papers, British Library, Add Mss 43514, WEG to Ripon, 4 October 1874, fols. 212–16. A copy is in GPBL, Add Mss 44286, fols. 212–16.

65. GPBL, Add Mss 44286, WEG to Ripon, 17 October 1874, fols. 215–16.

66. Essential reading on this topic is H. C. G. Matthew, "Gladstone, Vaticanism, and the Question of the East," in Derek Baker, ed., *Religious Motivation: Biographical and Sociological Problems for*

the Church Historian (Oxford, 1978), 417–42. Morley's chapter on Vaticanism also provides a helpful background; see his *Life of Gladstone*, 2:384–98.

67. Lord John Acton, in a letter to Granville, reported the circumstances of the insertion of the offending passage in "Ritual and Ritualism." Shortly after Gladstone had posted the manuscript to *Contemporary Review*, he left for a holiday in Germany in early September. While there, he found at an inn near Salzburg a newspaper with the public announcement of Ripon's conversion—a fact that Gladstone, of course, already knew from Ripon's wife. Apparently angered by this knowledge now made public, Gladstone sent off from Munich the offensive addition to his article on ritualism (Martin Collection, St. Deiniol's Library PRO Red 9/601, Acton to Granville, 2 December 1874). See also *Diaries*, vol. 8, 13 September 1874 and 525 n. 5; and Josef L. Altholz, "Gladstone and the Vatican Decrees," *Historian* 25 (1963), 317–18.

68. Dilke in a speech at Hammersmith on 8 Sept 1874 (Stephen Gwyn and Gertrude Tuckwell, *The Life of the Rt. Hon. Sir Charles W. Dilke* [London, 1917], 1:179). Argyll in a letter to Harcourt, quoted in John P. Rossi, "The Selection of Lord Hartington as Liberal Leader in the House of Commons, February, 1875," *Proceedings of the American Philosophical Society* 119, no. 4 (August 1975), 308–9.

69. See Harcourt's letters to Lord Edmond Fitzmaurice on 6 January 1875, to Goschen on 7 January 1875, and to Dilke on 20 January 1875, as found in Gardiner, *Life of Harcourt*, 1:285, 286, and 290.

70. Evidence relating to Gladstone's resignation may be found in GGP 2104, memo entitled "Reasons for Retirement" dated 9 January 1875; GGP 779, WEG to Catherine Gladstone, 11 January 1875, fol. 7; and Bassett, *Gladstone to His Wife*, 206–9.

71. T. A. Jenkins, *Gladstone, Whiggery and the Liberal Party, 1874-1886* (Oxford, 1988), 27, 28, and 31. Jenkins also notes Gladstone's "instinctive urge" to impose his authority upon the party, as well as the "exceptionally autocratic nature of his leadership" and his "dictatorial tendency."

72. Johnson, *Diary of Gathorne Hardy*, 9 June 1875, 239; Disraeli to Lady Bradford, tentatively dated 27 May 1875, but likely later, in Monypenny and Buckle, *Life of Disraeli*, 5:378.

73. *Diaries*, vol. 9, 16 January 1875.

74. Ibid., 30 March 1875.

75. Ibid., 29 December 1875.

Chapter 9: Gladstone Redivivus

1. *Diaries*, vol. 9, 30 March 1875.

2. He was so described by J. L. Garvin, *The Life of Joseph Chamberlain* (London, 1932), 1:239.

3. I have relied heavily on Shannon's *Gladstone and the Bulgarian Agitation, 1876*, for the following discussion.

4. Ibid., 92; Matthew, "Introduction," *Gladstone Diaries*, vol. 9, li; Ann Pottinger Saab, *Reluctant Icon: Gladstone, Bulgaria, and the Working Classes, 1856–1878* (Cambridge, Mass., 1991), especially chap. 5. The labor leader was Alfred Days, secretary of the Workmen's Hyde Park Demonstration Committee from Hackney. Saab follows Neil Smelser's *Theory of Collective Behavior* (New York, 1963) as a framework for understanding the Bulgarian agitation.

5. Agatha Ramm, ed., *The Political Correspondence of Mr. Gladstone and Lord Granville, 1876–1886* (Oxford, 1962), 27 Aug 1876, 1:3; and 29 Aug 1876, 1:3.

6. Quoted in Morley, *Life of Gladstone*, 2:420.

7. Ramm, *Correspondence of Gladstone and Granville, 1876–1886*, 3 October 1876, 1:10; Granville to WEG, 4 October 1876, 1:12; WEG to Granville, 7 October 1876, 1:13.

8. John P. Rossi, "The Transformation of the British Liberal Party: A Study of the Tactics of the Liberal Opposition, 1874–1880," in *Transactions of the American Philosophical Society*, new ser., 68, part 8 (1978), 38. For a thorough discussion of Gladstone's presumption as "unofficial" leader of the Liberal Party see Shannon, *Gladstone and the Bulgarian Agitation*, chap. 4.

9. Ramm, *Correspondence of Gladstone and Granville, 1876–1886*, 28 January 1877, 1:29.

10. Ibid., 23 April 1877, 1:35.

11. For Harcourt's reactions see Gwen and Tuckwell, *Life of Dilke*, 1:220; and Gardiner, *Life of*

Harcourt, 1:318. Granville's remarks are in Ramm, *Correspondence of Gladstone and Granville, 1876–1886*, 2 May 1877, 1:36.

12. Gwen and Tuckwell, *Life of Dilke*, 1:221.

13. Ramm, *Correspondence of Gladstone and Granville, 1876–1886*, 4 May 1877, 1:36.

14. *Diaries*, vol. 9, 7 May 1877.

15. Ibid., 16 May 1877. See Matthew's discussion of Gladstone's "passion for order" as revealed in his behavior during these years ("Introduction" to *Diaries*, vol. 9, lxxxiii).

16. Ibid., 23 May 1877 and 24 May 1877. The diary is filled with such references for the last half of the year.

17. Ibid., 18 October 1877.

18. As Shannon argues in his *Gladstone and the Bulgarian Agitation*, 274–81.

19. Ramm, *Correspondence of Gladstone and Granville, 1876–1886*, 11 October 1877, 1:55.

20. Ibid., 11 October 1877, 1:55; 31 October 1877, 1:56; 20 November 1877, 1:58. The specter of Home Rule that Gladstone raised must have caused Granville to swoon. He sent by the next day's post an expostulation: "What with the disjointed state of the Home Rulers, and the feeling of the nonconformists and others in England & Scotland, any understanding with him [Issac Butt, the parliamentary Home Rule leader] now, appears to me dangerous and premature" (ibid., 21 November 1877, 1:59).

21. *Times*, 8 November 1877.

22. *Diaries*, vol. 9, 7 November 1877.

23. *Diaries*, vol. 9, 24 February 1878 and 10 March 1878. Gladstone took all this in stride and suspected the hidden hand of Conservative organizers. There may have been some truth to this conjecture: see Hugh Cunningham, "Jingoism in 1877–78," *Victorian Studies* 14, no. 4 (June 1971), 429–53.

24. Monypenny and Buckle, *Life of Disraeli*, Disraeli to Queen Victoria, 3 November 1877, 6:194.

25. Gladstone's own estimate was 86,930; he kept precise records of crowd counts and length of speeches at each stop (see *Diaries*, vol. 9, 466).

26. Matthew has much of value to say about the Midlothian Campaign in his "Introduction," liii–lxix, *Diaries*, vol. 9.

27. W. E. Gladstone, *Midlothian Speeches, 1879*, ed. M. R. D. Foot (reprint, Leicester, 1971), 165.

28. Ibid., 65.

29. Matthew, "Introduction," *Diaries*, vol. 9, lxi.

30. Granville's letter in Ramm, *Correspondence of Gladstone and Granville, 1876–1886*, 1 February 1877, 1:30.

31. *Diaries*, vol. 9, 24 November 1879, 29 November 1879, 4 December 1879, 6 December 1879.

32. Morley, *Life of Gladstone*, 2:450 and 452.

33. Richard T. Shannon, "Midlothian: 100 Years After," in Peter J. Jagger, ed., *Gladstone, Politics and Religion* (New York, 1985), 88–103.

34. Monypenny and Buckle, *Life of Disraeli*, Disraeli to Lady Bradford, 28 November 1879, 6:503; Johnson, *Diary of Gathorne Hardy*, 27 November 1879, 428; Lord George Hamilton, *Parliamentary Reminiscences and Reflections, 1868 to 1885* (New York, 1917), 173.

35. John P. Rossi, "The Ripon Diary, 1878–80:3," *Recusant History* 12, no. 6 (1974), 28 November 1879, 273.

36. Details of the negotiations may be found in John P. Rossi, "'The Nestor of his Party'—Gladstone, Hartington and the Liberal Leadership Crisis, November 1879–January 1880," *Canadian Journal of History* 11, no. 2 (1976), 189–99.

37. These allegations are among the documents in *Wright v. Gladstone*, a case between Gladstone's sons and Captain Peter Wright, tried in 1927. See GGP 1972.

38. Hamilton Papers, British Library, Add Mss 48607B, Louisa Pepys to Hamilton, 7 May 1882, fols. 91–96; and W. W. Parkinson to WEG, 5 May 1882, fols. 97–99. Eddy Hamilton, Gladstone's private secretary during the second administration, was often called upon to resolve the suspicions that arose over the chief's "night walks." In this case, he sent letters to both Tottenham and Parkinson to the effect that had either of them overheard the conversation of the

couple they spied, they would have "placed a very different interpretation upon the event." For Hamilton's views of the incident at the duke of York's column see Bahlman, *Diary of Hamilton*, 1:269–70.

39. For the Thistlethwayte affair see Matthew, "Introduction," *Diaries*, vol. 5, lxi–lxv; vol. 7, ciii–cvii; and vol. 9, lxxxvii–lxxxix. Especially important is the series of letters from Gladstone to Thistlethwayte in the appendix to vol. 8 of the *Diaries*, 557–587, and in the appendix to vol. 12, 431–531. Details of Thistlethwayte's early life are briefly recounted in Cyril Pearl's not wholly reliable *Girl with the Swansdown Seat*, paperback ed. (New York, 1958), 120–22. Her portrait appears in this book, among many other illustrations, in what Pearl calls a "Galaxy of Soiled Doves." The portrait is reproduced, along with a photograph, in *Diaries*, vol. 6, pl. 3.

40. Ibid., vol. 6, 30 April 1865.

41. Ibid., vol. 7, 2 July 1869.

42. Ibid., vol. 8, WEG to Thistlethwayte, 16 December 1869, 579.

43. Ibid., 5 October 1869, 559.

44. Ibid., 18 October 1869, 563.

45. Matthew, "Introduction," *Diaries*, vol. 5, lxiii.

46. Ibid., vol. 7, ciii.

47. GGP 776, WEG to CG, 6 February 1865, fol. 172.

48. Matthew, "Introduction," *Diaries*, vol. 5, lxiii.

49. *Diaries*, vol. 7, 25 October 1869.

50. Ibid., vol. 8, WEG to Thistlethwayte, 19 October 1869, 564.

51. Ibid., 22 October 1869, 567.

52. Ibid., 23 October 1869, 569; and Matthew, "Introduction," *Diaries*, vol. 7, civ.

53. Ibid., vol. 7, 18 November 1869; for other diary entries in November see *Diaries*, passim.

54. Ibid., 28 October 1869.

55. Ibid., vol. 8, 575–76.

56. Ibid., vol. 7, 12 December 1869.

57. Ibid., vol. 8, WEG to Thistlethwayte, 16 December 1869, 579.

58. Ibid., 18 December 1869, 581.

59. Ibid., vol. 7, 13 December 1869.

60. Ibid., 19 December 1869 and 20 December 1869.

61. Ibid., 19 January 1870.

62. Ibid., vol. 8, WEG to Thistlethwayte, 22 April 1870, 585–87.

63. Ibid., vol. 7, 27 February 1870. See also Matthew, "Introduction," *Diaries*, vol. 9, lxxxviii. This was the first time Gladstone entered in his diary her residence, rather than her name, after a visit.

64. Excerpts from the diaries of Derby and Carnarvon are reprinted in Matthew, "Introduction," *Diaries*, vol. 7, cv. Carnarvon's assumptions about Gladstone's "passion" are surely too early; his comments about his madness were common enough among his political opponents.

65. *Diaries*, vol. 8, 11 February 1872.

66. Ibid., vol. 7, 17 April 1871, 20 April 1871, 29 April 1871.

67. Ibid., vol. 8, 17 November 1872.

68. Matthew, "Introduction," *Diaries*, vol. 9, lxxxvii–lxxxviii.

69. The diminishing affective role of Mrs. Thistlethwayte in Gladstone's life is obvious from the diaries in the late 1870s. She remained with her husband until he died in 1887. A copy of his death certificate is in GGP 1974. It is dated 7 Aug 1887 and reads, "Pistol shot Wound in Head Accidentally when carrying a loaded pistol found in a helpless condition on the floor and died in 14 hours." His death was ruled accidental, although suspicions must remain. Perhaps he died trying to summon a laggardly servant. But he was an experienced sportsman, and suicide seems at least a possibility.

70. If Disraeli's pleading and sometimes pathetic letters to her are any guide. Lady Bradford did not reciprocate his feelings. The examples are numerous in Zetland, *Letters of Disraeli to Lady Chesterfield and Lady Bradford*.

Chapter 10: "The Host of Pharaoh"

1. For a discussion of the election see Trevor O. Lloyd's *The General Election of 1880* (Oxford, 1968); Rossi, "The Transformation of the British Liberal Party," especially 109–26; and Blake, *Disraeli*, chap. 30. Election returns are taken from Lloyd.

2. T. A. Jenkins, in "Gladstone, the Whigs and the Leadership of the Liberal Party," *Historical Journal* 27, no 2 (1984), however, dismisses the assumption commonly held among historians that Gladstone was the inevitable prime minister after the election of 1880.

3. Fortesque, having served as chief secretary for Ireland in Gladstone's first ministry before his demotion to the Board of Trade, was brought in for Argyll as privy seal after Argyll's resignation over Ireland in 1881.

4. Ramm, *Correspondence of Gladstone and Granville, 1876–1886,* "Introduction," 1:xlii. Gladstone held only about half as many cabinet meetings as had Disraeli during parliamentary sessions.

5. Matthew characterizes Gladstone's governance and his health during the second administration in *Diaries,* "Introduction," vol. 10.

6. Matthew's phrase in ibid., liii.

7. The quotation is from a confidential letter to Sir Henry Ponsonby, the queen's secretary: see G. E. Buckle, ed., *The Letters of Queen Victoria,* 2d ser. (London, 1928), 30 April 1880, 3:91.

8. Paul Kennedy, *Strategy and Diplomacy, 1870–1945* (London, 1983), 21.

9. For the development of Gladstone's conciliatory policy in South Africa see D. M. Schreuder, *Gladstone and Kruger: Liberal Government and Colonial "Home Rule," 1880–85* (London, 1969).

10. A general background to Anglo-Russian rivalry in Central Asia may be found in Firuz Kazemzadeh, *Russia and Britain in Persia, 1864–1914* (New Haven, 1968); and Vartan Gregorian, *The Emergence of Modern Afghanistan: Politics of Reform and Modernization, 1880–1946* (Stanford, 1969).

11. See W. D. McIntyre, "British Policy in West Africa: The Ashanti Expedition of 1873–74," *Historical Journal* 5, no. 1 (1962), 19–46; and John Keegan, "The Ashanti Campaign, 1873–74," in Brian Bond, ed., *Victorian Military Campaigns* (London, 1967), 163–98.

12. The sultan was, in Gladstone's words, the "greatest of all liars upon earth" and a "bottomless pit of iniquity and fraud" (letters to Ripon and Argyll in *Diaries,* vol. 9, 10 September 1880, 579; and 26 October 1880, 603).

13. The most comprehensive discussion of this diplomatic episode remains W. N. Medlicott's *Bismarck, Gladstone, and the Concert of Europe* (London, 1956). As Medlicott observes, Gladstone was the "real driving force" for intervention throughout the crisis, and he showed "remarkable firmness in the pursuit of this policy" (138–56). This is borne out by the correspondence between Gladstone and Granville during the summer and autumn of 1880. See, for example, the series of letters about a proposed telegram to the sultan: Gladstone strengthened the wording to make it an ultimatum (Ramm, *Correspondence of Gladstone and Granville, 1876–1886,* 1:171–73).

14. The story is briefly told in Roger C. Thompson's *Australian Imperialism in the Pacific: The Expansionist Era, 1820–1920* (Melborne, 1980), chap. 4, "Queensland's Quest for New Guinea, 1883." See also John Legge, "Australia and New Guinea to the Establishment of the British Protectorate, 1884," *Historical Studies, Australia and New Zealand* 4 (1949–51), 34–47; and Marjorie G. Jacobs, "The Colonial Office and New Guinea, 1874–84," *Historical Studies, Australia and New Zealand* 5 (1951–53), 106–18.

15. Letter printed in full in Paul Knaplund, ed., "Gladstone-Gordon Correspondence, 1851–1896," *Transactions of the American Philosophical Society* 51, part 4 (1961), 88–89. Gordon was a younger son of Lord Aberdeen, the former prime minister, under whom Gladstone had once served.

16. *Diaries,* vol. 10, 13 June 1883, Cabinet Memos, 460.

17. GPBL, Add Mss 44142, Derby to WEG, 7 December 1883, fol. 14.

18. *Diaries,* vol. 11, 8 December 1883, 74.

19. Ibid., 6 August, 9 August 1884, 184 and 186; 21 January 1885, 281.

20. Paul M. Kennedy, *The Rise of Anglo-German Antagonism, 1860–1914* (London, 1980), 175, especially chaps. 9 and 10.

21. *Diaries,* vol. 11, 3 January 1885, 270.
22. For this exchange, see GPBL, Add Mss 44142, Derby's letters to WEG, 23 December 1884, fols. 106–7; 26 December 1884, fols. 108–9; 27 December 1884, fols. 110–11. WEG's to Derby is in ibid., 30 December 1884, fols. 113–14, partially printed in *Diaries,* vol. 11, 266 n. 9. The cabinet meeting that annexed Natal southward was held on 3 January 1885; see *Diaries,* vol. 11, 270.
23. Quoted here from Morley, *Life of Gladstone,* 3:56.
24. See A. H. H. Knightbridge, "Egypt in British Political Thought, 1875–1900," (Ph.D. diss., Oxford University, 1963). Ronald Robinson and John Gallagher (with Alice Denny), *Africa and the Victorians: The Climax of Imperialism,* remains stimulating reading. I have used the Anchor edition (New York, 1968); especially useful are chaps. 4–6.
25. Modern research, much of it based on Egyptian sources, has shown how moderate were the intentions of Arabi and his followers. See A. G. Hopkins, "The Victorians and Africa: A Reconsideration of the Occupation of Egypt, 1882," *Journal of African History* 27, no. 2 (1986), 363–91, especially 374–75. See also John S. Galbraith and Afaf Lufti al-sayyid-Marsot, "The British Occupation of Egypt: Another View," *International Journal of Middle East Studies* 9 (1978), 471–88; and Alexander Schölch, "The 'Men on the Spot' and the English Occupation of Egypt," *Historical Journal* 19, no. 3 (1976), 773–85.
26. Magnus, *Gladstone,* 445.
27. For Gladstone's remarks, see *Diaries,* vol. 10, WEG to Cardwell, 15 September 1882, 333; WEG to Madame Novikov, 15 September 1882, 334; and to Childers, 16 September 1882, 335.
28. Quoted in John V. Crangle, "The British Peace Movement and the Anglo-Egyptian War of 1882," *Quarterly Review of Historical Studies* 15 (1975–76), 144. See also M. E. Chamberlain, "British Public Opinion and the Invasion of Egypt, 1882," *Trivium* 16 (1981), 5–28. As Chamberlain notes, the peace movement—never very effective—was ignored by Gladstone.
29. Agatha Ramm, "Great Britain and France in Egypt, 1876–1882," in P. Gifford and W. R. Louis, eds., *France and Britain in Africa* (New Haven, 1971), 113.
30. Various explanations are discussed in Galbraith and Afaf Lufti al-Sayyid-Marsot, "British Occupation of Egypt," 478–81; and Ramm, "Great Britain and France," 105–8.
31. Marvin Schwartz, *The Politics of British Foreign Policy in the Era of Disraeli and Gladstone* (New York, 1985), chap. 6.
32. Matthew believes that Gladstone's "executive itch"—that tendency to exercise control over legislative affairs—also operated in his foreign and imperial policy (*Diaries,* vol. 10, "Introduction," xliv).
33. Quoted in Magnus, *Gladstone,* 288.
34. Ramm, *Correspondence of Gladstone and Granville, 1876–1886,* 1:384–85.
35. For this exchange see ibid., 386–87.
36. Ibid., WEG to Granville, 1 July 1882, 1:383.
37. CDBL, Add Mss 63690, 2 July 1882, fol. 164.
38. Matthew, *Diaries,* vol. 10, "Introduction," clxxii.
39. Gardiner, *Life of Harcourt,* 1:448; Walling, *Diaries of Bright,* 485; CDBL, Add Mss 63690, 8 July 1882, fol. 167; Gwynn and Tuckwell, *Life of Dilke,* 1:446–47. Gathorne Hardy (now Lord Cranbrook), that inveterate Gladstone watcher, took pleasure in noting Gladstone's "arrogance & ill humour" during the debate on 7 July (Johnson, *Diary of Gathorne Hardy,* 8 July 1882, 498).
40. *Diaries,* vol. 10, 8 July 1882, 294.
41. Leon Festinger pioneered the theory in his *Theory of Cognitive Dissonance* (Evanston, Ill., 1957). Although the theory of cognitive dissonance has become increasingly controversial, it is strongly defended by some social psychologists. See Elliot Aronson's *The Social Animal,* 2d ed. (San Francisco, 1976), chap. 4, and his more recent defense of the theory in the American Psychological Association's *Monitor* (August 1990), 10.
42. For this analysis of Gladstone's decision making, see also the suggestive work by Irving L. Janis and Leon Mann, *Decision Making: A Psychological Analysis of Conflict, Choice, and Commitment* (New York, 1977), especially 82–95.

43. The letters, dated 10 July to 14 July 1882, are in *Diaries*, vol. 10, 295–99. Quotations in the following paragraph can be found in this source.

44. Walling, *Diaries of Bright*, 14 July 1882, 487–88.

45. Ramm, *Correspondence of Gladstone and Granville, 1876–1886*, 1:22 September 1882, 429.

46. John S. Galbraith, "The Trial of Arabi Pasha," *Journal of Imperial and Commonwealth History* 7 (1979), 274–92. In a thorough piece of detective work, M. E. Chamberlain has made a plausible case for Arabi's innocence during the Alexandria riots: see "The Alexandria Massacre of 11 June 1882 and the British Occupation of Egypt," *Middle Eastern Studies* 13 (1977), 14–39. Indeed, it appears that Arabi himself, commanding units of the Egyptian army, put down the riots.

47. Magnus believes that Gladstone was suffering from depression; see his *Gladstone*, 291–92.

48. *Diaries*, vol. 10, 24 October 1882, 357–58.

49. Ramm, *Correspondence of Gladstone and Granville, 1876–1886*, 11 November 1882, 1:451.

50. *Diaries*, vol. 11, appendix 1, 659–60.

51. *Diaries*, vol. 10, 19 January 1883, 397.

52. Reproduced in Brooke and Sorensen, *PMP*, 4:63.

53. *Diaries*, vol. 10, 20 January 1883, 397. This was not entirely true. Gladstone harbored a suspicion that the cabinet was conspiring to keep him abroad so that they could pursue policy without him. See the exchange of letters between Gladstone and Granville in Ramm, *Correspondence of Gladstone and Granville, 1876–1886*, 2:11–12, 17–18, 20. Perhaps Gladstone's suspicions were exacerbated when he learned that the queen contemplated offering him a peerage, an unsolicited honor that would, in effect, banish him to the House of Lords.

54. *Diaries*, vol. 10, 26 February 1883, 409.

55. See O'Leary, *Elimination of Corrupt Practices*, chaps. 5 and 6.

56. The most recent account of Bradlaugh is Walter L. Arnstein's *The Bradlaugh Case: A Study in Late Victorian Opinion and Politics* (Oxford, 1965).

57. *Diaries*, vol. 9, WEG to the Speaker, H. B. W. Brand, 24 May 1880, 529.

58. Ibid., vol. 10, 28 March 1882, 227.

59. Dilke described Gladstone as "very angry" with his colleagues for proposing Bradlaugh's exclusion (Dilke Papers, British Library, Add Mss 43942, 21 February 1881, fol. 32). See also Carlingford's account of a cabinet meeting the following year during which Gladstone resisted his colleagues' efforts to act against Bradlaugh (CDBL, Add Mss 63690, 22 February 1882, fol. 67).

60. See Bassett, *Gladstone's Speeches*, 580–600.

61. Ibid., 599–600.

62. Morley, *Life of Gladstone*, 3:15.

63. Ibid., vol. 11, 23 August 1883.

64. Algernon West was one of Gladstone's secretaries during his first ministry; he served again during Gladstone's last ministry of 1892–94. An expert in patronage, he was awarded a KCB in 1886. His account of the *Pembroke Castle* voyage may be found in his *Recollections: 1832–1886* (New York, 1900), 330–40.

65. West, *Recollections*, 331. Tennant was to marry H. H. Asquith in 1894.

66. *Diaries*, vol. 11, 8–21 September 1883, 26–30, recount the voyage. Tennyson hinted broadly that he would not reject the offer of a barony, even though he had refused four times before. Gladstone was disposed to grant Tennyson's wish, but only after quizzing Hallam, Tennyson's son, about his father's willingness to appear in the House of Lords and occasionally vote on urgent matters of state (Robert Bernard Martin, *Tennyson: The Unquiet Heart* [Oxford, 1983], 541).

67. *Diaries*, vol. 11, 21 February 1883, 30.

68. For the cabinet see ibid., vol. 11, 25 October 1883, 48; letter to Catherine is in ibid., 26 October 1883, 49.

69. For an introduction to the origins of the reform legislation of the 1880s see William A. Hayes, *The Background and Passage of the Third Reform Act* (New York, 1982), chaps. 2 and 3.

70. CDBL, Add Mss, 25 October 1883, fol. 274. Derby thought this threat of resignation, made only to the cabinet, would be counterproductive if widely known. "Nobody will put himself out of

the way to serve a Minister who is politically dead," he wrote to Granville. (Quoted in Hayes, *Third Reform Act*, 104 n. 29.)

71. The complexities of redistribution and of the Reform Act generally may best be followed in Matthew, *Diaries*, "Introduction," vol. 10, cii–cix; and Mary E. J. Chadwick, "The Role of Redistribution in the Making of the Third Reform Act," *Historical Journal* 19, no. 3 (1976), 665–83. Neal Blewett, in "The Franchise in the United Kingdom, 1885–1918," *Past and Present*, no. 32 (December 1965), 27–56, has useful things to say about the act within the broader context of franchise reform. Andrew Jones's *The Politics of Reform, 1884* (Cambridge, England, 1972), is the most complete analysis, but it is also maddeningly allusive and elliptic. The concluding "Portrait Gallery" (appendix 4, 244–61) is, however, not to be missed.

72. Peter Marsh, in *The Discipline of Popular Government: Lord Salisbury's Domestic Statecraft, 1881–1902* (Hassocks, Sussex, 1978), 35–47, discusses Salisbury's tactics during the reform debates in the Lords.

73. For these letters see *Diaries*, vol. 11, 167–71.

74. Ibid., 8 July 1884.

75. See Dilke's journal in Gwynn and Tuckwell, *Life of Dilke*, 2:64.

76. Memos are in *Diaries*, vol. 11, 19 August 1884, 191–94; and 25 August 1884, 198–99.

77. Descriptions and extracts of Gladstone's speech are taken from the *Times*, 1 September 1884.

78. Why Salisbury, after months of stalling, should have compromised is a matter of historical dispute. Corrine C. Weston, in "Disunity on the Opposition Front Bench, 1884," *English Historical Review* 106, no. 418 (January 1991), 80–96, believes that the queen's decisive influence operating on a Conservative disunity undermined Salisbury's intransigence. John D. Fair, in "The Carnarvon Diaries and Royal Mediation in 1884", ibid., 97–116, sees no evidence of Conservative disunity and suggests that Salisbury's former mistrust of Liberal intentions was removed by *their* willingness to compromise. Most particularly, Fair believes that assurances from Gladstone may have been decisive. Peter Marsh, in his *Discipline of Popular Government*, 43, agrees.

79. Matthew, *Diaries*, vol. 10, "Introduction," cii and cix.

80. But Gladstone also believed that Britain's departure would leave unresolved a significant Egyptian problem, which he defined as "how to plant solidly western & beneficent institutions in the soil of a Mahomedan community?" *Diaries*, vol. 11, WEG to Rosebery, 15 November 1883, 59.

81. Knightbridge, "Egypt in British Political Thought", 256.

82. For information on the Madhi and Britain's involvement in the Sudan generally, see Mekki Shebeika, *British Policy in the Sudan, 1882–1902* (Oxford, 1952). This book draws on Egyptian and Sudanese sources, as well as standard British ones.

83. *Diaries*, vol. 11, WEG to Northbrook, 12 August 1884, 187.

84. CDBL, Add Mss 63692, 24 March 1884, fol. 126.

85. *Diaries*, vol. 11, 18 March 1884, 125.

86. CDBL, Add Mss 63692, 22 March 1884, fol. 125.

87. Gordon also informed the cabinet that he planned to send out his small garrison against the Mahdi to "show his force." This news "frightened us out of our senses," Dilke reported. See Gwynn and Tuckwell, *Life of Dilke*, 2:40.

88. The letters may be found in Buckle, *Letters of Queen Victoria*, 2d ser., 3:485 and 488.

89. Gladstone's exculpatory position was most carefully worked out in a postmortem of the Gordon affair, contained in a long memorandum, "The Military Position in the Soudan" (GPBL [Supplementary], Add Mss 56452, 9 April 1885, fols. 149–71).

90. Ibid., WEG to E. W. Benson, 12 May 1884, 145.

91. *Diaries*, vol. 11, 12 May 1884. Carlingford noted that Gladstone's speech did not make a good impression in part because "he had been violently excited in the course of it" (CDBL, Add Mss 63692, 12 May 1884, fol. 150).

92. According to Dilke, in Gwynn and Tuckwell, *Life of Dilke*, 2:34.

93. CDBL, Add Mss 63692, 30 May 1884, fol. 268.

94. Fitzmaurice, *Life of Granville*, 15 July 1884, 2:390.

95. Both generals kept journals during these final weeks. See *The Journals of Major-Gen. C. G. Gordon, C.B., at Khartoum*, ed. A. Egmont Hake (London, 1885); and *In Relief of Gordon: Lord Wolseley's Campaign Journal of the Khartoum Relief Expedition, 1884–1885*, ed. Adrian Preston (London, 1967). Not the least intriguing aspect of this Victorian imperial spectacle was the sight of two literary generals penning their way toward a rendezvous in the desert. See also Adrian Preston, "Wolsey, the Khartoum Relief Expedition, and the defense of India, 1885–1900," *Journal of Imperial and Commonwealth History* 6, no. 3 (May 1978), 254–80.

96. Lord Elton, *Gordon of Khartoum: The Life of General Charles George Gordon* (New York, 1955), 368–69. Elton presents a commonly accepted view of Gordon's death. Douglas H. Johnson, however, points out that by metaphorically dressing Gordon in white and presenting him as appropriately stoical and superior before hordes of native murderers, Victorian mythmakers could enshrine him as a martyr. Johnson believes it more likely that Gordon was killed directing his troops, most probably by accident in the general confusion of defending the palace. See Johnson's "The Death of Gordon: A Victorian Myth," *Journal of Imperial and Commonwealth History* 10, no. 3 (May 1982), 285–310.

97. *Diaries*, vol. 11, WEG to Northbrook, 6 January 1885, 272.

Chapter 11: *"A Dark and Dreary Cloud"*

1. Gordon also died to the accompaniment of much bad verse. See Richard Hill, "The Gordon Literature," *Durham University Journal*, new ser., 16, no. 3 (June 1955), 97–103; John M. Mac-Kenzie, *Propaganda and Empire: The Manipulation of British Public Opinion, 1880–1960* (Manchester, 1984).

2. "Hoarse as a raven," he wrote in the *Diaries*, vol. 11, 26 March 1885.

3. Ibid., 29 March 1885.

4. Ibid., 31 March 1885.

5. Carnarvon Papers, British Library, Add Mss 60915, 25 July 1880, fol. 12.

6. Noted by Matthew, *Diaries*, vol. 9, 564 n. 3.

7. Quotations in this paragraph from the *Diary* are in vol. 9, 23 June, 24 June, 8 July, 23 July, 31 July, and 31 July–3 August 1880. This last entry is of a rare kind: several days are conflated into one. A similar entry for 4–6 August occurred, when he noted that his lung congestion was relieved.

8. *Diaries*, vol. 9, 29 August 1880, 573.

9. Because of the timing of his illness, it is tempting to consider that Gladstone was employing a strategy of withdrawal in order to avoid the consequences of a certain defeat in the House of Lords over the disturbance bill. But the evidence seems conclusive that the stresses of overwork had only a direct physiological impact.

10. There has been considerable historical interest in the Land League. Among the most useful works are Samuel Clark, *Social Origins of the Irish Land War* (Princeton, 1979); Andrew W. Orridge, "Who Supported the Land War: An Aggregate-Data Analysis of Irish Agrarian Discontent, 1879–1882," *Economic and Social Review* 12, no. 3 (April 1981), 203–33; William L. Feingold, *The Revolt of the Tenantry: The Transformation of Local Government in Ireland, 1872–1886* (Boston, 1984); Janet K. TeBrake, "Irish Peasant Women in Revolt: The Land League Years," *Irish Historical Studies* 28, no. 109 (May 1992), 63–80; Jane McL. Cote, *Fanny and Anna Parnell: Ireland's Patriot Sisters* (New York, 1991); and Paul Bew, "The Land League Ideal: Achievements and Contradictions," in D. J. Drudy, ed., *Ireland: Land, Politics and People* (Cambridge, England, 1982).

11. Important biographies are: F. S. L. Lyons, *Charles Stewart Parnell* (New York, 1977); and R. F. Foster, *Charles Stewart Parnell: The Man and His Family*, 2d ed. (Hassocks, Sussex, 1979). See also the historiographical essay on the various interpretations of Parnell by D. George Boyce, "'The Portrait of the King Is the King': The Biographers of Charles Stewart Parnell," in D. George Boyce and Alan O'Day, eds., *Parnell in Perspective* (London, 1991).

12. Crucial to an understanding of the role of the Land League in the agrarian outrages is Towns-

hend's *Political Violence in Ireland,* especially chap. 3. Townshend's sophisticated analysis carefully reviews the arguments between those who believed then (or who believe now) that the Land League was intent on subverting the legitimate government in Ireland, and those who believed that the league was in the tradition of Irish agrarian movements that sought primarily redress of economic grievances. Townshend espouses the second point of view.

13. As revealed in *Florence Arnold-Forster's Irish Journal,* ed. T. W. Moody and Richard Hawkins with Margaret Moody (Oxford, 1988). For an analysis of the institutional failures of Dublin Castle see Kieran Flanagan, "The Chief Secretary's Office, 1853–1914: A Bureaucratic Enigma," *Irish Historical Studies* 24, no. 94 (November 1984), 197–225.

14. See his letters to Gladstone in *Earl Cowper, K.G.: A Memoir by His Wife* (1913), 13 November 1880, 427–28; and 23 November 1880, 434.

15. *Diaries,* vol. 9, WEG to Forster, 25 October 1880, 601.

16. Ibid., WEG to Forster, 9 December 1880, 635.

17. According to Dilke: see Gwynn and Tuckwell, *Life of Dilke,* 1:362.

18. *Diaries,* vol. 9, 9 December 1880, 634–35.

19. Garvin, *Life of Chamberlain,* Morley to Chamberlain, 31 December 1880, 1:332.

20. *Diaries,* vol. 9, 12 December 1880, 637.

21. Ibid., WEG to H. B. W. Brand, 15 December 1880, 643. See additionally the cabinet minutes of 15 November 1880, in ibid., 614.

22. GPBL, Add Mss 44194, Brand to WEG, 18 December 1880, fol. 230.

23. *Diaries,* vol. 10, 3 February 1881, 16. Fortesque agreed: he characterized the resolution as conferring "despotic powers" on the Speaker (CDBL, Add Mss 63689, 4 February 1881, fol. 78).

24. Garvin, *Life of Chamberlain,* 1:334.

25. Gwynn and Tuckwell, *Life of Dilke,* 1:365.

26. *Diaries,* vol. 10, 23 February 1881, 24. The Prince of Wales resided at Marlborough House.

27. Ibid., WEG to Hartington, 25 February 1881, 24.

28. Allen Warren, "Gladstone, Land and Social Reconstruction in Ireland, 1881–1887," *Parliamentary History* 2 (1983), 153–73. Warren's argument is developed at greater length in his Oxford D.Phil. dissertation of 1974, "The Irish Policies of the Second Gladstone Government, 1880–1885."

29. *Diaries,* vol. 9, WEG to Cowper, 24 November 1880, 620.

30. GPBL, Add Mss 44157, Forster to WEG, 5 November 1880, fol. 193.

31. *Diaries,* vol. 9, WEG to Childers, 10 December 1880, 636.

32. GPBL, Add Mss 44105, WEG to Argyll, 14 April 1881, fol. 66.

33. See especially Warren, "The Irish Policies of the Second Gladstone Government," chap. 3.

34. Ibid., 127, letter dated 16 May 1881.

35. *Diaries,* vol. 9, 25 December 1880, 652.

36. See Matthew's discussion in *Diaries,* vol. 10, "Introduction," cxiv–cxvi.

37. Ibid., WEG to Forster, 9 October 1881, 142.

38. Francis H. Herrick, "Gladstone, Newman, and Ireland in 1881," *Catholic Historical Review* 47, no. 3 (1 October 1961), 342–50. Granville Papers, Public Record Office (hereafter PRO) 30/29/149, Errington to Granville, 20 December 1881 (copy in Martin Collection, St. Deiniol's Library, Hawarden, 636, but apparently misdated as 1880).

39. *Diaries,* vol. 10, WEG to Chamberlain, 15 December 1881, 177; WEG to Harcourt, 16 December 1881, 178; WEG to Acton, 26 December 1881, 184.

40. The story is well told in Tom Corfe's *The Phoenix Park Murders: Conflict, Compromise and Tragedy in Ireland* (London, 1968).

41. Bailey, ed., *Diary of Lady Frederick Cavendish,* 2:318. Gladstone rejected any suggestion of personal responsibility in Cavendish's death. When he and Catherine arrived within hours to comfort Lucy, she implored him not to blame himself. "O no," he responded (perhaps too readily), "there can be no question of that" (ibid., 319).

42. "We got Gladstone, not without difficulty," Harcourt wrote Spencer on 8 May, "to consent that the Protection of Life Bill should take precedence over all other measures" (Gardiner, *Life of Harcourt,* 1:439). The assassinations did not, as many historians have claimed, provoke the gov-

ernment into coercive legislation, but they did have the effect of accelerating its introduction and most surely called forth harsher terms. See Lyons' comments in his *Parnell,* 211.

43. Fortesque recounts a cabinet discussion within a fortnight of an interview between Gladstone and O'Shea: Gladstone "was convinced that Parnell... desired to 'get back into legality'" (CDBL, Add Mss 63690, 10 June 1882, fol. 153).

44. See, for example, James Loughlin, *Gladstone, Home Rule and the Ulster Question, 1882–93* (Dublin, 1986), chap. 2, "Gladstone and the Liberal Conversion to Home Rule." F. S. L. Lyons also makes explicit his view of Gladstone's conversion as a "journey to Damascus" (in his *Ireland since the Famine,* paperback ed. [London, 1989], 184). Paul Bew, on the first page of his short biography of Parnell, speaks of Gladstone's "conversion" (*C. S. Parnell* [Dublin, 1980]). See, in addition, Magnus, *Gladstone,* 333.

45. Cooke and Vincent, *Governing Passion,* 55.

46. See this book, chapter 9, "Gladstone Redivivus."

47. Gladstone, *Midlothian Speeches,* 86–87.

48. *Diaries,* vol. 9, 598–99.

49. Ibid., 25 October 1880, 602.

50. See Matthew's discussion, *Diaries,* vol. 10, "Introduction," xcviii–xcix.

51. *Times,* 14 October 1881.

52. See C. H. D. Howard, "Joseph Chamberlain, Parnell, and the Irish 'Central Board' Scheme, 1884–5," *Irish Historical Studies* 8 (1953), 324–61.

53. *Lord Carlingford's Journal: Reflections of a Cabinet Minister, 1885,* ed. A. B. Cooke and J. R. Vincent (Oxford, 1971), 1 May 1885, 98.

54. Matthew, "Introduction," *Diaries,* vol. 10, cxxiv–cxxv.

55. *Diaries,* vol. 11, 335.

56. Ibid., vol. 9, WEG to Spencer, 9 May 1885, 337. See in addition the account of the Central Board episode in J. L. Hammond's *Gladstone and the Irish Nation* (London, 1938), 366–73, especially the unsent letter to Spencer dated 10–11 May 1885 on 371 n. 1.

57. The Minute may be found in *Diaries,* vol. 11, 21 May 1885, 343–44.

58. This is Richard Jay's opinion; see his *Chamberlain,* 108.

59. Gardiner, *Life of Harcourt,* journal for 20 May 1885, 1:526.

60. Bassett, *Gladstone to His Wife,* 1 May 1885, 246.

61. Lyons, *Parnell,* chap. 9, "Towards the Fulcrum."

62. This important letter to the queen may be found in Philip Guedalla, ed., *The Queen and Mr Gladstone* (New York, 1936), 23 May 1885, 663–66.

63. *Diaries,* vol. 11, WEG to Derby, 17 July 1885, 372.

64. Ibid., 4 August 1885, 379–80, for WEG's letter, and 5 August 1885, 380 n. 2, for O'Shea's response.

65. The process of Spencer's decision can be followed reasonably well by reading his correspondence in Gordon, *Red Earl,* vol. 2, chap. 1.

66. Ibid., Campbell-Bannerman to Spencer, 27 December 1885, 91. Campbell-Bannerman had served as Gladstone's chief secretary to Ireland in the final months of the second ministry.

67. For these letters see Holland, *Life of Devonshire,* Hartington to Granville, 8 August 1885, 2:77; ibid., 10 September 1885, 2:85.

68. Vincent, "Later Derby Diaries," 1 October 1885, 32.

69. Matthew believes that Gladstone "must have been pleased for it showed Parnell, and committed him on paper, as a rather moderate constitutionalist, flexible as to detail" (*Diaries,* vol. 10, "Introduction," cxl).

70. This outline for Gladstone's eventual Home Rule bill may be found in *Diaries,* vol. 11, 14 November 1885, 429–30. Jenkins, in *Gladstone, Whiggery, and the Liberal Party,* makes much of this document because it shows how early Gladstone had devised his Home Rule scheme: he thus refutes Cooke and Vincent, in *Governing Passion,* 54–56, who believe that Gladstone's commitment to Home Rule did not emerge until considerably later, in March 1886, and only then as a purely tactical political device.

71. In a letter marked "Secret": see *Diaries,* vol. 11, 14 November 1885, 430.

72. For this paragraph see Howard, *Political Memoir,* 179–80; D. A. Hamer, *Liberal Politics in the Age of Gladstone and Rosebery: A Study in Leadership and Policy* (Oxford, 1972), chap. 3 passim and 108–12; Jenkins, *Gladstone, Whiggery, and the Liberal Party,* 247–49; Loughlin, *Gladstone, Home Rule and Ulster,* chap. 7, "Gladstone's Concept of Irish Nationality and the Moral Crusade for Home Rule"; Matthew, *Diaries,* vol. 10, "Introduction," cxl and cxlv.

73. There is no comprehensive study of this important election. See, however, W. C. Lubenow, *Parliamentary Politics and the Home Rule Crisis: The British House of Commons in 1886* (Oxford, 1988), chap. 1, for an analysis of election returns.

74. Vincent, "Later Derby Diaries," 17 December 1885, 47. Derby saw a pattern in this behavior: "I know that when he decided on the dissolution of 1874, his then colleagues were completely taken by surprise: and what has been done may be repeated" (ibid.).

75. Holland, *Devonshire,* Hartington to Granville, 17 December 1885, 2:98.

76. Garvin, *Life of Chamberlain,* Chamberlain to Dilke, 17 December 1885, 2:141.

77. Gordon, *Red Earl,* Spencer to Granville, 17 December 1885, 2:83.

78. For Herbert's role in flying the Kite see his autobiography, *After Thirty Years,* part 2, chap. 7. This should be compared with the unexpurgated version in *Diaries,* vol. 11, appendix 1, sec. D, 660–67.

79. The quotation is from GPBL, Add Mss 56446, WEG to Granville, 18 December 1885, fol. 193.

80. In a letter to Hartington; see *Diaries,* vol. 11, 19 December 1885, 454.

81. Ibid., memo, 23 December 1885, 458.

82. GPBL, Add Mss 56446, 18 December 1885, fol. 194.

83. Marquess of Crewe, *Lord Rosebery* (New York, 1931), Spencer to Rosebery, 30 December 1885, 205.

84. Robert Rhodes James, *Rosebery* (London, 1963), 176. The letter was dated 2 January 1886.

85. For this exchange see Ramm, *Correspondence of Gladstone and Granville, 1876–1886,* Granville to WEG, 27 December 1885, 2:418–19; and ibid., WEG to Granville, 28 December 1885, 2:419.

86. GPBL, Add Mss 44191, 30 December 1885, fols. 59–62.

87. Holland, *Devonshire,* Hartington to WEG, 18 December 1885, 2:101; ibid., Hartington to Granville, 19 December 1885, 2:102; and ibid., 28 December 1885, 2:105.

88. Ibid., Hartington to WEG, 1 January 1886, 2:106–8. Other accounts of the meeting may be found in Gwynn and Tuckwell, *Life of Dilke,* 2:203.

89. *Diaries,* vol. 11, WEG to Hartington, 2 January 1886, 472.

90. Garvin, *Chamberlain,* Chamberlain to Harcourt, 8 January 1886, 2:163.

91. Gardiner, *Life of Harcourt,* 1:557–58; Garvin, *Life of Chamberlain,* Chamberlain to Harcourt, 6 January 1886, 2:162; Gordon, *Red Earl,* 8 January 1886, 2:454; Cooke and Vincent, *Governing Passion,* 322.

92. *Diaries,* vol. 11, 9 January 1886, 476.

93. Cooke and Vincent, *Governing Passion,* 323.

94. For Gladstone's difficulties in assembling his cabinet see Cooke and Vincent, *Governing Passion,* 334–71. O'Day's claim that Gladstone found the formation of his third government "easy" because the main appointments were filled "with alacrity" does not bear scrutiny (O'Day, *Parnell and the First Home Rule Episode,* 142–43).

95. For a comprehensive discussion of the linkage between Home Rule and land purchase see Warren, "Gladstone, Land, and Social Reconstruction in Ireland, 1881–1887."

96. Loughlin, *Gladstone, Home Rule and the Ulster Question,* 46. Loughlin believes that Gladstone was spurred on by his fear of revolution in Ireland. This seems exaggerated. Although the measure was certainly designed to promote social order, no evidence suggests that Gladstone gave any credence to the alarmist views of some of his contemporaries. Rather, it would seem that Gladstone was motivated by his need for control, not an extrinsic circumstance, to proceed quickly and decisively in order to quell anti–Home Rule feeling. (See Matthew, "Introduction," *Diaries,* vol. 10, cxlvii–cxlix).

97. See Matthew's discussion in his "Introduction," *Diaries,* vol. 10, cxlv–cxlix, and clix–clx; also O'Day, *Parnell and the First Home Rule Episode,* chaps. 7 and 8.

98. *Diaries*, vol. II, 8 April 1886, 526; Morley, *Gladstone*, 3:234; O'Day, *Parnell and the First Home Rule Episode*, 178.

99. Bassett, *Gladstone's Speeches*, 601–44, passim.

100. For the provisions and analysis of the bill see Matthew's "Introduction," in *Diaries*, vol. 10, cliv–clviii.

101. Johnson, *Diary of Gathorne Hardy*, 30 May 1886, 608.

102. Algar Labouchere Thorold, *The Life of Henry Labouchere* (New York, 1913), letter to Chamberlain, 29 May 1886, 351.

103. For the discussion that follows, see Matthew's discussion in *Diaries*, vol. 10, "Introduction," xli–xliv.

104. Citations in the preceding paragraph are from *Diaries*, vol. II, WEG to R. H. Hutton, 2 July 1886, 580; ibid., WEG to J. E. Barlow, 1 July 1886, 577; ibid., WEG to Peel, 23 June 1886, 573–74. Peel was the only Tory who had abstained on the Home Rule vote.

105. Palmer, *Memorials, Part 2: Personal and Political* (London, 1898), Selborne to Gordon, 9 July 1886, 2:228.

106. Bernard Mallet, *Thomas George, Earl of Northbrook, G.C.S.I.: A Memoir* (London, 1908), 30 July 1886, 233.

107. *Diaries*, vol. II, Acland to WEG, 13 June 1886, 571 n. 1. Gladstone professed not to understand Acland's objection (ibid., WEG to Acland, 15 June 1886, 571).

108. Could it be, he wondered further, "that old age is conducing to tenacity of office?" Quoted from Hamilton's diary in Feuchtwanger, *Gladstone*, 242–43.

109. Gordon, *Red Earl*, C. R. Spencer to Lord Spencer, 14 July 1886, 2:129–30.

110. These contradictory evaluations of the election were offered by the same historian: see Lubenow, *Parliamentary Politics and the Home Rule Crisis*, 291 and 293. The preponderance of his evidence in ibid., chap. 7, "The General Election of 1886," generally sustains the second point of view.

111. *Diaries*, vol. II, 8 July 1886.

112. Ibid., 20 July 1886.

Chapter 12: "The Stone of Sisyphus"

1. This point was perceptively made by Paul Smith in his review article, "Liberalism as Authority and Discipline," *Historical Journal* 32, no. 3 (1989), 726. Smith's work also informs the paragraph that follows.

2. See D. A. Hamer's suggestive analysis in his *Liberal Politics in the Age of Gladstone and Rosebery*, especially chaps. 3 and 6; the quotation here is from 57.

3. Ibid., 72 and 69.

4. A. W. Hutton and H. J. Cohen, eds., *The Speeches of the Right Hon. W. E. Gladstone* (London, 1902), 8.

5. Ibid., 68–97. See also *Diaries*, vol. 12, 7 November 1888.

6. *Diary of Gathorne Hardy*, 661, 663, and 710.

7. Hawarden Library, Red PRO 9/613, PRO/30/29/29A, Argyll to Granville, 22 June 1887. Argyll further condemned Gladstone's "fanatical sincerity, largely tinctured by dislike of opposition and the mere spirit of 'fight.' "

8. Quoted in Michael Barker, *Gladstone and Radicalism: The Reconstruction of Liberal Policy in Britain, 1885–94* (New York, 1975), 81.

9. Ibid.

10. Quoted in Gordon, *Red Earl*, 153 n. 1.

11. These numbers are taken from Curtis, *Coercion and Conciliation in Ireland*, 301.

12. The quotation is from *Diaries*, vol. 12, 20 November 1890.

13. Morley, *Gladstone*, 3:325.

14. *Diaries*, vol. 12, 21 November 1890.

15. Morley, *Gladstone*, 3:331. Other useful sources for this significant episode include Morley's *Rec-*

ollections (New York, 1917), 1:258–62; and Frank Callanan, *The Parnell Split, 1890–91* (Syracuse, 1992), chap. 1, "Divorce."

16. The quotation is from *Diaries*, vol. 12, 29 November 1890.

17. Quoted in Morley, *Gladstone*, 3:333; and repeated in a slightly different form to Edward Hamilton. See Dudley W. R. Bahlman, ed., *The Diary of Sir Edward Walter Hamilton, 1885–1906* (Hull, England, 1993), 130.

18. Historians are generally critical of Gladstone's action. Curtis calls it "hasty." Magnus believes it to be one of the "cardinal blunders" of Gladstone's life. Lyons thinks not only that the published letter was "extraordinarily precipitate" but that from it came the "real impetus to disaster." See Curtis, *Coercion and Conciliation*, 315–16; Magnus, *Gladstone*, 390–91; and Lyons, *Parnell*, 500. Callanan, in *The Parnell Split*, 20, is an exception. He believes that the emphasis placed on Gladstone's published letter is exaggerated and that the substance of the letter would have eventually become public knowledge.

19. As Matthew points out in *Diaries*, vol. 12, "Introduction," xli.

20. See Matthew's comment in *Diaries*, vol. 12, 340 n. 2.

21. Morley, *Gladstone*, 3:317. Gladstone's daughter Mary was particularly taken with Parnell's "refined and gentlemanlike" looks (Mary Gladstone, *Letters and Diaries*, 411; quoted in Lyons, *Parnell*, 450).

22. For this and the following quotations concerning Parnell's Hawarden visit see *Diaries*, vol. 12, 254 and 256.

23. Morley, *Gladstone*, letter dated 23 December 1890, 3:343.

24. Ibid., 3:344.

25. *Diaries*, vol. 13, WEG to Lord Spencer, 13 July 1892, 41.

26. Ibid., 15 July 1892.

27. Ibid., 12 February 1893.

28. Ibid., WEG to H. N. Gladstone, 31 January 1894.

29. Ibid., 5 September 1893.

30. Ibid., 17 June 1893.

31. Bahlman, *Diary of Hamilton*, 19 August 1892, 172.

32. Henry W. Lucy, *A Diary of the Home Rule Parliament, 1892–1895* (London, 1896), 161–62. See also ibid., 75, 111, and 152.

33. Useful for a discussion of Home Rule during Gladstone's fourth ministry are Matthew's analysis in *Diaries*, vol. 12, "Introduction," xlix–lxxiv; David Richard Brooks, "Gladstone's Fourth Ministry, 1892–94: Policies and Personalities" (Ph.D. diss., Cambridge University, 1975); and Loughlin, *Gladstone, Home Rule and the Ulster Question*, chap. 10.

34. Important as a background to the Uganda question are Robert Rhodes James, *Rosebery: A Biography of Archibald Philip, Fifth Earl of Rosebery* (London, 1963), chap. 8; and Robinson and Gallagher, *Africa and the Victorians*, chap. 11, "Uganda, the Rout of Liberalism."

35. *Diaries*, vol. 13, 22 September 1892, 85.

36. Ibid., WEG to Asquith, 23 September 1892, 86.

37. Ibid., WEG to Harcourt, 23 September 1892, 86.

38. Ibid., WEG to Morley, 26 September 1892, 92.

39. Ibid., WEG to Spencer, 26 September 1892, 93.

40. Horace G. Hutchinson, ed., *Private Diaries of the Rt. Hon. Sir Algernon West, G.C.B.* (London, 1922), 60. This second installment of West's recollections and diaries is indispensable to a study of Gladstone's fourth administration.

41. *Diaries*, vol. 13, WEG to Acton, 26 September 1892, 91.

42. Ibid., WEG to Harcourt, 24 September 1892, 89.

43. Although silent on the conflict between Gladstone and Rosebery, T. B. Miller provides a diplomatic context of the Egyptian question in "The Egyptian Question and British Foreign Policy, 1892–1894," *Journal of Modern History* 32, no. 1 (March 1960), 1–15.

44. *Diaries*, vol. 13, WEG to Rosebery, 20 January 1893.

45. Ibid., 21 January 1893.

46. Ibid., 30 January 1893.
47. Ibid., 5 February 1893.
48. As recorded by West in Hutchinson, *Diaries of West*, 148–49.
49. James, *Rosebery*, 283.
50. Gardiner, *Life of Harcourt*, Harcourt to WEG, 12 February 1893, 2:220–21. Gladstone soothed Harcourt's ruffled feathers by summoning a cabinet the following day (*Diaries*, vol. 13, WEG to Harcourt, 13 February 1893, 201).
51. *Diaries*, vol. 13, 4 March 1893.
52. Ibid., vol. 12, "Introduction," lxxvi–lxxx.
53. Hutchinson, *Diaries of West*, 32.
54. Bahlman, *Diary of Hamilton*, 30 October 1892, 177.
55. Calculated from the two tables entitled "Where Was He?" in *Diaries*, vol. 12, 533–35; and *Diaries*, vol. 13, 451–52.
56. For this paragraph see Susan Folkman, Richard S. Lazarus, Christie Dunkel-Schetter, Anita De Longir, and Rand J. Gruen, "Dynamics of a Stressful Encounter: Cognitive Appraisal, Coping, and Encounter Outcomes," *Journal of Personality and Social Psychology* 50, no. 5 (1986), 992–1003.
57. Pressures generated by the scare that affected the government's policy are set out in detail by Arthur J. Marder, *British Naval Policy, 1880–1905: The Anatomy of British Sea Power* (London, 1940), chap. 10, "The Navy Scare of 1893." See also Luke Trainor, "The Liberals and the Formation of Imperial Defence Policy, 1892–5," *Bulletin of the Institute of Historical Research* 42, no. 106 (November 1969), 188–200.
58. *Diaries*, vol. 13, WEG to Morley, 14 December 1893, 339; WEG to Rosebery, 18 December 1893, 341.
59. See, for example, his letter to WEG on 12 January 1893 in Gordon, *Red Earl*, 236.
60. *Diaries*, vol. 13, appendix 1, 433–37.
61. Ibid., 9 January 1894.
62. West was appalled at the conduct of the meeting and at Gladstone's behavior in general. "Posterity will say that he destroyed his party by proposing Home Rule, and that for the second time he destroyed it by abandoning it, and postponing for years a settlement. And it is for this that I have slaved for nearly two years!!" (Hutchinson, *Diaries of West*, 237).
63. See Bahlman, *Diary of Hamilton*, 9–11 February 1894, 221–34.
64. Hutchinson, *Diaries of West*, 247 and 248. For his part, Gladstone enjoyed the visit no more than West: he recorded in his diary on 29 January 1894 after a long conversation with West that "weary talks cast no light whatever on the matter" (*Diaries*, vol. 13, 20 January 1894).
65. Hutchinson, *Diaries of West*, 236.
66. Bahlman, *Diary of Hamilton*, 25 January 1894.
67. Ibid., 29 January 1894. On this day Hamilton relayed Acton's views to Harcourt: see Hamilton to Harcourt, 29 January 1894, in Gardiner, *Life of Harcourt*, 2:254.
68. Quoted from the Bryce Papers in James, *Rosebery*, 305.
69. Ibid., 5 February 1894.
70. Bahlman, *Diary of Hamilton*, 8 February 1894.
71. Hutchinson, *Diaries of West*, 273.
72. Rosebery's account of the events of January–March 1894 is set out in appendix 3 of James, *Rosebery*, 498–512. For Rosebery's view of Gladstone's proposal for a dissolution, see 503. A kinder view of Gladstone's proposal for a dissolution on the Lords can be found: see Sue Brown, "One Last Campaign from the GOM: Gladstone and the House of Lords in 1894," in Kinzer, ed., *The Gladstonian Turn of Mind*, 154–76.
73. *Diaries*, vol. 13, 437–39.
74. James, *Rosebery*, 504–5.
75. *Diaries*, vol. 13, WEG to Kimberley, 20 February 1894, 380. Rosebery, to whom Kimberley showed the letter, thought it "enigmatical" and claimed that he could not understand it (James, *Rosebery*, 505).

76. As recorded by both Hamilton (in Bahlman, *Diary of Hamilton,* 23 February 1894) and Rosebery (in James, *Rosebery,* 506).

77. See the notes of a meeting with Ponsonby, 22 February 1894, in *Diaries,* vol. 13, 381.

78. Ibid., appendix 1, 439–40.

79. Ibid., 4 and 17 May 1894.

80. Ibid., 25 July 1894, 416.

81. Ibid.

82. Ibid., 29 December 1896, 429.

83. See Vincent's introduction to his *Disraeli, Derby and the Conservative Party,* xv.

84. Felix Post, "Creativity and Psychopathology: A Study of 291 World-Famous Men," *British Journal of Psychiatry* 165 (1994), 22–34.

85. Magnus, *Gladstone,* 417.

86. Jonathan Parry, *The Rise and Fall of Liberal Government in Victorian Britain* (New Haven, 1994), 252, 255, 260, 302.

87. Michael J. Winstanley, *Gladstone and the Liberal Party,* Lancaster Pamphlets (London, 1990), 41, 61, 63.

88. Marquess of Crewe, *Rosebery,* 431, letter dated 7 October 1896. Rosebery always maintained, probably rightly, that Gladstone's speech was only the proximate cause of his resignation: internecine party squabbles, especially over the leadership, were also important to his decision. See James, *Rosebery,* chap. 2 passim. Rosebery was also tired of being "tied to Gladstonian chains," as he had begun to be many years earlier with the Midlothian Campaign (Bahlman, *Diary of Hamilton,* 330).

89. Asa Briggs, ed., *Gladstone's Boswell: Late Victorian Conversations by Lionel A. Tollemache* (Brighton, 1984); *The Personal Papers of Lord Rendel* (London, 1931). Tollemache, a former Liberal M.P., records conversations in 1896 when Gladstone visited Cannes. Rendel's diary is more useful on political matters; he was with Gladstone at Hawarden, London, Cannes, and elsewhere in the final years. Gladstone himself noted that after his retirement, his time was "mainly filled up with conversations: interesting though to a deaf man fatiguing" (*Diaries,* vol. 13, 27 July 1896, 426).

90. Hutchinson, *Diaries of West,* 323, 327.

91. Bahlman, *Diary of Hamilton,* 290, 320, 335.

92. Hutchinson, *Diaries of West,* 301.

93. Bahlman, *Diary of Hamilton,* 344.

94. British Library, Kilbracken papers, Add MSS 44901, WEG to Godley, 7 January 1898, fol. 100. Godley was created the first Baron Kilbracken in 1909.

Bibliography

Manuscript Collections

British Library Additional Manuscripts
  Aberdeen Papers
  Carlingford Papers
  Carnarvon Papers
  Dilke Papers
  Gladstone Papers
  Hamilton Papers
  Kilbracken Papers
  Ripon Papers
Christ Church, Oxford
  Phillimore Papers
St. Deiniol's Library, Hawarden
  Glynne-Gladstone Papers

Selected Works

Acland, A. H. D. (ed.), *Memoir and Letters of the Right Honourable Sir Thomas Dyke Acland* (London, 1902).

Altholz, Josef L., "Gladstone and the Vatican Decrees," *Historian* 25, no. 3 (1963), 312–24.

Anderson, Olive, "Loans versus Taxes: British Financial Policy in the Crimean War," *Economic History Review*, 2d ser, 16, no. 1 (1963), 314–27.

———, *A Liberal State at War: English Politics and Economics during the Crimean War* (New York, 1967).

Antonovsky, Anton, *Health, Stress, and Coping* (San Francisco, 1979).

Argyll, eighth duke of, George Douglas, *Autobiography and Memoirs*, ed. the dowager duchess of Argyll, 2 vols. (New York, 1906).

Armon-Jones, Claire, "The Social Functions of Emotion," in Rom Harré (ed.), *The Social Construction of Emotions* (Oxford, 1986).

Arnstein, Walter L., *The Bradlaugh Case: A Study in Late Victorian Opinion and Politics* (Oxford, 1965).

——, *Protestant versus Catholic in Mid-Victorian England* (Columbia, Mo., 1982).

Aronson, Elliot, *The Social Animal*, 2d ed. (San Francisco, 1976).

Ashwell, A. R., and Wilberforce, Reginald G., *Life of the Right Reverend Samuel Wilberforce, D.D.* (New York, 1883).

Averill, James R., "Studies on Anger and Aggression: Implications for Theories of Emotion," *American Psychologist* 38, no. 11 (November 1983), 1145–60.

Bagehot, Walter, "Mr Gladstone," in Norman St. John-Stevas (ed.), *Bagehot's Historical Essays*, paperback ed. (New York, 1965).

Bahlman, Dudley W. R. (ed.), *The Diary of Sir Edward Walter Hamilton, 1885–1906* (Hull, England, 1993).

Bailey, John (ed.), *The Diary of Lady Frederick Cavendish*, 2 vols. (London, 1927).

Bandura, Albert, *Aggression: A Social Learning Analysis* (Englewood Cliffs, N.J., 1973).

——, "Self-Efficacy: Toward a Unifying Theory of Behavioral Change," *Psychological Review* 84 (1977), 191–215.

——, *Social Learning Theory* (Englewood Cliffs, N.J., 1977).

——, "Self-Efficacy Mechanism in Human Agency," *American Psychologist* 37, no. 2 (February 1982), 122–47.

——, "The Psychology of Chance Encounters and Life Paths," *American Psychologist* 37, no. 7 (July 1982), 747–55.

Barker, Michael, *Gladstone and Radicalism: The Reconstruction of Liberal Policy in Britain, 1885–94* (New York, 1975).

Bartlett, C. J., "Clarendon, the Foreign Office, and the Hohenzollern Candidature, 1868–1870," *English Historical Review* 75, no. 295 (April 1960), 276–84.

Basset, Arthur Tilney, *Gladstone's Speeches* (London, 1916).

——, *Gladstone to His Wife* (London, 1936).

Battiscombe, Georgina, *Mrs. Gladstone: The Portrait of a Marriage* (London, 1954).

Beales, Derek, *England and Italy, 1859–60* (London, 1961).

——, "Gladstone and His Diary: 'Myself, the Worst of All Interlocutors,'" *Historical Journal* 25, no. 2 (1982), 463–69.

——, "Gladstone and His First Ministry," *Historical Journal* 26, no. 4 (1983), 987–98.

Bebbington, David W., "Gladstone and the Nonconformists: A Religious Affinity in Politics," in Derek Baker (ed.), *Studies in Church History*, vol. 12, *Church, Society, and Politics* (Oxford, 1975).

——, *Evangelicalism in Modern Britain: A History from the 1730s to the 1980s* (London, 1989).

Bell, P. M. H., *Disestablishment in Ireland and Wales* (London, 1969).

Bentley, James, *Ritualism and Politics in Victorian Britain: The Attempt to Legislate for Belief* (Oxford, 1978).

Bentley, Michael, *The Climax of Liberal Politics: British Liberalism in Theory and Practice, 1868–1918* (London, 1987).

——, "Gladstonian Liberals and Provincial Notables: Whitby Politics, 1868–80," *Historical Research* 64, no. 154 (June 1991), 172–85.

Best, G. F. A., "The Religious Difficulties of National Education in England, 1800–70," *Cambridge Historical Journal* 12, no. 2 (1956), 155–73.

Bew, Paul, *C. S. Parnell* (Dublin, 1980).

——, "The Land League Ideal: Achievements and Contradictions," in D. J. Drudy (ed.), *Ireland: Land, Politics and People* (Cambridge, England, 1982).

Biagini, Eugenio F., *Liberty, Retrenchment and Reform: Popular Liberalism in the Age of Gladstone, 1860–1880* (Cambridge, England, 1992).

Blake, Robert, *Disraeli* (New York, 1967).

Blewett, Neal, "The Franchise in the United Kingdom, 1885–1918," *Past and Present*, no. 32 (December 1965), 27–56.

Boyce, D. George, " 'The Portrait of the King Is the King': The Biographers of Charles Stewart Parnell," in D. George Boyce and Alan O'Day (eds.), *Parnell in Perspective* (London, 1991).

Briggs, Asa (ed.), *Gladstone's Boswell: Late Victorian Conversations by Lionel A. Tollemache* (Brighton, 1984).

Broadwell, Albert H., "The Gladstone Family," *Strand Magazine* 10, 215–21.

Brooke, John, and Sorensen, Mary (eds.), *The Prime Ministers' Papers Series: W. E. Gladstone*, vol. 4, *Autobiographical Memoranda, 1868–1894* (London: HMSO, 1981).

Brooks, David Richard, "Gladstone's Fourth Ministry, 1892–94: Policies and Personalities" (Ph.D. diss., Cambridge University, 1975).

Brown, Sue, "One Last Campaign from the GOM: Gladstone and the House of Lords in 1894," in Bruce L. Kinzer (ed.), *The Gladstonian Turn of Mind: Essays Presented to J. B. Conacher* (Toronto, 1985).

Bruce, Henry Austin, *Letters of the Rt. Hon. Henry Austin Bruce, Lord Aberdare of Duffryn* (Oxford, 1902).

Buckle, G. E. (ed.), *The Letters of Queen Victoria*, 2d ser. (London, 1928).

Butler, Perry, *Gladstone: Church, State, and Tractarianism: A Study of His Religious Ideas and Attitudes, 1809–1859* (Oxford, 1982).

Buxton, Sidney, *Finance and Politics: An Historical Study, 1783–1885* (London, 1888; reprinted in the Reprints of Economic Classics series [New York, 1966]).

Callanan, Frank, *The Parnell Split, 1890–91* (Syracuse, 1992).

Chadwick, Mary E. J., "The Role of Redistribution in the Making of the Third Reform Act," *Historical Journal* 19, no. 3 (1976), 665–83.

Chamberlain, Muriel E., "The Alexandria Massacre of 11 June 1882 and the British Occupation of Egypt," *Middle Eastern Studies* 13 (1977), 14–39.

———, "British Public Opinion and the Invasion of Egypt, 1882," *Trivium* 16 (1981), 5–28.

———, *Lord Aberdeen: A Political Biography* (London, 1983).

Chandos, John, *Boys Together: English Public Schools, 1800–1864* (New Haven, 1984).

Checkland, S. G., *The Gladstones: A Family Biography, 1764–1851* (Cambridge, England, 1971).

Clark, Samuel, *Social Origins of the Irish Land War* (Princeton, 1979).

Cocks, Geoffrey, "Contributions of Psychohistory to Understanding Politics," in Margaret G. Hermann (ed.), *Political Psychology: Contemporary Problems and Issues* (San Francisco, 1986).

Comerford, R. V., *The Fenians in Context: Irish Politics and Society, 1848–82* (Dublin, 1985).

Conacher, J. B., "Party Politics in the Age of Palmerston," in Philip Appleman (ed.), *1859: Entering an Age of Crisis* (Bloomington, 1959).

———, *The Aberdeen Coalition, 1852–1855: A Study in Mid-Nineteenth Century Party Politics* (Cambridge, England, 1968).

———, *Peelites and the Party System, 1846–52* (Newton Abbot, Devon, 1972).

———, *Britain and the Crimea, 1855–56: Problems of War and Peace* (New York, 1987).

Cook, Adrian, *The Alabama Claims: American Politics and Anglo-American Relations, 1865–1872* (Ithaca, N.Y., 1975).

Cooke, A. B., and Vincent, John, *The Governing Passion: Cabinet Government and Party Politics in Britain, 1885–86* (New York, 1974).

Cooke, A. B., and Vincent, J. R. (eds.), *Lord Carlingford's Journal: Reflections of a Cabinet Minister, 1885* (Oxford, 1971).

Corfe, Tom, *The Phoenix Park Murders: Conflict, Compromise and Tragedy in Ireland* (London, 1968).

Cote, Jane McL., *Fanny and Anna Parnell: Ireland's Patriot Sisters* (New York, 1991).

Cowling, Maurice, *1867: Disraeli, Gladstone, and Revolution: The Passing of the Second Reform Bill* (Cambridge, England, 1967).

Crangle, John V., "The British Peace Movement and the Anglo-Egyptian War of 1882," *Quarterly Review of Historical Studies* 15 (1975–76), 130–50.

Crewe, Marquess of, *Lord Rosebery* (New York, 1931).

Crosby, Faye, and Crosby, Travis L., "Psychobiography and Psychohistory," in Samuel Long (ed.), *The Handbook of Political Behavior*, vol. 1 (New York, 1981), 195–254.

Crosby, Travis L., *Sir Robert Peel's Administration, 1841–1846* (Newton Abbot, Devon, 1976).

———, *English Farmers and the Politics of Protection, 1815–1852* (Hassocks, Sussex, 1977).

———, "Gladstone's Decade of Crisis: Biography and the Life-Course Approach," *Journal of Political and Military Sociology* 12, no. 1 (Spring 1984), 12–17.

Cruickshank, Marjorie, *Church and State in English Education: 1870 to the Present Day* (London, 1963).

Cunningham, Hugh, "Jingoism in 1877–78," *Victorian Studies* 14, no. 4 (June 1971), 429–53.

Curtis, L. P., Jr., *Coercion and Conciliation in Ireland, 1880–1890: A Study in Conservative Unionism* (Princeton, 1963).

———, "Encumbered Wealth: Landed Indebtedness in Post-Famine Ireland," *American Historical Review* 85, no. 2 (April 1980), 332–67.

Davidoff, Leonore, "Class and Gender in Victorian England: The Diaries of Arthur J. Munby and Hannah Cullwick," *Feminist Studies* 5, no. 1 (Spring 1979), 86–141.

Denholm, Anthony F., "The Conversion of Lord Ripon in 1874," *Recusant History* 10 (April 1969), 111–18.

———, *Lord Ripon, 1827–1909: A Political Biography* (London, 1982).

Denison, John Evelyn (Lord Ossington), *Notes from My Journal When Speaker of the House of Commons* (London, 1900).

Drew, Mary, *Mrs. Gladstone* (New York, 1920).

Drus, E. (ed.), *A Journal of Events during the Gladstone Ministry, 1868–1874, by John, First Earl of Kimberley*, Camden Miscellany 21 (1957).

Earl Cowper, K.G., A Memoir by His Wife (privately printed, 1913).

Elder, Glen H., Jr., "Family History and the Life Course," *Journal of Family History* 2 (1977), 279–304.

Eldridge, C. C., "The Lincoln Divorce Case: A Study in Victorian Morality," *Trivium* 11 (1975).

Ellis, S. M., *A Mid-Victorian Pepys: The Letters and Memoirs of Sir William Hardman* (New York, 1923).

Ellison, Christopher G., "Religious Involvement and Subjective Well-Being," *Journal of Health and Social Behavior* 32 (March 1991), 80–99.

Elton, Lord, *Gordon of Khartoum: The Life of General Charles George Gordon* (New York, 1955).

Engel, Arthur J., " 'Immoral Intentions': The University of Oxford and the Problem of Prostitution, 1827–1914," *Victorian Studies* 23, no. 1 (Autumn 1979), 79–107.

Erickson, Arvel B., "Edward T. Cardwell: Peelite," *Transactions of the American Philosophical Society*, new ser., vol. 49, part 2 (1959), 67–95.

Erikson, Erik, *Childhood and Society* (New York, 1963).

F. A., "William Ewart Gladstone: A Study of Character," *London Society* 15, no. 86 (February 1869).

Fair, John D., "The Carnarvon Diaries and Royal Mediation in 1884," *English Historical Review* 106, no. 418 (January 1991), 97–116.

Feingold, William L., *The Revolt of the Tenantry: The Transformation of Local Government in Ireland, 1872–1886* (Boston, 1984).

Festinger, Leon, *A Theory of Cognitive Dissonance* (Evanston, Ill. 1957).

Feuchtwanger, E. J., *Gladstone* (New York, 1975).

Figgis, John Neville, and Laurence, Reginald Vere (eds.), *Selections from the Correspondence of the First Lord Acton* (London, 1917).

Finnegan, Frances, *Poverty and Prostitution: A Study of Victorian Prostitutes in York* (Cambridge, England, 1979).

Flanagan, Kieran, "The Chief Secretary's Office, 1853–1914: A Bureaucratic Enigma," *Irish Historical Studies* 24, no. 94 (November 1984), 197–225.

Folkman, Susan; Lazarus, Richard S.; Dunkel-Schetter, Christine; De Longir, Anita; and Gruen,

Rand J., "Dynamics of a Stressful Encounter: Cognitive Appraisal, Coping, and Encounter Outcomes," *Journal of Personality and Social Psychology* 50, no. 5 (1986), 992–1003.

Foot, M. R. D. (ed.), *The Gladstone Diaries*, vols. 1 and 2 (Oxford, 1968).

Foot, M. R. D., and Matthew, H. C. G. (eds.), *The Gladstone Diaries*, vols. 3 and 4 (Oxford, 1974).

Foster, R. F., *Charles Stewart Parnell: The Man and His Family*, 2d ed. (Hassocks, Sussex, 1979).

Galbraith, John S., "The Trial of Arabi Pasha," *Journal of Imperial and Commonwealth History* 7 (1979), 274–92.

Galbraith, John S., and Afaf Lufti al-sayyid-Marsot, "The British Occupation of Egypt: Another View," *International Journal of Middle East Studies* 9 (1978), 471–88.

Gallagher, Thomas F., " 'Cardwellian Mysteries': The Fate of the British Army Regulation Bill, 1871," *Historical Journal* 18, no. 2 (June 1975), 327–48.

———, "The Second Reform Movement, 1848–1867," *Albion* 12, no. 2 (Summer 1980), 147–63.

Gardiner, A. G., *The Life of Sir William Harcourt* (London, 1923).

Garratt, G. T., *The Two Mr. Gladstones* (London, 1936).

Garvin, J. L., *The Life of Joseph Chamberlain* (London, 1932).

Gash, Norman, *Sir Robert Peel: The Life of Sir Robert Peel after 1830* (London, 1972).

Gay, Peter, *The Bourgeois Experience: Victoria to Freud*, vol. 1, *Education of the Senses* (New York, 1984).

Gerard, Jessica, "Lady Bountiful: Women of the Landed Classes and Rural Philanthropy," *Victorian Studies* (Winter 1987), 183–210.

Gergen, Mary M., and Gergen, Kenneth J., "The Social Construction of Narrative Accounts," in Kenneth J. Gergen and Mary M. Gergen (eds.), *Historical Social Psychology* (Hillsdale, N.J., 1984).

Ghosh, P. R., "Disraelian Conservatism: A Financial Approach," *English Historical Review* 99, no. 391 (April 1984), 268–96.

Gladstone, Viscount, *After Thirty Years* (London, 1928).

Gladstone, William E., "Course of Commercial Policy at Home and Abroad," *Foreign and Colonial Quarterly Review* (January 1843).

———, *Quarterly Review* 99 (June and September 1856), 521–70.

———, "Prospects Political and Financial," *Quarterly Review* 101 (January 1857), 243–84.

———, *A Chapter of Autobiography* (London, 1868).

———, *Gleanings of Past Years* (London, 1879).

———, *Midlothian Speeches, 1879*, ed. M. R. D. Foot (Leicester, 1971).

Golby, John, "A Great Electioneer and His Motives: The Fourth Duke of Newcastle," *Historical Journal* 8, no. 2 (1965), 201–18.

Gordon, Arthur H. (ed.), Baron Stanmore, *Correspondence of George, Earl of Aberdeen, K.G., K.T., 1850–52* (n.p., n.d.).

Gordon, Peter, *The Red Earl: The Papers of the Fifth Earl Spencer, 1835–1910* (Northampton, 1981).

Gregorian, Vartan, *The Emergence of Modern Afghanistan: Politics of Reform and Modernization, 1880–1946* (Stanford, 1969).

Greven, Philip, *The Protestant Temperament: Patterns of Child-Rearing, Religious Experience, and the Self in Early America*, paperback ed. (Chicago, 1988).

Griffith, Elisabeth, *In Her Own Right: The Life of Elizabeth Cady Stanton* (New York, 1984).

Guedalla, Philip (ed.), *Gladstone and Palmerston: Being the Correspondence of Lord Palmerston with Mr Gladstone, 1851–1865* (New York, 1928).

———, *The Queen and Mr Gladstone* (New York, 1936).

Gwyn, Stephen, and Tuckwell, Gertrude, *The Life of the Rt. Hon. Sir Charles W. Dilke*, 2 vols. (London, 1917).

Hake, A. Egmont (ed.), *The Journals of Major-Gen. C. G. Gordon, C.B., at Khartoum* (London, 1885).

Hamer, D. A., *Liberal Politics in the Age of Gladstone and Rosebery: A Study in Leadership and Policy* (Oxford, 1972).

————, "Gladstone: The Making of a Political Myth," *Victorian Studies* 22, no. 1 (Autumn 1978), 29–50.

Hamilton, Lord George, *Parliamentary Reminiscences and Reflections, 1868 to 1885* (New York, 1917).

Hammond, J. L., *Gladstone and the Irish Nation* (London, 1938).

Hammond, J. L., and Foot, M. R. D., *Gladstone and Liberalism* (New York, 1966).

Hanham, H. J., *Elections and Party Management: Politics in the Time of Disraeli and Gladstone*, 2d ed. (Hassocks, Sussex, 1978).

Hawkins, Angus, *Parliament, Party and the Art of Politics in Britain, 1855–59* (Stanford, 1987).

Hayes, William A., *The Background and Passage of the Third Reform Act* (New York, 1982).

Helmstadter, Richard J., "Conscience and Politics: Gladstone's First Book," in Bruce L. Kinzer (ed.), *The Gladstonian Turn of Mind: Essays Presented to J. B. Conacher* (Toronto, 1985).

Herrick, Francis H., "Gladstone, Newman, and Ireland in 1881," *Catholic Historical Review* 47, no. 3 (October 1961), 342–50.

Hill, Richard, "The Gordon Literature," *Durham University Journal*, new ser., 16, no. 3 (June 1955), 97–103.

Himmelfarb, Gertrude, "The Politics of Democracy: The English Reform Act of 1867," *Journal of British Studies* 6, no. 1 (1966), 97–138.

Hopkins, A. G., "The Victorians and Africa: A Reconsideration of the Occupation of Egypt, 1882," *Journal of African History* 27, no. 2 (1986), 363–91.

Howard, C. H. D. "Joseph Chamberlain, Parnell, and the Irish 'Central Board' Scheme, 1884–5," *Irish Historical Studies* 8 (1953), 324–61.

Hudson, Derek, *Munby: Man of Two Worlds. The Life and Diaries of Arthur J. Munby, 1828–1910* (London, 1972).

Hutchinson, Horace G. (ed.), *Private Diaries of the Rt. Hon. Sir Algernon West, G.C.B.* (London, 1922).

Hutton, A. W., and Cohen, H. J. (eds.), *The Speeches of the Right Hon. W. E. Gladstone* (London, 1902).

Hyde, F. E., *Mr Gladstone at the Board of Trade* (n.p., 1934).

Iliasu, A. A., "The Cobden-Chevalier Commercial Treaty of 1860," *Historical Journal* 14, no. 1 (1971), 67–98.

Ingham, S. E., "The Disestablishment Movement in England, 1868–74," *Journal of Religious History* 3, no. 1 (June 1964), 38–60.

Jacobs, Marjorie G., "The Colonial Office and New Guinea, 1874–84," *Historical Studies, Australia and New Zealand* 5 (1951–53), 106–18.

Jagger, Peter J., *Gladstone: The Making of a Christian Politician*, Princeton Theological Monograph Series, vol. 28 (Allison Park, Penn., 1991).

Jalland, Patricia, "Mr Gladstone's Daughters: The Domestic Price of Victorian Politics," in Bruce L. Kinzer (ed), *The Gladstonian Turn of Mind: Essays Presented to J. B. Conacher* (Toronto, 1985).

James, Robert Rhodes, "Gladstone and the Greenwich Seat: The Dissolution of January 26th 1874," *History Today* 9, no. 5 (May 1959), 344–51.

————, *Rosebery: A Biography of Archibald Philip, Fifth Earl of Rosebery* (London, 1963).

Janis, Irving L., and Mann, Leon, *Decision Making: A Psychological Analysis of Conflict, Choice, and Commitment* (New York, 1977).

Jenkins, T. A., "Gladstone, the Whigs and the Leadership of the Liberal Party," *Historical Journal* 27, no. 2 (1984), 337–60.

————, *Gladstone, Whiggery and the Liberal Party, 1874–1886* (Oxford, 1988).

Jenkins, T. A. (ed.), *The Parliamentary Diaries of Sir John Trelawny, 1858–1865*, Camden Fourth Series 40 (London, 1990).

————, *The Parliamentary Diaries of Sir John Trelawny, 1868–73*, Camden Miscellany, Camden Fifth Series 3 (London, 1994), 329–513.

Johnson, Douglas H., "The Death of Gordon: A Victorian Myth," *Journal of Imperial and Commonwealth History* 10, no. 3 (May 1982), 285–310.

Johnson, Nancy E. (ed.), *The Diary of Gathorne Hardy, Later Lord Cranbrook, 1866–1892: Political Selections* (Oxford, 1981).

Jones, Andrew, *The Politics of Reform, 1884* (Cambridge, England, 1972).

Jones, J. R., "The Conservatives and Gladstone in 1855," *English Historical Review* 77, no. 302 (January 1962), 95–98.

Kazemzadeh, Firuz, *Russia and Britain in Persia, 1864–1914* (New Haven, 1968).

Keegan, John, "The Ashanti Campaign, 1873–74," in Brian Bond (ed.), *Victorian Military Campaigns* (London, 1967).

Kennedy, A. L. (ed.), *"My Dear Duchess": Social and Political Letters to the Duchess of Manchester, 1858–1869* (London, 1956).

Kennedy, Paul M., *The Rise of Anglo-German Antagonism, 1860–1914* (London, 1980).

———, *Strategy and Diplomacy, 1870–1945* (London, 1983).

Kilbracken, Lord, *Reminiscences of Lord Kilbracken* (London, 1931).

Kinzer, Bruce L., *The Ballot Question in Nineteenth-Century English Politics* (New York, 1972).

———, "The Un-Englishness of the Secret Ballot," *Albion* 10, no. 3 (Spring 1979), 237–56.

———, "John Stuart Mill and the Irish University Question," *Victorian Studies* 31, no. 1 (Autumn 1987), 59–77.

Knaplund, Paul (ed.), "Gladstone-Gordon Correspondence, 1851–1896," *Transactions of the American Philosophical Society* 51, part 4 (1961).

Knightbridge, A. H. H., "Egypt in British Political Thought, 1875–1900" (Ph.D. diss., Oxford University, 1963).

Knox, Bruce, "British Policy and the Ionian Islands, 1847–1864: Nationalism and Imperial Administration," *English Historical Review* 99, no. 392 (July 1984), 503–29.

Kobasa, Suzanne C., "Stressful Life Events, Personality, and Health: An Inquiry into Hardiness," in Alan Monat and Richard S. Lazarus (eds.), *Stress and Coping: An Anthology,* 2d ed. (New York, 1985).

Langer, Ellen, *The Psychology of Control* (Beverly Hills, 1983).

Lathbury, D. C. (ed.), *Correspondence on Church and Religion of William Ewart Gladstone* (London, 1910).

Lazarus, Richard S., *Psychological Stress and the Coping Process* (New York, 1966).

Lazarus, Richard S., and Folkman, Susan, *Stress, Appraisal and Coping* (New York, 1984).

Legge, John, "Australia and New Guinea to the Establishment of the British Protectorate, 1884," *Historical Studies, Australia and New Zealand* 4 (1949–51), 34–47.

Levinson, Dan, *The Seasons of a Man's Life* (New York, 1978).

Lloyd, Trevor O., *The General Election of 1880* (Oxford, 1968).

Loughlin, James, *Gladstone, Home Rule and the Ulster Question, 1882–93* (Dublin, 1986).

Lowenthal, M. F., and Chiriboga, D., "Social Stress and Adaptations: Toward A Life Course Perspective," in C. Eisdorfer and M. P. Lawton (eds.), *The Psychology of Adult Development and Aging* (Washington, D.C., 1973).

Lubenow, W. C., *Parliamentary Politics and the Home Rule Crisis: The British House of Commons in 1886* (Oxford, 1988).

Lucas, Reginald, *Lord Glenesk and the Morning Post* (London, 1910).

Lucy, Henry W., *A Diary of Two Parliaments* (London, 1886).

———, *A Diary of the Home Rule Parliament* (London, 1896).

———, *Memories of Eight Parliaments* (London, 1908).

Lynch, M. J., "Was Gladstone a Tractarian? W. E. Gladstone and the Oxford Movement, 1833–45," *Journal of Religious History* (Australia) 8, no. 4 (1975), 364–89.

Lyons, F. S. L., *Charles Stewart Parnell* (New York, 1977).

———, *Ireland since the Famine,* paperback ed. (London, 1989).

McCann, W. P., "Trade Unionists, Artisans and the 1870 Educational Act," *British Journal of Educational Studies* 18, no. 2 (June 1970), 134–50.

McCarthy, Justin, *The Story of Gladstone's Life* (London, 1898).

McIntyre, W. D., "British Policy in West Africa: The Ashanti Expedition of 1873–74," *Historical Journal* 5, no. 1 (1962), 19–46.

MacKenzie, John M., *Propaganda and Empire: The Manipulation of British Public Opinion, 1880–1960* (Manchester, 1984).

Maehl, William Henry, "Gladstone, the Liberals, and the Election of 1874," *Bulletin of the Institute of Historical Research* 36, no. 93 (May 1963), 53–69.

Magnus, Philip, *Gladstone: A Biography* (London, 1954).

Malatesta, Carol Z., and Izard, Carroll E., (eds.), *Emotion in Adult Development* (Beverly Hills, 1984).

Mallet, Bernard, *Thomas George, Earl of Northbrook, G.C.S.I.: A Memoir* (London, 1908).

Marcus, Stephen, *The Other Victorians*, paperback ed. (New York, 1985).

Marder, Arthur J., *British Naval Policy, 1880–1905* (London, 1940).

Marlow, Joyce, *Mr and Mrs Gladstone: An Intimate Biography* (London, 1977).

Marsh, Peter, *The Discipline of Popular Government: Lord Salisbury's Domestic Statecraft, 1881–1902* (Hassocks, Sussex, 1978).

———, *Joseph Chamberlain: Entrepreneur in Politics* (New Haven, 1994).

Martin, Robert Bernard, *Tennyson: The Unquiet Heart* (Oxford, 1983).

Mason, John W., "The Duke of Argyll and the Land Question in Late Nineteenth-Century Britain," *Victorian Studies* 21, no. 2 (Winter 1978), 149–70.

Masterman, Lucy (ed.), *Mary Gladstone (Mrs. Drew): Her Diaries and Letters*, 2d ed. (London, 1930).

Matthew, H. C. G., "Gladstone, Vaticanism, and the Question of the East," in Derek Baker (ed.), *Religious Motivation: Biographical and Sociological Problems for the Church Historian* (Oxford, 1978).

———, *Gladstone, 1809–1874* (Oxford, 1986).

———, "Rhetoric and Politics in Britain, 1860–1950," in P. J. Waller (ed.), *Politics and Social Change in Modern Britain: Essays Presented to A. F. Thompson* (Hassocks, Sussex, 1987).

Matthew, H. C. G. (ed.), *The Gladstone Diaries*, vols. 5–14 (Oxford, 1978–1994).

Mattlin, Jay A.; Wetherington, Elaine; and Kessler, Ronald C., "Situational Determinants of Coping and Coping Effectiveness," *Journal of Health and Social Behavior* 31 (March 1990), 103–22.

Maxwell, Sir Herbert, *Life and Letters of George William Frederick Fourth Earl of Clarendon* (London, 1913).

Medlicott, W. N., *Bismarck, Gladstone, and the Concert of Europe* (London, 1956).

Meyer, Bernard C., "Some Observations on the Rescue of Fallen Women," *Psychoanalytic Quarterly* 53, no. 2 (1984), 208–39.

Miller, T. B., "The Egyptian Question and British Foreign Policy, 1892–1894," *Journal of Modern History* 32, no. 1 (March 1960), 1–15.

Millman, Richard, *British Foreign Policy and the Coming of the Franco-Prussian War* (Oxford, 1965).

Monat, Alan, and Lazarus, Richard S., "Stress and Coping—Some Current Issues and Controversies," in Alan Monat and Richard S. Lazarus (eds.), *Stress and Coping: An Anthology*, 2d ed. (New York, 1985).

Moody, T. W., "The Irish University Question of the Nineteenth Century," *History* 43, no. 148 (June 1958), 90–109.

Moody, T. W., and Hawkins, Richard (eds.) with Moody, Margaret, *Florence Arnold-Forster's Irish Journal* (Oxford, 1988).

Morley, John, *The Life of William Ewart Gladstone* (London, 1912).

Munsell, F. Darrell, *The Unfortunate Duke* (Columbia, Mo., 1985).

Newsome, David, *The Parting of Friends: A Study of the Wilberforces and Henry Manning* (London, 1966).

Norman, E. R., *The Catholic Church and Ireland in the Age of Rebellion, 1859–1873* (London, 1965).

————, "The Maynooth Question of 1845," *Irish Historical Studies* 15 (1967), 407–37.

Ó Gráda, Cormac, "The Investment Behavior of Irish Landlords, 1850–75: Some Preliminary Findings," *Agricultural History Review* 23 (1975), 139–55.

————, "Irish Agricultural Output before and after the Famine," *Journal of European Economic History* 13, no. 1 (Spring 1984), 149–65.

O'Leary, Cornelius, *The Elimination of Corrupt Practices in British Elections, 1868–1911* (Oxford, 1962).

Orridge, Andrew W., "Who Supported the Land War: An Aggregate-Data Analysis of Irish Agrarian Discontent, 1879–1882," *Economic and Social Review* 12, no. 3 (April 1981), 203–33.

Owen, David, *English Philanthropy, 1660–1960* (Cambridge, Mass., 1964).

Palmer, Roundell (earl of Selborne), *Memorials, Part 2: Personal and Political, 1865–1895,* 2 vols. (London, 1898).

Park, Joseph H., *The English Reform Bill of 1867* (New York, 1920).

Parry, J. P., *Democracy and Religion: Gladstone and the Liberal Party, 1867–1875* (Cambridge, England, 1986).

————, *The Rise and Fall of Liberal Government in Victorian Britain* (New Haven, 1994).

Paul, Herbert Woodfield, *The Life of William Ewart Gladstone* (London, 1901).

Pearl, Cyril, *The Girl with the Swansdown Seat,* paperback ed. (New York, 1958).

Pointon, Marcia, "W. E. Gladstone as an Art Patron and Collector," *Victorian Studies* 19, no. 1 (September 1975), 73–98.

Post, Felix, "Creativity and Psychopathology: A Study of 291 World-Famous Men," *British Journal of Psychiatry* 165 (1994), 22–34.

Pratt, Edwin A., *Catherine Gladstone: Life, Good Works, and Political Efforts* (London, 1898).

Preston, Adrian, "Wolsey, the Khartoum Relief Expedition, and the Defense of India, 1885–1900," *Journal of Imperial and Commonwealth History* 6, no. 3 (May 1978), 254–80.

Preston, Adrian (ed.), *In Relief of Gordon: Lord Wolseley's Campaign Journal of the Khartoum Relief Expedition, 1884–1885* (London, 1967).

Prochaska, F. K., *Women and Philanthropy in Nineteenth-Century England* (Oxford, 1980).

Proudfoot, Lindsay, "The Management of a Great Estate: Patronage, Income and Expenditure on the Duke of Devonshire's Irish Property, c. 1816 to 1891," *Irish Economic and Social History* 13 (1986), 32–55.

Ramm, Agatha, "Great Britain and France in Egypt, 1876–1882," in P. Gifford and W. R. Louis (eds.), *France and Britain in Africa* (New Haven, 1971).

————, "The Parliamentary Context of Cabinet Government, 1868–1874," *English Historical Review* 99, no. 393 (October 1984), 739–69.

————, "Gladstone's Religion," *Historical Journal* 28, no. 2 (1985), 327–40.

Ramm, Agatha (ed.), *The Political Correspondence of Mr. Gladstone and Lord Granville, 1868–1876,* 2 vols., Camden Third Series 81 (London, 1952).

————, *The Political Correspondence of Mr. Gladstone and Lord Granville, 1876–1886,* 2 vols. (Oxford, 1962).

Reid, Sir Weymss, ed., *The Life of William Ewart Gladstone,* 2 vols. (New York, 1899).

Rendel, Lord, *The Personal Papers of Lord Rendel* (London, 1931).

Richards, N. J., "Religious Controversy and the School Boards, 1870–1902," *British Journal of Educational Studies* 18, no. 2 (June 1970), 180–96.

"Right Honourable William Gladstone, M.P., The," *Blackwood's Edinburgh Magazine,* 97, part 1, no. 592 (1865), 267.

Robbins, Alfred F., *The Early Public Life of William Ewart Gladstone* (New York, 1894).

Robertson, John M., "Gladstone: A Study," *Free Review,* 94.

Robinson, Ronald, and Gallagher, John, with Denny, Alice, *Africa and the Victorians: The Climax of Imperialism,* Anchor ed. (New York, 1968).

Roper, Henry, "W. E. Forster's Memorandum of 21 October, 1869: A Re-examination," *British Journal of Educational Studies* 21, no. 1 (February 1973), 64–75.

——, "Toward an Elementary Education Act for England and Wales, 1865–1868," *British Journal of Educational Studies* 23, no. 2 (June 1975), 181–208.

Rossi, John P., "The Ripon Diary, 1878–80:3," *Recusant History* 12, no. 6 (1974), 261–301.

——, "The Selection of Lord Hartington as Liberal Leader in the House of Commons, February, 1875," *Proceedings of the American Philosophical Society* 119, no. 4 (August 1975), 307–14.

——, " 'The Nestor of His Party'—Gladstone, Hartington and the Liberal Leadership Crisis: November 1879–January 1880," *Canadian Journal of History* 11, no. 2 (1976), 189–99.

——, "The Transformation of the British Liberal Party: A Study of the Tactics of the Liberal Opposition, 1874–1880," *Transactions of the American Philosophical Society,* new ser., 68, part 8 (1978).

Russell, George W. E., *The Right Honourable William Ewart Gladstone* (London, 1891).

——, "Mr. Morley's Gladstone," *Independent Review* 1, no. 2 (November 1903), 329–42.

Saab, Ann Pottinger, *Reluctant Icon: Gladstone, Bulgaria, and the Working Classes, 1856–1878* (Cambridge, Mass., 1991).

Salisbury, Lord, *Quarterly Review* 120 (July and October 1866).

Sandiford, Keith A. P., "W. E. Gladstone and Liberal-Nationalist Movements," *Albion* 13, no. 1 (Spring 1981), 27–42.

Schölch, Alexander, "The 'Men on the Spot' and the English Occupation of Egypt," *Historical Journal* 19, no. 3 (1976), 773–85.

Schreuder, D. M., *Gladstone and Kruger: Liberal Government and Colonial 'Home Rule,' 1880–85* (London, 1969).

——, "Gladstone and Italian Unification, 1848–70: The Making of a Liberal?" *English Historical Review* 85, no. 336 (July 1970), 475–501.

——, "Gladstone as 'Troublemaker': Liberal Foreign Policy and the German Annexation of Alsace-Lorraine, 1870–1871," *Journal of British Studies* 17, no. 2 (Spring 1978), 106–35.

——, "Gladstone and the Conscience of the State," in Peter Marsh (ed.), *The Conscience of the Victorian State* (Syracuse, 1979).

Schwartz, Marvin, *The Politics of British Foreign Policy in the Era of Disraeli and Gladstone* (New York, 1985).

Searby, P., "Gladstone in West Derby Hundred: The Liberal Campaign in South-West Lancashire in 1868," *Transactions of the Historical Society of Lancashire and Cheshire* (1959–60), 139–66.

Shanley, Mary Lyndon, " 'One Must Ride Behind': Married Women's Rights and the Divorce Act of 1857," *Victorian Studies* 25 (Spring 1982), 255–76.

——, *Feminism, Marriage, and the Law in Victorian England, 1850–1895* (Princeton, 1989).

Shannon, Richard T., *Gladstone and the Bulgarian Agitation, 1876* (London, 1963).

——, *Gladstone: volume 1, 1809–1865* (London, 1982).

——, "Midlothian: 100 Years After," in Peter J. Jagger (ed.), *Gladstone, Politics and Religion* (New York, 1985).

Shebeika, Mekki, *British Policy in the Sudan, 1882–1902* (Oxford, 1952).

Sherwood, Michael, *The Logic of Explanation in Psychoanalysis* (New York, 1969).

Shkolnik, Esther Simon, "Petticoat Power: The Political Influence of Mrs. Gladstone," *Historian* 42, no. 4 (1980), 631–47.

Smith, F. B., *The Making of the Second Reform Bill* (Cambridge, England, 1966).

Smith, Paul, *Disraelian Conservatism and Social Reform* (London, 1967).

——, "Liberalism as Authority and Discipline," *Historical Journal* 32, no. 3 (1989), 723–37.

Stanley, Liz (ed.), *The Diaries of Hannah Cullwick, Victorian Maidservant* (New Brunswick, N.J., 1984).

Stanmore, Lord, *Sidney Herbert, Lord Herbert of Lea: A Memoir* (London, 1906).

Stead, W. T., "Mr. Gladstone at Eighty-Six," *McClure's Magazine* 7, no. 3 (August 1896), 196–200.

Stearns, Carol Zisowitz, and Stearns, Peter N., *Anger: The Struggle for Emotional Control in America's History* (Chicago, 1986).

Steele, E. D., *Irish Land and British Politics: Tenant-Right and Nationality, 1865–1870* (Cambridge, 1974).

———, *Palmerston and Liberalism, 1855–1865* (Cambridge, 1991).

Strachey, Lytton, and Fulford, Roger (eds.), *The Greville Memoirs* (London, 1938).

Stuart, C. H., "The Formation of the Coalition Cabinet of 1852," *Transactions of the Royal Historical Society*, 5th ser., 4 (1954), 45–68.

Sutherland, Gillian, *Policy-Making in Elementary Education, 1870–1895* (London, 1973).

TeBrake, Janet K., "Irish Peasant Women in Revolt: The Land League Years," *Irish Historical Studies* 28, no. 109 (May 1992), 63–80.

Temmel, Matthew R., "Gladstone's Resignation of the Liberal Leadership, 1874–1875," *Journal of British Studies* 16, no. 1 (1976), 153–75.

Thompson, Roger C., *Australian Imperialism in the Pacific: The Expansionist Era, 1820–1920* (Melbourne, 1980).

Thorold, Algar Labouchere, *The Life of Henry Labouchere* (New York, 1913).

Townshend, Charles, *Political Violence in Ireland: Government and Resistance since 1848*, paperback ed. (Oxford, 1983).

Trainor, Luke, "The Liberals and the Formation of Imperial Defence Policy, 1892–5," *Bulletin of the Institute of Historical Research* 42, no. 106 (November 1969), 188–200.

Trudgill, Eric, *Madonnas and Magdalens: The Origins and Development of Victorian Sexual Attitudes* (New York, 1976).

Tucker, Albert V., "Army and Society in England, 1870–1900: A Reassessment of the Cardwell Reforms," *Journal of British Studies* 2, no. 2 (May 1963), 110–41.

Vaillant, George, *Adaptation to Life* (Boston, 1977).

Vaughan, W. E., "An Assessment of the Economic Performance of Irish Landlords, 1851–81," in F. S. L. Lyons and R. A. J. Hawkins (eds.), *Ireland under the Union: Varieties of Tension* (Oxford, 1980).

Veysey, A. Geoffrey, "Sir Stephen Glynne," *Journal of the Flintshire Historical Society* 30 (1981–2), 151–70.

Vidler, Alec R., *The Orb and the Cross* (London, 1945).

Vincent, John (ed.), *Disraeli, Derby and the Conservative Party: Journals and Memoirs of Edward Henry, Lord Stanley, 1849–1869* (New York, 1978).

———, *A Selection from the Diaries of Edward Henry Stanley, Fifteenth Earl of Derby (1826–93), between September 1869 and March 1878*, Camden Fifth Series 4 (London, 1994).

Wakeford, John, *The Cloistered Elite: A Sociological Analysis of the English Public Boarding School* (London, 1969).

Walkowitz, Judith R., *Prostitution and Victorian Society: Women, Class, and the State* (Cambridge, England, 1980).

———, *City of Dreadful Delight: Narratives of Sexual Danger in Late-Victorian London* (Chicago, 1992).

Walling, R. A. J., *The Diaries of John Bright* (1930).

Warren, Allen, "The Irish Policies of the Second Gladstone Government, 1880–1885" (D.Phil. diss., Oxford University, 1974).

———, "Gladstone, Land and Social Reconstruction in Ireland, 1881–1887," *Parliamentary History* 2 (1983), 153–73.

Weeks, Jeffrey, *Sex, Politics, and Society* (London, 1981).

West, Sir Algernon, *Recollections: 1832 to 1886* (New York, 1900).

Weston, Corrine C., "Disunity on the Opposition Front Bench, 1884," *English Historical Review* 106, no. 418 (January 1991), 80–96.

Wilkinson, Rupert, *Gentlemanly Power: British Leadership and the Public School Tradition* (London, 1964).

Winstanley, Michael J., *Gladstone and the Liberal Party*, Lancaster Pamphlets (London, 1990).

Wolf, Lucien, *Life of the First Marquess of Ripon* (London, 1921).

Woodall, Robert, "Orsini and the Fall of Palmerston," *History Today* (October 1976), 636–43.

Woodhouse, Margaret, "The Marriage and Divorce Bill of 1857," *American Journal of Legal History* 3 (1959), 260–75.

Zetland, Marquess of (ed.), *The Letters of Disraeli to Lady Chesterfield and Lady Bradford* (New York, 1929).

Index